The World of
the Japanese Garden

THE WORLD OF

From

by LORAINE KUCK

THE JAPANESE GARDEN

Chinese Origins to Modern Landscape Art

with color photographs by TAKEJI IWAMIYA

WEATHERHILL : *New York & Tokyo*

The title-page decoration, showing a portion of an idealized garden in the literary-man style (see page 242), has been reproduced from a copy of Kitamura Enkin's Tsukiyama Teizoden *(see pages 237-38) in the collection of Shuji Hisatsune.*

FIRST EDITION, 1968
REPRINTED WITH CORRECTIONS, 1980

Published by John Weatherhill, Inc., of New York and Tokyo, with editorial offices at 7-6-13 Roppongi, Minato-ku, Tokyo 106. Protected by copyright under terms of the International Copyright Union; all rights reserved. Printed and first published in Japan.

LCC CARD NO. 68-26951   ISBN 0-8348-0029-2

Table of Contents

PART FOUR

PLATES ILLUSTRATING THE TEXT

page 271

*

List of Illustrations

*(Credits for the illustrations, given below in parentheses,
indicate the photographer, where known, or the source.)*

7

PLATES ILLUSTRATING THE TEXT

For Chapter 1

For Chapter 2

For Chapter 5

For Chapter 7

Preface

SOME readers may discern hovering behind the present volume the ghost of an earlier work, and perhaps even recognize some of its phraseology, for this new work started out to be a revision of my previous book on the subject, *The Art of Japanese Gardens* (1941). It quickly became apparent, however, that far too many changes were needed if the new book was to be what I felt it should be. So a completely new work has resulted. Nevertheless, all the basic subject matter of the first has been retained, while much that is new has been added, for many new things have come to light in the intervening period. Also, interesting things have been taking place in Japanese landscape developments during the postwar period.

Moreover, since this book is a chronological story for readers and not merely an album of pictures with unorganized captions, it has seemed desirable to focus Japan's unique gardens into the total world picture of gardens. For this purpose, a short background was needed. And to clarify the background further, it was necessary to find out as much as possible about the origin of the naturalistic garden pattern of the Far East—that is, to trace the story of how China's gardens came into being. Considerable searching has made it possible to extend an original two chapters on this subject into four. I have been unable to find any other systematic attempt to trace Chinese garden developments, and I hope my efforts may lead someone better qualified to search further into this fascinating subject.

I have visited and studied all the surviving Japanese gardens that I discuss. Looking at them from the standpoint of Western landscape architecture, I have sometimes seen things in ways that differ from the conventional Japanese approach. But I have tried, all the same, to see these gardens with Japanese eyes and respond to them with Japanese feeling. And this I have tried to make clear to readers unfamiliar with them.

For knowledge of the origin and history of these gardens, I have had to rely, as always, on the research of Japanese scholars who have worked in this field: men who broke away from the repetitious inaccuracies of the old "Secret Books" on garden making and in this century began to search for real facts in diaries and records contemporary with the creation of the gardens. My debt to these scholars is great, and they are named in the Acknowledgments at the end of the book.

Since this book is not intended for Japanese readers but for those who may have no familiarity with, or only vague ideas about, Japanese history and culture, I have tried to paint in a clarifying background. I have included the many persons, as far as known, who took part in the scene: the emperors, princes, prelates, artists, and priests, the dictators, generals, oligarchs, and common people who, along with their times, their ideas, and their feelings, produced these gardens—most of them as conscious works of art. I have also placed emphasis on the traditions of Japanese esthetics as they found expression in the art of garden making in both old and new Japan.

A few technical points need to be noted. For the word order of Japanese personal names, I have adopted the system of giving the names of all pre-Meiji (before 1868) figures in the order of surname first, given name last—for example, Tokugawa Ieyasu—and those of post-1868 figures in Western style—for example, Mirei Shigemori. In certain Chinese and Japanese place names I have not hesitated to be redundant. For example, I say "the Lu-shan mountains" and "Saiho-ji temple," even though -shan itself means mountain in Chinese and -ji means temple in Japanese. This follows the usage of English-speaking Westerners in the Orient who tend to accept local names in full and then, for smoother identification, add their own supplements.

Rather than interrupt the narrative flow with footnotes, I have relegated all notes to the end of the book. The bibliography has been purposely made selective rather than comprehensive, since it is designed to suit the needs of the general reader and to include the more readily accessible among the sources that I have used in writing the book, together with a few others that are of special interest and value.

One other feature that has emerged as this work assumed book form is the color photography by Takeji Iwamiya. An artist who is generally regarded as one of Japan's most able photographers, he is known particularly for his fine studies of Japanese gardens. Anyone who has ever tried to get good photographs of these gardens is aware that they are probably the world's most difficult subjects. The amorphous leafiness which pervades them, often with almost no distinct contrasts, makes it extremely difficult to attain clarity and to catch their basic esthetic qualities.

But in work covering more than twenty years, Mr. Iwamiya has succeeded in doing just this. From his large collection—the gleanings of many springs and autumns of color, many summers and winters of seasonal changes—he has selected for this book a group of photographs that best represent his own answer to the question: What is a Japanese garden? Although it so happens that all his photographs were taken in the Kyoto area, cradle of Japanese gardening and the part of Japan that he knows and loves best, Mr. Iwamiya has not tried to show only famous gardens, nor to give an overall idea of what any particular garden looks like in its entirety. Rather, by choosing small, significant details, details that have remained persistently in his memory over the years, he has tried to suggest his answer to a difficult question. And, indeed, his selection of details, which are revealed with artistic sensitivity and superb photographic clarity, has communicated his answer more clearly than words could do. I feel these photographs provide a sort of counterpoint to the text, a dimension of vivid immediacy which is the next best thing to a walk through the gardens themselves.

14

Mr. Iwamiya's subjective studies, then, are scattered through the main text, inviting the reader to pause occasionally for a moment of visual contemplation, while those photographs more directly illustrating subjects touched on in the text have, with the exception of a few color plates preceding Mr. Iwamiya's, been gathered together at the end of the book for ease of reference.

PART ONE

Introduction

CHAPTER ONE

Japan Discovers
the Gardens of China

I N THE year A.D. 607 one of the most stupendous landscape parks the world has ever seen was being constructed in China. The emperor, known to history as Sui Yang Ti, was building it near his capital in the city of Lo-yang.

"To create his Western Park," says a chronicle,[1] "the ground was broken over an area two hundred *li* in circuit (about seventy-five miles) and the labor of a million workers, on the average, was required. Within the park were constructed sixteen courts [residential palaces built around interior courtyards]. Earth and rock were brought to make hills, and the ground was excavated for the Five Lakes and Four Seas."

The record continues by relating that each lake covered an extensive area. In each, earth and rocks were piled up to form hilly islands. Of the four large lakes or "seas," the Northern Sea was the most extensive, being some thirteen miles in circuit. Within it were three island-peaks, representing three mystic isles of ancient Chinese belief. Upon these islands were built gaily colored pavilions, towers, terraces, and colonnades. Canals were dug connecting all the lakes. When they were completed, pleasure barges could go through the whole system. The prows of these boats were decoratively extended into the heads of dragons or mythical phoenixes, and the sterns suggested their tails.

The undertaking was carried out in an imperious manner. In addition to huge levies of forced manpower, the record states, "a proclamation was issued directing that all those in the vicinity [of the capital] possessing plants, trees, birds and beasts should dispatch them to the park. From everywhere, then, were collected innumerable quantities of flowers, herbs, plants, trees, birds, beasts, fishes and frogs, and even these were not fully sufficient." Full-grown forest trees were brought to the site on specially constructed carts and replanted in the park.

As the park approached completion, the record comments, "with the lake shore bending and turning, and the broad expanse of the water, there were a thousand prospects, and a variegated beauty unequaled in the world of men." A few years later, referring to the year 610, it says, dropping into poetic mood: "The garden's verdure, trees, birds, and animals had multiplied to the point of luxuriant abundance. Peach walks and plum byways met beneath kingfisher-green shadows. Golden gibbons and green deer sped by.

"A highway was laid from the imperial palace [in the capital] to the Western Park, set out with tall pines and lofty willows. The emperor would often visit the park on the spur of the moment, going, making his lodging and returning the same night."[2]

The attraction is not unexpected. Each of the sixteen pleasure palaces in the park housed twenty concubines. "All were beautiful, respectful, virtuous and lovely of face. Each group was chosen in turn by the emperor as the recipient of his imperial favors."[3]

We know the beauty of this imperial garden was not exaggerated because its reflection, as in a long mirror, has come down the centuries to be seen in still-existing imperial Chinese gardens. Landscape design and architecture in China have been almost incredibly conservative throughout the centuries, with few major changes taking place.[4] Surviving buildings and gardens which were constructed before the twentieth century must appear in most ways very much as such things have always appeared. And to go back even before the time of Sui Yang Ti's garden, his vast park itself was only one in a line of such great estates that had been coming into existence for over a thousand years before.

Today in China two such great lake-and-hill gardens still remain. They were built by the last imperial Chinese dynasties and must, in their general effect, be something like visual counterparts of Sui Yang Ti's Western Park. The writer had the good fortune to go through these imperial Peking gardens in 1931, shortly after they had been opened to the public and before vandalism and neglect had loosed their destructive forces upon them.

One, the new Summer Palace, lies a few miles outside Peking. Originally, it was the site of the great imperial park called Yuan Ming Yuan,[5] largely destroyed by European troops in 1860 as an act of reprisal. What remains is a section reconstructed in the late nineteenth century by the old empress dowager of the Manchu dynasty. This new Summer Palace rises on a hillside above a wide lake (Plate 51). It is an ascending congeries of terraces, courtyards, individual palace halls, pavilions, roofed corridors, and steps. The lake, shimmering below, holds a distant island, reached by a marble bridge, its many arches often doubled in the dark water below.

The second imperial garden which still exists in Peking is probably even more like Sui Yang Ti's Western Park. Once it was even called the Western Park (showing the continuity of tradition), since it lies west of the Winter Palace in the Forbidden City. The latter is a great square enclosure in the center of Peking, its high red walls about a mile long on each side. Within, facing the monumental main gate, are the three Halls of State of the former Chinese empire. Behind them, in a private section, are the residential palaces, one for each of the ruler's ladies. He could easily slip away from his official duties to enjoy the quiet beauty of the adjoining great park.

This park is now known as the Park of the Sea Palaces, for it holds three large lakes, called "seas," with various palace-style buildings scattered around their shores. The three lakes are named the Northern Sea, the Middle Sea, and the Southern Sea. The largest, the Northern Sea or Pei Hai, is some three miles around. The opposite shore, as seen across the gleaming waters, must be half a mile away. This is small compared to Sui Yang Ti's Northern Sea, which was thirteen miles around. His lake, if we accept the figures in the chronicle, would just about have covered the entire city of Peking.

Carrying on tradition, even in the twentieth century, the old empress dowager of the

Manchus used to enjoy being poled about on this lake with her ladies.[6] Her barge, gaily designed like a small floating pavilion, I saw moored in its cavernous boathouse on the edge of the water.

In summer, this lake's surface is largely covered by acres of nelumbium lotus. The huge leaves often crowd together into a billowing new surface, several feet above the water. The great pink lilies rise above the leaves in August, their papery petals encircling a center of rich golden stamens. The leaves are shaped like an immense rounded bowl with rippled edges. The interior of the leaf is a curious translucent bluish green, due to a waxen surface. When drops of rain or dew collect in these jade bowls, surface tension pulls up the water into crystalline globules. And if the leaf sways, these jewel-like drops roll back and forth like crystal beads. When acres of these leaves rock together in some light breeze, sheets of electric-blue light sometimes flash across the field, refracted from the waxen surfaces.

At one end of Peking's Northern Sea rises a large hilly island, its peak now crowned by a white stupa in Lamaist style (Plate 50). The island is about a mile around, bordered by a path, partly shaded by immense old weeping willows. In spring, the late afternoon sun turns these trees into green-gold. And as the breeze ripples the clear surface of the water, the reflections of their long, slender branches seem to corkscrew forward, spiraling rhythmically and continuously.

In the twelfth century, Marco Polo, who visited the court of Kubilai Khan, wrote that this hilly island had been created out of the material excavated after Kubilai ordered the lake enlarged. Marco also tells how this great khan caused the island slopes to be planted with full-grown trees, mostly evergreens.[7] One ancient juniper has been pointed out as a possible survivor of these originals. In summer, other trees cover the island with their green shade. In spring, where its slopes are sunny, they are sheeted with small lavender-blue wild flowers, called the Second Month Orchids.[8]

Various pavilions, terraces, monuments, and picturesque little kiosks are scattered over the island's tree-shaded slopes. These small structures are among the originals from which the chinoiserie kiosks of eighteenth-century Europe were derived.[9]

The outer shore of this island, overlooking the main body of the lake, is faced with a long, curving terrace of creamy white marble. This is topped by a balustrade of the same material, intricately carved. The terrace holds a long colonnade, its tiled roof upheld by vermilion-red pillars, its ceiling painted in designs of gold, white, malachite green, and deep lapis-lazuli blue. From this terrace one can look across to the farther shore, where five small pavilions with upcurved roofs seem to float on the water (Plate 52). They may suggest the claws of a sleeping dragon.[10]

One large section of the island hillside is covered with an extensive rockery. Here are the "piled-up rocks" we found mentioned on Sui Yang Ti's islands. The stones in Peking are usually enormous, rough, and irregular, placed so as to exaggerate their grotesque effects. A path winds among them from which, here and there, caverns open eerily, leading into the hillside. The whole effect of this stone-covered hillside is weird and fantastic. We shall come to understand it later.

The great pleasure park of Sui Yang Ti in the seventh century is important to the story

21

of Japanese gardens because the first imperial Japanese landscape gardens appear to stem directly from it.

During the autumn of A.D. 607 there arrived in the Sui capital of Lo-yang the first official embassy from the still-primitive island kingdom of Japan. Up to that time, most of what the Japanese had heard about Chinese civilization had trickled in, secondhand, through Korea. (This peninsula had earlier been a Chinese colony.) The head of this Japanese embassy to the Chinese capital was named Ono no Imoko. He had been sent to learn all he could about Japan's fabulous continental neighbor.

We can picture Ono no Imoko and his suite walking the streets of the Sui capital, gazing with awe at the size and beauty of the red-pillared Halls of State when he was received at court and listening to the accounts of vast enterprises elsewhere.[11] Probably his curiosity took him out to the site of the Western Park, where he could see the armies of men working around the lakes, with the rocky peaks rising on the islands in the Northern Sea, the forests of trees being moved in, and the sixteen pleasure palaces going up around the shores. He must also have become aware of the resentment of the people at the monstrous levies of manpower being drawn off for these imperial extravagances—resentment that, in another ten years, was to rise into an open rebellion which brought the short-lived Sui dynasty to an end.

But among the ideas that Ono no Imoko must have taken back to the Japanese court was the Chinese concept that imperial rule demands for its proper setting a monumental architecture and great lake gardens. At any rate, it is only four years after this first Japanese embassy to China that we find mention of a landscaped lake garden being constructed in front of the Japanese imperial palace. It was the first thing of its kind ever seen in Japan.

CHAPTER TWO

Mediterranean, Persian, and Indian Contrasts

BEFORE following Ono no Imoko on his return to Japan, it is worth stopping to attempt an understanding of the great landscape park he had seen under construction at Lo-yang. It is also interesting to compare its origin with that of garden estates of the Mediterranean world and Europe, which are so wholly different, with their geometrically formal paths, pools and fountains, clipped trees, flower beds, and lawns.

The question will inevitably arise, did these two ways of laying out gardens ever have any influence on each other? Briefly, the answer to this question is that they did not. Each had its own origin and went its individual way, separated by great deserts and mountains, until, in the fifteenth century, Europe finally made direct contact with the Far East by sea.

Forerunners of the modern European garden came into existence around the Mediterranean. It is an area that is generally dry and in places a true desert. In some sections, brief winter rains may bring on glorious masses of wild flowers—those biblical "lilies of the field" which include narcissus, anemones, ranunculus, tulips, hyacinths, cyclamen, and others. They bloom tumultuously for a brief period in spring, but as summer closes down, hot and dry, the spring flowers, as in Persia, "vanish with the rose" and the landscape again becomes sere and brown. Garden designers, consequently, have sought some means of making their immediate environment more livable than as nature created it.

The world's first real ornamental gardens seem to have come into existence in Egypt. There civilization had developed perhaps a millennium before it did in China, so that the Mediterranean style is the older. Because pictures of these earliest gardens have survived in the dry sands of Egypt, it is still possible to see what they were like by looking at the scenes painted for their owners on tomb walls (Plate 1).[1] These tombs were built for Egyptian nobles who owned the estates and hoped to continue a shadowy existence on a shadowy counterpart estate in the next world.

The country home of such an Egyptian landowner was, first of all, a practical farm. His house stood near the banks of the Nile, on a generous plot of land with necessary outbuildings, all enclosed by a high wall. To maintain it at all seasons, but especially when the Nile was low, a good-sized reservoir was necessary.[2] It appears that these bodies of water became the center of the world's first ornamental gardens.

The reservoir, square or rectangular, was placed in front of the house, where the sight of water could provide a pleasant outlook. To create shade and produce fruits, trees were planted around the reservoir in neat rows. These were mostly date palms and sycomore figs *(Ficus sycomorus)*. Grapes for wine were grown on long trellises, also parallel to the walls and the rows of trees. Any remaining spaces were filled in with garden beds, probably used largely for vegetables. The reason for the straight, neat rows is obvious. It was to facilitate irrigation from the reservoir. We can assume, I think, that this functional need to irrigate was the beginning of all formal design.

The pool was stocked with fish, and in it were grown Egyptian water lilies. These lilies are referred to classically as "lotus" although that name now belongs botanically to the nelumbium lilies of Asia. Egyptian water lilies, botanically, were nympheas, with floating leaves and blue or white flowers growing close to the water's surface. The Egyptians adored these flowers. We see the blossoms carried in their hands, wound around their heads, and even laid on their food. The massive pillars of their architecture sometimes carried capitals inspired by the shape of the buds.

Egyptian ornamental gardening was further developed on the sloping banks of the reservoirs when small flowering plants were grown there. Because pictures showing these plants are highly stylized, it is difficult to be sure but probably they were mostly blue cornflowers and red poppies, which we know were grown later in such gardens.

The style of garden which thus grew out of a practical farmstead was developed, finally, into a pure pleasure garden. But always the basic outline remained, with a formal pool holding lilies and fish, other flowers along the banks and beside the garden paths, and rows of trees to create shade. It was a thoroughly practical style, not only for Egypt but for all the dry Mediterranean world, and eventually its pattern spread over all that area and far beyond it, even to Persia and India.

Babylonia, Assyria, and Persia had possessed walled hunting parks from very early times. These were sparsely wooded or partly planted areas stocked with animals for royal sport. The Persians called such half-natural parks "paradises," a word which originally meant simply an enclosed area.[3] At some early time, certain Near Eastern storytellers placed one of their myths of man's creation in such a park, calling it "Eden." It was only in a later age, however, that the present allegorical meaning came to be attached to the word "paradise."

In the seventh century B.C. the Assyrians came down and conquered Egypt. There they saw the formal Egyptian gardens and carried back to Mesopotamia the first ideas of a planned design.[4] Later the triumphant Persians eliminated the Assyrians, and then they, too, swept into Egypt as conquerors. The idea of a garden laid out in a geometric pattern was taken to Iran and there developed into a new, distinctive form. The Persians also took back something of the Egyptian love for the blue water lily, for among the sculptured reliefs on the walls of the great palace of Darius at Persepolis we can still see lines of guests at the New Year's festival, each man holding a water lily in his hand.[5]

The Persian garden has been called the most distinctive product of Persian culture.[6] The making of a garden evidently fascinated noble and peasant alike. Even kings took a personal interest. Cyrus told the Greek Lysander that he himself had designed his garden at

Sardis and had even set out some of the trees. Lysander, looking at the king's gorgeous robes, found this hard to believe.[7]

The early Persian gardens were probably much like those of Egypt, but in time certain changes developed. The garden area came to be divided into four parts by crossed canals. Where they intersected, a pool or building was usually placed. The four-part idea seems to have reflected a primitive concept of the world, which was thought to be divided into such quarters—a derivation indicated by decorations on very early Iranian pottery.[8] The crossed-canal design is called the *chahar-bagh* or "four gardens" and became widely spread over all this part of the world, even to some distant oases in Central Asia. Complexity was added when each square was further subdivided. Or, if there was a sufficient slope, terraces with the water falling in cascades from one to the next were created. If the water pressure was sufficient, as from a lake above, rows of small water jets were often used down the center of the canal or along its banks.

Persian interest in growing flowers for the poolside was probably much greater than had been that of the Egyptians, for the plantings of the latter were quite limited in variety. The Persians are believed to have been the world's first people to make a special pursuit of the cultivation of flowers. Many of Europe's familiar garden plants were first brought from the fields of Persia. Later, when close contacts developed between Persia and China, there was a considerable exchange of plants, so that many flowers and fruits now appear to have been native to both areas. The narcissus, for example, which became one of China's traditional flowers, is really a native of Persia.

When the Muslim Arabs took over Persia in the seventh century A.D. the Persian garden style was carried back to the Mediterranean, and then, by way of North Africa and Sicily, it was taken on to Spain.[9] Today the gardens of the Moorish Alhambra and Generalife in Granada tell clearly of their Persian origins, with their central canals, their small jets of water, and their flower borders. The patios of Mexico and the southwestern United States are their distant descendants.

Other parts of Europe had received a concept of the formal garden by a different route. Imperial Rome took the basic pattern directly from Egypt and added sheared hedges and trees. Renaissance Italy developed this classical form in creating such great estates as Villa d'Este and Frascati. The cloister garden carried formality into medieval Europe. Eventually the style came to have such vast expressions as Versailles, with its grand canal, great terraces, and fountains. In England the pattern of straight lines and geometric curves was accepted through the seventeenth century.

Thus the geometric garden pattern of Europe and the Near East is, in a sense, an architectural extension of the house. Its lines are controlled by the architect's square and compass, all its elements shaped and modified by man's handiwork. The ground was leveled and terraced, not left in natural contours. Water lay in geometric pools or was caused to fall in cascades or spurt in jets or spring from fountains, rather than to remain as a natural stream. Stones were cut into such useful pieces as copings and benches or carved into statues. Walks were paved or graveled and extended in a direct straight line. Or, if curved, they were geometrically controlled.

However, by the eighteenth century, the English had had enough of geometry. They had come to realize that their own green countryside, with its trees, was really a garden. They tore out much of the old formal garden structuring and brought the lawn and trees right up to the house. Controversy over these two garden styles occupies much of the eighteenth-century English literature. The case for the naturalistic garden was considerably reinforced when it was learned that the great imperial gardens in Peking were all in a naturalistic manner. What was called the Anglo-Chinese garden then became the rage, for a time, all over Europe.

The Persian garden pattern moved not only west to Spain but also eastward into neighboring India. As early as the fourth century B.C., we hear of a large park belonging to King Chandragupta (321–296), ruler of the powerful and highly developed Maurya empire. A Greek ambassador to his court, named Megasthenes, wrote that in the center of Chandragupta's capital, near the present city of Patna, the king had a large park with pools and many fine trees, some brought from distant places. Tame peacocks and pheasants wandered about in it.[10] We know that Chandragupta's rule came after a long period of close and friendly relations between India and Persia during which India had adapted many Persian institutions and aspects of Persian culture. There is every reason to think that Chandragupta's imperial garden was laid out in the Persian manner—as were also his palace buildings, which Megasthenes describes as unmistakably in the Persian style of Persepolis.[11] From this early time on, I think, we can assume that at least on the level of palaces and courts the formal garden style was well established in India.

Private estates had doubtless been developed very early in India, although probably in a more casual, homelike manner than the formal Persian garden. A home place is described by the famous poet Kalidasa, who lived in the fourth or fifth century A.D. His description tells us that this garden had as its central feature a large pool, evidently used principally for bathing but also holding water lilies. Steps descending into the water were for the convenience of bathers, as is still seen in India. This pool had evidently been excavated rather deeply, and the material taken out had been piled into a bank or low hill beside it and topped by some handsome rocks. It was called a "pleasure hill." Kalidasa also mentions an arbor with creepers, a gate, and a surrounding tall hedge of bananas, which gave privacy. He wrote:

> There to the north of the Lord of Wealth's house is our home,
> Noted easily from a distance by its portal, handsome as the King of
>   Gods' bow [the rainbow].
> There also is a pond with stairway, built of emerald [colored] stones,
> [Its surface] woven with lotus buds in gold, on stems gleaming
>   like a cat's-eye beryl.
> Sightly golden banana trees surround its banks,
> And beside it rises a hill of pleasure, its top fabricated with
>   beautiful sapphire [colored] stones.
> Here grows the crimson *ashoka* with trembling shoots, and the hand-
>   some *keshara,*
> And nearby the *madhavi* covers an arbor surrounded by *kuravaka.*[12]

26

These plants are still seen commonly in Indian gardens, the first two being fine flowering trees, one red, the other white. The arbor cover is a vine with fragrant white flowers, and the last is a red amaranth.

The Persian formal garden was brought once more into India some centuries later by the Mughal conquerors. Their leader, Babur, a descendant of Turkish nomads who had overrun Iran, settled in Agra in 1526. He was a lover of the Persian garden and left examples of it wherever he stopped for very long. By this time, of course, this garden style had undergone many refinements and changes, among them the introduction of cascades and jets of water wherever a sloping site made it possible. The beauty of some of the surviving Mughal gardens in India makes it rather easy to understand why Babur was not at all interested in a naturalistic landscape style, as brought out in his memoirs.[13] He mentions acquiring an estate in the hills near Kabul which possessed a winding natural stream. This he ordered reconstructed into a channeled watercourse. Several other valleys with natural streams he also turned into formal layouts with straight canals, cascades, and pavilions.

It was Babur's descendant, Shah Jahan, who built the Taj Mahal at Agra as a memorial and tomb for his queen. In front of it was laid out a large, typically formal garden (Plate 56). The crossing canals of the original "four gardens" pattern can still be traced in the long, impressive central channel that leads up to the building and a cross axis canal halfway up. Under British control the flower beds which originally lined these waterways were not kept up, and the area has come to be merely grassed, with the trees planted at random. Now, however, a straight line of evergreens borders the central channel once more.

However, this approach canal, with its bordering walks and center line of ornamental jet heads, is a basic part of the overall building concept, creating the tremendous first impression one receives. At the end of this long waterway, the white cluster of pointed domes and slender minarets rise gleaming against the blue sky. Sometimes, in the lowering sun of a late afternoon, they lie in rosy, mystic reflection in the long mirror of the water.[14]

Halfway up this central axis, where the cross canal intersects it, there is a large square pool. It surrounds a marble terrace just above the water level. This forms a base for a second terrace that rises to about shoulder height, its top reached by several steps. Here, in the center of this raised block, lies a deep, square pool, dark in comparison with the white-lined channels. On this eminence one can sit on marble benches and enjoy the whole prospect of building, sky, and water. In the dark square of the pool at our feet four white water lilies seem to float. They are carved of marble and are attached to nearly invisible pipe standards so that from the center of each flower a tiny jet of water can spurt out.

From very early times retreats and hermitages existed in the forests at the foot of the Himalayas, frequented by men seeking to escape from the world's distractions and to attain wisdom. Among the trees that often shaded such places was a giant fig with distinctive, heart-shaped leaves. Under one of these trees, about the year 528 B.C., an Indian prince named Gotama sat in meditation. In his youth he had been protected from knowledge of the world's ills but had come to learn of them by chance. Greatly distressed by the sight of sickness, suffering, and death, he gave up his princely life to seek ways of preventing these evils.

For a long time he sat lost in thought, sheltered by the giant fig tree, until suddenly,

27

great intuitive understanding came to him and he became, in the words of his time, an enlightened teacher—that is, a *buddha*. The tree *(Ficus religiosa)* has come to be known as the *bodhi* or Tree of Enlightenment and is sacred to his followers everywhere.

Wandering about after this experience, perhaps in a daze, he came to an area called the Gathering Place of Sages—that is, the Deer Park of Isipatana. There he found several monkish companions, and to them he described his experience and began to expound his new ideas on how humanity could seek relief from suffering.[15] The Deer Park, as the place of the first sermon, is thus known to every Buddhist. Many years later a great temple garden in Japan was named for it.

The teachings of the gentle, enlightened prince-monk grew slowly into a great religion, with all the accretions, schisms, and sectarianism of a spreading, complex system. Gotama himself ceased, in some places, to be remembered as the historic teacher and became a god, the Buddha. Other gods clustered around him. In time some were identified with him; sometimes they even displaced him. One of the most revered of these was Amitabha, Lord of Light, whom the Japanese call Amida.

In scriptures designed to appeal to simple folk, unable to grasp more transcendental concepts or unable, for practical reasons, to devote their lives to the good works that Gotama taught, Amida is described as waiting in his Western Pure Land to receive all who shall call on him, even once, in true and simple faith. The Sukhavati scriptures,[16] in lush and turgid prose, describe Amida's paradise garden, filled with gem-laden trees and golden sands. There, in a celestial palace on the edge of a lily-filled lake, the heavenly hosts await devout souls who are to be reborn to bliss on a blossom seat in this lake.

The sacred flower of these Buddhist scriptures was again the blue water lily. We can see it clearly depicted about the same period in exquisite Buddhist paintings in the cave temples at Ajanta, carried in the hand of a young prince known as the "Beautiful Bodhisattva."

Buddhism was taken in all directions by earnest Indian missionaries. In the first century A.D. some of them trudged all the interminable desert miles to China, crossing Central Asia on the ancient road north of the Himalayas. They usually joined caravans which were returning to China after taking silk to Afghanistan and Parthia. The Indian missionaries carried in their scanty baggage the Buddhist scriptures, among them the sutras of Amida's paradise. In time, the Chinese responded to the appeal of Amida's benevolence and were thrilled by the written descriptions of the celestial lake garden and its palaces.

But the Chinese could never know of the kingly gardens of India which had inspired the sutra's fervid descriptions, for only books could be carried over the Silk Road. These books held no precise details, only the ecstatic reiterations of golden-leaved trees and gemlike fruit. It is doubtful if the Chinese were ever at all interested in the actual gardens of India or thought of them as different from their own. For by the time those stories reached China, that country had long possessed a well-developed garden style of its own, based on a naturalistic pattern of lakes, islands, and peaks. The sutra stories had no influence whatever on this pattern.[17] On the contrary, when the Chinese eventually came to depict the Amida story in paintings, they used their own Chinese imperial palaces for the setting.

Pictures of this paradise as visualized by Chinese monks of the seventh, eighth, and ninth centuries still remain on the walls of certain desert cave chapels along the ancient silk route.[18] In that dry atmosphere they have survived, as in Egypt. The frescos show the earliest pictures to be painted contemporaneously of a Chinese lake garden and its palaces. There was no attempt on the part of these artists to set the story in any Indian environment. Instead, they did as the Italian Renaissance artists were to do—illustrated the scriptures in terms of their own age.

In these frescos we see in the background a splendid Chinese palace with trees growing casually here and there. In front, a platform projects on supports out into the lake, with the heavenly hosts seated on it, like a Chinese ruler and his court. Steps lead down into the water in which the lilies grow. On some of the blossoms are to be seen the newborn souls.

But the flowers in these Chinese paintings are no longer the floating water lilies. They have become the nelumbium lotus of China and the Far East, their bowl-like leaves lifted high above the water, their pink or white flowers on tall stems (Plates 54, 55). It is this flower, with its wider, rounded petals, that enters so extensively into Buddhist art of China and Japan as a symbol of the soul's ascent from mud and slime to the glory of flowering in the sun, and also as a seat for holy beings (Plate 53).[19] The blue water lily was not known in China and Japan until comparatively modern times.

PART TWO

Chinese Origins

CHAPTER THREE

Early Chinese
Hunting Parks

THE earliest garden style created by the Chinese was not based, like the Egyptian's, on a desire to shut away a desert but on the beauties of verdant nature, inspired by one of earth's most flowery spots. Chinese civilization came into existence along the rivers of the great North China plain. In earliest times this area was covered with a luxuriant forest, alternating with stretches of flowery grassland or prairie.

The richness and variety of the primeval Chinese forests have never been exceeded. They contained almost every kind of conifer, hardwood, and fruit tree, with magnificent stands of bamboo in the south. As the land was cleared for planting, hundreds of species must have been lost, like the gingko tree, which now remains only in cultivation. But with all its losses, China still has more kinds of trees than all the rest of the temperate world put together.[1]

It was a land of flowers. The plain has been farmed intensively for over forty centuries, and much of it today could almost be described as a dust bowl. Yet even today the wild flowers appear after rains wherever they can find a bit of undisturbed land—a cliff edge, along a stream, beside a path. In the hills near Peking it is still possible to climb a rocky path in late summer and see the astonishing sight of familiar garden flowers blooming all along the way. Zinnias, pinks, asters, scabiosa, larkspur, gentians, Michaelmas daisies, wild chrysanthemums, and many others grow on a scale few Occidental gardens could attempt.

They appear in mounting masses of color—jungles of pale yellow and deep blue beside the stream; sheets of pink, mauve, and lavender spread across an open glade; drifts of white among rocks; and spikes of pale blue among clumps of orange by a rocky wall.

In the North China spring, the first warmth of the returning sun causes fruit trees to burst into a sudden petally wonderland. So also do species of forsythia, dogwood, daphne, magnolia, viburnum, philadelphus, azalea, rhododendron, and hundreds of other woody shrubs. Summer flowers include peonies, hydrangeas, crepe myrtle, roses, mallow, lotus, many kinds of lilies, and the blue-flowering paulownia tree.

The love of flowers has been deep and widespread in the Chinese people. In no other great art of the world have flowers played such a major part as they do in Chinese art and its derived arts in Japan. Over the centuries, the Chinese have compiled many volumes on horticulture. They have been transplanting full grown trees for over fifteen hundred years, and for at least a thousand they have been growing tree miniatures in pots. Yet when they came to make landscape gardens, they did not emphasize flowers. Flowers took their place only as one of the phases of a natural scene. This has not deterred the Chinese people from growing flowers in pots for their courts and terraces and developing horticultural hobbies for their pleasure.

No pictures of China's earliest gardens survive, as such pictures do in Egypt. But the Chinese have been a literate, artistic, and conservative people, and their culture has never been superseded nor seriously displaced by another. Traditions and forms, therefore, have remained consistent. In their records are many references to ancient construction, and in their art are many illustrations derived from times past. Taken together, these can probably give us a fairly clear idea of how the earliest Chinese gardens began and what they looked like.

The early Chinese people were not only agriculturists but also hunters, for many animals lived in the forests and grasslands. Animals have been a basic element in Chinese art and even a part of Chinese gardens. Birds and butterflies, fish, frogs, and even small animals like rabbits have been considered an integral part of gardens. And menageries of larger, more exotic animals were usually a part of imperial parks, even up to the last ones in Peking and Manchuria.

Primitive Chinese people lived in roofed holes scooped in the ground. Eventually they came to evolve a manner of house building much like that still to be seen on Chinese farms. Clay models of houses, dating back two thousand years, make it clear how little have been the basic changes in house design since then. The early house was a simple structure of wood framing, its walls filled in with mud bricks and its roof thatched. To raise it above the damp fields, it stood on a platform of pounded earth. The building turned its solid back to the cold north and opened its southern front to a yard or court which was enclosed by side buildings and by high walls of pounded earth. Simple gardens first appeared in these courtyards, and to this day the gardens of ordinary people in China are found in them.

We catch a glimpse of one of the early homesteads in certain songs in the *Book of Odes,* the *Shih Ching*. These were collected perhaps a thousand years before the Christian era and are the earliest literature of China. In one, the girl sings to her lover:

> I beg of you, Chung Tsu,
> Do not climb into our homestead,
> Do not break the willows we have planted.
> Not that I mind about the willows,
> But I am afraid of my father and mother.
> Chung Tsu I dearly love;
> But of what my father and mother would say
> Indeed I am afraid.[2]

Planting a willow tree near the house may have had some magic significance, such as warding off fire, for willow trees grow along all the watercourses of China, and even today the twin ideas of water and willows seem almost inseparable. But I think we can be sure that the grace and beauty of this tree were also appreciated, as they still are. In this homestead, the willow was evidently planted near the wall—where the lover might have broken it in scrambling over. It was put there to be out of the way of the central working space, as we often see trees today in Japanese farmyards, which were created on much the same pattern.

In time this early type of construction became expanded to impressive proportions in royal palaces, ancestral halls, and temples. The wood framing developed into stately pillars of cypress and pine, often painted with vermilion-red lacquer. The roof became large and massive, made of gleaming green, yellow, or blue glazed tiles. Sometimes the building was two-storied, or small towers might go up considerably higher at the corners. Like the lesser residences, the structure stood facing south on a high, raised platform. Auxiliary buildings were placed left and right and sometimes behind, on an axis. When the palace stood informally in a natural setting, the terrace might be asymmetrical, built out into the edge of a lake, or it might overhang a ravine. In more urban situations the main ceremonial building faced a spacious courtyard, paved and without plantings, designed to hold many people in ceremonial formation. In the case of imperial Halls of State, where officials were lined up on important occasions, this level forecourt would accommodate hundreds.

As in the Near East, the early Chinese kings and nobles had enclosed hunting parks. They were probably created after agriculture had begun to reduce the forest areas and scatter the game. A curious but significant diagram of such early parks can probably be seen in a written character which was one of the first ways in which the word for park—that is, *yuan*—was set down, possibly around 1500 B.C. It includes the character for tree, which in pictographic writing showed a stylized tree made up of trunk, branches, and roots. When two trees were placed side by side, the meaning was "grove" or "forest"; three trees signified the adjective "luxuriant." The word for park was written by placing four trees within a square. The square is taken to represent an enclosing wall, and the four tree characters have the significance of "many trees."[3]

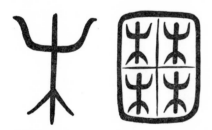

Fig. 1. *The Chinese character for "tree" (left) as used in inscriptions on ancient bronze castings. This in turn became an element in what was probably the first diagram ever made of a Chinese park, the pictograph standing for the word "park" (right), found in the Great Seal Script on the Stone Drums.*

The use of the wall around these parks marked the beginning of Chinese landscape development—that is, the treatment of outdoor space by man for his own use and enjoyment. But although the old written character shows four trees neatly arranged within the square, the Chinese never superimposed such formality on their parks, as did the Persians after discovering formality in Egypt. Rather, in their gardens the Chinese have always held to the theme of nature. Nothing they knew of could be more beautiful than the natural

35

lakes and streams, the wooded hills and flowery meadows of their early land. Later, when they came to know better their awe-inspiring mountains, these too were incorporated into the garden picture.

Nature, in time, was handled as an art theme, the garden being subjected to the laws of design, including rhythm, scale, harmonic balance, proportion, unity, and emphasis. Sometimes the garden treatment included abridgment, stylization, and symbolism. But always, in garden layouts, man's handiwork remained subordinated to the theme of nature. This is exactly opposite to the Mediterranean pattern.

However, it should be mentioned that the Chinese did later sometimes use water and trees in geometric arrangements when these were part of an architectural complex. Water was often introduced in squared tanks or similar forms or in geometrically laid out canals. Smaller courtyards, in particular, might use trees, shrubs, and vines grown in raised beds enclosed by low retaining walls of stone or tile. But even these courts were almost never laid out with axial formality.

In taking over stretches of landscape for their hunting parks, the rulers undoubtedly chose the finest stands of forest, the most picturesque lakes, streams, and meadows. In due course, these hunting parks—especially if they were not too far from a capital city—became royal country estates and pleasure parks and consequently the settings for some of China's most magnificent palaces.

In the centuries preceding the Christian era, China had become divided politically into a number of smaller states, most of them generally engaged in desultory war with each other. Each petty ruler had his own palace and probably his park. This is evident from the fact that when, by 221 B.C., these states had, one by one, been subjugated and brought under a single rule, the successful warlord who thus made himself the First Emperor celebrated his triumph by reproducing in his park along the bank of the Wei River the palace halls of each of the vanquished princes.[4]

This First Emperor (221–210 B.C.), who is known to history as Ch'in Shih Huang Ti, set up his capital on the Wei River near the site later known as Ch'ang-an and today as Sian. On the opposite side of the river he possessed a large hunting preserve called the Shang-lin Park. Deciding that his old Hall of State and other government buildings were too small for his new greatness, he began the O-fang Palace. Its great Hall of State is reported to have been 500 feet deep and 500 paces wide, and its front courtyard could accommodate a vast number of officials lined up at important ceremonies. The building was also appropriately high, for it is recorded that flagpoles, some 35 feet high (that is, 50 Han feet) could be set up below, meaning, it seems, without touching the eaves.[5]

The O-fang Palace buildings were enclosed by a massive wall, while a covered road and special bridge connected the estate with the capital city across the river. Another road ran south to a mountaintop where the First Emperor planned to construct his tomb. The vast size and splendor of the O-fang Palace buildings have come down in Chinese history as the very archetype of imperial magnificence, a goal to be equaled by any ruler who could command the means and the manpower.

Yet with all the reported wonder of the bridges, walls, roads, and buildings, there is not a word recorded at this time about the development of the Shang-lin Park itself. We must conclude, therefore, that up to the fourth century B.C. the Chinese were concerned with building stately, but had not, as yet, begun to garden finely.

Landscape development, probably, was not really necessary at this time, for there must have still been preserved around the natural lakes and streams of the imperial parks much of the primeval woodland and the flowery meadows of early China. We can judge this by a quotation from Mencius (around 373–288 B.C.), who refers to the destruction of the forests in these words: "The trees of the New Mountain were once beautiful. Being situated, however, on the borders of a large State, they were hewn down with axes . . . and could they retain their beauty? Still, they were not without buds and sprouts springing forth; but then came the cattle and goats and browsed upon them. To these things is owing the bare and stripped appearance which, when the people see it, they think was never finely wooded."[6]

Not until man has destroyed natural beauty and created in its place monotonous fields, bare hills, and ugly cities does he feel a need to replace nature with gardens.

CHAPTER FOUR

Development of
Lakes and Islands

THE First Emperor died before the O-fang Palace was finished. Out of the civil wars that followed, there finally emerged the great dynasty of Han. It became China's first long-continued empire, lasting about 400 years (206 B.C. to A.D. 220). Eventually, Han jurisdiction extended from Korea to Afghanistan, and its power as well as its size was comparable to that of its great contemporary, the Roman empire. The two never made official contacts, but they knew of each other through the traffic in silk across Central Asia and from the outposts of each near the Oxus River.

Kao Tsu, a warlord who made himself emperor by founding the Han dynasty, was of frugal peasant stock. In 200 B.C., although he was still fighting, he commissioned his prime minister Hsiao Ho to build a suitable palace in his new capital city of Ch'ang-an. Remembering the grandeur of the great O-fang Palace, this commissioner began construction of the Wei-yang Palace on a magnificent scale. When it was partly finished, the emperor returned from a campaign and came to inspect it. He was angry at the tremendous scale and said: "The country is not yet entirely subjugated, and our final success or failure is still uncertain. Yet you, Ho, are putting up these palace buildings on a scale beyond measure."

Hsiao Ho replied: "The Son of Heaven has the whole country for his household. Without great and magnificent buildings, there would be no way of making himself imposing and majestic, so that later generations need add nothing to them."[1]

The emperor was satisfied with this reasoning and soon took possession of the new palace. The philosophy that imperial greatness and stability might be maintained through majestic buildings and great parks was to be accepted down the centuries to the last imperial construction in Peking, which may still be seen.

The early part of the Han period was a time of energetic expansion. Old restraints had been thrown off, and the country was prosperous. A feeling of joyous exuberance permeated this age, easily seen exemplified in its art. Certain reliefs show high-stepping horses carrying riders or drawing light chariots at a furious pace (Plate 58). The Han people, like these horses and their drivers, it seems to me, felt they were going places and doing things. We learn of these doings in a poem describing certain murals, in deep reds and blues, with fantastic crowds of mythical and historic personages, all in great action.[2]

38

The new freedom to enlarge and create was applied also to the making of parks and imperial estates. It reached its peak under the Han emperor Wu (140–89 B.C.), who laid out many new areas and enlarged and developed older ones. Among the latter was that same Wei-yang Palace, whose original size had so dismayed his great grandfather, founder of the dynasty.

This palace lay inside the city wall, much as the Forbidden City lies inside Peking. Its inner walls enclosed the Hall of State, where the emperor received foreign ambassadors. It was some 400 feet wide and 110 feet deep. Today, the corresponding hall in Peking is only 200 feet wide and a hundred feet deep.[3] Yet this building looms up with impressive size in the imperial enclosure. It is thought that lack of sufficiently large timbers, due to deforestation, accounts for the reduction in size of the present building.

The rear section of the Wei-yang enclosure was a private area (as in Peking) where the emperor lived with his empress and various ladies. Each had an individual palace residence, the various buildings set apart by garden spaces. The original precincts of the Wei-yang Palace were extended by Emperor Wu beyond the city wall to include a large pleasure park, the whole being more than seven miles around (Plate 5). There were twelve lakes and five hills in the park as well as forty-three buildings for various purposes. Inside the the residential area, within the walls, there was a single lake and hill.[4]

While the lakes and hills in the great park were probably all of nearly natural form, it is likely that the lake inside the city was largely aided by artificial construction. There must have been a source for the water—a natural stream or perhaps a canal. Its course could have been widened and excavated so as to form the lake, and the material taken out of this lake could then have been used for the "hill," which was probably little more than a good-sized bank, planted with trees.

Another great enclosure within the city was the Ch'ang-lo Palace, dating back to the beginning of the Han period. Usually this was occupied by the empress dowager and the ladies who had been favored by the late emperor. Like the others, it was of impressive proportions, occupying about one-ninth of the space within the city walls. In such an area there must have been extensive open areas for planting.

The old Shang-lin Park across the river, in which a century before had stood the great O-fang Palace of the first Ch'in emperor, was extended by Emperor Wu to 300 li (about 100 miles) in both directions. It was really an immense royal hunting preserve, used primarily to supply the court with game, fish, and birds. The gamekeepers lived in several villages, while seventy lodges accommodated the court and guests at a great annual hunt in the autumn. On that hunt thousands of animals were slain for feasting and for the sacrifices.[5]

New imperial estates developed by the emperor Wu outside the city walls included the Ch'ien-chang Palace. It was linked to the Wei-yang Palace by a two-storied covered arcade. Also newly built was the Kan-ch'uan Palace, about 75 miles away. The names of all these palaces have come down in Chinese tradition as synonymous with beauty and imperial grandeur. All had fine buildings, groves, streams, and hills.[6]

Full accounts of these Han parks and palaces were compiled later. The city of Ch'ang-an eventually had to be abandoned as a Han capital, but when, long afterward, the T'ang dynasty came back to the vicinity of this site to re-establish its capital city, there seems to have been a good deal of curiosity about the monuments left on the old site nearby. Studies were made, old traditions were examined, and the results were compiled into various records.[7] However, by the time these later records were made, the creation of man-made landscapes had become common practice. But T'ang writers on the Han period seem to have assumed that such artificial landscape practices had been followed also at earlier periods. Examination of early contemporary Han records does not bear this out, for there seems to have been very little artificial landscaping at that time.[8]

The most important contribution to Chinese garden art in the Han period was probably made by Emperor Wu in his attempt to imitate certain Mystic Isles of the Blest believed to lie off the coast of Shantung. The story of these isles had originated much earlier, in the coastal provinces where the people were seafarers. The stories were doubtless inspired by the fact that not very far away, off the coast of Korea, there are, in fact, many islands both large and small. On those misty seas they might easily appear sometimes to vanish.

The tale of the Mystic Isles[9] relates that somewhere off the coast of Shantung there were once five islands called P'eng-lai, Ying-chou, Fang-hu, Yuan-ch'iao, and Tai-yu. They were large mountainous islands, their summits towering up thousands of feet, their sides steep and precipitous. Thick groves of trees grew on the high plateaus, while rich verdure trailed down their misty blue valleys. All the birds and beasts living on these islands were purest white, while the trees bore pearls and other gems. Every flower was fragrant, and the fruits brought immortality to those who ate them.

Along the shores of these islands, and on high leveled terraces, were many pleasure halls of gold, silver, and jade. In these dwelt the Immortals, the happy ones who do not die. The Immortals or *hsien* were not gods, but human men and women who, by one magic means or another, had achieved a state in which youth is eternal, sickness, age, and death unknown. The hsien also possessed other superhuman powers, such as the ability to float or fly through the air. Sometimes they preferred to ride on the backs of giant cranes. The Immortals lived wherever they wished, but thousands chose to spend their time on the isles in happy companionship with each other.

Now, in the beginning, the five islands had not been firmly fixed to the sea bottom but were floating. They rocked and drifted about, and these movements so annoyed the hsien that they complained to the Supreme Ruler of the Universe. He commanded fifteen enormous tortoises to support the islands firmly on their backs. This plan worked for a long time, but one day a giant, setting out on his travels, had not taken many strides when he

1. One of the world's earliest gardens as painted more than three thousand years ago on the walls of an ▶
Egyptian tomb near Thebes (dated Dynasty XVIII, between 1420 and 1375 B.C.). Such gardens combined practicality with beauty. The rectangular pool held fish and ducks as well as the blue Egyptian water lily. On its edges were set out small flowering plants which probably included red poppies and blue cornflowers. Fruit and shade trees were grown in straight lines around the water. Among them, in this scene, the date palm and the sycamore fig can be identified. Other contemporary garden paintings reveal that such pools were sometimes used to supply irrigation water to the garden. This usage, combined with a general Egyptian preference for geometric layout, accounts for the straight-line planning which became the prototype for Europe's formal gardens. (Reproduced as "The Pool in the Garden" in Ancient Egyptian Painting, *1936, by N. M. Davies and A. Gardiner)*

came to the region of the five islands. With one cast of his net he gathered up six of the tortoises and, carrying them on his back, returned to his country. Robbed thus of their support, two of the islands drifted away and were lost.[10]

Actual belief in the three remaining isles, P'eng-lai, Ying-chou, and Fang-hu, was widespread in the early pre-Christian centuries, and the hope of learning the secret of immortality by reaching them was strong. One of the most credulous of the hopefuls had been the hard-headed First Emperor of Ch'in. He visited the seacoast more than once and sent several ships to find the islands and bring back some of the fruits of immortality. However, on their return the ships reported that although the peaks might be sighted, as in a cloud, they sank beneath the waves when a ship approached closer or a wind arose and blew them away.[11]

Another credulous ruler who would have liked to attain immortality was the emperor Wu of Han himself. Knowing the failures of his predecessors in reaching the isles, he conceived the possibility of enticing the Immortals to his own estates, where, presumably, they might have been induced to part with the secrets of immortality. This plan was undertaken in the large Tai-i lake. It lay west of the capital city of Ch'ang-an and north of the great country estate of Ch'ien-chang.

This huge lake held a number of rocky islands in which the imagination of the time saw fantastic animals. One of these rocks is said to have been as large as a whale.[12] Other rocks may have suggested the giant sea tortoises of the tale. More likely, this lake was chosen because already there was in it, on a central island, a tall towerlike structure called Chien T'ai. It was so picturesque and beautiful, rising in the middle of the lake, it could have served as a palace for the Immortals.[13]

Around this tower, on three islands in the lake, Emperor Wu caused to be constructed halls and courts which were named—to suggest the Mystic Isles—the P'eng-lai Palace, the Ying-chou Palace, and the Fang-hu Palace. The poet and historian Pan Ku (A.D. 32–93), who lived in the century immediately following Emperor Wu and, one must assume, had seen the Tai-i lake and its islands, wrote a rhapsodic prose poem on the scene. He took a certain poetic license in his choice of words to enhance the supernatural feeling of this place. Viewing it from a certain point, he says:

"Before, stretches the lake T'ang-chung; behind, Lake Tai-i. Their waves can be seen as high as those of the limitless sea, breaking against the rocks of the fairy shores, half submerged in water. With a crash they hurl themselves against the fairy rocks covering the isles Ying-chou and Fang-hu, while P'eng-lai rises between them. Then the magic grasses flour-

◄ *2. Of all the paradises that men have dreamed of, none seems to have had a more lasting appeal than that of the lovely Mystic Isles of the Immortals in the Eastern Ocean. Long after all belief in them had vanished, artists and craftsmen continued to use the theme, apparently for sheer joy in a congenial subject. Takahashi Sohei, an artist of the Edo period, produced this form of the fantasy in the style of his time. (Collection of Kan'ichiro Ishibashi, Tokyo)*

◄ *3. Another Edo-period artist, perhaps the celebrated Korin, here echoes the Mystic Isles theme in a shimadai painting for auspicious occasions showing symbols of happiness and longevity—tortoise, crane, pine, bamboo, and plum—that have also found their way into garden art. The island of such paintings was often patterned on the Mystic Isles. (Private collection, Tokyo)*

43

ish in winter, supernatural trees thrust up in clumps. The rocks are precipitous, the cliffs towering, metals and rocks form high jutting peaks. There the emperor [Wu] raised two statues of immortals holding bowls to collect the dew; these statues he placed on two columns of bronze, which rose far above the impurities of the dusty world."[14]

While waiting for the Immortals to come, Emperor Wu spent his time discussing Taoist theories on ways to attain immortality. Unfortunately, in spite of all efforts to attract them, the hsien never came. Emperor Wu and all other Chinese emperors have proved to be mortal.

However, the lovely Mystic Isles, both the originals and their imitations, appear to have achieved something like immortality themselves. Of all the paradises that man has dreamed of, none seems to have had a more lasting appeal than this one. Long after all belief in the isles had vanished, artists and craftsmen continued to use the theme, apparently for sheer joy in a congenial subject (Plates 2, 3). To this day, small *shikishi* paintings, depicting the fantastic forms of the isles or the misty green-and-blue beauty of P'eng-lai (called Horai-zan in Japan) may often be picked up in the art section of a modern Japanese department store. And in old Japanese garden lakes, one can still sometimes dimly see the outlines of a giant tortoise holding an island firm above the flood (Plate 57).

Descriptions of that other paradise, the celestial lake garden of the Buddha Amida, reached China during the latter part of the Han period. These came in books carried over the Silk Road. The people of the Han period, however, were too busy with the affairs of this world to pay much attention to promises about the next one. It took later disaster to turn their thoughts that way. But when, at last, this happened, Buddhism introduced another concept which eventually found its image as an island in Chinese garden lakes. Here we can look forward for a moment and compare this later Buddhist island to the Isles of the Immortals.

Hinduism and Buddhism, originating along the lower slopes of the vast Himalaya Mountains, very logically conceived of the universe as centering around a stupendous central peak which supported the heavens above and was surrounded below by the world, made up of nine vast mountain ranges and eight oceans. The peak was known as Great Meru or Sumeru, and the entire concept was sometimes tagged as the Nine Mountains and Eight Seas.

The foreign, otherworldly concepts of Buddhism, when presented to the Chinese, were at first pictured by them in terms of their own mystic Taoism, that unworldly Way which was opposed to the proper conventionalities as taught by Confucius. It is probable, there-fore, that Mount Sumeru was early conceived of as very like the towering peaks of the Immortals' Isles. But later, when pious people turned over their estates to be converted into Buddhist monasteries, it is likely that the new abbots renamed existing islands on such estates from the rich imagery of their sacred scriptures. It is certain, at any rate, that in due course islands in Buddhist precincts came to be known as Sumeru or, as the Japanese came to call them, Shumisen.

Nevertheless, the difference between islands derived from these two concepts seems to have been mostly a matter of names, although there may have been a period when there was some real difference in their structure. The garden Isles of the Immortals had at first, as we have seen, been developed in typical Chinese fashion, with strong emphasis on the buildings. Later that portion of the tale touching on the giant tortoises was remembered, and there were tortoise islands. Even the cranes who ferried the Immortals to the isles eventually became a longevity symbol and found themselves also represented as islets.

On the other hand, Mount Sumeru, having been derived from awe-inspiring nature, emphasized its rocks and other natural aspects. One description of a "Mount Sumeru" erection in T'ang times states: "Its four faces were made up of sublime rocks and towering precipices. Pearly birds and rare beasts, groves of trees and plants of exquisite beauty grew upon it. There were images of gods and Buddhas. It was something people had never heard the like of and was regarded as miraculous." It has been suggested that the "pearly birds" may have been ceramics.[15]

Looking back over the landscape development of the Han period we see, then, that in the beginning chief emphasis was given to islands. This is logical, for islands, by their nature, are always focal points of interest. Inevitably they hold something of mystery and entice-ment, arising from their isolation, while the appeal of their beauty is doubled by the magic of reflection. In a land like North China, which was comparatively level, with many rivers and lakes, it was natural that islands should have become the first center of developing landscape interest. The lake-and-island pattern, therefore, was the first to emerge in the history of Chinese gardens.

The great imperial parks of the early Han period were designed for emperors and princes only. They were largely an expression of the power and glory of empire, and no attempt by a rich commoner to own an extensive estate was tolerated. This is brought out in an account of a rich merchant, Yuan Kuang-han of Mao-ling.

He had stored cash by the million and had eight to nine hundred slaves. He acquired land at the foot of the northern mountains, four li from east to west and five li from north to south (something over a square mile in area). There was a swiftly flowing stream and stones "joined like mountains," more than a hundred feet high and stretching along for several li. He raised white parrots and purple mandarin ducks. Yaks, grey gaurs, and other strange animals and precious birds were gathered in it. Sand was collected into islands and violent waters (a cascade?) produced waves which went on into the river. Many strange trees and curious plants were cultivated. Houses were scattered here and there or arranged into groups, some with many-storied buildings, and having wooden passageways connect-ing them.

It is hardly a surprise to learn that a little later this commoner "committed a crime" and was executed. His birds, beasts, plants, and trees were all transferred to Emperor Wu's Shang-lin Park.[16]

Nevertheless, the creation of private estates was to be one of the next important steps in the development of Chinese gardens.

45

CHAPTER FIVE

Addition of
Mountains and Rocks

THE early imperial parks, with their stretches of natural forest and grassland, their rivers, lakes, and islands, were simple and uncomplicated expressions of nature, used mostly for the lusty sport of hunting. Yet the Chinese seem always to have possessed a strong subjective feeling for the beauties of nature. Their earliest songs took aspects of nature as metaphors to reflect symbolic parallels in the acts and feelings of men:

> Gorgeous in their beauty
> Are the flowers of the cherry.
>
> Are they not magnificent in their dignity—
> The carriages of the royal bride?[1]

Harmony with nature was an intuitive basic philosophy for survival, with the feeling that man should strive to put himself into harmony with nature's ways, rather than to contend against them. In a much-quoted statement, Confucius (551–479 B.C.) once said: "The wise find pleasure in water; the virtuous find pleasure in hills. The wise are active; the virtuous, tranquil. The wise are joyful; the virtuous are long-lived."[2]

The phrase "hills and water" has become for China and Japan the term for "landscape." It was later to be extended to cover paintings of landscapes and also landscape gardens. What Confucius (who lived in a period of danger and duplicity) appears to be saying is that active outings to the tranquility of hills and streams bring not only deep joy to the sensitive person but a refreshment to body and spirit that could even prolong life.

This early, rather vague feeling for nature changed into highly developed consciousness when China's vast mountains in the south and west became generally better known, and when catastrophe created in the people a mood to turn away from the world of men.

The Han dynasty, which was to endure for four hundred years, was broken about halfway through when the throne was usurped for a short time (A.D. 8–23). With the restoration of the imperial line, the capital was moved away from Ch'ang-an, with its tradition of great palaces, to Lo-yang. This city was some 125 miles eastward, near the Yellow River. The Han dynasty was never again so powerful as it had been before the usurpation, and we hear no more of such great imperial parks as were built by the emperor Wu.

46

However, the country was prosperous, and the desire of wealthy commoners like Yuan Kuang-han to own fine estates appears to have increased, while the imperial power was not strong enough to suppress those who attempted to do so. One of the most famous of the early private estates was that in the Golden Valley, the Chin Ku Yuan, built near the end of the third century.

By then the last Han emperor, who had been a puppet in the hands of a warlord, had been deposed, and the great empire had broken into three kingdoms, all fighting each other. It was during this extended period of danger and uncertainty that the estate in the Golden Valley was awarded to a faithful officer, Shih Ch'ung.

"In the year 290," Shih Ch'ung writes, "I was called to the aid of the Marshal [Chan Lu], who had charge of all the military affairs in Chin Chou and Hsi Chin. I had a villa in the Golden Valley [Chin Ku] in Ho-yang. It was ten li from the city [of Lo-yang]. The ground went up in places and down in others. [That is, it was hilly or rolling.] There were clear waters and verdant woods, plenty of fruit trees, bamboos, pines, herbs for medicines, and grasses. I had rice fields covering [an extensive acreage], two hundred sheep and all kinds of chickens, pigs, ducks, and geese. I had a mill and fish ponds, and [for storage] caves in the earth. I had all the things that can please the eye and heart."[3]

"When I was fifty years old," he continues, "I left my position, and during my later years I have indulged myself quite freely. I liked forests and natural scenery, so I escaped to my villa [the Golden Valley] in Ho-yang. The place lies below a long bank and beside a clear stream. Nearby there are forests of a thousand trunks. The water encircles my residence and there are pavilions, halls, and ponds with birds and fishes. When I go out I shoot birds and catch fish. When I come in I have the pleasure of reading and lute playing. In my house are people who can play the *chin shih* [Chinese harp]."[4]

Shih Ch'ung tells of entertaining with a prolonged house party an official friend who was about to leave for another city. Although they tried to be gay, he remarks, "thinking of the brevity of life, we were aware that we did not know when we should die."

Their premonitions were well founded. Only a few years later disaster came to Lo-yang. In the constant struggle for power the nomadic horsemen of the northern steppes had been enlisted as auxiliaries by one side. These barbarians were always hovering outside the Great Wall (which had originally been built to prevent their forays). Like the Goths, they eventually turned into invaders, and in A.D. 311 they captured the Chinese emperor, sacked and burned Lo-yang, and massacred thousands.

Even before this happened, however, the master of the Golden Valley had been assassinated because he would not give up his favorite concubine. It is probably the romantic aspects of this story that have perpetuated the Golden Valley in legend and art as a place of fabulous beauty and extravagance. Centuries later, imaginary pictures of it were still being painted. But from the master's own words it appears to have been only a pleasantly large and well-developed estate. It was not, at any rate, an elaborate landscape garden.

The invading barbarians continued their devastation, and in 316 also captured and destroyed Ch'ang-an, the other great city of the empire. After that, all North China lay under their control.

During these periods of danger, escape became the main thought of the times, escape not

47

only from bodily dangers but from the mental turmoil that accompanied the destruction of a world. Many people went into the hills, where horsemen could not follow. After the fall of the capital remaining members of the court and many families of the scholarly governing classes fled southward. Beyond the barrier of the mighty Yangtze River they set up a new capital on the site of present-day Nanking. During the following centuries this southern area remained comparatively peaceful although plagued by a series of short-lived governments known as the Six Dynasties.

Up to that time, this southern region had been a cultural outland. But with the coming of the scholarly gentry it gradually became a fully civilized part of China. New phases of culture came into being there, influenced in part by the warmer climate and the green beauty of the hills and valleys. Among these new things were gentlemen's country estates and rustic retreats in the hills.

Another way in which escape was sought from the turmoil of the age was through the peace and quiet of religion. Buddhism, with its otherworldliness, now became extremely popular and attracted thousands as monks and nuns. Many new monasteries had to be constructed to hold them. At first these new centers were built largely in the southern mountains, where safety and isolation made for quiet and peace of mind.

These new mountain temples required water from a spring or stream, and woodlands nearby to provide timber and fuel. Shelter from wind and storms was often sought in the lee of rocky cliffs, and at such sites also would have been found stones for building. These several items being among the more important aspects of fine scenery, the new institutions often came to occupy very picturesque spots.[5] In time the presence of temple buildings became typical of the more accessible parts of China's mountain landscapes.

The shock of the great empire's disintegration had affected most profoundly those minds which were sensitive and thoughtful. Released from their responsibilities to its social order, and repulsed by spectacles of cruelty and stupidity, many such men turned away from their old ideas. Previous thinking had been largely associated with Confucianism, a system of political ethics and social orderliness. Now, to many men Confucianism seemed to have failed, and they turned to Taoism, that opposing system of Chinese philosophy which preached political inaction and personal individualism as the Way. Men whose thoughts took this turn often left civilization to wander in the mountains. All of those who came to the hills discovered there a new world of grandeur and beauty, holding permanent spiritual values to which they could cling and respond.

China's mountains may well be the most spectacularly beautiful and awe-inspiring of any in the world. The highlands of Asia are not volcanic but are vast uplifted folds of the earth's crust, cracked and tilted into almost incredible peaks and precipices. The great chasms have been deepened by eroding waters which dash and roar among the rocks below. Tributary streams from some high, hanging valley may leap to join the main stream in a single arc of white foam. Or the falling waters may be shattered into cataracts against jagged cliffs.

On the ridges of these mountains, or wherever a foothold exists, luxuriant forests crowd together. Occasionally a single aged tree—twisted, storm-tossed, and broken—may cling to a dangerous cliffside, becoming the symbol of human life triumphant over difficulties.

48

On all but the most vertical of the lower mountain slopes grow luxuriant jungles of flowering shrubs, while annuals and grasses fill in the open glades below.

Not far from where ancient Chinese civilization began, there rises abruptly from the level plain the mountain called Hua-shan (Plate 61). Farther south and west is the great peak of Omei-shan. On each there have been temples for centuries. The path which pilgrims take to reach these and other temples is still a flowery way. Above the scarlet lilies, campanulas, jasmine, and forget-me-nots of the lower slopes, the rhododendrons turn whole mountainsides into solid masses of color. Acres of pale pink reflect a silvery sheen. Yellows create patches of sunshine. Brilliant scarlets sweep like flames across the mountainsides, and whites tumble in foaming cascades down the slopes. Here and there, like dissonant notes of music, patches of purple and magenta may spark these other colors into added brilliance.

The pilgrim, trudging his way upward, soon leaves behind the sweltering heat of the plains and the sibilance of insects. He feels the fresh coolness of the mountains and is suddenly aware of their vast stillness. Above him rise the pines and other conifers, and soon their pungence swirls about him like incense ascending to heaven. Clouds and mist may suddenly close in around him, whitely blinding out all view. When they lift again, the landscape below is partially revealed through tenuous veils of drifting cloud. Far away, the silvery pattern of a great river writhes its dragon way across the plain. At his feet, an awesome chasm opens, its sides a sheer mile or more in depth. Somewhere below roars a hidden river. And in the far distance, above the mist, grim old peaks ascend into the sky out of nothingness.

It is a scene that was to be depicted by China's landscape painters in a thousand variations. It would find its way into Chinese poetry and be given impressionistic form in Chinese and Japanese garden art. For out of such scenes rose slowly a cult of the wilderness, a worship of nature, in which men sought to understand the world, the universe, and themselves through contemplation or by identifying themselves as a minute but integral part of the cosmos. Gardens of the coming age were to include those which embodied such esoteric relationships with nature. These came into being parallel with the art of landscape painting and more or less as a phase of it.

Up to the Six Dynasties, Chinese painting had depicted almost exclusively the figures of men and animals. Now began the painting of landscape. Of this type, the greatest masterpieces were to be produced later, in the T'ang and Sung periods (seventh to late thirteenth century). Later still, in Japan, landscape painting was to have an autumnal season of greatness in the fifteenth century.

It was during these epochs of great landscape painting that the greatest gardens were also produced in both countries. The painter used brush, paper, and ink to achieve his effects and express his concepts. The landscape garden maker took rocks, water, and trees to produce three-dimensional forms of the same idea. During the early part of the Six Dynasties, landscape painting and garden making were just starting on this course. But the cult of nature seems to have had its earliest expression in words, whether in prose or in poetry.

One of the great painters of this age was Ku K'ai-chih (344–406). A paragraph he wrote reveals how landscape impressed him. He had been on a visit to a picturesque part of southern China, K'ai-chi, and on his return he was asked what it was like. He summed up his impressions in these terms:

> A thousand cliffs vie in beauty,
> Ten thousand gorges compete in their rushing [waters].
> The grasses and trees which screen them
> Are like rising clouds and dense vapors.[6]

An example of how landscape painting came down from the mountains is found in the life of a famous painter and critic named Tsung Ping (375–443). His biography states: "Tsung Ping loved landscapes. In the west he ascended Mounts Ching and Wu; in the south he climbed the peak of Heng. On the last he built for himself a hut, cherishing the idea of a peaceful [life there]. Then he fell ill and went home to Chiang-ling. He said, lamenting, 'I am old and in poor health as well; I fear it would be difficult for me to roam the famous mountains [any longer]. Now I can only clarify my desires by meditation on the *Tao* and wander in my dreams.' All that he experienced in his travels he painted on his walls."[7]

Tsung Ping was able to express his feeling for landscape not only in wall paintings but in words also. I quote Alexander Soper's comment on a rather remarkable statement that is attributed to him: "Under his name is preserved a so-called 'Preface to Painting,' in which the point of view of the creative nature worshiper is already well expressed. The whole treatise is interesting, both for its historical primacy in the field of theory and for its own sake. . . . One cannot be sure of following Tsung Ping's thought everywhere, but its sense is clear enough in crucial passages.

" 'Landscapes (he says) have a material existence, and yet reach into a spiritual domain.' The wild beauty of their forms, the 'peaks and precipices rising sheer and high, the cloudy forest lying dense and vast,' have brought to the wise and virtuous recluses of the past an unending pleasure, a 'joy which is of the soul, and of the soul only.' One approach to the *Tao* is by inward concentration alone; another, almost the same, is through the beauty of mountains and water. 'In such a way, the beauty of Mount Sung and Mount Hua, the very mystery of the Dark Spirit of the Universe, all may be captured within a single picture.' In statements such as these, the sublimity of Nature and its representation in art are joined mystically with the eternal beyond all forms."[8]

The mention of Tsung Ping's mountain hut is one of the earliest references to a custom that was to become widespread down the centuries, that of a scholar building a rustic retreat where he might get away from life's complications and stay for longer or shorter periods. These retreats were not always in the deep mountains but sometimes near the edge of a lake or stream. Many pictures showing such retreats are found among Chinese paint-

4. The romantic beauties of Hangchow in South China, with its villas around the lake, its islands, temples, and half-moon bridges, remained in the memory of the Japanese long after their country had become a hermit nation and its people were forbidden to travel abroad. Artists of the Edo period continued to paint its charms with nostalgia, as did Ike no Taiga, about the time of the American Revolution, in the screen painting of which this is a detail. (Tokyo National Museum) ▶

未央宮

ings. Generally, somewhere, is included the small figure of the scholar, engaged in his preoccupation with nature and usually attended by a servant.

Probably the clearest description of one of the Chinese mountain retreats, and a revelation of the state of mind that went with them, was set down later by an official of the T'ang dynasty. His name was Po Chu-i, and he was one of China's greatest poets.

Like most Chinese officials, Po Chu-i (772–864) went through periods of political favor and disfavor at court. During one of his periods of disfavor he was sent to a distant post on the Yangtze River. His headquarters was in the city of Kiu-kiang, then called Chiang-chou, about ten miles from the Lu-shan mountains. During his stay in this district he built for himself in those hills a retreat which he called the Grass Cottage, because it was thatched.[9]

It had two or three rooms and four windows. A doorway, opening to the north, admitted wind against the summer heat, while high rafters on the south admitted sunshine against the winter cold. The woodwork was hewn but not painted, the walls mud-plastered but not given a white finish. Steps were of natural stones, windows filled with lattices of bamboo and covered with paper. Hangings were of homespun, all in keeping. (This is a fairly accurate description still of a traditional Japanese tea hut. Such structures trace their descent back to these rustic retreats in the Chinese mountains.)

Po Chu-i's record continues: Inside the cottage were placed four wooden couches, two plain screens, a lacquered lute, and of books—Confucian, Taoist, and Buddhist—two or three scrolls each. "Since then, the poet has come to set these things first of all: to lift up his eyes and see the mountains; to lower them and listen to the stream; to look about him at bamboos, willows, clouds, and rocks, from morn till nightfall. One night's lodging brings rest to the body; two nights give peace to the heart; after three nights the drooping and depressed no longer know either trouble. If one asked the reason, the answer is simply —the place."

The description of the mountain garden which follows is revealing in that much of it is not actual garden but the natural environs of the Grass Cottage. Immediately in front of the building—that is, to the south—there was a leveled area, about a hundred feet square, probably enclosed by a wall. Across the upper part of this was a flat terrace. Beyond the terrace, and something under half its size, lay a square pool surrounded by mountain bamboo and wild herbs. In the pool, Po Chu-i planted the tubers of white lotus and stocked it with white fish.

South of the level courtyard one came to a rocky torrent, narrowed by the projection of ancient pines and old fir trees. They were almost eighteen spans in circumference and many feet in height, "their tall heads touching the clouds, their branches drooping over the water like low-hanging streamers, like an umbrella, or like dragon-snakes." Under these conifers swung a dense growth of vines and creepers "through whose interwoven shade the light of the sun and moon could not penetrate, and under which the winds of summer

◄ *5. Park of the Wei-yang Palace of the Han period in China as imagined by a painter who lived some centuries later—but still close enough to have a good idea, probably, of what it could have been like. The emperor of China appears under an umbrella of state, standing on a bridge and watching the approach of a dragon-headed boat lighted by rows of lanterns. The painting is believed to be a fairly late (Ming) copy of an original by the famous landscape painter Li Ssu-shun (651–710). (British Museum, London)* at full tide blew cool as autumn." The path which ran through this copse was covered with white pebbles.

Five paces to the north (that is, behind the cottage) the clearing ended at a cliff in which steps had been cut so that one could ascend. This slope was covered with a confusion of rocks and wild plants. "A green shadow covers and enfolds it, accented by the dripping red of some fruit whose name I do not know. . . . Then there is the 'Flying Spring' planted around with tea bushes. A lover of such things need only start a fire and boil water to spend a whole day there."

East of the cottage a small cascade fell down the cliff, flowing over ledges, around corners, and finally passing off through a stone gutter. "At dusk and dawn, and at midnight, its dripping sounds like the bangles of an artful beauty, tinkling accompaniment to the playing of lute and zither. . . ."

On the west, the cottage backed against the base of the great north precipice. A stairway of split bamboo, like a scaffold, led up its face. Another spring, dividing into thin veins of water, ran down to drip from the eaves and trickle over the ledges, "the drops bound together and intermingling like strung pearls, like falling dew, then as fine mist, scattering far on the breeze."

The poet adds: "In these four directions, staff and sandal, ear and eye may win [to such scenes as these]: in spring, the variegated embroidery of valley flowers; in summer, clouds and a torrent rushing through a rocky defile; in autumn, the Tiger Ravine under the moon; in winter, the snow-covered Fragrant Censer Peak, cold and gleaming in obscurity. Dusk and dawn cherish and display a thousand changes, a myriad appearances, never to be wholly caught in words. . . ."[10]

As we have noted, Po Chu-i was writing about natural scenery rather than a man-made garden. Yet this description by a skilled and sensitive artist does convey to us the intense pleasure in nature's beauties felt by those who lingered in the hills. And his words convey to us the picture of an area which was to have a profound effect on Chinese gardens. For it was this very spot in the Lu-shan mountains that had much to do with the second phase of Chinese garden development, the introduction of rocks and mountains into its pattern.

The Lu-shan range (where was formerly the popular foreign summer resort of Ku-ling) is a comparatively small, isolated group of mountains rising abruptly from the rolling green valley of the Yangtze River (Plate 59). Its peaks are much lower than those of the vast mountains farther west, but they are similarly sharp and precipitous. As seen from the river, their blue outlines are so picturesque as to seem almost like an artificial scenic set.

By the late fourth century there had settled in these mountains a famous monk named Hui Yuan (344–417). He was regarded as the greatest cleric of his day and is remembered as being virtually the founder, in China, of the cult of Amida—that beneficent Buddhist deity who receives faithful souls into his heavenly lotus garden.

Hui Yuan attracted around him a group of thoughtful men. Not all were Buddhist monks, but all were seeking understanding and knowledge. The group was known as the White Lotus Society, and its lay members came and went as they could. The name White Lotus must have been selected because of Hui Yuan's devotion to Amida. Probably also there was a pool near his monastery in which these flowers were grown (as Po Chu-i was to grow them later, doubtless in memory of the monk). The society was probably named after the white flowering variety of this plant rather than its commoner pink form—the dawn lily of the Aryans—because the white suggested greater purity and spirituality (Plate 60).

A patron had erected for Hui Yuan in 316 a temple called the Eastern Forest Monastery. (Later there was to be its twin, the Western Forest Monastery. Both were still in existence at the time of Po Chu-i.) Members of the White Lotus Society who were not monks usually built small houses for themselves somewhere in its vicinity—places, no doubt, much like the Grass Cottage. The monastery stood in a very picturesque spot. Behind and above it towered the tallest of the Lu-shan peaks, called from its form the Incense Burner (or, more poetically, the Peak of the Fragrant Censer). The building stood near a great ravine lined with waterfalls. The description of the grounds in Hui Yuan's biography continues:

"There were piled-up layers of rock on which pines were densely growing; clear rivulets flowed down on either side of the steps, and white clouds filled its rooms. Inside the monastery [grounds] Hui Yuan developed a special grove for meditation. The mist condensed on the trees and dripped onto the paths, which were covered with moss. Every spot seen by the eye and trodden by the foot was full of a spiritual purity and majesty."[11]

Mossy paths and a grove developed for meditation do not indicate very extensive garden developments by man around the monastery. Rather, Hui Yuan was making use, for the most part, of the natural beauties already there. Yet he is regarded as a master designer of monastery gardens.[12] His part, it seems to me, was to emphasize man's relationship to these beauties. If he encouraged meditation outdoors in groves, rather than indoors in a monastery hall, it must mean that he wanted his followers to find in the "peaks and precipices rising sheer and high, the cloudy forest lying dense and vast" that "joy which is of the soul and of the soul only" and to sense something of the "Dark Spirit of the Universe." These are the phrases of Tsung Ping, who was at one time a member of the White Lotus Society. I believe we can take his words as expressing a feeling that prevailed in the group.

Hui Yuan evidently thought of the whole mountain as the monastery's "garden," even as Po Chu-i was to regard the same mountainside as the "garden" of his Grass Cottage. I think it is doubtful if either of them had a very clear concept of "garden" as apart from the natural environment.

This brings out an attitude on the part of all Oriental garden makers that is uniquely of the Far East—the feeling that the area on which they are working should be made to seem a part of an overall ideal environment, whether or not any such environment actually exists. Oriental gardens are often enclosed by walls which can be conspicuous and ornamental adjuncts to the garden. But these walls are practical, not mental, enclosures. Physically they may shut away the garden from what is around it. But they are not intended to shut it away from nature and give the enclosure over to man. This is the very opposite of the purpose of the wall in Mediterranean gardens.

It is said that when Hui Yuan's lay followers left the mountain they took with them ideas for their own gardens. On the Lu-shan they had become conscious of the beauty and grandeur of peaks, precipices, and waterfalls and had come to know the joy of living with these things. It was such ideas that they took away and sometimes applied to their own country places. "This marks the first known instance of the spread of landscape ideas from one center," in the opinion of Professor Wu Shih-chang.[13]

We can trace this in several members of the White Lotus Society. Among them is Hsieh Ling-yun (385–433), known as one of China's fine poets and painters. He was descended from one of the old scholarly families which had fled from the invading barbarians several generations before and had settled south of the Yangtze. He owned a small country place within view of Lu-shan, which he describes in these words:

> I placed my house against a northern slope,
> And opened its [southern] doors toward the stream.
> The rushing torrent I used instead of a well.
> I planted hibiscus instead of a surrounding wall,
> Above them, from my window I can see masses of mountains.[14]

Here the mountains had entered the garden. Not bodily, as yet, but in a way the Japanese would later describe as "borrowing scenery." Seated in his study window, Hsieh Ling-yun could gaze at the fantastic blue outlines of the Lu-shan and wander in imagination through the scenic beauty of remembered waterfalls and woodlands.

In thus calling upon his imagination to supply details of the landscape picture, Hsieh Ling-yun was among those initiating another aspect of Oriental garden art. It is one that has proved particularly baffling to Europeans when they have come up against it—the demand that an observer complete the landscape picture in his mind, when there is present only a token suggestion of landscape. The token may be a single rock, to suggest a peak, or several rugged stones placed together to suggest a distant range or rocky cliff. Such token stones have sometimes been described as "miniature mountains," but they were never intended to be taken at their face value as miniatures. They can, of course, be taken merely as attractive stones, to be enjoyed for their intrinsic beauty, within the scale of the garden. But any imaginative dimension built into them is strictly a subjective thing in the mind of the individual beholder.

Also living near the Lu-shan in the days of Hui Yuan was another poet and writer who may, or may not, have visited the mountain. At any rate, his thinking appears to have been often strongly in accord with that of the White Lotus members. He was T'ao Ch'ien, sometimes called T'ao Yuan-ming (378–427). Qualified to be an official, he had accepted a government position but soon found he wanted only to return to life in the country.

He evidently tried to become what might be called a gentleman dirt farmer, but was not very successful at that, chiefly, it seems, because he was too fond of leisurely and happy contemplation of trees, flowers, fields, and the distant Lu-shan peaks. His description of his country place gives a very clear picture of the southern Chinese countryside at that time.

> I cultivated rough land in the south
> And, keeping to simple ways, I returned to my fields and gardens.
>
> I have some ten *mou* of land,
> And a thatched house of eight or nine rooms.

Birch and willows shade the back eaves,
Peach and plum spread their branches in the front courtyard.

Villages lie in the distance,
Smoke rises like mist from faraway fields,
Dogs bark in hidden lanes,
And roosters crow from the tops of mulberry trees.

Inside my house there is no worldly hubbub,
There is space, and I have leisure.
For a long time I was in a cage
But now I am back with nature.[15]

T'ao Ch'ien has been regarded down the centuries as the archetype of China's nature lover, because he did not need to seek isolation in the wilds but could find complete detachment and fulfillment in a simple country courtyard. Since his day, scholars have quoted his lines:

I built my hut in a zone of human habitation,
Yet near me there sounds no noise of horse or coach.

Would you know how that is possible?

A heart that is distant creates a wilderness around it.
I pluck chrysanthemums under the eastern hedge,
Then gaze long at the distant southern hills.[16]

Here again the mountains have entered the garden. But I think the importance of this verse lies in its emphasis on the garden as a place of retreat. It might well be that these very words did much to crystallize the Oriental garden into a place of escape. Busy officials who could not get away to the actual wilds came to create a bit of nature in their city courtyards. There they could go for a time and throw off the pressures that they faced outside. This has been one of the basic urges behind a great deal of Chinese garden making.

It was from the green, romantic southern countryside, therefore, with its steep mountains, its rocks and waterfalls, that there derived that intense interest in natural stones which has become the special attribute of Far Eastern gardens. The use of rocks in these gardens, in their own unaltered forms, to create works of art as landscape patterns, or even as abstractions of pure design, is the unique contribution of these gardens to the world's artistic materials and techniques.[17]

From the southern mountains also, Chinese garden art gained its third dimension. Width and depth had been part of the old, widely spreading lake-and-island parks of the northern plain. Now, with the hills, came perpendicularity. The natural gardens of the hill monasteries—not only Hui Yuan's, but many others—were characterized by their peaks, their rocky cliffs, their leaping waterfalls—all of them lines of verticality. When, as inevitably they did, the mountains merged with the lake-and-island pattern, these three dimensions completed the necessary outline of the fully mature Chinese garden.

57

CHAPTER SIX

The First Man-made Landscapes

NORTH China slowly recovered from the invasions of the northern horsemen. Its two capital cities, though damaged, remained centers of population and sophistication. Chinese culture was too great and too strong to be destroyed, nor even long disrupted, by a few thousand mounted barbarians.

The invading tribes, however, settled down in the country and established themselves as the rulers. But before long (as had happened before and would take place again) Chinese civilization began to exert its quiet but powerful persuasions upon them. The invaders gave up their barbaric ways and adopted the dress, language, customs, and even the ways of thinking of their Chinese subjects. Intermarriage was not infrequent, and after several hundred years the newcomers had virtually disappeared among the Chinese population. For a long time, however, contention continued between the various barbarian tribal leaders, so that in North China boundaries and powers were frequently shifted, while the peace was uneasy and often broken.

An example of how the new rulers adopted Chinese ways is furnished by Shih Hu, khan of five barbarian tribes. He was one of the rulers of the Later Chao (334–49). Some distance east of his stronghold lay a "Flowery Grove Park." The record states: "In spite of the remonstrances of all his ministers, Shih Hu . . . directed Chang Ch'ung, President of the Board, to send 160,000 men and women with 10,000 carts into the surrounding territory to bring earth to construct a wall of ten li around the Flowery Grove Park. Chang Ch'ung, in a single night, set up three of the 'Four Quarters' gates, and digging through Pei-ching, diverted the course of the Chang River into the Flowery Grove Park. . . . In this park Shih Hu had planted every variety of fruit that was liked by his people. . . . Within the park there was the Thousand Goldpiece Embankment; upon this were set two copper dragons facing each other, and the water from the Chang was diverted through their mouths to form the Celestial Spring, and then to flow through all the imperial waterways."[1]

Devices like the copper dragons go back to the Han period. A wall of ten li (say three miles) does not enclose a very large park by past imperial standards. And in this case, we should judge, it was not a very good park, either. In spite of the excessive demands upon the populace, this ruler seems to have lacked, as we might expect, not only the real power to do more but also the necessary taste.

However, when the T'o-pa Tartars took over the rule of North China, calling it the Wei empire, a government was established that lasted over 150 years (398–557). Eventually the Wei rulers became Chinese in all but name. Under them the country was generally prosperous and peaceful. Prosperity was due partly to the caravan trade over the old Silk Road that continued to move across Central Asia to Afghanistan. Part of the trading was done with several thriving desert oasis kingdoms along the way, but silk and other goods were also transshipped to India, Persia, and even the Mediterranean.

The returning caravans brought back to China, among more tangible things, a great freight of Buddhist influence. Many missionaries from India and the oasis cities came to China, while a few Chinese pilgrims were able to make the long round trip to India, seeking better understanding of the sacred texts. The Wei rulers became ardent Buddhists, often extending their patronage to the Indian missionaries and fostering Buddhist construction. In 494 the Wei emperor finally felt himself so secure in Chinese ways that he moved his capital from the north down to Lo-yang, the very heart of old China. Nearby he and his successors sponsored, among other things, the building of Buddhist cave temples filled with images and paintings. Buddhist sculpture made during the Wei period and found partly in these caves includes much of the greatest art in this form that China has produced.

By the fifth century the intense feeling for nature generated by escape to the hills had attained wide and popular proportions. In Alexander Soper's words, "The cult of the wilderness, of the lonely hermitage, of height and steepness, of rock and forest and water, had gained so much prestige that it no longer represented the dreams of the discontented and dispossessed alone. It was fashionable, and an exciting new interest for the great and secure at home, in cities, and in courts."[2]

Excursions into the hills became the fashionable thing. An amusing anecdote illustrates how the appreciation of the wilderness was regarded as a gentlemanly accomplishment. One of the northern rulers asked an official how he compared himself to the prime minister. "In political affairs I am no better," modestly replied the official. "But I may say that I excel him in the appreciation of scenery."[3]

The painting of landscape pictures particularly benefited from this widespread interest. As a result, such painting was given a great impetus. These pictures are now generally regarded as the form in which Chinese art has reached its greatest achievements. Many Western critics are coming to regard them as among the greatest painting the world has produced, and by some they are considered as possibly the greatest of all.

The making of landscape gardens followed the painters' interest, benefiting from the cult of natural scenery. The two arts, painting and gardens, developed in parallel, slowly and experimentally, until both reached their climax in the Sung period.

The actual construction of gardens to suggest landscape, as opposed to the use of naturally existing scenic elements, must have started when landowners took note of the natural beauties remaining on their property and began to preserve and enhance them. Perhaps a path was cleared over the slopes to a scenic outlook or to a woodland cascade; perhaps the trees were preserved, a choked spring or stream cleaned out, or a swampy spot excavated into a lake. Remnants of the original forests and natural countryside must still have been fairly common in the fifth and sixth centuries, for overpopulation had not yet smoothed all the land to monotonous agriculture. Evidence of this is found in the fourth-century villa of the Golden Valley, previously described.

The owner, it will be recalled, mentions its rice fields and mill, its pigs, ducks, chickens, and fishponds. But he also states that his place possessed land "that was high in places and low in others"—that is, hilly or rolling. There were clear waters and verdant woods with bamboos, pines, fruit trees, grasses, and herbs (probably wild flowers). He also notes that there had been built halls, ponds, and pavilions for beauty and enjoyment.

However, when a piece of land did not possess such features, human labor began to supply them. During the reign of Emperor Hsuan Wu (500–515) we hear of Ju Hao, "who was by nature a subtle craftsman." He fashioned a hill west of T'ien Yuan Chih to make another Flowery Grove. "He chose fine rocks from the quarries of Pei-mang and Nan-shan, transplanted bamboo from Ju and Ying, directed the construction of two-storied pavilions, set in order, above and below, and laid out trees, all to give the impression of rustic wildness."[4] Here the construction of artificial landscapes was well on its way. It is significant, I think, that even at this early date, Ju Hao "chose fine rocks," showing the very early interest in such things.

The Wei rulers obviously had no objections to anyone building a fine country estate and mansion if he could afford it, and many did. This is made clear from certain Buddhist gift records, for it became the custom for wealthy people to "acquire merit" by turning over certain of their estates for Buddhist uses. We are fortunate in having among these gift records a rather full description of what was evidently one of the best of such early sixth-century estates.

Under date of the Wei emperor Hsiao Ming (516–27) is mentioned the gift of an estate known as the "Hill of Bright Beauty" (Chang Yang Shan) by one Chang Lun.[5] He was minister of agriculture and also junior preceptor to the heir apparent. Chang Lun, it is said, was by nature gay and extravagant, and a great fancier of mansions, robes, and equipages. He also had a taste for garden making, so that his parks, groves, hills, and streams were regarded as more beautiful than those of any prince of the time.

The Hill of Bright Beauty possessed "ranges rising in steep succession above its independent peaks and ridges; with deep ravines and caverns, wound through by tortuous trails, all as if the work of nature itself. So lofty were the forests and so huge the trees, that the sun and moon could not penetrate their shadowed obscurity; so luxuriant were the vines and creepers in their festooning that the wind and mist could not sweep beneath them. The craggy paths seemed to halt against a rock and then go forward; the lofty torrents to turn on their course and once more be straightened."[6]

This description possesses a definite "literary" quality with its paired and balanced clauses and artistic exaggerations. Allowance must be made for this poetic license. "Ranges rising in steep succession . . . independent peaks and ridges . . . deep ravines and caverns"— these terms belong to the phraseology of the wilderness cult, but we can be sure something was actually there to inspire the words. However, the impressive size of these peaks and ravines could only have existed in the imagination of the beholder. The obvious success with which the construction of the garden was accomplished gives evidence that not only had garden craftsmanship been achieved but also that artistry had entered the garden by this time.

If we examine the techniques of construction necessarily involved in making Chang Lun's garden, we may follow the progress of garden construction up to that time. We know the place was a suburban estate not far outside the walls of Lo-yang. The city lies near where two tributaries converge into the Yellow River, so there has always been water available for gardens. The place may have occupied a natural slope with a spring or stream flowing through it, for this would have been the simplest way to create the "lofty torrents." Or water could have been brought in a conduit from up-river.

Additional evidence that it was probably a natural site is the lack of any mention of a lake. Had the hills been artificially constructed, it would almost certainly have required that they be made of the material excavated from the bed of a lake. Finally, the size of the trees and the luxuriance of the undergrowth indicate that the site was a natural one, and these were probably part of the original woodland.

Had the peaks and ridges and deep ravines been entirely man-made, it would have required the bringing of many rocks to the site. This is always a difficult and expensive undertaking. The abundance of these peaks and ridges suggests again that they were natural features to begin with and that Chang Lun's success as a garden maker lay in the way he had handled and developed what was on the site, making the tortuous trails and craggy paths "all as if the work of nature itself."

A stroll up the path of this garden, a stop to look up at the tumbling waterfall, perhaps a rest in a small pavilion near the top, with an outlook over the countryside beyond the walls, would obviously have been delightful. It was a garden which, in effect, has been duplicated many thousands of times in the centuries since.

Thus, by the end of the sixth century, all the basic elements of the full Chinese landscape garden had been evolved—the extensive imperial park, the mountain-inspired rock garden, and the private estate—each with nature as its theme. There remained to be created only the pure abstraction, inspired in Sung times by Zen Buddhism, which today can be studied only in Japan.

By the end of the Northern Wei kingdom (557), the time was approaching when the north and the south of China would be once more brought together into a single great empire, which would rise to new heights of splendor and glory. This unification was effected by the short-lived Sui dynasty (589–618). It served as a curtain raiser to the great period of the T'ang dynasty.

With the Sui, we come again to the year 607, when the second emperor of the line, Sui Yang Ti, was building his vast Western Park outside Lo-yang. With his "five lakes and four seas" it is evident now that he had revived and was once more following the great imperial tradition of spreading lake-and-island parks. But the reference to "piled-up rocks" on the islands in these shows that the influence of the mountains had been assimilated into the lake-and-island pattern.

It is especially interesting to note that he was also creating in his Northern Sea three island peaks in imitation of the three Mystic Isles of tradition. And on them he was constructing terraces, arbors, and pavilions, even as Emperor Wu of Han had built them almost seven hundred years before in the hope of attracting the Immortals. Here is evidence that the tradition of these isles, as a feature of garden lakes, had long been launched on its course down the centuries, even to the present day.

I cannot leave the subject of Chinese gardens without touching on the people who made them, summed up, for me, in one man who represents and humanizes them all. He is our T'ang official, the poet Po Chu-i, master of the Grass Cottage on Lu-shan, who directed the planting of white lotus in its pool and saw the encircling landscape as part of the cottage garden.

He was a man who admitted that he could never stop making gardens, whether by planting his official yamen as the governor of a province or, in private retirement, creating his own estate. He served as governor of Hangchow and helped to beautify that bit of "heaven below" around its willow-fringed lake. He was also governor of Soochow, that other garden city of the south.

As a young official, working at his first job in the capital city of Ch'ang-an, he rented as bachelor quarters a small pavilion on an old estate. Behind it he discovered the remains of a bamboo grove. This he cleared and tended until new shoots came out and the spot was once more green and shady. In what must have been the rather dreary courtyard of his city office, he once planted some pine trees and bamboos. Years later, he revisited this office, to find the trees grown and himself grey-headed.[7]

He once wrote to a friend: "From youth to old age, the whitewashed cottage of poverty, or the vermilion gates of affluence, have each seemed to last but a day in turn. But to build up a terrace with dirt spilled from a basket; to pile up a hill with rocks carried by a pole; to make a pool with water borne in a dipper—joy in such garden making has always held me like an obsession."[8]

PART THREE

The Gardens of Japan

CHAPTER SEVEN

A Garden for
an Empress

THE Japanese envoy to the Sui court, Ono no Imoko, had been sent to China to learn all he could about the great continental neighbor. He must have found the scale of the imperial undertakings there nothing less than staggering, for he had come from a land where even the palace of the ruler had, until lately, been little more than a wooden cottage.

The ruling sovereign who had sent Ono no Imoko to China was the empress Suiko, his kinswoman.[1] Her palace stood near the head of the Inland Sea on the beautiful Nara plain. Today, as always, fields of growing rice wave over this plain almost as far as the eye can see. At the time of Ono's departure, there already had begun to rise above these fields the strange, exotic sight of several large buildings in Chinese style, with red pillars and soaring tiled roofs.[2] They were evidence that Japan had already learned a good deal about Chinese civilization and had begun to adopt certain of its aspects.

Japan had learned of China through Korea, a peninsula which projects from the Chinese mainland toward the Japanese islands. The peninsula had been developed as a Chinese colony under the far-flung power of the Han dynasty. The seafaring Japanese had maintained varying relations with the people of the peninsula, learning early that by trading— or possibly raiding—its seacoast they could obtain many pleasing products of Chinese origin: such things as metal swords and polished bronze mirrors. The Japanese prized these so highly that they sometimes placed them in the tombs of their chieftains, where modern excavators have found them.

By the sixth century many Japanese leaders had a fair idea of the outward aspects of Chinese civilization. And along with this understanding had come a desire for more of China's material products and for the knowledge and skill that produced them. Korean craftsmen and artists were being induced to come to Japan to work and teach. Also, by way of Korea, had come Buddhism. It proved a powerful carrier of Chinese art and culture.

The Chinese authorities looked upon Ono no Imoko as just another of the many barbarian vassals who were regularly arriving to pay their respects to the Chinese court. He was received, his gifts accepted, and a return embassy arranged to accompany him home.[3]

The Chinese foreign office, it appears, was sufficiently interested in the Eastern Islands to want some first-hand information. Perhaps there may still have been a lingering interest in the Mystic Isles. During the time this Chinese embassy remained in Japan we may be sure that among the innumerable questions put to its members would have been some on the subject of parks and palaces. The answers would doubtless have made clear, once more, the Chinese belief that impressive architecture and spreading parks were demanded to support imperial greatness.

When the Chinese diplomats returned home, Ono no Imoko went again to China with them. This time he was accompanied by a group of other Japanese scholars.[4] There is a tradition that after he came back he founded the art of flower arrangement in Japan, an art which had its origin in the placing of flowers on Buddhist altars.

We know of no gardens as such existing in Japan up to this time. The earliest mention in the Japanese records of a cultivated garden concerns the search for a site on which to erect a shrine to the imperial ancestress, the Sun Goddess. The recorded myth[5] relates that a heavenly princess was sent to earth to find a suitable spot. She went far and wide, never satisfied, until finally she came to the district of Ise near the eastern seacoast. There she found a "Lord of Garden Making" (Sono Tsukuru Kami). The shrine to the Sun Goddess was eventually placed near his garden. In this story, "garden" obviously refers to the growing of practical plants—for food, medicines, and dyes. The "Lord of Garden Making" was probably the remembrance of an early agricultural specialist in a land still largely devoted to hunting and rice culture.

Today, as for ages past, this shrine to the Sun Goddess at Ise is the holiest spot in Japan (Plates 64, 66). It is a simple, unpainted wooden building of prehistoric design, standing in the midst of a magnificent primeval forest near a small river. The modern world is checked at the edge of this forest. People walk quietly along its graveled paths, to bow their heads at the inner gates before the buildings. On their return they linger to enjoy the beauty of great trees, the glossy green of low undergrowth, the glimmering vistas of the river. It seems to me this quiet enjoyment of natural beauty is a real, if unrecognized, part of the religious feeling present. For the Shinto gods were nature spirits. A sense of pleasure in nature, a close relationship with it, has been, and still is, I think, one of the most profound and fundamental traits of Japanese personality.

It is not strange that this should be so. Japan is one of earth's beauty spots, a land of gentle loveliness, with mountains enveloped in misty green, with many little rivers and a magnificent coastline. It is totally different from the endless level plains and vast, tilted precipices of China. Among the hills are many pointed green cones to indicate the volcanic origin of the islands. Vast Fuji-no-yama, the newest and greatest of these cones, is one of the few to rise above its forest skirts, and its enormous converging lines are incredibly high, grey, and smooth. The volcanic rocks of the canyons are often beautifully molded and twisted from nature's crucible. Many have been partly smoothed by water. Others, after centuries of quiescence, are patterned with lichens and moss.

Japanese civilization developed on the Pacific side of the main island, where the climate is mild and pleasant, well sheltered from Siberian cold. The year is ushered in with a long spring, surging with the excitement of blossoming trees and the flowering of native

66

camellias and azaleas. Summers are lushly tropical, vivid with emerald green and shrill with the voices of cicadas. Autumn brings long weeks of mellow quiet, with the warm haze of prolonged Indian summer hanging over the hills. Wild chrysanthemums bloom, and the scarlet and gold of maples and sumac turn ravines into rich brocades. In winter, the lightly sifted snows are never powdery cold, but wet and clinging, and even the slender branches of willows are wrapped in white as they hang over the cold green of streams.

Throughout the country crystal springs seep from mossy hillsides, for gentle rains fall at all seasons. They flow down small valleys to join frantic little rivers that have cut rocky gorges in the hills and now dash whitely among the boulders at the bottom. These rushing streams tumble frequently into tall plumes of white, falling across granite cliffs. The canyon walls are mossy from spray and draped in ferns. When rivers reach the coastal plain they become meandering channels of dark water in broad beds of yellow sand.

The Inland Sea, a wide channel of blue water, separates three of the larger Japanese islands. The seacoast is often spectacularly beautiful, with precipitous cliffs descending into deep water, or with scalloped sandy bays marked off by pine-covered headlands. Islets, often a single great rock, may rise in these bays with one or more pines clinging to them, twisted and weatherbeaten.

Wherever the land can be leveled it has been turned into a mosaic of small irregular fields, each enclosed by a dyke. Seen from above, the effect of such fields is like the pattern of leaden moldings in a stained glass window. By a system of incredibly complex water management, each little field becomes in summer a tiny pond holding a few inches of water for the growing rice. As the plants become tall, the dykes disappear under a smooth expanse of waving green. When the crop is cut and the fields are drained, the dykes reappear. Skill in handling water goes back to dim periods of prehistory. And when artificial lakes, streams, and cascades were wanted later for landscape gardens, their making was never a problem.

The very early people venerated hills, rocks, and trees as the abode of spirits (Plate 65). Certain spots were considered sacred and were marked off by a rope of rice straw—a custom continued in some places to the present day.[6] The strong feeling of awareness for these natural elements was the foundation on which was easily developed an interest in the Chinese idea of creating a garden landscape in the pattern of nature (Plates 62, 63).

When that time came, the techniques of building hills and handling rocks were by no means a novelty. For early chiefs and their princesses were buried in huge grave mounds (Plate 67) which were literally small hills, and these were often surrounded by water in the form of a wide moat, actually a lake.[7] A number of these tumuli are found near Nara, but many others, more simple, are widespread throughout the country. Veneration for these mounds has prevented most of them from being excavated. But when certain ones were broken into by accident, they were studied. The mounds, enclosing the stone-lined tombs, were built up largely from soil taken from the moat. The water has continued to flow around them, and the construction has survived more than fifteen centuries.[8]

Only four years after Ono no Imoko's first trip to China, under date of 612, the Japanese records mention the arrival in the capital of a Korean craftsman whose face and body were

67

blotched with white. His appearance was objectionable to the Japanese, who may have thought him a leper. He was called Michiko no Takumi, but they sometimes referred to him as Shikomaro, the Ugly Artisan. They planned to get rid of him by casting him away on an island in the sea, but he protested, saying: "If you dislike my spotted skin, you should not breed horses and cattle that are spotted with white. Moreover, I have a small talent. I can make the figures of hills and mountains. If you keep me and make use of me, it would be to the advantage of the country. Why should you waste me by casting me away on an island in the sea?"[9]

It was realized, then, that this man must be a garden craftsman in the Chinese and Korean manner they had heard about. It was decided to overlook his appearance and call on his talents to create a garden for the empress in the Chinese manner. He was ordered to build a "bridge of Wu"—that is, a bridge in the Chinese style—and a "Shumisen" in the southern courtyard of the palace.

From this order it seems clear that the Japanese may already have made some attempt to create for the empress a lake-and-island setting in the Chinese manner. Her palace may have been one of the elegant Chinese halls, although these structures were more often reserved for the temples of the new Buddhist deities. Whether or not there was a Chinese hall facing south in the traditional manner, it is probable that she actually lived in the more comfortable native style—as did many modern Japanese long after they had acquired European-type houses.

The southern courtyard of the palace would have been that portion of the grounds lying before the main hall, and the order for a bridge clearly indicates the presence of a pond or lake there. This water probably served also as a protective moat, for there seems to be evidence that the dwellings of early Japanese emperors were generally surrounded by water.[10] The order for a bridge in the Chinese style seems to indicate also the presence of an island, to be reached by the bridge. A "bridge of Wu" would have been in the ornamental high-arched style of Tʻang, lacquered red with vermilion. The lake was probably surrounded by a growth of pine trees and native shrubs, and the effect would have been very picturesque.

Just what was meant at that time by a "Shumisen" is uncertain. The word, it will be recalled, is the Japanese designation for Mount Sumeru, that vast peak which, according to Hindu and Buddhistic belief, centers and upholds the universe. In later Japanese garden construction a Shumisen was a rocky islet in a garden pond. It has been assumed that the Ugly Artisan constructed such a naturalistic island of "piled-up rocks" in the imperial lake.

However, I have found new light thrown on the subject by studying what appears to be an actual Shumisen of the empress Suiko's period (Plates 68-69). It is a rock monument in the form of a rounded, blunt-pointed cone, about eight feet high. Three layers of carved granite are fitted together to form the structure, with evidence that originally there was a fourth layer. Crudely chiseled around the surfaces of this cone are wavy lines which suggest receding mountain ranges, rising higher and higher and growing fainter near the top. The actual peak of the stone might be Great Meru itself, rising above its surrounding mountains.

This stone structure now stands in the grounds of the Tokyo National Museum.[11] It

68

was dug up in 1903 on a site near Nara not far from the empress Suiko's palace. The site where it was found is believed to be that of a garden which belonged to her uncle, a powerful court noble named Soga no Umako.[12] In the national record an entry dated eight years after the story of Michiko refers to Soga as "Lord of the Island."[13] This title is clarified by his obituary notice several years later: "He possessed a house by the Asuka River where he built a garden with a small pond and in the pond an island. Therefore, he was often spoken of as 'Lord of the Island.' "[14]

There must have been something extraordinary about this island to create for its owner a popular title. If we assume that the island held this rocky cone, a closer examination reveals a possibility for its fame. The "mountain" is hollow, with the bottom stone cut out so that it becomes a large bowl. The next stone above is roughly doughnut-shaped. (The missing stone would have been a ring also.) The capstone that forms the peak is in the form of an acorn. Cut through its back to the open center is a squarish hole. If water were to be introduced into this opening (say by means of a bamboo conduit) it would fall through the center and fill the bowl. It would then gush out in four directions through four small openings in the bottom stone.[15] The whole structure, therefore, is a sort of ingenious fountain.

Since Soga was first called "Lord of the Island" only eight years after the Ugly Artisan worked on the garden of the empress, it is possible, even probable, that he worked also on Soga's estate. Perhaps we can see in this rocky structure exactly what he meant when he said he knew how to "make the figures of hills and mountains."[16] Whatever its background, this rocky mountain is certainly a Shumisen. It may well be the only surviving remnant anywhere of a T'ang-period Chinese or Korean garden ornament embodying the holy mountain.[17]

There was, however, nothing original in the idea of bringing water into a garden through such a fountain. Dr. Seiroku Noma writes of this aspect of the structure: "Such strange and clever devices were in use in Chinese palaces as early as the Han dynasty."[18] It will be recalled, similarly, that in the description of the Flowery Park of the barbarian ruler Shih Hu in the fourth century mention is made of two copper dragons through which a stream was made to issue into all the waterways of his garden.

It is interesting to note that, for a long time after the empress Suiko's first lake-and-island garden was built, the term used in Japan to designate a landscape garden was simply the word for island, *shima*. This pattern remained the basic form of a Japanese landscape garden for the next several centuries. And, with modifications, it has remained a basic form to the present day.

CHAPTER EIGHT

Nara Copies
of Chinese Gardens

A S LONG as Japanese chieftains lived in simple wooden houses like the shrine of the Sun Goddess there were few problems involved in the custom of moving out and rebuilding on a different site when the old chief died. But when palaces and temples were constructed in the stately and expensive Chinese style, moving became a different matter. After the empress Suiko's death, several such moves were made. But when the city, now called Nara, became the capital of Japan in 710, it remained so for seven reigns—about seventy-five years.

Nara, the city that rose from the rice fields, was unlike anything the Japanese had seen before. It was as much like the Chinese T'ang capital, Ch'ang-an, as the Japanese could make it. Carefully laid out on this Chinese plan was its wide central avenue, running north and south between the imperial palace and the city's main gate. Crossing this avenue like a gridiron were nine secondary avenues with many smaller streets branching off. Just such a city plan, with its straight avenues and right angles, may still be seen in Peking, and vestiges of such an original remain in Kyoto.[1]

Nara's imperial enclosure occupied the northern end of the city and held the government buildings. Clustered near the foot of some hills were a number of great religious establishments, each a complex of buildings, some with pagodas. All this, with the mansions of the nobility, made the city a place of wonder and awe to the people. Sir George Sansom remarks: ". . . Though Nara was a copy, it was more splendid than anything that had ever before been known in Japan. Even today a visitor to its ancient site can with but little effort of imagination reconstruct its vanished glories from the remains of its great temples and their treasures, peopling its palaces with courtiers in ceremonial robes, its holy edifices with priests who chanted litanies in a strange tongue, its workshops with artists from China and Korea and their eager Japanese pupils, who wrought the exquisite shapes of gods in bronze and wood and lacquer. . . .

"It is difficult to realise how complete a revolution was effected in all departments of life in the capital. Life in the country went on as before. Peasants grew their rice, fed their silkworms, grudged their taxes and worshipped their native gods. But in the city all was new, all was foreign. The very architecture of the palaces and temples was Chinese . . . the costume of the courtiers, their etiquette, their ranks and appellations were borrowed from China. . . . It is hard to find a parallel for this curious phenomenon of a small society, busily digesting and assimilating a superior foreign culture not imposed from without by conquest or proximity, but voluntarily, even enthusiastically, adopted."[2]

The great religious foundations, both Shinto and Buddhist, had extensive grounds. Today the precincts of several of these have been thrown together to form Nara Park. A herd of tame deer wanders about in this park, much to the delight of visitors. Surviving in it are several of the original eighth-century structures, among them an imperial treasure house, the Shoso-in. It still holds the gifts—personal possessions of the emperor Shomu— presented by his widow to the Temple of the Great Buddha. Among the contents are several items touching on gardens.

One is a painting of a noble lady sitting on a rock in a garden under a picturesque small tree (Plate 72). The painting is in the rather fanciful Chinese style of the period, very evident in the treatment of the rock on which she sits. It is much curved and convoluted, totally unnatural. It is true that stones with round pothole openings and curved edges were popular in Chinese gardens, but in depicting them the painters sometimes let their brushes run away with them. This picture probably does no more than indicate that Japanese artists were aware of trends in Chinese garden fashions.

Also in the Shoso-in treasure house is a sort of tray garden or miniature landscape made entirely from pieces of wood. It is based on a length of cryptomeria wood, about three feet long, with borders cut to simulate the much-indented shores of an island. Pieces of wood with rough natural surfaces are set up to create a fantastic landscape with towering pinnacles and craggy cliffs. This ornament makes it clear that Japanese were acquainted with China's interest in rugged natural scenery and also with the various ways in which it could be depicted.

We know there were many gardens in Nara, although the only known remnant remaining from the eighth century is a trace of pebbles which reveals where there was the shoreline of a pond near the imperial palace. These pebbles were found during excavations made in 1957.[3] I think we may be sure that the Nara gardens were as much like their Chinese T'ang prototypes as possible—as was the city plan and its architecture. Their principal feature, of course, would have been a large pond or lake with an island. On the level, well-watered Nara plain such bodies of water would not have been difficult to build. Rocks on the island and shore would have been part of the necessary pattern, with trees and flowering shrubs. And on these lakes would have been the pleasure barges, with their picturesque dragon or phoenix heads and spreading tails.

Confirmation of all these things is found in poems of the period. They were written by the people who lived on these estates and described in poetic language what they saw. Most of the poems are found in a collection called the *Man'yoshu* brought together near the end of the eighth century. Here we can find mentioned the sparkle of a garden lake, the reflection of a rock, the green rain of young willows, and the fragrance of wisteria. Since it was the custom to attach short notes to these poems, telling the conditions under which they were written, it is frequently possible to visualize the scene in considerable detail.

71

Thus on a March day in the year 730, a group of high-born gentlemen sat in a garden in Nara. They were delighting in the early coming of spring and expressing this delight by writing short poems. They were especially pleased with the blooming of the Andromeda shrub *(Pieris japonica),* whose dainty white flowers are individually much like lilies-of-the-valley (Plate 71). This plant is one of Japan's earliest spring bloomers and is still the commonest shrub grown in Nara Park because the deer will not nibble its leaves.

Of the poems written on this occasion, several were later considered good enough to be included in the *Man'yoshu* anthology. Wrote Otomo no Yakamochi, mentioning the pond:

> The pond water
> Reflects the fragrance
> Of perfect Andromeda flowers.
> Let me put them in my sleeve.[4]

Another, Ikako no Mabito, saw the fleeting beauty of these flowers as a reflection of the Buddhist feeling that all beauty is ephemeral. He lets us know there were rocks by the pond:

> In the shadow of the rocks
> The pond water
> Glows with the color
> Of Andromeda flowers.
> Must these fall?[5]

We get our clearest picture of this garden from the poem of Mikata no Ohogimi, who mentions the island:

> When I look at your island
> Where the love bird dwells
> I see today also
> The Andromeda blooming.[6]

To the Japanese, the "love bird" is the brightly colored little mandarin duck, which is monogamous.

The *Man'yoshu* poems also mention violets, cherry blossoms, azaleas, wisteria, and the green of young willows. Following are two of Aston's translations.[7]

> The rippling wisteria
> That I planted by my house
> As a memento
> Of thee whom I love
> Is at length in blossom.

6. Designs created with sand, Daisen-in, Kyoto. ▶

7 (overleaf). Portion of the "Moss Temple" garden, Saiho-ji, Kyoto. ▶

72

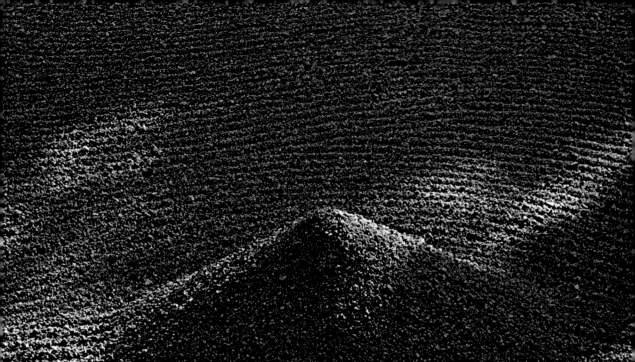

Before the wind of spring
Has tangled the fine threads
Of the green willow—
Now would I show it
To my love.

Other poem-pictures of Nara gardens, giving additional details, can be found in a second anthology of the period called the *Kaifuso*.[8] Thus, at another spring garden party, given this time by the minister of the left, Nagaya Ohogimi, one of the guests, Otsu Renju, was inspired to compose this whimsical piece:

Sunlight sparkles on the dancing water,
Spring warms the garden wall
Plum buds smile like red lips,
But the gate-willow has not yet
Grown her eyebrows.

In another of these poems we have definite mention of the pleasure boats which floated around the garden lake in the Chinese manner. This poem is by Ishikawa Sekusaku.

Clear and deep-brimming is the pond,
Fresh is the garden with opening flowers,
Frolicking birds skim the waves, then scatter—
Pleasure boats wander among the isles.

Additional details may be picked up in single lines from other poems in the *Man'yoshu*. "Pearly pebbles on the seashore where the pine shadows are sharp"[9] does not refer to the real seashore, but to a garden shoreline in Nara, thirty miles from the coast. "Garden stones glowing in the mellow light of autumn" reveals that the Japanese had come to have a strong appreciation of the beauty of rocks (Plate 72). It might, in the future, even surpass that felt by the Chinese.

◄ *8. Rocks through snow, Ryoan-ji, Kyoto.*

◄ *9. Famous dry cascade and pools, upper garden, Saiho-ji, Kyoto.*

CHAPTER NINE

Great Estates in Heian,
Capital of Peace and Tranquility

WHY the grand new city of Nara, only seventy-five years old, should have been abandoned as the capital city of the country is still something of a mystery. The usual assumption is that undue influence on secular affairs was being exerted by the great Buddhist institutions. At any rate, it was decided to move the imperial palace, and a site some thirty miles away was finally selected.

The new situation was, and still is, unusually beautiful. The city lies in a round valley enclosed on three sides by hills. On the northeast they lift to a notched green peak, Mount Hiei (Hiei-zan). A monastery had recently been built on this peak, and it was believed its holy influences would ward off the evils traditionally expected from that quarter.

Today, as always, two rivers meander over the gently sloping floor of the bowl-shaped valley. The city was originally laid out between them but has grown widely since then. Around the city, the valley floor is still a mosaic of dyked fields, each little patch blossoming in spring with a crop of a different color. In summer, the dykes disappear under the uniform green of young rice shoots; in autumn the land is golden with harvest; in winter the empty brown fields are spiked with conical straw ricks and touched white with frost.

The city built in this beautiful spot was named Heian-kyo, the Capital of Peace and Tranquility. Poets have since referred to it as the City of Purple Mountains and Crystal Streams, from its circle of hills and the many little waterways that course through the town. But during a thousand years of history it was generally spoken of simply as the Capital—Miyako. Today it is called Kyoto.

The city was laid out as a large rectangle, some three and a half miles deep and three miles wide. Within its northern boundary was set apart a second area, forming the imperial enclosure or Daidairi. This area was something under a mile square, and within it were all the imperial buildings—the Great Hall of State, the government offices and shrines, the palace of the emperor, and the apartments of the palace ladies.[1] Like Nara, it was comparable to its model in China, the city of Ch'ang-an.

We can judge the magnificence of the Daidairi's buildings, done in the eighth-century Chinese style, by those of the present-day Heian Shrine (Plates 17, 73). The latter was erected in 1894 to celebrate the 1,100th anniversary of the founding of the city. The main building of the Heian Shrine reproduces, as nearly as modern knowledge permits, the Great Hall of State of the Daidairi. This shrine is dedicated to the emperor who made the move to the new location, the emperor Kammu. He is now regarded as the tutelary deity of Kyoto.

When the city was first built there was no space within the imperial enclosure for a large garden. But just south of it there was laid out, a few years later, in the year 800, a large lake-and-island park in the imperial Chinese manner. Known as the Divine Spring Garden or Shinsen-en, this was long the largest and finest garden in the capital. Poems and references scattered through old records testify to its beauty, but detailed descriptions are vague. We know, however, it covered thirty-three acres and contained a large lake (kept filled by the "divine spring"). There was also a hill, and a large pavilion in Chinese style. Maples, willows, and cherry trees grew on it.[2] One record presents this brief picture: "The honorable path is clean-swept, and the shadows of willows lie long across it. . . . A sandy white beach winds around the lake. All is calm and clear. The eye catches a pure spring bubbling up to run off in a narrow streamlet. If we climb the low hill, we may often catch sight of birds among the trees. Should we work our way through the undergrowth, we startle the wood doves. . . . In the dragon pond glimmer the sun, moon, and stars. . . ."[3]

Another record continues: "The red-leaved grove is wide. In the pond the water brims deeply, even at the edges. . . . It seems like a small River Wu. . . . Clerks and court officials often steal away secretly from their duties to visit it. . . . One cannot look at this garden long enough, for its beauties are ineffable. . . . Darkness always seems to drive one home before one is ready. . . ."[4]

The emperor and the court often came to this garden, and all manner of entertainments were given in it—banquets, poem parties, wrestling matches, and military exercises. To accommodate the emperor and others of high rank, on the shore of the lake stood a pavilion called Kenrin-kaku, the Pavilion of the Imperial Seat. It consisted of a main building with arcades extending like arms, right and left.

Today, on a quiet street in Kyoto, a little pond is all that remains of the Divine Spring Garden, the once glorious first imperial garden (Plate 75). During the civil wars of the middle ages the place was overrun and destroyed and its very existence finally forgotten—until modern scholarship realized that a little natural pond in an old part of the city must be a remnant, its divine or perpetual spring still functioning to keep it supplied with water. For some years the spot was maintained as a little public park with a few fine trees along its banks. But when a severe typhoon destroyed these trees about 1960 the spot was redeveloped to memorialize its historic past. The pond is now neatly walled, and in the center a small square island holds a little shrine to the emperor Kammu.

In the centuries that followed their construction, the palace and other buildings within the imperial enclosure were swept by fire again and again. During the periods of rebuilding, the emperors had to live for considerable periods outside in the house of some noble relative. Finally they came to make their residence permanently in outside mansions. In time, one of these was developed into the present imperial palace of Kyoto, some distance east of the original Daidairi. But for long the emperors returned to the Great Hall of State, rebuilt there, for their enthronement ceremonies. Finally this, too, was again burned but not rebuilt, since difficult times had come to the country. During the period of civil wars the imperial enclosure and the Divine Spring Garden became a neglected wilderness.

Many of the court nobles owned country estates, and some of these have survived better than gardens built in the city. The earliest one that remains in anything like its original size and form is Saga-no-in, the estate to which the emperor Saga retired in 823. This emperor was known for his devotion to all things Chinese, so we can assume this garden, with its large lake and islands, was as much like the current gardens of T'ang China as it could be made.

Outings on the lake in gay pleasure boats were often enjoyed. We can visualize such a boating party with the help of a present-day festival which takes place annually in Kyoto.[5] A group of the city's literati, interested in preserving old ways, re-enact the scene by donning the costumes of Heian courtiers and going out in gaily decorated boats (Plate 76). The prow of such a boat would be finished by the head of a dragon or that of a mythical *hoō*, bird of good omen.[6]

While they were being poled about the water, those on board played old-style music on the flute or composed poems on the beauty of the landscape. Later, they might go ashore on an island where they would write down their poems in bold Chinese characters on long strips of colored paper. These would be read aloud later.

Today, some eleven hundred years after its construction, the emperor Saga's estate consists of a large old pond holding two small, half-drowned islands and a rocky islet on which turtles sun themselves. The pond, now called Osawa-ike, owes its preservation to the fact that the estate was early converted into a Buddhist foundation, the temple called Daikaku-ji. Temple buildings, reconstructed later, still stand on the banks of the lake.

Like all these country estates, Saga-no-in was situated in a highly picturesque spot. Forested hills encircle it on three sides, extending protecting arms. The green hillsides are beautiful at all seasons, whether under the snows of winter or the hazy heat of summer. The countryside falls away beyond the lake, its rice fields glimmering with delicate green in spring or with dusty gold in the level sun of autumn.

Cherry and maple trees today border the large old pond. When clouds of pink petals or tiny bright maple leaves drift down to the ancient green water, the path around it becomes a favorite rendezvous with Kyoto people. A pleasant melancholy hangs over the scene, derived from its beauty and the awareness of passing centuries. This feeling is still perfectly expressed in a poem written about four hundred years after the garden was built, when it had been neglected but was still beautiful.

> Although the scene
> At Osawa-ike is old,
> The same bright autumn moon
> Casts down its lucid light.[7]

Our interest in the emperor Saga's estate returns to the islands, since these are the earliest known remains of a Japanese garden on its original site.[8] There are two fairly large islands of mounded earth, possibly knolls left in the lake bed when it was excavated. The larger island, irregularly broad and pointed, lies fairly close to the shoreline. The second, almost round, lies off the point of the first. Both are overgrown with grasses and reeds, and a few pine trees rise on the larger island. Between these two is a rocky islet onto whose broad slanting side the small turtles crawl to sun themselves.

Some years ago, when the pond was emptied for repairs, Mr. Mirei Shigemori, who has been a lifelong student of Kyoto gardens, was able to make a detailed study of these islands. He found that the water level had been raised, reducing the size of the large islands. It also hid the fact that the single rocky islet visible was but one of a chain of five which originally stretched between the two islands.

The surviving islet is made up of three stones, each carefully placed. The largest, a rock of considerable size, stands nearly upright, leaning against a second one almost as large. A third stone, smaller than either, firms their position on the pond bottom. The stones which once made up the other four islets in this chain have toppled over and washed out of position and out of line. But there is evidence that they were arranged once in generally similar form to the one remaining. Since in other old garden lakes there are islets made in this general style, it is taken to be typical of that period.

Such straight lines of five or more islets are also found in a number of other very old gardens, showing that it was an accepted form. Its meaning—and such a form was peculiar enough to have had a meaning—is unknown. It remains one of the mysteries of Japanese garden history. The stones are always too far apart, too pointed, or too irregular to have served any practical purpose (such as stepping stones or foundation rocks). Such chains today are called "night mooring stones" or *yo-domari,* suggesting a line of cargo junks anchored for the night in some safe haven. This name, however, has the feeling of a later explanation and one much too simple and obvious. Remembering the devotion of the emperor Saga to all things Chinese, it seems probable that this design came directly from T'ang China. Its explanation may come to light sometime.

Two other features of the emperor Saga's estate are of interest. One is the way the pond bottom is finished—with small stones tightly packed together in clay. This is a technique that has survived the centuries. It is typical of this period, and traces of it often indicate whether or not certain old lakes date back to Heian times.

The second feature is a cascade, built into the hillside on the north bank of the pond. It was rediscovered by Mr. Shigemori after having been forgotten for centuries. A poem written about it when the garden had long been neglected and was in ruins tells us that it had been remembered, however, for a long time:

> While the sound
> Of the cascade
> Long since has ceased,
> We still hear the murmur
> Of its name.[9]

After examining what remains of the stones in this cascade Mr. Shigemori ventures to think that it never did hold any water but was built from the beginning as a "dry cascade." Such cascades look as if the water had temporarily dried up but will resume flowing after the next rain. The effect is gained by the graphic arrangement of the stones. The style was

81

used when there was no source of flowing water. Until this example was discovered it was not realized that Japan might have utilized the dry technique so early. It suggests also that China might have furnished the prototype, something not hitherto considered.

Estates as large and fine as the emperor Saga's were rare in the early ninth century. But during the next three hundred years, more and more of the court nobles built fine country places in the most picturesque spots they could find around Kyoto. There was, for instance, a famous place called Riverbank Villa—that is, Kawara-no-in.[10] It was built by the minister of the left, Minamoto no Toru, about 872. He was one of the numerous younger sons of the emperor Saga and may have been raised on the shores of Osawa pond. But he had achieved his position as minister by his own efforts.

His estate stood on the bank of the Kamo River on the east side of the city. Descriptions of its situation make it appear to have been the original garden occupying the site where now is the garden called Shosei-in, the property of the Higashi Hongan-ji temple. Today, Shosei-in fills a large city block near the Kyoto railway station. It is set apart from the dust and noise of the neighborhood by a high, brownish wall. Tall trees rise above this wall, and behind it is a lake of considerable size with several large islands. Among the rock arrangements on these islands are some in typical Heian style.

Part of the original Riverbank Villa was laid out, it is said, to suggest the scenery around the town of Shiogama in the far north of Japan. Shiogama means "salt caldron," and the story goes that the owner of Riverbank Villa ordered sea water brought all the thirty miles from the coast so it could be boiled down into salt on his estate. While the fires were burning, he could watch the ever-changing flutter of smoke against the sky. The esthetic appreciation of fluttering smoke was characteristic of the refined pastimes of the Heian court.

The authority for this story seems to rest chiefly on a poem and its note. After the death of the minister of the left, the poet states, he visited Riverbank Villa, saw the place called Shiogama, and felt moved to write:

> Departed the prince—
> Vanished the smoke
> Of Shiogama;
> Lonely the beach
> Along its length.[11]

Still another of these large old estates survives as the garden of Kanju-ji temple, east of the city. The original owner, a noble named Miyamichi Iyamasa, chose a picturesque spot in the midst of a quiet sunlit valley, with little hills forming a distant bowl-like rim. One small peak, nearer at hand, rises up as if purposely put across the far side of the lake to center the view.

Miyamichi's daughter married a member of the important Fujiwara family, and their daughter became the youthful consort of the emperor Uda. When this took place, Miyamichi, the grandfather, was a man of wealth and power. He built this estate at the end of

10. Stone cargo junk on river of sand, Daisen-in, Kyoto. ▶

the tenth century, about the time his granddaughter became mother of the prince who later was to be the emperor Daigo.

This estate has more nearly maintained its original feeling than any other of the period.[12] There were five islands in the broad lake, recalling the original five Mystic Isles and, as at Saga-no-in, a waterfall, There are comparatively few stones, and some of these have been disarranged from their original positions. But the garden must always have been as quiet and beautiful as it is today, with long jade shadows stretching across the clear water, and the song of birds in the stillness. In an old manuscript is found a line of poetic description: "Mandarin ducks come to float on the precious jade pool of this garden, their purple and vermilion mantles spreading the hues of a thousand autumns."[13]

Even yet, the priest tells us, these little ducks come to this pond, as they must have been doing, literally, for a thousand autumns.

◄ *11. Sand sculpture: "The Moon Facing Height," Silver Pavilion, Kyoto.*

CHAPTER TEN

Gardens for
Prince Genji's Ladies

THE court of Heian continued in peace and tranquility in Kyoto for over 350 years, reaching a pinnacle of glory and romance in the eleventh and twelfth centuries. This was a period of luxury and elegance in which the court nobles vied with one another in building splendid houses and gardens and in giving magnificent entertainments.

Since the days when Nara was the capital, Japan had been dominated by a single great family, the Fujiwaras. The head of this clan held the hereditary office of regent and was all-powerful. Under him, all high government offices were filled by Fujiwara men, and all the empresses were Fujiwara ladies, usually the regent's own daughters. Maids-of-honor and ladies-in-waiting were other Fujiwara women, of slightly lower rank.

One of these ladies of the court is known to us as Murasaki. She was the author of a novel which pictures in wonderful detail the court life she knew in the eleventh century. We can read it in an English translation as *The Tale of Genji*.[1] In its pages we see a group of romantic, sentimental, and highly refined people for whom love and the appreciation of beauty were principal occupations. Nights were one romantic affair after another; days, a succession of esthetic pastimes. They were sensitively aware of every beauty and change in the outdoors. In them the inherent Japanese love of nature took its sunniest, gayest, and most open forms. They built their houses so that, when they chose, they could practically sit outdoors in them. And they laid out their gardens to show nature in her brightest and happiest moods.

We do not know the real name of the lady-in-waiting who wrote *The Tale of Genji*, but she was generally called after the heroine of her story, Murasaki or Violet. She possessed a fine literary gift and had learned something of the Chinese language as a girl. These accomplishments were then regarded as only suited to a man, but when she was left a young widow at about twenty-five, her learning secured for her an appointment as tutor to the empress. The latter, a girl of only sixteen, was the daughter of the regent Fujiwara Michinaga. Although Murasaki's literary endeavors were regarded as something of a joke about the court, she was not unattractive, as evidenced by the fact that when her kinsman, the regent, came to visit his imperial daughter, he usually tried to make love to the pretty lady-in-waiting. From Murasaki's diary we gather he was not very successful in these overtures.[2]

This regent, Michinaga, brought the fortunes of the Fujiwara clan and of the Heian court to their highest point. In Murasaki's novel her hero, Prince Genji, is obviously modeled after Michinaga in position and importance. But her diary makes it clear that the personality of the regent is not portrayed in the character of the prince.

In the story Prince Genji in his youth had been a great lady's man. In his maturity the various women he had wooed became his consorts. Each then lived in her own establishment, a wing of the magnificent mansion he built when he became powerful at court.

The prototype regent, Michinaga, who is noted in history for his extravagant mansions and gardens, had built himself a great town house in Kyoto and villas in the nearby countryside, at Uji and Katsura. Murasaki's descriptions of Genji's estates must have been compounded from what she had seen of these and others. Rearranging her materials to suit her story, she had her prince create around the apartments of each lady a garden designed to meet her special tastes. As her manuscript circulated around the court, its readers were probably able to identify many of the original places she describes.

Of Genji's mansion built in town it is written:[3] "He effected great improvement in the appearance of the grounds by a judicious handling of knoll and lake, for though such features were already there in abundance, he found it necessary here to cut away a slope, there to dam a stream, that each occupant of the various quarters might look out of her windows upon such a prospect as pleased her best. To the southeast he raised the level of the ground, and on this bank planted a profusion of early flowering trees. At the foot of this slope the lake curved with especial beauty, and in the foreground, just beneath the windows, he planted borders of cinquefoil, of red-plum, cherry, wistaria, kerria, rock-azalea, and other such plants as are at their best in springtime; for he knew that Murasaki [his favorite] was in especial a lover of the spring; while here and there, in places where they would not obstruct his main plan, autumn beds were cleverly interwoven with the rest."

The Lady Akikonomu preferred the autumn: "Akikonomu's garden was full of such trees as in autumn-time turn to the deepest hue. The stream above the waterfall was cleared out and deepened to a considerable distance; and that the noise of the cascade might carry further, he set great boulders in mid-stream, against which the current crashed and broke."

A garden which would be most agreeable in summer was made for the "Lady from the Village of Falling Flowers": "In the northeastern garden there was a cool spring, the neighbourhood of which seemed likely to yield an agreeable refuge from the summer heat. In the borders near the house upon this side he planted Chinese bamboos, and a little further off, tall-stemmed forest-trees whose thick leaves roofed airy tunnels of shade, pleasant as those of the most lovely upland wood. This garden was fenced with hedges of the white deutzia flower, the orange tree 'whose scent reawakes forgotten love,' the briar-rose, and the giant peony; with many other sorts of bush and tall flower so skilfully spread about among them that neither spring nor autumn would ever lack in bravery."

For the Lady of Akashi, mother of Genji's only daughter, he built a garden that would be most beautiful in winter. "To the north of Lady Akashi's rooms rose a high embankment, behind which lay the storehouses and granaries, screened also by a close-set wall of pine-trees, planted there on purpose that she might have the pleasure of seeing them when their boughs were laden with snow; and for her delight in the earlier days of the winter there was a great bed of chrysanthemums, which he pictured her enjoying on some morning when all the garden was white with frost."

It is interesting to note here that the service area of the estate was separated from the residence by a high embankment. The horses were kept some distance away, behind a wall also. A racecourse was laid out for the master's pleasure in this vicinity.

"On the east a great space was walled off, behind which rose the Racing Lodge; in front of it the race-course was marked off with ozier hurdles; and as he would be resident here during the sports of the fifth month [June], all along the stream at this point he planted the appropriate purple irises."

The heroine's spring garden is more completely pictured a little later when the account of a boating party is given. It is interesting to notice how the guests appreciated the stone artistry discovered on the island. Only a person who had herself taken part in such an excursion, could, I think, have written this detailed description.[4]

"Towards the end of the third month [April], when out in the country the orchards were no longer at their best and the song of the wild bird had lost its first freshness, Murasaki's Spring Garden seemed only to become every day more enchanting. The little wood on the hill beyond the lake, and the bridge that joined the two islands, the mossy banks that seemed to grow greener not every day but every hour—could anything have looked more tempting? 'If only one could get there!' sighed the young people of the household; and at last Genji decided that there must be boats on the lake. They were built in the Chinese style. Everyone was in such a hurry to get on board that very little time was spent in decorating them, and they were put into use almost as soon as they would float. . . .

"It was possible to go by water all the way to the Spring Garden, first rowing along the Southern Lake, then passing through a narrow channel straight towards a toy mountain which seemed to bar all further progress. But in reality there was a way round, and eventually the party found itself at the Fishing Pavilion [on the main lake]. Here they picked up Murasaki's ladies, who were waiting at the Pavilion by appointment. . . . The lake, as they now put out towards the middle of it, seemed immensely large, and those on board, to whom the whole experience was new and deliciously exciting, could hardly believe that they were not heading for some undiscovered land. At last however the rowers brought them close in under the rocky bank of the channel between the two large islands, and on closer examination they discovered to their delight that the shape of every little ledge and crag of stone had been as carefully devised as if a painter had traced them with his brush. Here and there in the distance the topmost boughs of an orchard showed above the mist, so heavily laden with blossom that it looked as though a bright carpet were spread in mid-air. Far away they could just catch sight of Murasaki's apartments, marked by the deeper green of the willow boughs that swept her courtyards, and by the shimmer of her flowering orchards, which even at this distance seemed to shed their fragrance amid the isles and

12. Autumn wild flowers (bellflower, Platycodon grandiflorum) temporarily overgrowing the austerity of a garden, Hoshun-in of Daitoku-ji, Kyoto. ▶

rocks. In the world outside, the cherry-blossom was almost over; but here it seemed to laugh at decay, and round the Palace even the wistaria that ran along the covered alleys and porticos was all in bloom, but not a flower past its best; while here, where the boats were tied, mountain-kerria poured its yellow blossom over the rocky cliffs in a torrent of colour that was mirrored in the waters of the lake below. . . ."

The native golden-flowered kerria shrub, with its slender drooping stems and fresh green foliage, is now known around the world and is still grown occasionally in the gardens of its native land. But the extensive use of flowering trees and shrubs, as seen here in the Heian gardens, was later replaced to a considerable extent by the use of greenery alone.

To study these great estates in more detail we can turn to two other contemporary records, one a book on garden making, the other a painting. The book is the *Sakuteiki* or *Treatise on Garden Making*,[5] written near the end of the period by one of the most important gentlemen of the court. At that time, garden planning was a gentleman's accomplishment. The *Sakuteiki* mentions, for instance, that the great estate of Kaya-no-in was designed by its owner, the regent Yorimichi (Michinaga's son). Also we note in Murasaki's story that Prince Genji himself planned his estate, and there is a description of Genji "standing in his shirt-sleeves instructing the workmen how to utilize the little spring of water that issued near the gallery of the eastern wing."[6] The directions in the *Sakuteiki* are, therefore, written as notes from one gentleman to another.

This book sums up the theories of garden design prevalent about the middle of the eleventh century. It reveals the immensely conscious understanding that made nature the only possible pattern for a garden. It also reveals how far the Japanese had departed by then from that exact copying of Chinese gardens which had marked their earlier years. They had come to look at their own hills, valleys, and rivers and now used the more gentle contours of these things as inspiration for their garden landscapes. The *Sakuteiki* also makes it clear that there was full understanding of the artistic principles which underlie good garden design.

The mansion of an important Heian noble, constructed in the style known as *shinden*, was not a single building but a complex of structures connected by outdoor arcades which were roofed and raised to floor level. The separate buildings were often the apartments of the ladies of the household, each wife or ward having her own establishment, including a retinue of ladies and maids. The ground between these buildings was usually landscaped with trees, flowering shrubs, moss, and sand (Plate 26).

Small open courts called *tsubo*, which were left in front of some of the more important apartments, were carefully developed into little gardens. Their plantings were sometimes augmented with tubs of flowering plants, such as cherry trees, plums, or wisteria, in the Chinese manner. Ladies whose rooms faced these small courts were often called by the name of the flower dominating them, and this flower was sometimes also used as a decorative motif in the rooms—stenciled or embroidered on curtains and screens. Readers of *The Tale of Genji* will recall the Lady Fujitsubo (She of the Wisteria Chamber).

◄ *13. Moss and sand as ground covers, Funda-in (Sesshu-in) of Tofuku-ji, Kyoto.*

The main hall of the mansion opened toward the lake and was flanked on either side by wing buildings.[7] These three faced a spacious courtyard and garden running down to the water's edge. It was enclosed on the sides by covered arcades which ran forward from either side building and ended in picturesque little kiosks overhanging the water. These end pavilions were known as the Fishing Hall and the Spring Hall. The lake shore, which swept outward in a graceful curve before the building, turned back to bring the waterline under the two pavilions. Such a curve still remains before a surviving building of the period, the splendid Phoenix Hall of Byodo-in temple (Plate 81).

The center of the forecourt in front of the main hall was kept clear, but the sides were landscaped. The open center was used as a place to stage entertainments and also "to accommodate the many people who come to pay their respects" to the lord of the mansion, in the words of the *Sakuteiki*. He received them sitting at the front of the hall facing out. Its walls could be raised by top hinges and hooked to the ceiling, making it almost an open pavilion. The courtyard was deeply covered with sand or rounded river pebbles to prevent muddiness underfoot. On special occasions, when entertainments were taking place, the ladies viewed them by peeping from behind the side curtains.

We can see just such a scene in a scroll picture painted in the twelfth century (Plate 79). It is called the *Calendar of Festivals* or *Nenju Gyoji*.[8] For the month of May the event was a cockfight. We see it being staged before the main hall. Two striped marquees have been set up on either side of the courtyard, and the attendants are bustling about in a great state of preparation and excitement. This painting also shows the naturalistic landscaping that was developed around the edges of the courtyard. There are small hillocks, rocks, a little stream, trees, and flowering plants. The trees are of a flowering variety, carefully pruned and maintained in their natural forms, although these forms are given somewhat picturesque emphasis.

The most important feature of this forecourt landscaping was the little streamlet (Plates 77-78). It entered the main court from under one of the bridgelike galleries connecting the wing buildings. Before this, it had circulated among the gardens of the rear buildings. It usually originated in a cascade on a slope somewhere behind the estate, and on its way to the lake it might fall into other cascades. The *Sakuteiki* classifies waterfalls into various forms, including those in which the water drops off one side; in which it is divided into two parts at the top; in which the face of the fall is seen at an angle; in which it falls in a smooth flow "like a piece of hanging silk"; in which it is divided into many falling threads by numerous irregularities at the lip; in which it is compounded into several falls or steps.

After the little stream entered the front courtyard it might flow around some rocks on its banks, divide at a tiny island, and be crossed by a small bridge in front of one of the gates into the garden. Small flowering plants and grasses grew along its banks.

The *Sakuteiki* is much concerned over the direction in which this stream should flow. Here superstition enters the subject of garden design. Various authorities are quoted, who all tend to show that the stream should rise in the north and east and flow toward the south and west. A quotation from an unspecified Chinese classic says: "A proper watercourse is one which travels from the east to the west, passing through the south, for this is the course of the sun. A watercourse from west to east is wrong."

This left-to-right direction (as one sits in the central hall) has been largely preserved and may be seen in most gardens of the present day. But nowhere has one of the original streamlets been preserved, for they were all artificially made and highly contrived—not strong enough to resist the centuries. However, an imitation of one, made in the sixteenth century around Sambo-in temple, may give us an idea of what they looked like (Plates 77–78).

Out in the lake, as viewed from the main hall, there was a central island which was rather close to the near shore. It seems often to have served as a place for musicians to sit and play, the music drifting over the water. It was connected to the shore by an arched vermilion-red Chinese bridge. The *Sakuteiki* says of this bridge: "It should not be set straight on the main axis [of the central hall] but slightly aslant, so that its eastern supports will be in line with the pillars of the western wing. . . . The under supports of the bridge should be hidden by piled-up rocks."[9] If there were other islands, any bridges connecting them were low and level. Small islands might be simply large single rocks.

The important subject of rock placement is dealt with at length in this book. Its directions are derived either from sharp observation of nature, from esthetics, or, occasionally, from geomancy. The threat of good or bad fortune was sometimes used to reinforce a natural or an esthetic law, as in this case: "Do not set upright a stone which naturally was flat, or vice versa; violations of this will surely bring evil fortune."

Stones should be useful as well as artistic: "The usual places to set rocks are: where the stream emerges into the courtyard; where it curves around a hillock; where it empties into the pond; where it bends in passing a building. Other stones should be set out only after due consideration, lest they spoil the effect. Within the stream itself the most suitable place for stones is at the bend, for two reasons: first, the esthetic effect, second, to prevent the point of land from being washed away. Elsewhere in the stream, too many stones should not be laid. While these might look well enough from near at hand, from any distance an overabundance of rocks will make the course seem one of stone rather than of water."

This general layout was followed not only for the mansions of great nobles but for more modest establishments also. On one occasion Prince Genji is unexpectedly forced to spend the night in the home of one of his gentlemen-in-waiting, Ki no Kami. His coming has caused a flurry of preparation in the house, and we read: "The eastern side of the hall was opened and swept and an elevated mat hastily placed in it for the prince. The garden streamlet had been designed unusually well to suggest coolness. The place was enclosed by a brushwood fence in country style [apparently in place of the more elaborate arcades], and the plantings in the court had been carefully arranged. The murmur of insects was borne on the cool evening breeze, while the whirling of fireflies delighted the onlookers. The prince and his attendants drank wine, seated where they could see the pond rippling under the eastern kiosk. . . . Ki no Kami was surprised and delighted by the visit, thinking it a great honour to his streamlet."[10]

The shinden style of mansion, with its picturesque end pavilions over the water, was modified in later periods. But the story of Prince Genji and the *Sakuteiki* have been read by all succeeding generations. With them the artistic influence of the Heian courtiers, and their fine taste, have affected the whole culture of Japan, including its gardens.

CHAPTER ELEVEN

Gardens of
Kamakura Warriors

FOR nearly three hundred years, the city of Heian, Capital of Peace and Tranquility, justified its name. But the gay, brilliant, and effeminate court depicted by Murasaki was its climax. Even in her day, quarrels for land and power were beginning in distant provinces, although no hint of this strife reached her pages. Yet in the next century, armed conflict was to enter the capital itself, and a child emperor was to perish in a great battle on the Inland Sea.

To maintain order, the Fujiwaras had come to rely on two military families, the Taira and the Minamoto. It was only a matter of time until these virile military men should realize it was they, not their effeminate employers, who held the real power. This came to pass in the second half of the twelfth century, when, by a series of adroit moves backed up by military force, the leader of the Tairas made himself the real master of Kyoto in place of the Fujiwara regent.

Autocratic and tyrannical, the Taira leader maintained a state of opulence rivaling that of the Fujiwara courtiers. His great estate, the Rokuhara, lay along the eastern bank of the river. It was a hated place, and all trace of it has disappeared. Just across the road, however, there is still an old pond garden that has been identified as the estate of his son, Taira Shigemori.[1] Known as Sekisui-en (Plate 83), this garden lay almost forgotten for centuries behind the high white walls of Myoho-in temple. Today a hospital stands at the street end of the long old pond, and patients may look up its green vistas to the Eastern Hills beyond. Tall trees enclose the water; in summer it is dappled with lily pads, and its edges are crowded with lush reeds and water grasses.

The winding shape of this water—inevitably called a "dragon pond"—is a departure from the broad, sunny lakes of the Heian courtiers which had preceded it. The lake is large enough for boating in the courtly manner, but this winding shape is something new. Its shores were evidently planned also for strolling along a beckoning path. Fujiwara court ladies, in their rich but cumbersome costumes, were not given to outdoor walking.

14. Free-form patterns of moss on sand, Sambo-in of Daigo-ji, Kyoto. ▶

Here, then, we seem to see the influence of more active people, the military men and their ladies. In time, the stroll garden became an established pattern, and the dragon-shaped pond was to be followed in several gardens of the succeeding period.

The stream which still supplies this lake flows down from a small valley in the pictur-esque green hills behind. Perhaps the winding form of the lake was suggested, or neces-sitated, by the curves of the original stream. If so, its bed must have been considerably broadened, deepened, and leveled out to make the lake.

As the lake was dug out, several islands were left, and their height may have been raised by some of the earth removed. One island is broadly pointed, almost similar in outline to the large island in the emperor Saga's lake made several centuries before. Lying off the tip of this large island is now a point of land which looks as if it had originally been a small round island. It would have been identical in position and in relative size to the small island which lies off the point of the large island in Saga's lake. Extending out from the face of the large island is a line of five rocky islets. This is one of the somewhat mysterious "night mooring stone" arrangements. Here, centuries later, we seem to have an almost exact duplication of the pattern of islands in the older garden, showing a remarkable continuity of tradition.

There are indications that Taira Shigemori built his original mansion in this garden near the shore, facing the large island and its five stone islets. From this site could have been seen a cascade on the opposite shore, through which the water probably entered the garden. The cascade stones are now much disarranged by trees which have grown up among them. The bottom of the pond is pebbled.

A second large island in this lake seems to be headed, as it were, toward the mansion. This one appears to have been a "tortoise" island, in which a large, upright stone suggested the raised head of a swimming sea creature. The island was oval, and originally around its perimeter, in imitation of flippers and tail, were other stones, more or less graphically arranged. Today these stones have washed out of position, and only an expert could detect the original form.[2]

With the presence of a tortoise island we are back to the ancient Chinese tale of the Mystic Isles, which were originally floating but whose movements were stabilized by giant tortoises. Only the sea creatures are here remembered. Forgotten is the story of the Immortals and their halls of jade. There is gentle whimsy in such a concept in a garden lake. At first glance, we see only a little island in a pond. When we look again we wonder —do we, perhaps, make out something more: a large creature, head above the surface, flippers barely moving? Another look and the thought vanishes, and it is, after all, only a little rocky island overgrown with weeds and bushes.

Probably the tortoise island originated in China, although I do not know of any relic or reference to such a thing there. It must have appealed strongly to the Japanese sense of humor. Possibly also it was regarded as a fortunate symbol of longevity. At any rate, such islands continued to be built down the centuries, some of them created with realism and, occasionally, with real artistry.

◄ *15. Rill through seminatural forest, Gio-ji, Kyoto.*

With the Tairas gathering up all the prizes of wealth and power, it was not to be expected that the other military family, the Minamoto, would stand quietly by for long. They soon found an excuse to attack the Tairas and, after a conflict of several years, were victorious under their leader Yoritomo.[3]

To avoid the enervating court influences which had undermined his late rivals, the victorious Yoritomo moved his headquarters to the beach town of Kamakura, some three hundred miles northeast of Kyoto. It was the district where his baronial fief was situated. Yoritomo's vassals, the provincial barons, made virtues of frugality, simplicity, and hardihood. Luxurious living and fine estates were no part of their ambitions, at least in the early decades of military rule. In those years of the late twelfth and early thirteenth centuries, the tramp of armored knights was heard on both sides of the world, for the Kamakura period in Japan was coincidental with the Third Crusade in Europe, and Yoritomo was a contemporary of England's Richard the Lion-Hearted.

Country knights, newly arrived in Kamakura with their foot soldiers and other followers, must have gazed with wonder and respect at many of the activities going on there. Religion was flourishing, as it often does in periods of turmoil and danger. The roofs of new shrines and temples were rising above the pine trees. At one site there was an unusual amount of activity. A huge mold was being constructed in which was to be cast a gigantic bronze image. It would be a figure of the Buddhist deity Amida, he who welcomes believing souls to a lotus seat in his celestial lake garden. Today, this massive figure is known as the Great Buddha of Kamakura.

On street corners of the town, followers of the militant monk Nichiren thundered against the abuses of the times, while those of the gentle monk Honen preached for simple folk a doctrine of salvation through faith in Amida. And as time went on, there were seen, more and more, the priests of a new religious sect called Zen. It was coming in from China, where it was being developed under the current Sung dynasty. Many of the Japanese warriors were becoming greatly interested in Zen.

Through this military and churchly crowd there would occasionally pass a figure in silken gown and small black cap, conspicuously neither of army nor of church—a civilian courtier up from Kyoto. A number of such men, having no taste for empty office, took service under the Kamakura government. Their long experience in administration did much to make the new rule a success. And with them the courtly culture, hitherto closely confined to Kyoto, began to make some contacts with the population at large—among other ways, through gardens.

While Yoritomo, as the actual ruler, or shogun, held power in Kamakura, the emperor's court in Kyoto continued its existence, outwardly much as always. Its offices were still filled with Fujiwara men who hoped for better times when the military upstarts should somehow be put in their places. This never happened. Nevertheless, down the centuries, this imperial court continued to exist, usually almost without political power, often impoverished, but clinging to the prescribed pattern of its ways, its refinements, its ceremonies, and its social distinctions. It never lost a certain prestige which has made it the fountainhead of honors and titles, eagerly sought and humbly accepted by actual rulers. The refining influences of this court in time subtly penetrated throughout the nation and colored the whole of its cultural fabric. Warriors, while at first despising courtly effeminacy, again and again came to accept courtly manners and courtly traditions of art and esthetics.

The warriors themselves contributed new and virile influences to the national culture. And a little later, when Zen Buddhism was stronger, this new sect reoriented many cultural expressions. But there has remained always a certain fundamental pattern laid down by the Heian court. Founded upon Chinese T'ang culture, this pattern was softened by the Japanese love of beauty in nature, joined to a ceremonious refinement of manner and a tendency to view all things in terms of esthetic appreciation and art.

After Yoritomo had established himself in Kamakura, he had still to conquer a northern branch of the Fujiwara family which had not submitted to him. A hundred years before, this branch had developed large estates in the far northern end of the country. Near what is now the village of Hiraizumi, these Fujiwaras had built their mansions and family temples, reproducing in them some of the magnificence found in the capital. In fact, nothing now remains around Kyoto that surpasses in faded splendor one of their surviving temple buildings, the Golden Hall of Chuson-ji. Another of their temples, called Moötsu-ji, possessed a chapel inspired by the surviving Phoenix Hall at Uji and, like that, set in a large landscaped lake garden.

It was inevitable that Yoritomo should attack and conquer this northern stronghold and annex its riches. But he could not have foreseen that he would be overwhelmed by the beauty of the lovely lake garden and of Moötsu-ji, its temple—even to constructing a replica when he returned to Kamakura.

Arriving at Moötsu-ji through the stately gates on the southern side of its lake, Yoritomo would have seen lying directly before him a vermilion-red bridge leading across the lake to a central island. A second bridge went on straight to the opposite shore, and the path then continued across a forecourt to the central entrance of the temple hall.[4]

This building, which was also colored vermilion red, must have been much like the surviving Phoenix Hall at Uji, which helps us to picture it among the green trees of the north. It had two stories and therefore was sometimes referred to as Nikai-do or the Two-storied Hall. Its central unit was flanked on either side by a pair of structures corresponding to the end pavilions of the shinden hall. But those of Moötsu-ji were modified for religious purposes and derived from China. One was a bell tower, holding a cylindrical Buddhist bell whose mellow tones announced the services. The other was a drum tower in which the passing hours were marked by the roll of a large drum. Among other auxiliary structures within the precincts was a small pagoda to the goddess Benten, rising on the central island. Also on this island was a small shrine to the deity Daikoku.

The axial formality of the approach, from the gates, straight across the two bridges, and then up to the building, was unusual. But apart from that, the garden held the usual characteristics of its time. Through the forecourt between building and lake, a streamlet meandered down to the water, its banks marked by stones. Other stones rose above the lake surface, one group being a straight line of "night mooring" islets. Another was the head of a tortoise island. More rocks outlined a jutting peninsula and, at one point on the shore, a high bank or rocky "hill" held the usual cascade.

99

Today, the old pond of Moötsu-ji lies dreaming, long shadows of the cryptomerias still stretching across its mirror surface (Plate 84). But the gay red bridges and buildings have vanished. Their foundation stones, however, may yet be found, to indicate where they stood. In fact, the stonework in this garden is better preserved in its original form than in any other relic of the period. Even the course of the streamlet can probably be traced in a surviving ditch lined with half-buried rocks.

Yoritomo began building his replica of Moötsu-ji in 1189, the very year he returned from the northern campaign.[5] Although he was an advocate of frugality and simplicity in personal living, he was willing to lavish large sums on religious establishments. The new temple was named Eifuku-ji but was popularly called Nikai-do (Two-storied Hall). It lay in a picturesque half circle of Kamakura's pine-covered hills, enclosing a quiet site for the lake.

Our interest in this replica garden lies chiefly in the fact that it is by far the best documented of any of the early landscaping projects. Its story can be found scattered through the entries of an official daily chronicle of the times, the *Mirror of the East*.[6] Here we find the first full account of how such a large undertaking was carried out.

After the temple building was started, three years had to pass before it was sufficiently advanced to justify starting intensive work on the garden. In the meantime there had been gathered together the necessary rocks. Also, suitable trees had been located and marked for transplanting at the proper time. Yoritomo demanded that each of his vassals in the neighboring provinces locate large, fine rocks and bring them to the site. Each vassal was also required to send three men to work on the job.[7]

When the time came to begin work, the chronicle mentions, huge stones, waiting to be put into place, were "piled up like hills" around the edge of the garden. Finally, an entry on the 24th day of the 8th month (September, according to the old calendar), 1192, reads: "Today excavating began on the pond of Nikai-do. Natural conditions around this site are very well suited to a landscape garden."

This comment by the chronicler is interesting evidence that he himself was interested in garden making. Doubtless he was one of the civilian officials up from Kyoto who had a background in such things. This also probably accounts for the continued entries in the record on this subject.

Yoritomo continued his personal interest in this temple project. He had selected a man of experience to design and direct the garden construction, a priest of the Tendai sect, whom we know only by his priestly name of Jogen. Like the chronicler, he must have come from Kyoto, where he had learned this art as a gentleman's accomplishment. He and the chronicler would have known each other, and the latter must have come to the site often to watch his friend's progress.

Yoritomo also visited the garden site often to inspect the progress of the work. He evidently accepted without question the courtly precept that garden making was a suitable occupation for persons of the highest position. He must also have had very definite ideas of what he liked and did not like, for while, on one occasion, he approved of the way

16. Pond bank stylized with cobbles, Sento Palace, Kyoto. ▶

Jogen had been putting in rocks, on another visit he asked the priest to change the position of some of the upright stones.

Someone who has had a chance to observe the making of a Japanese garden, especially before World War II, can reconstruct without difficulty this scene in Kamakura in 1192.[8]

The greater part of the future garden area would have been a wide, raw excavation where the future lake would be. Swarming everywhere were the workmen, some digging the earth with their mattocks; others, in pairs, carrying it away in rope nets slung on a pole between them. Standing in the midst of this activity, a quiet figure, would be Jogen, his clerical gown probably tucked up around his waist. Certain men would bring up a great rock to its approximate site. At a wave of Jogen's hand, it would be raised or lowered, twisted or turned, with many grunts and chanteys of concerted action. A tall tripod of tree trunks, with block and tackle, aids this movement today, and something of the sort must always have been used.

At last, when the stone seemed just right to Jogen, if the shogun was watching, he would turn for final approval. Perhaps the stone would be shifted just a little more. Then, when it was exactly right in its artistic relation to other stones near it, and to the whole balance and rhythm of the garden, it would be fixed into place by tamping with earth and pebbles.

This business of moving rocks seems to have fascinated certain of the young warriors. Raised in the country, they had probably never seen anything like it before. It challenged their strength, and the record tells how they tried their hand at moving stones. One, Hatakeyama Shigetada, succeeded in moving a stone ten feet long. We can picture this horseplay, the grinning workmen gathered around to see the fun; the tolerant Jogen pointing where the stone was to go; the determined young brave, red-faced and sweating, tugging and heaving at the huge stone; his triumph when he succeeded; the admiring murmurs of the crowd. And among them, the chronicler, noting in his mind that the incident was something to put into the day's record.

The planting of trees and shrubs is not mentioned. That was too routine and, compared to the stonework, of little importance. However, a number of full-sized trees were doubtless moved in. The technique of successfully transplanting such trees goes back, as we have seen, to distant centuries in China. Most of the trees transplanted into Eifuku-ji would have been the picturesque and ubiquitous pines from neighboring hillsides.

But Eifuku-ji also held cherries and flowering Japanese apricot trees.[9] We know, because they are mentioned in an entry some twenty years later, when Yoritomo was dead, and the new ruler (who was interested in erasing the memory of his achievements) ordered some of the temple's cherry trees moved to his personal estate. At the time of the original transplanting, a corner of the garden (as happens today) would have been used as a base yard for trees, with almost a forest of balled plants gathered and waiting to be put out. Their roots were tightly bound into a ball of earth by networks of yellow rice-straw rope.

With such intensive work, the garden itself was completed in only three months' time. On the 20th day of the 11th month, to celebrate the event, Yoritomo's wife, the strong-

◀ *17. Pond and Chinese bridge-pavilion on a winter morning, Heian Shrine, Kyoto.*

minded Lady Masako, visited the temple. The first Buddhist service was held five days later. "This place," exclaimed the chronicler, "is as beautiful as Amida's paradise."[10]

The temple of Eifuku-ji stood for over two hundred years, but in the turbulent middle ages it was burned and never rebuilt. Gradually its neglected and silted pond slipped back into rice fields. Only in the 1930's was its story traced and its site located. Excavations revealed most of the original islands and shoreline, and further restoration was planned. But with the coming of World War II these plans evidently had to be abandoned. When I visited the site in 1961 the pond area was again covered with rice stubble and giant reeds, with here and there a half-buried stone showing. New suburban houses were being built around the edge. Only an upright stone marker at one corner carried an identification of the site of Yoritomo's garden (Plate 82).

CHAPTER TWELVE

The Western Paradise: Saiho-ji

TO COMPARE the beauty of a garden to Amida's Paradise was a natural turn of thought in twelfth-century Japan. Early forms of Buddhism had demanded that devotees spend their time in religious good works, usually by becoming a monk or a nun in their old age. Since this was impossible or impractical for most people, a form of belief that offered salvation through faith alone held hope for many. Such a belief was founded upon the Buddhist deity Amida, who, it will be recalled, refused to accept Buddhahood until all beings should also be saved with him. As preached by the monk Honen, all a believer had to do to be sure of rebirth in his paradise was to call upon Amida in true and simple faith. The sect soon attracted overwhelming numbers.

Amida's heaven was supposed to lie to the west; hence it was often referred to as the Western Paradise. And since it was a land of purity and goodness, in contrast to this foul and sinful world, it was also called the Pure Land or Jodo. Amida's heavenly palace and lake garden was a concept to inspire artists, and its imagery entered largely into late Heian and Kamakura art. A natural form for such imagery was a lake garden on this earth, and certain gardens in Japan were designed on this theme. Among them was that of Saiho-ji temple, near Kyoto. It has remained one of the greatest and finest gardens ever created in that country.

The centuries have rolled gently over this old temple garden tucked away in a fold of the hills west of Kyoto, leaving it by far the best preserved of any built up to the thirteenth century. Kyoto people call Saiho-ji the Moss Temple, Koke-dera, for it lies in a spot particularly favorable to the growth of mosses. Sheltered alike from cold north winds and the hot western sun, with a heavy clay soil that holds moisture, the mosses have taken possession of the garden in such variety and profusion that they eclipse in interest the more showy plants.

As we enter the garden through a small gate, our first impression is one of size. It covers about four and a half acres. The place seems a forest, deeply shadowed, with dark water gleaming in its depths. There is no carefully organized landscape picture here. The place is a stroll garden, like that around Taira Shigemori's dragon pond. As we go along the path which leads off among the moss and trees, the garden will be revealed to us bit by bit. It is as if we were looking at one of the long Oriental scroll paintings, as it is slowly unrolled, studied, and rerolled.

Passing down the path, we are scarcely aware of the garden's boundaries. A wooded hill rises behind, and when we look for other limits, our sight is baffled by the dim parallel lines of giant bamboo stalks. A wide planting of these surrounds one side of the garden. Everywhere the trees spring up, large and small, to cast a light shade over the mossy ground. They are quite untrained, different in this from the artfully cultivated specimens of a later period. They are mostly broadleaved evergreens, although here and there are conifers and the delicate tracery of Japanese maples.

The tree trunks are mottled with greyish-green lichens, creating a mysterious haze through their parallel trunks. In May scarlet azaleas flame in the shadows. The huge blue-green bowls of the lotus sway over the pond in July. In autumn the maples burn a mellow crimson against the azure sky. And in winter the mosses, still green, hold promise of spring in their velvet depths.

Once there were cherry trees in this garden, splendid enough, when in bloom, to lure court nobles all the way from Kyoto. We read in a contemporary diary[1] of the visit of the ex-emperor Kogon in the spring of 1347. The cherry blossoms were at their best, and to view them better the party took to boats on the pond. One courtier suggested music, and soon the thin melody of flute and zithern floated up to the petaled branches. Toward evening, everyone left the boats and the ex-emperor took his seat under one of the blooming trees. Ten tall lanterns, on standards, threw soft light up to the masses of flowers overhead, which flushed radiantly against the starry darkness of the sky.

The present path curves through a glade and lifts to a slight eminence occupied by an old ceremonial teahouse. Everywhere the mosses carpet the ground, undulating away in hummocky waves of emerald, jade, and bronzy green (Plates 7, 87). Often there seems to be a translucent azure highlight over certain patterns of growth. The mosses mold smooth green banks to the pool and throw verdant shadows into rock crevices. Over forty species and varieties are said to grow here.[2] Some are like finest velvet. Others are coarse and a full two inches high, like tiny conifers creating a fairy forest. Patterns of varying colors and textures spread over the ground—on mats of duller green, mysterious circles of jade; or undefined blotches appear in overtones of grey and yellow.

A side path branches across the moss to a small bridge leading to an island. The bridge is made of logs, its top covered with earth, all now mossy. The water seen from the bridge is crystal clear, but the bottom is emerald green from threadlike waterplants growing on the sandy bed. The limpid surface of the water is stippled with golden sunlight, and the tree trunks seem twice their length in the shimmering mirror.

In excavating for this lake, a large, squarish island was left and divided into two parts by a narrow channel. The lake hereabouts, therefore, is roughly a circular ring of water, very irregular in shape and presenting vistas of rocky islets, shadowy coves, and rolling mossy banks. There are indications that the lake was once much larger, extending over what is now the bamboo grove beyond. It must have been this extended portion that was used for boating. It would also show a greater similarity to the lakes of Heian mansions, to which this garden was still close in time.

106

The banks of the large, rounded, central island do not hold any "shore protecting" stones, which is a rather unusual circumstance. They are simply molded of clay, over which the mosses now roll in rounded greenery. The bottom of the pond is also made of this puddled clay. Both are part of the original construction, and the way they have survived is a tribute to the remarkable techniques of the original builders. However, rocks are numerous around the shores of the second largest island, while others are used to create several rocky islets. The latter appear to have been of the turtle and crane styles.

The rockwork around the second largest island is very much like that found on a similar island in the Gold Pavilion garden not many miles away, and it is also in the general style of rockwork found on the hillside above, indicating that both upper and lower gardens here were made at the same time. Frequently appearing in this rockwork is the "trinity style," in which a larger central stone is flanked by two others, one on either side. This was derived from the trinity of Buddhist figures in which the central image is similarly flanked.

In a small upper pond somewhat apart from the main lake, Saiho-ji has its own example of the straight-line "night mooring stones" (Plate 86). Here they are much smaller than we have seen them in older, larger lakes and are set up in two lines. It looks very much as if this were a vestigial tribute to an older tradition which was wearing thin. It has been suggested that here these stones might be nothing more than one-time foundations for some building which overhung this small pond. Since the stones are sometimes pointed and all are irregularly spaced, this seems very unlikely. Whatever their significance, they are singularly ornamental, especially in summer, when small grasses and wild flowers grow out of their crevices, to be reflected back in the quiet, shallow water.

Saiho-ji's garden holds a distinctly double character. Above the lower lake garden rises a mossy hillside with rocks and trees, separated by a wall and ornamental gateway. We pass through this gate and ascend a path of stepping stones. It winds through mosses as verdant and thick as those below, following a sunny glade, so perfect as to seem theatrical, or as if we had slipped back to the age of the gods. Eve might be sunning herself on that mossy bank, or Izanami, her Japanese counterpart, be standing, long-haired, in those shadows.

The original layout of this hillside garden cannot now be determined, for only three individual rock creations remain, scattered over the mossy slopes. They are still in good condition and are masterpieces of their kind.

The first one we come to is a rocky "island" in a sea of moss. It is a group of rather large stones which might be mistaken for a mere pile of rocks left there after some building operation. In fact, few of the people who go through the garden give this heap a second look. But as we pause, our eye is caught by something familiar. A second look and we see it—a huge tortoise, floating in the mossy sea, head back, flippers at rest (Plate 88). To the eye of the imagination he is quite plain; in the cold eye of realism he disappears. Of the many tortoise islands made up to this time in Heian lakes none is as graphic today as this one.

A second arrangement in the hillside garden has been built up around a natural woodland spring. Cold and clear, the water seeps from the ground, and large stones have been arranged to dramatize and make it useful. Above the point where the water emerges, a large flat-faced rock has been set into the hill to hold back the earth. The water collects below it in a small pool, about six inches deep, clear and shadowy. The pool is lined with clay, and a flat stone has been placed over the clay to form the bottom. Large wing stones, right and left, also keep the earth from washing in. Across the front of the pool are low, flat kneeling stones, about a foot high. The excess water runs away between then in a tiny rill. Deepset in the mossy hillside, this spring seems completely natural, irresistibly inviting one to kneel and drink. It became the prototype for various springs of water to be used in making tea.

Beyond the spring, certain large, flat-topped stones hold furry rugs of coarse, matted moss, flung over them by the centuries. Some visitors have assumed these flat stones were used as outdoor meditation seats. But the chronicles state clearly that those who came to meditate used the small chapel, which probably stood where its successor stands today. The flat-topped stones of Saiho-ji, both here and elsewhere, are very characteristic of its style, as we shall see.

Beyond the small chapel we come to the dry cascade, the high spot and climax of the garden (Plate 85). The place is mysterious with the shadows of tall trees, so that at first the large rocks, blotched with lichens, which mount the hillside are sometimes difficult to distinguish clearly. Eventually we make out what appears to be a rocky cascade formed of great boulders. They look as if the topsoil had been washed away by falling water, revealing the basic rocks of the hillside. No water trickles over them now, nor has it ever done so. Yet the feeling persists that water must have created this fall and sometime will flow here again.

At the foot of the cascade are two "pools" on successive levels, outlined in smaller stones. The lower pool washes to our feet. Only moss has ever brimmed here, as it does today, but somehow the green surfaces seem to ripple like water touched from above by a fall.

The atmosphere of this place is one of great serenity and quiet. We feel as if we had, indeed, left the foul world far below.

As we stand looking at this rock re-creation, the thought crosses our mind, "Can this, after all, be natural?" Then we notice how the earth has been washed away from under several of the lower rocks, leaving exposed the foundations of small stones on which they were based. And we know that every rock in sight was placed just as we see it, with super-lative artistry and skill. Each stone is so right in its position we are hardly aware of the effort that went into their placement.

Saiho-ji's rocks are natural "mountain stones," probably found somewhere in these hills but not, apparently, on this particular site, for there are no signs of any natural out-croppings here (Plate 9). The rocks are mostly of granite, large, rugged, and irregular. Yet closer observation reveals that a large number of them again have flat tops. This is not a common feature of rocks, and it tells of the large amount of careful selection and rejection that was done in assembling those finally used here. Perhaps a tendency toward natural cleavage in these stones may have made this selection a little easier. It is interesting to know that Saiho-ji's flat-topped stones originated a style and a pattern which later dominated a whole period of garden art.

As we study the effect of their repeated level lines and surfaces, we realize how much their horizontality contributes to the strong sense of serenity dominating this place. Yet it is not this horizontality alone that produces the feeling. Every other stone present also contributes toward it, because each has been placed in its most stable position—prone or on its broadest base. The latent power of these quiescent rocks, the strength of nature here in repose, is what gives this spot its feeling of utter tranquility.

It is noteworthy that there is a total absence in this cascade, or in any other stone arrangement in this garden, of any upstanding rock or soaring stone. The maker of this garden was not interested in creating any suggestion of a larger landscape in the fourth dimension of the imagination. He was concerned only with nature, idealized Japanese nature, right on this hillside and in scale with it. The only call on the imagination is to see water swirling down the cascade. The whole creation is integrated into its environment.

It has long been thought that Saiho-ji's garden was made in the second half of the fourteenth century by the great Zen ecclesiastic, Muso Kokushi. It now appears the garden was a hundred and fifty years old before he ever came to rehabilitate it and add to it a number of new buildings. The internal evidence of its design and construction indicates so strongly that the garden was made long before Muso's day that Mr. Shigemori sought through a mass of legends, traditions, and stories to find any kernels of truth among them.[3] The real story, as he believes it can be reconstructed, makes fascinating reading.

Saiho-ji's origin is associated with Matsuo Shrine, a Shinto foundation, which still stands in the hills about a third of a mile from the garden. The shrine was built by members of the Hata family to honor a Shinto ancestor whom they had adopted. And the head of the family was the shrine's hereditary high priest, an office which, in Shinto, may be more patriarchal than religious.

This Hata family, to judge by its name, had originally been either Chinese or Korean. The founder was probably one of those craftsmen brought to Japan to teach the civilized arts and crafts. Being skilled and energetic, his descendants, in due course, became possessed of extensive lands near present-day Kyoto, which they developed for rice culture by constructing dams and irrigation systems. General land development was their specialty, but they also carried on many other enterprises and were exceedingly wealthy.

It is believed that, when plans were afoot in the eighth century to move the capital to the present Kyoto site, this family made the move possible by largely underwriting its expense, donating land and the materials for palace construction. It was greatly to their advantage to have the court and its generous patronge nearby.

Up to this time the Hatas had remained commoners. But in the immemorial manner of wealth, Hata heiresses came to marry court titles, and the family became affiliated with the courtly Fujiwara clan. Later, in the Kamakura period, when the military had assumed power and, among other things, were taking manors from helpless Fujiwara nobles, the Hatas seem to have held on to their property with a firm hand. For they were able to construct, even at that time, this temple and its garden, which is one of the most expensive ever made in Japan.

About the time Yoritomo was building Eifuku-ji temple and garden in Kamakura, the hereditary high priest of Matsuo Shrine was one Fujiwara Morokazu. He was an ardent follower of Amida and conceived the idea of building a Jodo temple near Matsuo and inducing the famous monk Honen to come as its founder. The spot favored for this undertaking seems to have been hallowed by an ancient hermitage once existing there, which legend has confused with Saiho-ji's beginning.[4] Tradition also says that the deity of Matsuo, endorsing the idea of the Jodo temple, indicated its preference for a site by appearing on a large stone. This is still pointed out to the credulous.

Here, during the Kenkyu era (1190–98), Fujiwara Morokazu built twin temples to the glory of Amida and gave a manor for their upkeep. These facts, labeled "History of Saiho-ji," were cut on a stone marker some years later and put up by the priest Jikusen.[5]

The twin temples illustrated the dual concepts of the Jodo sect: this sinful world and that Pure Land. The Temple of [Aloofness from] the Foul World, or Edo-ji, was placed on the hillside. The Temple of the Westward Direction or Saiho-ji (hence, by implication, of Amida's Paradise) was constructed on the level ground just below, where there would be room to re-create Amida's celestial lake. The hillside temple of Edo-ji early disappeared, leaving its garden as part of Saiho-ji's precincts and giving it the dual character we see today.

Many floods and freshets have washed over Saiho-ji in the eight hundred years since it was first constructed, and several times the garden has been partially reconstructed. But the fact that it has survived and has maintained much of its original stonework is testimony to the thoroughness of its primary construction, done by men wise in the ways of land and water. Every detail was carried out in the very best manner possible. All this must have demanded an extended period for building and, since the garden is large, must have added much to its cost. This was also increased by the fact that no suitable stones occurred on the site, but all had to be brought in.

Additional confirmation of Saiho-ji's construction in the late twelfth century is found in its internal feeling and the style of its rockwork. We have pointed out that the designer was not interested in creating any larger landscape in the mind of the beholder by using soaring rocks in the Chinese manner. He was interested only in re-creating Japanese nature and integrating it into the existing setting. In this he was carrying out exactly the admonitions of that treatise on garden making, the *Sakuteiki*, which, it will be recalled, was written just about the same time that Saiho-ji was built. It emphasizes as one of its chief themes the need to study nature and then re-create it (always, of course, as art, not as exact imitation).

We do not know who the designer of Saiho-ji was, nor are we exactly certain as to the name of the author of the *Sakuteiki*. But in a small society like that of Kyoto's courtly nobility it is more than likely they were acquainted, were even friends through their common interest in garden design. If, however, their ages made a friendship impossible, both at any rate expressed the feeling common at this period, the turn away from Chinese art to nature in Japan. Saiho-ji's rockwork is the most purely Japanese expression of rock artistry that is known.

This might have been anticipated. For the past three hundred years the Japanese had been slowly moving away from the imitation of things Chinese. They had been laying the foundations of their own cultural forms and developing their own artistic expressions out of the elements of T'ang culture. For a considerable time official relations with China had almost ceased. China had been going through another period of revolution, as the great T'ang dynasty fell and the new period of Sung rule was established in South China. Fresh troubles with the northern barbarians had complicated the beginnings of Sung. But by the time Saiho-ji was built, Southern Sung was already producing new creative ferments in painting which were later to electrify Japanese art and gardens. But before these influences reached the islands in force, there was to be the usual long lag.

In the meantime, the years rolled on over Saiho-ji, its mosses probably growing ever thicker and greener. Finally, nearly a hundred and fifty years had passed since its construction. During this period the Hata-Fujiwara family evidently continued to give it some care, even as the head of the family remained the hereditary high priest of nearby Matsuo Shrine. The family also remained in control of the extensive lands and fortune of the one-time Hata family.

In 1337 the family head was Fujiwara Chikahide, probably a several-times grandson of Saiho-ji's founder. Chikahide was an important personage, governor of Settsu Province, wealthy and powerful. Being as ardently interested in the new Buddhist sect of Zen as his forebear had been in the cult of Amida, he evidently conceived the idea of rehabilitating the mossy old Jodo temple on the hillside and converting it into a center for the new sect. This he would do if he could persuade the great Zen ecclesiastic Muso Kokushi to come and officiate awhile as its first honorary abbot.

Muso the State Priest (1275–1351) was one of the most powerful and astute men of his time. The period was again one of military troubles, for the regime at Kamakura had been overthrown, and a new general, Ashikaga Takauji, was trying to control the country. Muso Kokushi was his supporter and advisor and is generally credited as one of those who helped to make the new government a success.

Since the provincial governor, Chikahide, was also a supporter of the new general, it proved not too difficult to arrange for Muso Kokushi to come to the new-old family temple. We can surmise that its mossy seclusion and beauty may have entered into his decision. After he settled there, he changed the written characters of its name so that, although they continued to be pronounced Saiho-ji, the syllables meant Temple of Western Fragrance, a Zen allusion, rather than Temple of the Westward Direction, its old Jodo name.

Following Muso's suggestions, the garden was rehabilitated and several buildings either reconstructed or added new.[6] These structures were not large halls but small pavilions and studios, one high on the hill, as a lookout, others scattered about. They were evidently all of excellent design, for they met the highly exacting taste of a later generation. So much admired were they that several were copied. We can catch a glimpse of one, the Ruri-den, in the only replica which survives, the so-called Silver Pavilion in the garden of that name. This we shall come to in due course along with other ways in which Saiho-ji's garden influenced later estates.

All of Saiho-ji's buildings were burnt in the civil wars of the middle ages. The present main building, or Founders' Hall, is about a century old. There are two tea cottages, one of which, the Shonan-tei, is under government protection as a "national treasure." But none of these is like the structures erected for Muso Kokushi.

Saiho-ji was built to express the Jodo concept of Amida's celestial garden. But over the years other feeling has crept in. The curious effect of the moss, the lichen-marked tree trunks, the dark gleaming water with its long reflections, all combine to create a feeling of the centuries rolling over. And with this has come the mood of great tranquility that Japanese artists call *yugen*. Yugen is called into being by atmosphere, one of hazy unreality that creates in a mind attuned to it the feeling of kinship with nature, the sense of one's spirit merging with the spirits of other natural things and the eternal behind them all. This is the basic feeling of Oriental mysticism, fostered consciously by Zen. From this time on, it was to play a large part in Japanese gardens, with the garden artists striving consciously to put it into their work.

Saiho-ji, therefore, marks a definite change in garden development, with the disappearance of the old, gay, open Heian pleasure park, while it foreshadows the new subjective feeling in gardens of the coming age.

CHAPTER THIRTEEN

The Sung Dynasty Influence:
Tenryu-ji and Kitayama-dono

NEW meaning and artistry were soon to come to Japanese gardens when communications with China were once more fully established. To understand these developments we must know what had been going on in China in the meantime.

The great T'ang dynasty had come to an end in 908, brought on by internal rebellion. Ch'ang-an, which had been for centuries the splendid capital, was ruined and depopulated. For over fifty years North China remained in a state of anarchy under a series of petty rulers. However, below the Yangtze River the southern regions, as once before, were relatively peaceful, and there T'ang culture and its arts continued.

One of the northern rulers had selected as his capital the city of K'ai-feng, situated on the northern plain. It remained as the capital when a new general made China once more into a single united empire, the Sung dynasty. The century and a half that K'ai-feng was the seat of government is known as the period of Northern Sung (960–1125). It was a period of high culture and refined civilization. The Sung rulers were pacifists, more interested in the arts and philosophy than in war and expansion of territory. But Tartar nomads who had earlier penetrated below the Great Wall during the period of anarchy had remained as rulers of a limited area around Peking.

The fifth Sung ruler, the emperor Hui Tsung (reigned 1101–26), is regarded as one of the most interesting men in Chinese history. A painter of real talent himself, he presided over an academy of artists and was an enthusiastic collector of pictures, porcelains, and other art. His interests also included gardens, of which there were many in K'ai-feng. But the finest of all was the great imperial landscape park known as Ken Yu or Eastern Hill.[1] Here had been assembled a vast number of natural rocks, along with rare trees, plants, and animals, incorporated into a series of landscape features. The effect could not have been very different from that of its successor in Peking today, the Park of the Sea Palaces, previously described. It is probably safe to assume that under Hui Tsung's artistic guidance Ken Yu was the most beautiful garden ever seen in China.

While lengthy descriptions tell of its beauty in poetic terms, we can catch a glimpse of what some of its stone artistry was actually like in a surviving painting of the time. The picture does not show Ken Yu but probably some private princely garden in the city. The painter who did this picture was one of those in the emperor's academy. His name was Su Han-ch'en, and he was the recipient of honors from this emperor and the two following.[2] The picture in which we are interested shows a garden terrace with two young children playing at the foot of a high, thin rock (Plate 98). They are deeply absorbed in watching a large cricket on a stool. The children are delightful, but interest is focused and held by the fantastic rock that towers behind them.

The tall, slender stone is surrounded by a flowering bush of changeable rose mallow (*Hibiscus mutabilis*) while small chrysanthemums spill over the ground. Estimating by the size of the children, the stone rose about six feet and was about one foot wide. (Several feet must have been underground to hold it erect.) It probably was made of sandstone or shale, since layers and cleavages are visible in its sheer face and broken top. The rock probably came from some river bed or old lake, for near its base can be seen what seem to be several incipient "potholes" (rounded holes worn by a small stone rotating in a rock pocket through water action). In time, rocks thus carved into fantastic rounded holes by pothole action came to be the most sought after of all Chinese garden rocks. They were numerous in Ken Yu.

Since Su Han-ch'en was a genre painter, I think we can assume that this picture is approximately the portrait of a real rock which stood somewhere in K'ai-feng. It reveals to us in the most graphic way the style and the original artistry of Sung garden rockwork.

Studying this stone from the standpoint of a garden maker, we realize that it was actually a long, flat slab. Had it been left on the ground, or used otherwise horizontally, it would have attracted little attention. But someone with great imagination caused it to be set upright, its broken top forming a pointed peak. In this position, the stone suddenly takes on impressive importance, due to its proportions.

If we look at this stone for just what it is, we see only a striking rock ornament on a terrace, surrounded by flowers. But if we look at it with our creative imagination, we suddenly see in it one of those vast precipices so often a part of China's tilted mountains. Here the garden maker has accomplished with one rock exactly what the landscape painters did with their brushes and ink. That is, he has caught the very essence of these vast natural formations. We can see this plainly when we compare the stone in this painting with a great natural precipice like that in a painting by Fan K'uan (Plate 97). The garden rock and the landscape painting are treatments of virtually the same subject, done in two different but related media.

In 1126 the Tartars from Peking swept down on K'ai-feng, captured the emperor and many of his court, and carried them off to captivity in Manchuria. The peace-loving Sungs, unprepared to resist, withdrew south of the Yangtze River and established a new capital in the city of Hangchow. The period that followed is known as the Southern Sung (1127–1279).

Many of the artists who had worked in the K'ai-feng academy, including Su Han-ch'en, later gathered in Hangchow. Possibly it was there he painted the picture of a lady sitting at her dressing table on a terrace in early spring (Plate 90). This picture not only reveals the amenities of life in Hangchow but also shows us a terrace developed with potted plants, a picturesque tree, and an ornamental rock.

Hangchow, standing on the edge of picturesque West Lake, became the most beautiful and romantic of all Chinese capital cities (Plate 95). There has been a saying ever since: "Heaven above, Hangchow below."

This seemed to be almost as much deserved as ever when I saw it shortly before World War II. The silvery lake lay among small, sharply pointed green hills covered with broad-leaved evergreens, bamboos, and conifers. The hills were still pricked by little, upstanding pagodas, showing where monasteries stood among them. Villas lined the shore, reminding one of the scenes on the blue-and-white willow-pattern ware (Plate 89). Gardens following the lake's edge still doubled in its surface the tip-tilted corners of little pavilion roofs and the sapphire, turquoise, and rose hues of their glazed tile walls. The lake's smooth surface was dotted by small green islands and crossed by a long willow-fringed causeway. This was broken at intervals by arched, half-moon bridges whose dark shadows in the water completed a full-moon circle. There is a tradition that Po Chu-i, the garden lover and poet of T'ang, contributed to the beautifying of this district when he was its governor.

In Peking, during the Sung period, the Tartars came more and more to adopt the ways of their Chinese subjects. But farther north a new and quite different menace was appearing—the Mongols. These nomads are regarded as among the most savage and pitiless people known to history. They totally destroyed cities and their inhabitants who opposed them. When they took Peking, they turned it into their own capital, calling their dynasty the Yuan. In 1276 they took Hangchow, but since the city had not resisted them, it was not destroyed. Marco Polo, who worked later for the Mongol emperor Kubilai Khan, saw Hangchow after its glory had been greatly diminished. But he still regarded it as one of the finest cities in the world.

In later centuries, Hangchow was often visited by China-bound Japanese artists and students. Among them, in the fifteenth century, was the painter Sesshu, who found that by the time he arrived, the great master landscape painters of the Sung period were gone. He had hoped to study with them, but he wrote on his return to Japan that he had found no teachers in China except its mountains and rivers. Many of his paintings, however, continued to be done in the style of the old Sung masters (Plate 96). There is also in existence a painting, probably by Sesshu or one of his followers, showing Hangchow and its lake at the time of his visit. Much later, miniature copies of the causeway that crosses the lake appeared in Japanese gardens.

A resurgence of native Chinese power ended the Mongol Yuan dynasty after only eighty-eight years (1368). There followed the Chinese Ming dynasty, with Peking again as its capital. The existing imperial landscape park there is believed to have been directly inspired by Ken Yu, the imperial garden in K'ai-feng.

In Japan, in the old garden of Tenryu-ji temple, near Kyoto, there remain today three examples of rock artistry that are unmistakably in Sung style. Evidence indicates they might have been made by some Chinese rock craftsman who had fled to Japan, perhaps to escape the Mongols. If this should be so, they are, as far as we know, the only surviving examples of contemporary Sung rock artistry.

The temple of Tenryu-ji stands a few miles outside Kyoto in the popular river resort of Arashiyama. Ever since the ninth century, when the emperor Saga built his Chinese lake garden in this neighborhood, Kyoto courtiers had been creating their estates nearby also. And for the past five hundred years, the people of Kyoto have still been coming to Arashi-yama to enjoy the cherry blossoms in spring and the maple colorings in autumn.

The temple garden in which the three Sung-style rock arrangements are found is small, less than an acre (Plate 94). Its pond, lying behind the main building, is only a hundred and fifty feet wide and two hundred feet long. The opposite shore is formed by artificial hillocks or banks, now so overgrown with trees that they merge into the greenery of natural hills in the distance, obscuring a once famous view of the river and of a picturesque hill known as Kame-yama. Later, this hill gave its name to the estate. On the pond shore, opposite the building, are a stone bridge, a large cascade, and a rocky island. While other fine stone arrangements are found in this garden, the bridge, cascade, and island stand conspicuously apart from them in artistry.

We can best see these three on a stroll around the lake. We come first to the massive cascade built into the artificial hillside at the head of a small inlet from the lake. Over this inlet passes the bridge carrying the footpath that encircles the pond. Just beyond the bridge, out in the water, is the island.

The bridge is made of three flat, uncut stones, laid end to end like planks (Plate 92). Where the ends join, they are supported by single natural stones rising from the water. Possibly the supporting stones are chipped to hold the plank stones more securely, but no hint of this is visible. This bridge of natural stone is in complete harmony with the other two rock groups, but it introduces here, without any sense of intrusion, the presence of man into this natural landscape.

The cascade is best seen by looking up at it from the bridge which crosses its foot. It towers above us, huge and bold, its top about fourteen feet above the water. The main fall, rising from the lake, is a single high, flat rock face, seven feet tall and four feet wide. This is supported and enclosed on either side by enormous rugged boulders. Rising from the water, they turn the little inlet into a short, rocky fjord.

Above this main fall there is a sloping area of swirling rapids. Here, one of the stones, vaguely resembling a fish, is known as the carp stone. It is several feet long and is supposed to illustrate an old Chinese belief that golden carp, ascending the rapids in the upper Yellow River, became dragons if they succeeded in reaching the top. The belief became an allegory of man's struggle to achieve greatness. Because of this belief, the rapids of the Yellow River were known as the Dragon's Gate (Lung Men), and this name was bestowed on this cascade also.[3]

Above the rapids in the Tenryu-ji garden is a second fall, with a precipitous face about three feet high. At the very top, the whole structure is crowned by a huge pointed rock peak. In every line this rugged, powerful cascade suggests the dynamic movement of water. Yet there is not a drop in it. Investigation behind reveals that the whole structure stands on an artificial mound, with no water sources whatever.[4] Yet the feeling of water surging through it is so strong it seems that water must have created it.

18. Bridge carrying circulatory path across lake inlet, Shugaku-in, Kyoto. ▶

19 (overleaf). The Gold Pavilion in a traditional snow setting, Kyoto. ▶

The cascade is put together, of course, without cement. The stones stand by their own weight, with a mixture of clay and small pebbles around them.[5] This construction has held since the thirteenth century—doubtless aided by the fact that no freshet has ever washed through it.

Turning toward the lake, we view the island, a rocky peak which rises starkly above the water's surface (Plate 91). It is made up of seven stones, with the central peak a tall, pointed pinnacle, leaning slightly. Its top is about five feet above the water. Placed firmly against it are two flat-topped rocks which provide support and strongly contrasting lines. Three lower stones of differing heights, with nearly level tops, cluster about the base, opposite the leaning pinnacle. They give it balance and stability. The seventh stone, of medium height and nearly flat, also stands somewhat apart in the water.

From whatever point on the lake shore we view this arrangement, it presents always a balanced, harmonic form. This is a supremely difficult accomplishment, for composition in the round requires infinitely greater art than when a single front is presented. Tenryu-ji's islet is one of the finest creations in the whole range of Japanese garden artistry, a masterpiece unsurpassed in any other single arrangement.

Basically, this peak is an abstraction in pure form. But perhaps our imagination sees in it also a vast mountain rising from the sea—P'eng-lai, one of the Mystic Isles, with its high terraces on which the Immortals had their palaces. The name Horai, the Japanese rendering of P'eng-lai, has been given to a traditional style of island, exemplified in this one with its leaning top. The Horai style became a formula, with only a vague remembrance of the Immortals and their peaks.

As we look at Tenryu-ji's island and cascade, marked by their upward-soaring thrust, we contrast them with the tranquil, quiescent rocks of Saiho-ji's naturalistic cascade, integrated into its own hillside. Not for one moment would we suspect these rocks of Tenryu-ji of being nature's handiwork. They were created as art, bold and rugged—designed, perhaps, to excite the imagination and carry it far away from Japan's softly contoured mountains to the never-never land of vast Chinese landscape, its painting, and its traditions.

To know the way in which these fully matured examples of Sung rock artistry suddenly appeared in Japan, at a time when the rounded naturalism of Saiho-ji was dominant, we must look into the story of this site.[6]

As early as the ninth century a certain Prince Kaneaki had built a villa there. Later the place became known as Danrin-ji when the empress Danrin retired to it after she became a Buddhist nun. Some decades after this, in 1256, the ex-emperor Gosaga moved here permanently after a series of fires had destroyed his Kyoto palace. The place was then renamed Kameyama-dono after the picturesque small mountain just behind it. It was developed into proper magnificence for the ex-emperor, and a new garden was made, probably the one which still survives as part of the present Tenryu-ji precincts. Under Gosaga the place was the center of court life for over forty years, since he continued to

◄ *20. Rock base above pond, supporting pillar of an overhanging structure, Joshoko-ji, Kyoto.*

administer the powers of the throne from retirement. One of the many princelings who were raised on this estate was a great-grandson who became the emperor Godaigo, important to its later story.

During this period the military government in Kamakura was flourishing, but in Kyoto most of the nobles were feeling the loss of incomes. However, one noble family was still rich and powerful—the Saionji branch of the Fujiwaras. It was the head of this family, Saneuji, who had originally paid for the improvements to Gosaga's estate, the reason being that his own daughter, Kitsuko, was the imperial consort. The wealth and power of the noble Saionji family derived from the fact that, a generation earlier, Kinstune, the family head, had elected to become the eyes and ears at court of the Kamakura military government. Being plentifully rewarded for this service, he chose to build lavish villas and give fine entertainments.

The finest of his new estates lay at the foot of some low, wooded hills just north of Kyoto. It was, therefore, called the North Hill Villa, or Kitayama-dono.[7] Its garden, with its large lake dug from the rice fields, was probably the last of the great Heian-style lake gardens to be built. And since it was made at the time when the cult of Amida was popular, it is believed this lake illustrated the theme of Amida's celestial lake garden. Today, it is part of the precincts of the Gold Pavilion temple.

Water still enters this lake through a high, rocky cascade which extends up the hillside for about forty feet toward a pond-reservoir above (Plate 93). Like the later cascade at Tenryu-ji, this one is also unmistakably an example of Sung rockwork. The two are, in fact, so much alike that experts believe they could well have been the work of the same man. Both have high falls, an interval of swirling rapids, and a carp stone.

Kintsune's lake (now that of the Gold Pavilion garden) was partially completed in 1224. In that year a visitor, the famous poet Teika, described it in his diary. The style of the rockwork immediately caught his attention. "Everything has been constructed after modern ideas," he wrote. "Every object is rare and precious. The forty-five-foot waterfall, the jade-green pond, the clear water of the spring—there is nothing to compare to them."[8]

These "modern ideas" must have been the Sung influence. Here, it appears, the artistic thought of contemporary China had entered Japan, even while Emperor Hui Tsung was still reigning in K'ai-feng. When we learn that Kintsune was carrying on a sort of trade with South China to acquire rare and precious things for his new house, the way in which this influence could have entered is clear. Such desultory Japanese trade with China had continued, even though official relations between China and Japan had long ceased.[9]

We can see, then, how it would have been possible for some wandering Chinese rock artist to have reached Japan at that early time and been engaged by Kintsune to direct the building of his cascade. This man might have been a Zen monk who (as was not unusual) happened to be also an artist. Such men were being invited to Japan at that time because of a strong interest in the Zen sect of Buddhism on the part of military men.

Some three decades later, when Kintsune's son was improving the retiring estate of his son-in-law, the ex-emperor Gosaga, he also followed the new Sung style. We can picture this father creating for his daughter a small version of the North Hill Villa, where she had lived as a child. Perhaps the same old Chinese rock artist was still available to do this work.

Or another could have been found to make a replica of the Kitayama cascade and to build the stone bridge and the Isle of the Immortals in the new garden.

The carp stones found in both gardens form another interesting connection between them. In Kitayama (the older garden) the stone is at the lake level, probably put there simply as a bit of Chinese tradition. But later, in the cascade made for the retired emperor and empress, the magic fish has achieved the upper level of the fall, soon, presumably, to take off as a dragon. This advanced position was doubtless a graceful gesture to the imperial status. That this stone was an important detail is evident from the fact that both cascades were called by the traditional Chinese name, Dragon Gate Cascade or, in Japanese, Ryumon no Taki.

The relationship of the smaller, later Tenryu-ji garden to the older one, Kitayama, is evident also in other ways. Tenryu-ji's pond, although small, is obviously a reduced version of the Heian-style lake garden, with the same open, sunny atmosphere about it that reflected the old, carefree life of the courtiers. It is much too small for boating, but the atmosphere of a lake designed for boating is there.

The ponds of both estates have shorelines interrupted by large peninsulas. These serve to prevent the monotony of a circular outline. The "shore protecting" stones which outline the large peninsula in the foreground of Tenryu-ji are in a later style, as are other stones around the edge of the water, for fire and neglect later forced the reconstruction of the shore. But the bottom of the pond is still covered with the clay and pebbles characteristic of an older period, and there is no reason to think the general size and form of the pond have ever been much changed.

Today, in midsummer, the quiet surface of the water at Tenryu-ji is crowded with native lily pads, and their small golden blossoms push up to open in the sunlight. In autumn, when leaves and flowers sink below the surface, the dark mirror reflects the gold and scarlet of foliage. Then, in the mirrorlike surface, each small rocky islet rests on its own perfect reflection, and we understand why such rocks are sometimes called "floating stones."

Because Tenryu-ji is a greatly reduced version of the old shinden lake garden, and because the path around the lake, with its bridge, foreshadows the coming popularity of the stroll style, this place is strongly transitional between the old and the later modes. Gardens made afterward were generally to be much smaller and were to have their details better developed and better integrated.

This trend can be noted by looking at Tenryu-ji garden from the porch of the building. It divides easily into three parts, a background, a middle ground, and a foreground. The background is made up of the large trees and the once visible river and natural hills behind. The middle ground is the lake and its enclosing hillocks. The foreground is a stretch of level sand between the building and the near edge of the lake. This corresponds to the forecourt of the old shinden mansion. As we shall see in due course, there is evidence that the layout of this garden came later to serve as a prototype for garden makers who had lost inspiration and were trying to make rules to take its place.

The time came when the retired emperors no longer lived on this estate, and it was falling into neglect. This was the time when the state priest, Muso Kokushi, was acting as abbot of the old Moss Temple, Saiho-ji, not far away, and the aspiring general, Takauji, was attempting to overthrow the Kamakura government and set up a new military dictatorship with himself at its head. We can picture Muso, as he went back and forth to Saiho-ji, passing the old estate and realizing how perfectly its many fine buildings could be converted into a new Zen foundation—which he had hopes of establishing.

At that time the ruling emperor was Godaigo (1287–1339), who had lived as a young prince at the old place. A man of force, he was taking advantage of the unsettled times to attempt to restore political power to the throne. After some success, however, he had been forced by Takauji to flee from Kyoto and set up his court in the mountains south of Nara. There he suddenly died, and Takauji was in great fear of his vengeful ghost.

Muso Kokushi suggested that this spirit might be laid and given rest if it could be enshrined in a holy temple. He must also have pointed out how ideal for this purpose would be the old estate where the late emperor had lived as a youth. The result was the establishment of the Temple of the Heavenly Dragon, Tenryu-ji, with the spirit of Godaigo enshrined. Although "Heavenly Dragon" here meant the late emperor, it is believed the nomenclature was suggested by the Dragon Gate Cascade behind the pond.

Muso Kokushi, of course, was the founding abbot of this institution, and the old place entered a new and important phase of its existence, one that still continues although none of the original buildings remain. Muso adapted the various halls to ecclesiastical usage and added only a pagoda and his inevitable summerhouse. This he called the Dragon Gate Pavilion, because it must have looked down upon the cascade. His own apartments overlooked the garden, which, of course, had been cleaned and restored. The temple still possesses a note in his handwriting in which he jotted down a subject for a poem which he hoped to write when he had more time for such things: "On looking over to Arashiyama on a snowy day from the abbot's apartments," it runs.[10]

Later tradition has made Muso Kokushi the designer of this garden of Tenryu-ji,[11] even as it makes him the designer and builder of Saiho-ji. But it would have been as impossible for him to do the one as the other.

In those troubled times there was no time, no money, and no men for such things. Moreover, the styles of the two gardens are as different as they could possibly be. Saiho-ji displays the epitome of Japanese naturalism in its rock artistry; Tenryu-ji exhibits (with the exception of the Kitayama estate) the first appearance in Japan of Sung rock artistry, and that in fully developed form. No man was likely to have been the master of both styles. All Muso did was to rehabilitate both gardens and put up some new small buildings in each.

By the next century, Sung art was to come in a great flood to Japan. It would reorient Japanese art and inspire the greatest period of artistic achievement that country has known.

CHAPTER FOURTEEN

Mansions of Muromachi:
The Gold Pavilion

ASHIKAGA Takauji was victorious over the Kamakura government, and in 1338 he became the shogun or military ruler. This started a new dynasty of *de facto* rulers in his family which is known as the Ashikaga shogunate. Since the intrigues of the court had played a large part in this national upheaval, Takauji found it expedient to make the headquarters of his new government not Kamakura but Kyoto, where he could keep an eye on the court.

After he and his vassal barons had settled there, the old city presented an appearance quite different from that of its former days. Then the court nobles had always been the chief sights of the town, riding in their high, two-wheeled, black-lacquered coaches drawn by slow-stepping oxen, attended by outriders. But with the coming of the military lords this was changed. These lords were now the wealthy element in the community. In their gold-crested helmets and lacquered armour laced with silken cords, they were now the glittering and conspicuous figures on the streets of Kyoto.

In Kamakura, a hundred and fifty years before, the military leaders had despised courtly effeminacy and had made virtues of extreme simplicity and hardihood. Their military mansions had included quarters for armed followers and stables for horses. Only small landscape gardens were developed in front of the main room, and garden making was not one of the things military men held important.

This had now changed. As the barons settled in the city they began to acquire fine town houses and country villas in the manner of the court nobles. Their activities were marked by that love of show characteristic of the newly rich everywhere. We read, for instance, of Ko no Moronao, one of Takauji's generals, who "made over an old mansion, constructed a 'Chinese gate,' a hall with end pavilions, and some tall buildings. It made a very grand sight."[1]

We get a further glimpse of Kyoto streets as the same record continues with a description of Ko no Moronao's garden. "Large stones were brought for the lake edge from the provinces of Ise, Saiga, Shima, and others. Axles on the carts squeaked and often broke. Oxen panted and lolled their tongues." The trees and plants for this garden were also collected from different places, made famous by well-known poems.

The court aristocrats viewed all these goings-on with the typical disdain of the old regime. With lands largely usurped and incomes meager, these nobles yet held themselves aloof, living with whatever of slender elegance they could manage. Nevertheless, as they still controlled access to the court and its honors, they were often approached by aspiring barons who desired social rank and court position. It is said that a chief source of income for needy aristocrats at this time came from their efforts toward procuring honorary court titles.

As time went on, the old Kyoto culture of these aristocrats began to impose its restraining taste on the newcomers, subduing their exuberance. Another restraining influence was Zen and its strong associations with art. This philosophy was becoming better understood, giving meaning to much creative work. Zen canons of taste have been summed up as the avoidance of the trite, the obvious, and the emphatic.

Thus, patterned and restrained by the old courtly nobility (which had derived its ideas and forms from T'ang China), electrified by the beauty of Sung art, given depth by Zen influences, and finally strengthened by the warriors' vigor, during the next decades inspiration and technique reached maturity together, producing gardens which for sheer beauty and artistry have never been excelled in any period or in any country.

Takauji and his successor, the second Ashikaga shogun, were too busy consolidating their position to have much time for fine estates. It was Takauji's grandson Yoshimitsu (1358-1409), the third shogun, who took the lead in building these gardens. He was a true product of his time, with a keen interest in art. Yoshimitsu was also a sincere student of Zen. As a young man he had once astonished a gay party of courtiers at the mossy old temple of Saiho-ji by leaving the pleasure seekers on the lake and going up the hillside to meditate with his Zen master.

The mansion and estate that Yoshimitsu built as his palace and shogunal headquarters stood in the northeastern part of the city, which, ever since that day, has been the best residential district of Kyoto. The place was called Muromachi Hall after the broad avenue on which it fronted. Government headquarters centered in this place also, and so there derived from it the name—Muromachi—by which historians designate the period during which the Ashikaga shoguns held power—that is, the period from 1338 to 1573.

Muromachi Hall was a splendid mansion that stood in a great lake garden.[2] It held such quantities of flowering trees it was popularly called the Flowery Palace, Hana no Gosho. In Japanese poetic language the word "flowers" always means cherry blossoms unless otherwise specified. Among those of the Flowery Palace were some of the weeping variety, we know, for there is a record[3] which tells how the young trees were given by a court noble to the shogun.

We can picture this garden when April opened the buds, the flower-laden trees appearing like a drift of pink mist around the lake, or like a delicate rain of color reflected in the shimmering dark water. To describe the scene adequately the same record goes back to the ancient tale of the Immortals' Isles with the words, "A vision of the Three Isles and a ship sailing to them could not be fairer than this."[4]

This harking back to the old tale was characteristic of the times. A new fad for things Chinese was sweeping the elite of Japan, the result of a new, active trade with China which had been officially inaugurated by Takauji. He had sponsored this when he needed money and fine things to complete his Tenryu-ji temple. Every ship now brought in exquisite Sung paintings, porcelains, and other art, which were eagerly acquired and carefully studied and appreciated by wealthy dilettantes.

Yoshimitsu took the lead in this, gathering around him connoisseurs, artists, and poets. He sometimes wore Chinese costume and had himself carried about in a Chinese palanquin. A great revival of interest in Chinese verse also marked the times, led by Zen priests who had visited China, staying chiefly at the monasteries around the lake at Hangchow. As one result of this, many Chinese literary allusions crept into the gardens in the naming of stones and islands, and a famous pavilion was to be built on a Chinese model.

The style set by Yoshimitsu in building the Flowery Palace was followed by his great vassals. We read of fine estates put up in the Muromachi district by such powerful barons as the lords Hosokawa and Ouchi. All held lakes, islands, bridges, and pavilions.

Yoshimitsu was on excellent terms with the court also and contributed generously to its support. Once, for a considerable period, the emperor even resided in the Flowery Palace after the mansion in which he was living had burned. It had been centuries since the emperors had lived in the original Daidairi, the old imperial enclosure of early Heian. Fires had devastated it again and again, and finally the rulers came to make their homes permanently on private outside estates.

One of these mansions, not far from the house of Ko no Moronao, belonged to a Fujiwara family whose daughters often became imperial consorts. It was called the Tsuchimikado-dono. Over a long period of years this place was finally settled upon as the permanent residence of the emperors. Of all the great estates which lay near the Flowery Palace, therefore, this is the only one to survive to the present day.[5] Its outlines are approximately those of the present Kyoto Imperial Palace, although nothing remains of the early Tsuchimikado-dono. The present palace buildings are a replica of those of Heian, while the present imperial garden dates from a reconstruction of the eighteenth century.

All the other great estates in the Muromachi district were later ruined in the Onin wars and disappeared, as houses and shops encroached on their precincts. But on the edge of town some places which had been developed as country retreats were more fortunate. Foremost among these was the one Yoshimitsu took over and developed as his own retiring place.

This was no other than the old North Hill Villa, Kitayama-dono, first constructed about 175 years before for Saionji Kintsune. Having been favorites of the Kamakura regime, the Saionji family had doubtless come upon hard times when that government was overthrown. They were probably glad enough to let Yoshimitsu have the Kitayama estate when he showed an interest in it.

He began its redevelopment about the time he was able to retire, 1394. He then turned over the Flowery Palace and the ceremonial part of the shogunal office to his nine-year-old son and, taking holy orders, moved to his new estate. There he continued to hold the power of the office but was freed from irksome official ceremonies.

The old North Hill Villa he rebuilt into a splendid country retreat, partly ecclesiastical, calling it the Deer Park or Rokuon. This was not a reference to any real deer in the park but a harking back to the old Buddhist scriptures which tell of the Deer Park of Isipatana, in ancient India, where Gotama first spoke to his followers after enlightenment.

Although the new estate was monastic in theory, Yoshimitsu rebuilt extravagantly. The original residence of Kintsune had stood on level ground near the entrance—the site now occupied by the current complex of Rokuon-ji buildings. Kintsune's residence had evidently been in typical shinden style, with arcades extending forward to the lake on either side of the main hall and at least one of them ending in the usual "fishing hall."

Yoshimitsu changed this considerably. Eliminating the fishing hall, he built beyond it, out in the lake, a large three-storied structure in Chinese style. It stood some twenty feet beyond the original pavilion.[6] Because the ceiling of the upper story was gilded, it came to be called the Gold Pavilion (Plate 104). All of Yoshimitsu's other buildings were later swept away by fire and vandalism, but the three-storied Chinese pavilion in the lake survived until after World War II. In 1950 it was burned by a disturbed student monk. An exact replica has since been rebuilt (Plates 19, 102). But the rebuilders took all too literally the romantic name of Gold Pavilion and covered the surfaces of the two upper stories with gold leaf.

As of this writing, the new building stands, an incredible blaze of gold, creating an atmosphere completely false to the restraint of its original Zen conception. However, thousands have flocked to see it, bringing a shower of real gold to the temple. Purists hope and believe that the exterior gilding cannot last forever, and that eventually the gold leaf will curl up and blow away, leaving the structure in the simple, unpainted wood of its predecessor.

The old structure, dingy with its five and a half centuries, had stood almost inconspicuously against its green background of trees and hills. Modern visitors sometimes wondered why it should rank as one of Japan's three great architectural treasures, along with the splendid old Phoenix Hall at Uji and the incredible eighth-century Horyu-ji monastery near Nara. Yet when one walked around the lake, viewing it from various angles (as it was meant to be seen from a boat), one understood Sir George Sansom when he said: "It is both a technical and an artistic triumph. . . . Its beauty . . . relies upon a harmony and a delicacy of proportion so just that because of its very rightness it leaves no impression upon a careless observer."[7]

This beauty could be appreciated best when it was seen on a winter morning, with the snow lying deep and untouched on rocks and roofs, the trees drooping under great loads of feathery whiteness. Against the powdered green of the hillside, the building stood out in sudden startling loveliness, its slender grace and delicate curving lines etched above the frozen lake. It is understandable why the classical way to see it had long been under these conditions.

The general design of this building came from South China. Somewhat similar buildings are often seen in Sung paintings, and small temples of a very similar design are still known. One, in Likiang, Yunnan Province, standing in a lake as does the Gold Pavilion, might easily be mistaken for it at first glance.[8] Drawings and sketches for the general outline of the original building may have been brought to Yoshimitsu by some traveled Zen monk, or possibly they were made by a Chinese artist living in Japan. Details of the building, especially the interior, were developed in Japanese style. The construction of such a building at this time was part of the wave of Sung influence which was then flooding into Japan.

If we wish to imagine it in the days when Yoshimitsu was its owner, the newly built replica is of great help, for its newness is comparable to that of Yoshimitsu's time. The lower unpainted story of the new structure is white and fragrant with its freshly cut wood. Its satiny finish and exquisite joinery are like fine cabinetwork.

It is believed that Yoshimitsu used the lower story as a reception room in which he received special guests, such as artists and scholarly monks. The second story was a study to which they might retire for discussions on art and esthetics. From its balcony they could enjoy the best view of the garden. The top story, with its gilded ceiling and bell-shaped windows, was probably a small, private Zen chapel. Seated in the second story of the pavilion, Yoshimitsu and his friends probably handled, studied, and admired the splendid examples of Sung paintings and porcelain just arrived from China by the latest ship. Probably, here, too, they drank tea in ceremonial fashion.

Tradition states that the water Yoshimitsu used for his tea came from the two rocky springs which are now special features of the garden. They lie at the foot of the hillside, set about with stones and reached by a path. The first is a squared recess in the slope, its flat roof a slab of rock which rests on upright stones lining the recess. It is in the pattern of the spring at Saiho-ji, but larger and bolder, as we should expect a rocky spring to be if made at this time. Cool and inviting, the water glistens as it trickles down the mossy wall behind into the rockbound pool. The second spring is an open pool lying in an angle of the hillside, surrounded by massive rocks. A small thatched roof keeps leaves from falling into the water. Both pools have flat kneeling stones in front for dipping up the water.

Beyond the springs on this hillside is the old Dragon Gate Cascade, made for Kinstune 175 years before Yoshimitsu's day (Plate 93). Lying at the base of the fall is the famous carp stone, starting its ascent to dragonhood. Over the nine-foot facer rock of the cascade pours a small stream of water from an upper reservoir. It now hits the twisted carp stone, spatters in a silver shower, and then runs away to the present edge of the lake. Originally this cascade must have stood almost on the lake shore, as at Tenryu-ji. Now a large area of what was formerly the pond has been filled in by the accumulated silt of centuries, and the ground—moss-covered and tree-shaded—extends from the foot of the hillside over to the pavilion itself.

The whole estate now covers some four and a half acres, with the lake taking up about one-third of this space. It is still the Jodo lake of the North Hill Villa except that more islands were probably added by Yoshimitsu.

No matter what the season, this garden is beautiful. The lake is rimmed by fine tremendous trees, which nevertheless do not seem to shut it in. For at one end, above them, rises a small pointed green peak, exactly the right size to fit into the landscape picture. It is known, from its shape, as Silk Hat Hill—that is, Kinugasa-yama. Rising against the sky at the foot of the lake, this little peak is definitely a part of its design.[9]

The lake spreads mirrorlike, holding reflections of this peak, the trees, and islands. In spring, azaleas cast scarlet shadows into the water, while purple irises bloom in shallows along the shore. In summer, the water's surface is patterned with the green circles of native lily pads. In autumn, tall reeds rally their pointed spears around the islets, and on the distant shore maples blaze gorgeously. In winter's grey light, the white flakes whirl lazily above the silvery surface of the water, piling up in silent whiteness on every rock and tree. An ineffable quietness and peace hangs over this garden, not to be caught by anything tangible, but so real it is the inner essence of the scene (Plate 103).

Although this estate was developed on the magnificent scale of Yoshimitsu's day, based on a Saionji foundation, it was done with the freedom, freshness, and simplicity of an art in its youthful period. There is spaciousness here, a regal grandeur, an artistic delicacy about it, not equaled in any other garden in Japan. These factors together have produced a work which may well be the finest of the estate gardens which Japan has created.

There is every reason to believe that Yoshimitsu was his own designer. No mention in the records is made of another, nor is anyone else known who was capable of doing it. No doubt he sought suggestions and help from the connoisseurs with whom he consorted. But it would be directly in the tradition of great garden making in Japan if the plan had been quite his own.

It is interesting to inquire into the techniques and details by which some of the effects are gained. On the outer or valley side of the garden, the lake is supported by an embankment formed of the excavated material. Toward the right, this bank rises into an artificial hillock with its broad rounded top some fifteen feet above the water. This rising ground swings right, around the lake, and joins a spur descending from the natural hillside behind the pavilion, so that the whole garden seems embraced and protected.

A path follows around the lake, but it was never an important part of the garden. Boating, not walking, was the diversion provided for here. This fact is made clear by the placement of some of the finest rock arrangements at places where they can only be seen from a boat—that is, on the far side of a large island.

This brings to mind the description of the boating party in *The Tale of Genji,* in which similar rock arrangements were discovered by the participants. It is believed there may have been a conscious harking back to this story in the Gold Pavilion lake. The records mention many boating parties here. Floating over the patterned surface of the water, guests must have felt keen enjoyment in the rocks and islands, the graceful form of the pavilion rising from the water, and the pointed outline of little Silk Hat Hill beyond the end of the lake.

From the pavilion, the size of the lake appears much larger than it really is (Plates 100, 101). This is achieved by bold and clever handling of vistas and perspectives. It is not until we consider the height of the trees on the opposite shore that we realize how close to us they really are. The principal device used to secure this effect is division of the lake into two parts, of which the inner, near half is filled with interesting rocks and islands to keep the eye busy, while behind it the outer half is empty and dimly seen, suggesting vaguely illimitable distances.

The lake is divided by means of a peninsula jutting out from the right shore and a long island which continues its line. The peninsula turns the lake's virtually oval shape into an approximate heart outline. A vista to the opposite shore is left open between the island and

130

the peninsula. Through this the lake seems to open into a wide sweep of clear water.

In the distance beyond the central island are a few lesser islands and rocky islets. They are deceptively small, to enhance the perspective, while the far shore of the lake has almost no stones visible on it. This is in strong contrast to the near shore of the central island and the peninsula, which hold many. It is as if the other side of the lake were too far away for its details to be seen.

The inner half of the lake holds no fewer than five smaller islands and a number of rocky islets.[10] Among the latter is one called the "Nine Mountains and Eight Seas." Here is the old Shumisen wearing a descriptive subtitle. It is simply a limestone rock about a foot above the water, shaped like a miniature mountain peak, with canyons worn in its flanks.

Some of the other rocks are of immense size, a fact especially visible when the lake is drained (Plate 99). We cannot now identify the famous one acquired by Kintsune in 1229 that took seventeen oxen to move.[11] Others among these immense stones were gifts from Yoshimitsu's vassals. (A great stone of fine shape and texture was considered a fit gift for a prince.) The names of some of the donors—Akamatsu, Hatakeyama, Hosokawa—still identify certain of these gift rocks, written on small wooden signs placed beside them.

The practice of boating seems to explain a straight line of squared stones extending parallel to the pavilion's platform. They seem to be in just the right position to prevent a boat drawn up beside it from swinging away. Yet sometimes they are regarded as a form of the old yo-domari, the night mooring stones, or a line of boats headed toward the Immortals' Isles.

The large central island that continues the line of the peninsula, dividing the lake into its inner and outer parts, lies in front of the pavilion. It holds a grove of small pine trees, kept trimmed to suitable scale, and its shoreline is marked by fine groups of stones. Some of these arrangements, centered by a large stone flanked by smaller ones, lie on the far side of the island, where, as mentioned, they can only be seen from a boat.

Most of the other islands are of the tortoise type, the upraised heads of the creatures and their half-submerged flippers being unusually graphic. Two such islands, one called the "Coming Tortoise" and the other the "Going Tortoise," lie to the right of the pavilion. In front of the building, one of two quite small islands is also a tortoise, but its partner is called a "crane island."

In the figure of the crane appears the second of the longevity creatures associated with the Immortals of the Mystic Isles. Cranes, it will be recalled, sometimes carried the Immortals on their backs to the isles. A Han garden record mentions a "crane island," but we do not know if this had any symbolic meaning. In Japan there were probably crane islands before this one in the Gold Pavilion lake, but earlier references to them are vague. It was probably the renewed Chinese influence that caused so many tortoise islands to be placed around the Gold Pavilion, and perhaps the crane island had a Hangchow prototype.

Unlike tortoise islands, crane islands seem to have had no recognizable pattern, at least at that time. This one is only a group of large stones of medium height with flat tops. Later, crane islands were made of upstanding rocks, the general effect being one of perpendicularity, in contrast to the horizontality of tortoise islands. In these upstanding islets no amount of imagination could see a bird depicted graphically, as the tortoise can be seen.

131

Their function seems to have been wholly artistic, to provide vertical contrast to the tortoise.

The theme of the crane seems to have been important in this garden. We can note it in an account of the grand imperial house party that Yoshimitsu gave for the emperor and the court after the estate was finished in 1408. This visit became one of the most famous excursions of Japanese court history. When the emperor Gokomatsu accepted the invitation to spend twenty days on the new estate, it was the first time in history that the honor of such a visit had been bestowed on anyone not a court noble.

The splendor of this occasion is revealed in contemporary records.[12] It took place in April when the cherry blossoms were at their peak of perfection. The emperor left his palace in great state, attended by a long procession of courtiers and nobles. Throngs of common people lined the streets between the palace gate and that of the Deer Park to see the procession as it passed. Arrived at the villa gate, the party moved up an outer avenue through lines of blooming cherry trees, of both single and double varieties. The days of the visit were filled with all manner of entertainment—feasting, drinking, dancing, music, boating, and the composition of poems. Of special interest is the mention of an exhibition of miniature gardens, each only a few feet square, in which were constructed islands, cascades, mountains with pine trees, turtles, and cranes.

On the third evening of the visit there was a boating party on the lake, followed by the writing of poems in the pavilion. The emperor went in one boat, Yoshimitsu in another, and still others were filled with princes and courtiers. Fragrant pine-knot fires were lighted in iron baskets swung from stands along the shore, a form of illumination which may still be seen at old festivals. Music by a group of players in a separate boat swept across the water, and the glowing lights were reflected from the pink blossoming trees into the polished black mirror of the lake.

Subjects for the poems were given out as the boats started. Poems in the Chinese language were to use "spring" as the rhyming word and to be on the subject of "an imperial feast amid reflections of cherry blossoms and the terraced pavilion in the pond." In Japanese they were to be about "cranes beside the pond at an imperial outing."

I have seen the wild cranes standing in this garden almost like statuary. Perhaps they came that day in 1408, a circumstance that would have been considered singularly propitious because of its happy augury of longevity.

When the thin, wavering music of flute and *sho* stopped, the boats pulled into the pavilion landing, and the poems were read inside. As might have been expected, most of those whose poems were acclaimed were court nobles, long practiced in this art. The poem of Fujiwara Shigemitsu has come down to us, expressive of the wish for long life and happiness:

> In the water
> Under the pines on the shore

21. *Island with small artfully trained pine trees, Sento Palace, Kyoto.* ▶
22. *Water lilies, horsetail reeds, and iris; inner pond, Heian Shrine, Kyoto.* ▶

132

Stand the friendly cranes;
A thousand and eight thousand years
Will they live on.[13]

But in spite of this good omen Yoshimitsu did not live much longer. Only two months after his grand party he was dead. At his wish the magnificent estate was turned into a Buddhist memorial temple and has come down the centuries as such to the present day.

◄ *23. Teahouse on pond bank planted with azaleas clipped to suggest rocks, Toji-in, Kyoto.*

135

CHAPTER FIFTEEN

Mansions of Muromachi:
The Silver Pavilion

THE son Yoshimitsu had left as a child shogun in the Flowery Palace grew into a youth interested only in the esthetic pleasures his father had enjoyed in his later years. Successive shoguns held similar interests, leaving government to their guardians and advisors—those great barons who contended for power during the next decades. The names of these lords appear often in garden annals, for the building of fine estates was one of their chief expressions of prestige. Behind this was their desire for more wealth and power, through lands and men. Among them, however, no single individual was able to make himself stronger than the rest and so displace the weak Ashikaga shoguns. This unstable equilibrium created a half century of peace after Yoshimitsu's death, during which the arts reached probably the highest point they have attained in Japan.

The capital was a rich and brilliant city during this period, filled not only with the fine estates of court nobles and great barons but also with hundreds of lesser residences of a high order. "Even men who made medicine and fortunetelling their professions and petty officials like secretaries had stately residences," says a commentator. "There were some two hundred such buildings constructed entirely of white pine and having four-post gates [that is, gates with flanking entrances for persons of inferior rank]. Then there were a hundred provincial nobles, great and small, each of whom had a stately residence, so that there were, altogether, from six to seven thousand houses of a fine type in the capital."[1]

The riches necessary to maintain the city in this state were derived, of course, from the common people, who were taxed exorbitantly. Japanese peasants have always been long-suffering under oppression, but during this period they were often goaded into desperate demonstrations of resistance. These riots usually followed a natural calamity, a drought or flood, which had destroyed the crops and brought on famine. In the wake of famines came epidemics, when thousand of the sick and starving crowded into the brilliant capital, hoping for help. Little or nothing was done for them, and the records mention hundreds dying daily in the streets. Because of these things, the name of the Ashikaga shoguns is synonymous in Japanese history with callous indifference and maladministration. But the shoguns under whom this happened had become only figureheads of government.

The wealthy and favored, indifferent to the sufferings of the poor, continued to build their fine houses and gardens. It was during this time, and doubtless due in large measure to the increase in moderately sized houses, that domestic architecture underwent considerable change. The old shinden had been simplified into the military mansion of Kamakura. Now another modification, derived from the needs of scholarly priests, created the *sho-in* style. The sho-in itself was a library or study, the chief room in a small residence temple. It was characterized by a low writing table built into a window embrasure. Another architectural feature that became widespread about this time was the tokonoma or recessed alcove built against or into an inner wall. Although its exact origins are unknown, one theory is that it might have been derived from the shrine or small altar that was often built into one wall of the sho-in. At first used in private houses as a place for receiving important guests, it later came to serve its present function as a place for displaying a hanging scroll or other work of art, with an incense burner or flower arrangement on a shelf at the side or on the raised floor of the alcove.

In the new architecture, doors, which in the shinden had been hinged at the top and hooked to the ceiling to open, became a series of sliding panels. Other sliding panels formed inside partitions. They were of light construction faced with paper and were often decorated by a painting that extended over the entire length of the wall when all the panels were in place. Thick cushionlike mats of straw, which had been used only as seats on the boarded floors of the shinden, were now used solidly over the entire floor.

Large houses were still a group of buildings, but they were not grouped so symmetrically as formerly, and the end pavilions disappeared from the edge of the lake. Gardens in general became smaller, in most cases occupying an enclosed area overlooked by the principal room of the house. More and more they were laid out simply to form a picture for this room.

Certain diarists of the time have left us glimpses of the construction of some of the great Muromachi estates. From such accounts we realize how much more difficult it is, physically, to create a landscape picture with trees, water, and rocks than it is to paint the same thing with brush, ink, and silk. Before ever a pond could be dug and the garden artist proceed with the hard-enough task of arranging his stones and trees, he had to be sure he possessed these things. Since there were, as yet, no commercial purveyors of rocks and trees, they usually had to come from gardens already in existence. Each time a new and important garden was made, older ones were apt to suffer losses. Saiho-ji, Tenryu-ji, and the Gold Pavilion all show where stones have been removed.

But while large and artistic rocks could, of course, be found in the mountains and brought to the garden site if enough energy were expended, nothing could hurry the growth of a tree. Therefore powerful personages took trees wherever they could find them. The gardens of small temples, and of retainers who had received favors, seem to have furnished most of the trees. The records hold plenty of evidence that these lesser folk objected to having their gardens raided in this high-handed manner and resisted it whenever they could.[2]

An incident is related in connection with the construction of a new imperial garden being made at the expense of one of the shoguns. Word had been sent out that trees should be "offered" by the temple of Daikomyo-ji at Fushimi and some of its subtemples, noted for their flowering trees. Three small subtemples complied, but a fourth protested to the shogun. However, the decision came back, "Obey the order."

A little later rumors were heard at the court of a much-cherished tree, probably a juniper, which was the pride and special adornment of a small subtemple garden. Court gardeners were sent to find it. They searched everywhere, in temple grounds and even in private gardens nearby. When it was found, they dug it up and took it away without ceremony. "The people were very much annoyed," remarks the record.

However, some of the gifts sent to these new gardens were given sincerely enough as compliments from one high personage to another. An example of this appears in the diary of Prince Sadafusa.

He was living quietly in retirement in Fushimi, enjoying the usual gentlemen's interest in the arts. In 1433 he sent a gift of pine trees and fish to the sixth shogun, Yoshinori, who was rehabilitating Yoshimitsu's old Flowery Palace. He also passed on to him three "sea stones" which had recently been presented to him by a certain abbot. That very night, after their arrival, a letter came from the shogun saying he was delighted, as these stones were the best he had received.

The number of men engaged at times in building these gardens is astounding, although the figures probably should not be accepted too literally. Lord Akamatsu detailed eighteen hundred of his retainers to bring stones from Uzumasa, a few miles away, to this same shogunal garden. At another time, three thousand of Lord Hosokawa's men moved rocks for another estate the shogun was building.

Serious incidents sometimes developed in the course of these operations. During the transportation of some plum trees presented by Lord Kuroda, a large branch of one was broken. The shogun was very angry and imprisoned three of the gardeners. Five young Kuroda knights, who evidently were responsible for the accident, were ordered arrested. Three of them fled into exile, and two others committed suicide.

The brilliance of the Muromachi period reached its climax under the eighth shogun, Yoshimasa. He was a grandson of the builder of the Gold Pavilion. Born in 1435, he became a child shogun on the death of his brother. He was brought up in the splendid mansions of his family and nourished on the esthetic traditions which pervaded them. When he is only fifteen years old, we see him presiding over a company of artists and poets gathered in a recently finished hall to paint pictures for its sliding screens and write poems in its honor.

Under such conditions, Yoshimasa could hardly have become other than what he was, a dilettante and man of taste. He is often compared to his contemporary across the world in Florence, Lorenzo de' Medici. Wrapped up in these artistic pursuits, he was not interested in the affairs of the country. Social history, in the past, has severely censured him as an indifferent ruler, but cultural history now gives him his due as the patron under whom, in many respects, Japanese arts reached their peak.

He gathered about him a coterie of artists, poets, and scholars. Most of them were Zen monks, since the church at that time offered the best retreat and background to men of such tastes. It was an age in which talent was sometimes recognized over birth and position, so that even aristocratic nobles from the court mingled with men of similar tastes from the military classes and, in a few cases, of even lower status.

These men whom Yoshimasa gathered about him in the latter part of the fifteenth century differed from those his grandfather had invited to the Gold Pavilion in being more sure of themselves, more conscious of what they were doing and of their opinions. In Yoshimitsu's day, all thought had turned toward China, for its greatness had been regarded as without peer. Now, although there was still much trafficking and travel back and forth, the Japanese felt themselves to be possible competitors in many ways.

They were, in fact, creating art which, in some of its aspects, was equal to the best which had come out of China. The Muromachi period was the age of great painters in Japan, of men who carried on with full competence the best of the fallen Sung traditions. And out of this were growing distinctive schools of Japanese artistry. They were marked, as always when the Japanese cease copying and begin to express themselves, by a turn toward nature —the soft and gentle nature of Japanese landscape—and by delicacy, refinement, and attention to detail.

Probably the most distinctive of the arts which took form under Yoshimasa's patronage was the tea ceremony. There had been a religious tea-drinking ceremony in Sung China, designed, by inducing wakefulness, to prepare those participating in it for Zen meditation. Tea drinking had also been used for what seems to have been a sort of guessing game of literary allusions. Out of these cultural associations, the Zen monk Shuko devised the Japanese tea ceremony. It was a secular, esthetic exercise of elegant simplicity, designed to create the proper atmosphere for group discussions of art, leading to finer appreciation and understanding. In its Muromachi form, the tea ceremony was probably free from that formalism which marked its later development. But it seems to have been performed in a setting designed to enhance its object. Still standing is a small room in one of the buildings put up by Yoshimasa which is believed to have been the first place definitely set aside for the tea ceremony.

While all the arts were fostered under Yoshimasa, those connected with building were particularly stimulated by his delight in constructing houses and gardens. Among the estates which he made over was the Takakura mansion, where his mother, a Fujiwara lady, resided. This he turned into a copy of Saiho-ji's moss garden, which at that time was regarded as the most beautiful place around Kyoto.

There seems, indeed, to have been almost a cult of admiration for Saiho-ji, led by the shogun himself. It must have been particularly beautiful then. Nearly a hundred and fifty years had passed since Muso Kokushi had converted the old gardens of Amida's Paradise, and of Aloofness from the Foul World, into that of the Temple of Western Fragrance. The small buildings which he had scattered through it must have mellowed and the mosses have become ever greener and thicker as the years rolled over.

Yoshimasa often visited Saiho-ji. We read of this in an official record kept by the priest of a small subtemple of Shokoku-ji called Onryoken.[3] This record gives us frequent and graphic glimpses into the life of the shogun. He had first gone to the Moss Temple in 1460 when the cherry blossoms were out and had been entranced by its beauty. He had returned

139

in the autumn to pay his respects on Muso Kokushi's death anniversary and a month later had come again to see the maples at their best. During the next five years he visited the garden regularly three or four times a year. On one of these occasions the Onryoken scribe notes that Yoshimasa exclaimed, "The beauty of this garden never diminishes!"

By the time he was thirty, Yoshimasa had exhausted all the possibilities of existing shogunal estates and was planning an entirely new villa to which he might retire, as his grandfather had retired to the Gold Pavilion. A site was found at the foot of the Eastern Hills which seemed to offer all that was wanted. The scribe of Onryoken, who was sent to see and report on it, wrote: "There are undulating hills and clear water. Clouds and mist mingle together. There is a pine gate and rock garden. The place has a quiet beauty far from the dust of the town. . . . In front rise several hilltops, forming an outlook. On the left side, water runs down and has been very usefully conducted to the small temple [which was already on the site]."[4]

These words could describe the place today, nearly five centuries after they were written. As a preliminary step, in 1466 Yoshimasa provided for the removal of the small temple already on the site. Plans were afoot to turn this area into a splendid estate, when suddenly everything was stopped by the outbreak of civil war in the very center of the capital (1466).

The years of uneasy peace between the great barons had at last ended, and two of the strongest, Yamana and Hosokawa, were contending openly for supremacy. Their underlying aims were masked, of course, by other excuses, and the Ashikaga shogunate was not threatened at the time. It was still useful, to one side or the other, in creating the fiction of legality, as that side was able to control its edicts.

As the fighting had begun in the Onin era, it is known as the Onin civil war. It was the most destructive Japan had known, for it centered where there was the most to be destroyed, the very heart of the rich Muromachi district. The two factions faced each other with the old Flowery Palace and the temple of Shokoku-ji between them. The mansions belonging to the two sides served as temporary strongholds, but as the fighting swayed back and forth one by one they were destroyed.

The period of fighting dragged on inconclusively, for months, for years, finally for a full decade. At the end of that time, Kyoto lay in complete ruin, not a single important building having escaped. Even isolated places like the Gold Pavilion estate and Saiho-ji temple had been looted and burned by lawless elements.

Quiet came at last to the city with the deaths of the two leaders. But in the provinces warfare continued spasmodically. Almost any baron who felt himself strong enough to win turned to prey on his neighbor. Kyoto tried to pull itself together, but during the years that followed it was entered again and again by marauding groups.

During the Onin war, even the residence of the emperor had fallen almost into ruins. Its rehabilitation was the most pressing construction facing Yoshimasa when at last it was possible to start some rebuilding. Not until this had been accomplished, under the extremely difficult and upset conditions of the times, could he turn his thoughts to his own long-postponed villa. In 1482, a full eighteen years after the estate at the foot of the Eastern Hills had been planned, its construction was once more undertaken.

But things could no longer be done on the spacious and elaborate scale of former days.

Nevertheless, Yoshimasa clung as closely as possible to the old elegance, and whatever he did was as perfectly done as possible, from the artistic viewpoint. Accounts of the construction seem almost pathetically meager compared to the grandeur of the past. But finally it was partly finished, and Yoshimasa moved in during the second year. The garden itself had hardly been started at that time.

Twelve wooden structures had been planned, and eventually all were completed. They included a monumental gate, a "dragon-backed" or curved bridge, a covered corridor, a chapel, a study, the reception hall, and several pavilions for such purposes as the incense ceremony and watching the game of *kemari*. Judging from the two of these buildings which survive, they were modest structures, very different from the gorgeous halls of former days. Yet their size and design were not entirely conditioned by economic necessity. Yoshimasa was deep in Zen esthetics, which made almost a cult of the simple and natural. If he built with restraint and understatement, it was largely from choice.

The garden was never entirely completed to Yoshimasa's satisfaction. Only a few stones, a few trees seem to have been available from time to time. Many of the stones and some of the trees came from the ruined Flowery Palace not far away, as men could be found to move them. But most of the trees seem to have been brought all the twenty-five miles from Nara, where fire had not devastated the gardens. Occasionally some lord would make a generous gesture by detailing his men for a few days to move stones and trees. Thus in 1488 Lord Asakura allowed three thousand of his men to work at moving pine trees from the Flowery Palace.[5] Some of this number were armored guards, a comment on the still unsettled conditions. Other plants mentioned as going into the garden are cherry trees, azaleas, prunus, camellias, and yews.

That Yoshimasa delighted in these flowering plants is evident from an anecdote set down in the Rokuon record. The scribe had been on a short journey and on his return was telling Yoshimasa what he had seen. He mentioned that the *ume* or "white plums"[6] had been at their best as he passed through Omi Province. Said Yoshimasa, no doubt smiling complacently, "White plums are at their best in my garden too."[7]

During Yoshimasa's life the estate was known as the Eastern Hill Villa or Higashiyama-dono, a name paralleling that of the North Hill Villa of his grandfather. And, also paralleling that older place, the new garden has come down the years under the popular name of Silver Pavilion Temple or Ginkaku-ji. This name is derived from one of the two original buildings still standing in it. Its correct name today is Jisho-ji, after Yoshimasa's spiritual name, given when the estate became a memorial temple after his death. It still has this status.

During the past hundred years it has often been said that this garden was designed by Soami, one of the artists in the coterie of connoisseurs that Yoshimasa gathered around him. Soami came of a family of artists which had served the shoguns since the days of the Gold Pavilion, and he was undoubtedly an important painter of the time. But there is no evidence contemporary with the garden that he had anything whatever to do with the design.[8] Without the fact being stated in words, all the records indicate that Yoshimasa followed the traditional custom of planning it himself, although he often asked advice from scholars and artists.

141

In carrying out the rockwork he was fortunate in having the best garden craftsmen to help him. The leading figure among them was on old man known as Kawara-mono Zen'ami. The prefix *kawara-mono* means literally "riverbank person" and indicated someone belonging to the outcast class, the group then known as *eta*. These people, who were affiliated with no clan, were in some ways lower than serfs. They lived in the no-man's land along riverbanks and had to do the meanest of work. This included butchering, which Buddhist teachings against the taking of life made abhorrent. But since they were available as laborers the riverbank people seem often to have been employed to do the heavy work in gardens, until, in time, the name became synonymous with a garden workman.[9]

As might be expected, occasionally one of these persons possessed ability and talent, and in time some felt themselves capable of designing. This was the beginning of a class of professional garden makers which undertook to plan and carry out an entire garden. Before that, as we have seen, garden planning was a dilettante interest of estate owners and talented monks.

Foremost among the kawara-mono was Zen'ami, who had spent a long lifetime working on the great Muromachi estates. His name appears as the maker of their gardens in several temple records in the latter part of the fifteenth century. This in itself is strong evidence of the regard in which he was held, for people of his class were not ordinarily mentioned in such records. One journal speaks of him as the "greatest in the world in stone placement"[10] and remarks in the same entry that he lived to be ninety-seven years old. (He died in 1483.) The family background is fully revealed when his grandson, who became something of a scholar, is quoted as saying that he regretted he had been born in the house of a butcher.

Yoshimasa had employed Zen'ami now and then over a period of years. For instance, he had once ordered him to make a garden for the scribe's own temple of Onryoken. When it was completed, this garden was described in its record with the words "Its artistry is exquisite."[11] Before the Onin war, the shogun had sent Zen'ami, among others, to inspect and report on the then proposed site at the foot of the Eastern Hills. When work on it finally began, nearly twenty years later, the old man had recently died. Although no entry makes direct mention of the point, it seems certain that his son, or grandson, both of whom had been trained in such work, was in charge of the workers and directed the arrangements.

Knowing Yoshimasa's admiration for Saiho-ji, it is no surprise to learn that he modeled his new estate after that old garden. By that time the Temple of Western Fragrance was in ruins, but no person knew better than Yoshimasa how it had looked in its days of perfection. His Eastern Hill Villa, therefore, had a pond garden of complex form below and a rustic rock garden on the hillside above. On this hillside Zen'ami's crew built a woodland spring (Plate 109) which, stone for stone, is almost a duplicate of the one which had been put into the temple garden of Aloofness from the Foul World some four centuries before.[12] It has the same large boulder set into the hillside to form a back wall, the same wing stones enclosing the pool, and, in front, the same flat rocks on which to kneel or stand. As at

24. Aged weeping cherry tree with traditional supports, Joshoko-ji, Kyoto. ▶

Saiho-ji, the water lies cool and clear in a circle of small stones, and a large flat stone forms the bottom. Excess water trickles out between the front stones and flows away down a small graveled rill.

This spring and the other rocks which were part of Yoshimasa's hillside garden were buried for a considerable period under earth washed down from the slopes above. In 1931, however, after examination of the old documents had given a clue to the existence of the upper garden, a search was made and the spring excavated.[13] The original paths and the sites of other buildings were also found.

The pond garden below is enclosed, like Saiho-ji's, by buildings, while the green hills rise behind. These hills have been owned by the estate from the beginning and have been left undisturbed, so that the garden trees blend into the natural forest on the slopes. The eye is led up and over their tapestried greens to where the topmost trees stand silhouetted against the skyline. This line curves and dips to a point, and this dip, in some curious way, becomes the focal point of the whole garden.

Such an upward view is not infrequent in Japanese gardens, although extremely rare in the Occident. In Japan, not content with incorporating the natural hills, the garden concept took in the very heavens. And when the full moon rises over this eastern hillside, the place reaches its peak of fulfillment. To enhance the beauty of moonlight, the garden contains no artificial lights. Yoshimasa composed a poem on the moonrise which is known to almost every cultivated Japanese.

> My lodge is at the foot
> Of the Moon Waiting Hill—
> Almost I regret
> When the shortening hill shadow
> At length disappears.[14]

Highly characteristic of Zen taste and feeling is the suggestion implied in this poem that the anticipation of beauty is better than its full realization.

In the level garden below, the pond is comparatively small and of very complicated shape, with several small islands which increase its complexities. In part, its present form is certainly different and smaller than it was originally, although it could never have been a large lake. Probably it covered a level area, now filled with trees and moss, which extends into the south side. Mention of a boathouse suggests the old traditions, but we hear of no boating parties, and it seems possible that in the beginning, as today, the chief way to enjoy this garden was by strolling through it.

To follow the winding path through the garden, crossing bridges and passing by the cascade, provides a series of ever-changing views. Azaleas pour from among the stones which enclose the shoreline and islands, and trees lean out to cast green reflections into the translucent depths of the water. The pond is called the Brocade Mirror, Kinkyo-cho. No better term could suggest its patterned loveliness.

The walk through this garden can be likened to following through one of the long

◀ *25. Japanese maple in climactic coloring, Shugaku-in, Kyoto.*

Oriental landscape scrolls. Such paintings are viewed in sections as the scroll is unrolled by the left hand and rerolled by the right, so that we seem to move forward through the landscape depicted. In strolling through this garden, we see one scene melt into another as we advance, just as do the continuous parts of such a painting.

The structure known as the Silver Pavilion, which has given its name to the estate, stands at one side of the lake (Plate 107). It is not large and has only two stories, nor is it so impressive as its predecessor, the Gold Pavilion. It does not occupy any such commanding position, but, darkened by the weather of its five hundred years, it stands quietly among the trees. Its popular name is derived from a report, apparently without foundation, that Yoshimasa intended to put silver on it, as his grandfather had gilded the interior of the Gold Pavilion. It houses an image of Kannon, the compassionate Buddhist deity, hence it is usually mentioned in the records as the Kannon Hall. But this building was also used as a chapel for Zen meditation, as indicated by the typical Zen name of the lower story, Soul Emptying Hall or Shinko-den.

The Rokuon diary makes it clear that the Silver Pavilion was inspired by one of the small structures, called the Ruri-den, which Muso Kokushi had built in Saiho-ji's garden. Its simplicity and restraint were in accord with Zen ideas.

From the balcony of this pavilion may be obtained the best single view of the garden (Plate 110), much as it must have been in Yoshimasa's day, for it still faces the dramatic skyline with its notch where the moon rises. Here it must have been that Yoshimasa sat as he composed the moon-waiting poem.

Out of the twelve original structures, the second to survive is a small Amida chapel called the East Seeking Hall—that is, Togu-do. The name refers to the search from the East—this world—for Amida's Western Paradise. In keeping with the old association of lotuses in the paradise garden, these plants were originally grown in the pond before this building. In the rear of the Togu-do is the small room of only four and a half mats which, it is believed, may have been designed expressly for Shuko's tea ceremony.

The pond area in front of the Togu-do seems to have come through the garden's later vicissitudes in better shape than any other section. Especially good here is the circle of rocks enclosing a small island lying just in front of the building. These rock arrangements exemplify the pure Muromachi techniques. The large stones have strong, flat tops and straight sides, showing the Saiho-ji influence. And for occasional contrast there are some with points. The groupings show more sophistication than do those of Saiho-ji. Most are dominated by the old, basic lines of the triangle, the trinity arrangement, in which a larger stone in the center is balanced by two smaller ones supporting it on either side. Muromachi style clearly shows its derivation from both the soaring artistry of Sung and the flat-topped quiescence of Saiho-ji.

The path which winds through the garden today crosses this island by two bridges. One is believed to date from Yoshimasa's time, for it immediately recalls the bridge in Tenryu-ji, with its two long, flat plank stones, laid end to end and supported where they join by stones rising from the water (Plate 105).

The second bridge was originally a wooden structure in arched form, called the Dragon Back Bridge. The space is now spanned by a single massive monolithic rock, a piece of

THE SILVER PAVILION

granite eight feet long and two feet wide (Plate 108). It was installed here during the later reconstruction and is typical of the later period.

The cascade was part of the original design. Reminiscent of the Gold Pavilion's cascade, it stands on a hillside, with a natural stream coming down from above. The rock face of the main fall is about ten feet high and four feet wide, supported on either side by large stones. The water forms a small pool at the base of this main rock, then runs off to join the lake at a slightly lower level. The cascade is called the Moon Washing Spring, Sengetsu-sen, a name suggesting that the moon's image, dancing in the pool, is being washed in the water.

Only eight years after he had finally begun his Eastern Hill Villa, Yoshimasa died, in 1490. The faithful scribe who was with him at the last speaks of him in the diary as "that man of incomparable taste."[15] He also noted that the estate was converted that very day into a subtemple of Shokoku-ji, the original Ashikaga memorial foundation.

The great days of Muromachi ended with Yoshimasa. Artists who had remained with him in the city scattered to find patronage from powerful barons in the provinces. And with them, Kyoto art was carried to a wider field.

For a few years the estate in the Eastern Hills was probably kept up, for Yoshimasa's son, the new shogun, came to live in it—and shortly created a scandal by bringing women to its monastic precincts. In 1501, a short eleven years after Yoshimasa's death, someone who visited the place found it looted and going to ruin.

For the greater part of the next century, that sixteenth which is the darkest in Japan's history, the garden lay disintegrating. It had never been as well made as the garden at Saiho-ji, its prototype done by the land-skilled Hatas, and could not resist the years as the older garden has done.

About 1585 an impoverished court noble, Kono Sakahisa, took possession and apparently did a little to rehabilitate the place. By the time he died, conditions had so improved that Shokoku-ji temple was once more able to assume control.

With a strong peace at last restored and reconstruction started in Kyoto, the rebuilding of Yoshimasa's estate-temple was undertaken, probably about 1615. Work continued for some years. The garden, however, had evidently gone so completely to pieces that much of it had to be entirely reconstructed. The original outline of the lake seems to have been considerably reduced, as previously noted, and new rockwork was put in around this new outline. But where parts of the old rockwork still remained in good shape, as around the island, it was left untouched. Fortunately, at the time of the reconstruction, garden artistry was at a high level.[16]

Today, the most arresting features of the Silver Pavilion garden are two piles of white sand (Plate 111). One is a large truncated cone; the other a wide, flat expanse, some two feet thick. These white and bulky piles appear startling in the sylvan setting of the garden and invariably provoke the inquiry: What are they? What do they mean?

There seems to be no answer. They have no meaning and they came there, apparently, by chance. The cone, with its flat top, is called the Moon Facing Height, Kogetsu-dai (Plate 11). It is sixteen feet in diameter on the ground, six feet high, and five feet in diameter across the top. The second, the wide, flat pile of sand, is called the Silver Sand

147

Sea or Ginsha-nada. It is roughly diamond-shaped, its sides beveled, its top kept molded into squared ridges, probably meant to suggest formalized ocean waves (Plate 204).

A search through the records throws almost no light on how these curiosities came into existence. Documents contemporary with the original construction of the garden do not mention them, which seems good evidence that they were no part of the first plan—at least in their present form. Mention of the Silver Sand Sea occurs in a poem written before 1576.[17] So some spread of sand to suggest this name evidently existed before the garden was reconstructed. In all probability it was simply an expanse of white sand covering the ground before the main building, a style often seen in other Zen temples and having its distant origin, probably, in the spread of sand over the forecourt of the Heian hall.

The cone could have been originally merely a pile of extra sand, left there to be drawn upon as needed in renewing the spread or the paths. Such functional piles of sand may be seen in a number of later Zen gardens, for instance in the *hojo* (abbot's quarters) garden of Daitoku-ji temple and in Daisen-in (Plates 6, 106).

A clue as to how the two in Yoshimasa's garden attained their present bulky size may be found in a group of old books in which famous gardens are described and illustrated by woodcuts.[18] These books were published from the seventeenth to the nineteenth century. The drawings in successive books show the sand piles getting higher and higher, as if each time fresh sand was brought in for renewal a little extra was added, the piles thus growing almost imperceptibly.

Today, Japanese critics generally agree that these sand heaps are inharmonious with the existing garden. The cone is too large to be anything but intrusive in this sylvan setting, while the expanse of the Silver Sand Sea interferes with the view of the garden from the main building. Moreover, the symbolic suggestion of water in its etched waves is incongruous with the actual water in the pond.

Yet by themselves, these sand piles are not without a certain abstract, esthetic beauty, especially in moonlight. Then their clear white forms shine in strong and pleasing contrast to the dark trees whose shadows fall across their smooth surfaces. The round top of the cone, when seen from the second story of the pavilion, might suggest the reflection of the full moon. In moonlight, too, the procession of silent waves across the Silver Sand Sea has a certain ghostly beauty of its own—the ghost, perhaps, of all rhythmic wave motion.

CHAPTER SIXTEEN

Zen Gardens: From
Painting to Landscaping

O F ALL the great estates built in the Muromachi period only the Gold and Silver
Pavilion gardens of Yoshimitsu and Yoshimasa remain today. Yet many small
temples also had gardens built for them in this period, like the one in which the scribes of
Onryoken lived. Many of these survive, which is fortunate, for it was in them that gardening reached its apex as fine art and as the expression of a philosophy.

The great estate gardens possessed beauty and artistry, but they were meant, first of all,
to provide a setting for the mansion of a great and important person. So they were landscape gardens first and works of art only secondarily. On the contrary, small temple
gardens had as their one and only purpose the aiding of contemplation, leading, it was
hoped, to enlightenment. Zen scholars, those artists and mystics who designed these small
gardens, were free to do almost exactly as they pleased. And since it was an age of artistic
ferment, it often pleased them to experiment with this garden medium. Artists created
landscape pictures from stones and sand, as like as possible to the painted Chinese landscapes they executed with their brushes; scholars symbolized their philosophy; and mystics
expressed their relationship with the Infinite. They created art first and gardens afterward.

A few paintings by the Sung masters had first arrived in Japan in their own day—that is,
the Kamakura period—when the Zen monks who traveled back and forth between the
two countries sometimes brought such pictures home with them. Later, Mongol disrup-
tions brought many fine pieces of art into the Chinese market, and some of these reached
Japan. Most of them came by way of the trade inaugurated by Takauji in connection with
the decorating of Tenryu-ji temple. We have glimpsed the Muromachi connoisseurs in the
Gold Pavilion delightedly poring over these newly arrived treasures.

This sophisticated Sung art, falling into the well-prepared soil of Muromachi, came to
a second flowering in Japan, belated but perfect, in the fifteenth century. Although separated both in time and in space, the Japanese Muromachi painters may be regarded as an
integral part of the Chinese Sung school. Later, the distinctively Japanese school of Kano
painting developed. But the early Muromachi masters were, to all intents and purposes,
Sung artists.[1]

Their pictures were executed by a special technique. They were drawn by a soft brush

149

with black ink (charcoal mixed with sizing and water) on semi-absorbent paper or white silk. The ink color could be made to range from faintest grey to wet black. Sometimes the pictures were also tinted lightly with green, blue, red, or yellow. The brush was handled as in brush writing, each stroke necessarily firm, definite, and final. There was no erasing a false line nor covering it with a second.

The brushwork could be varied, ranging through washes, lines, dots, and splashes. The strokes were delicately fine or broad or dashingly bold. Simple as were these materials, in the hands of a master they were capable of suggesting the mistiness of distant mountains or rivers, the bold forms of rocks and crags, the dark textures of pines, and the whiteness of a waterfall.

The landscape pictures are painted from the viewpoint of one who has climbed to high places and now looks back and down over the panorama below him, and up to the heights still ahead (Plate 112). Vast cliffs and peaks, often spoken of by Western critics as "chimney spires," soar in the background; weatherbeaten pines may cling to the rocks, and a river or lake may flow through the scene. Often a steep path can be seen winding upward. And on it, hardly discernible at first, are often the minute figures of pilgrims toiling upward, or seated, contemplating the scene below. Buildings and boats are frequently present in these pictures, but, like the figures, they never dominate the scene—as human elements are likely to do in Occidental landscape paintings.

Such pictures, and the gardens derived from them, are filled with Zen symbolism. Interpreted in one way, they present a picture of man's spiritual life. Thus the dark valleys stand for his cramped physical existence, from which he seeks to lift himself. Boats on the river, houses, and villages are signs of mundane life. A monastery where dwell those who aspire to higher things often rears its stately roof on somewhat higher ground.

The path and the climbing pilgrims indicate the long hard way to the soaring peaks of enlightenment. The philosopher-artist must himself have gone a certain distance along this way in order to look back and grasp its significance. But always the peaks soar above him, challenging him onward and upward. The tiny figures of men in this tremendous setting suggest the relative importance of man in the cosmos. Though he may be small, he is still an integral and harmonious part of the whole.

Behind this objective symbolism there lies, in these pictures, an even deeper meaning, something which can hardly be expressed in words but must be sensed. It is the attempt of the Zen artist, who was also a mystic, to reach through to an inner essence. The great landscape pictures have about them a universal quality. They are not the representation of a specific scene but seem to hold the quality of all landscape. That is, in drawing a mountain, a rock, or a waterfall, the Zen artist did not make a portrait of an individual thing. He studied many and sought to find and depict the quality that was common to all. As he succeeded in finding the essence of all rocks, all mountains, all trees, and in recording it so others might feel it also, he was successful as painter and philosopher.

The decade of Onin warfare in Kyoto drove a large part of its population into the provinces. Artists and scholars, except for the few who found refuge with the shogun, sought shelter in distant temples or settled at the provincial seats of feudal lords who acted as their patrons. A great deal of Muromachi art was thus created outside the capital and left scattered over the nation. Among such works are paintings and gardens made by the artist Sesshu (Plate 114).

Sesshu (1420–1506) was a Zen monk who, like that earlier garden lover Muso Kokushi, spent most of his life wandering from temple to temple, in Kyoto, Kamakura, and the western provinces.[2] But, unlike Muso, Sesshu had no interest in politics. He became a national figure purely as an artist, his fame resting on his superlative paintings (Plates 96, 112, 113, 201).

However, like the other artists of his day, he tried his hand at various contemporary art forms, composing verses, performing the incense ceremony, and making gardens. He seems to have been also an expert judge of art, and along with it something of a business-man, for he is spoken of as the "purchaser priest."[3] The China trade was still largely in the hands of Zen monks, and Sesshu appears to have acted sometimes as appraiser and buyer of art brought in from China. This connoisseurship is probably what obtained for him the opportunity to go at last to China, a trip that was doubtless the ambition of most Zen monks. Among Sesshu's patrons was the great baron Masahiro, Lord Ouchi, who was deeply interested in art and esthetics.

The Ouchi family controlled wide provinces at the western end of Japan, their castle seat being in the town of Yamaguchi. During the Onin war and later, this town achieved an urbanity which had hitherto been found only in the capital. Much of the trade with China went in and out of Hakata, in near-by Kyushu. Sesshu sailed from there in 1468, the year after the Onin war broke out in Kyoto. It is believed he was commissioned by Lord Ouchi to go to China and buy rare art objects.[4]

We can imagine Sesshu's anticipation as he set sail. It was his hope to find a Chinese teacher of painting who could still create masterpieces like those he had so long admired and studied and who could teach him secrets of this art. But by the time he arrived in China the Sung period was long past. Even the Mongol hordes had been driven back to their northern steppes, and China had risen again to a great era under the native Ming dynasty. But Ming genius did not blossom in painting; it found its best expression in new outlets—in drama, ceramics, and architecture, with Peking as its masterpiece. Landscape painting in the Ming period was becoming increasingly formalized and pedantic.

Sesshu went to Hangchow, the beautiful old Sung capital on West Lake. But by the time he arrived its great artists had gone. Instead of the master-painters he sought, Sesshu himself was hailed as a great artist and given high Zen honors.[5] This praise was hardly exaggerated, for Sesshu was unquestionably the supreme painter of the Muromachi period. His finest work was done, however, after he returned to Japan, carrying the inspiration of China's great mountains and rivers and the knowledge that no man living was his peer.

When he came once more to the shores of Japan, the Onin war was still wasting Kyoto. There was no reason why he should go to the capital, so he settled in Lord Ouchi's domains in western Japan. The remaining forty years of his long life were spent in this part of the country, the time filled with painting, teaching, and visits from old friends—those other monks and artists who had left the ruined capital and wandered to the west.

Sesshu's wanderlust never allowed him to stay many years in one place. He lived in various districts, in temples, or in studio-residences which he had built for himself. One of the latter, outside Yamaguchi and within view of its castle, is described by the monk Keigo, who visited him in 1488. Sesshu called his house the Heaven-Created Painting Pavilion—that is, Tenkai Zuga-ro. Keigo's description of it is written in traditional Chinese phrases. He even followed conventional Chinese garden descriptions to the extent of mentioning "unusual birds and strange animals" which, as we have seen, might once have been a part of Chinese gardens but were unlikely to have been seen in those of Japan. Keigo's lines give us a glimpse of the atmosphere in which the Muromachi artists lived and created their paintings and gardens. He wrote:

"From afar it appears rustic, with mysterious rocks and winding streams. A step inside transports one into a world entirely different from the city. Here, too, the artist put up a tablet inscribed 'Heaven-Created Painting.' The house faces the castle's north window. If one opens the door, one can see the rising and setting sun, clouds and sudden fog, haze and mist, curling smoke, the sky covered with storms, wind, the darkness of rain, and the crystal purity of snow and moonlight. Wherever one looks, variety meets the eye. More than a thousand, ten thousand changes, varying with the instant. . . . The wise Lord [Ouchi] often walks here and curious scholars and groups of officials gather also. The venerable Sesshu sits on his bamboo seat and reed cushion, or busies himself with his daily work, drawing water, or preparing incense for burning.

"A stream murmurs over here. There, large stones rise to a precipice. Rare plants and strange flowers achieve great loveliness. Unusual birds and strange animals appear and disappear. The cry of birds is heard; highly colored fish swim about; butterflies cluster 'round. During the heat of a midsummer day, the host and his guests exchange poems over their wine. The wind and moon are also visitors. All these things are present at the Heaven-Created Painting Pavilion."[6]

This obviously described the natural setting of a mountain retreat, not a landscaped garden. It brings to mind Po Chu-i's description of the environs of the Grass Cottage on Lu-shan. Nevertheless, Sesshu is known as a maker of gardens as well as a painter. Four gardens attributed to him still survive, scattered over western Japan. No documentary evidence proves beyond doubt that he made these four, but he is known to have lived in the vicinity of each. At any rate, whoever made them was, like him, a great Muromachi artist filled with the spirit of the age and possessed of its abilities. Sesshu we may think of as the archetype of such men.

Two of the four Sesshu gardens belong to the small temples of Mampuku-ji and Iko-ji in the village of Masuda near the north seacoast. Here Sesshu spent the last years of his life. Another garden, Kiseki-bo, is in the little mountain village of Hikosan in northern Kyushu. Its isolation has saved it from change, so that it is regarded as the best preserved of the gardens attributed to him. The garden of Joei-ji temple, near Yamaguchi, was probably made by Sesshu when he was under the patronage of Lord Ouchi, about 1490 (Plates 115–17).

Joei-ji's garden covers some seven acres and is laid out in the pond-and-island style. It has an unusually wide stretch of level foreground lying between the building that overlooks it and the near edge of the water. On the far side of the pond, the ground rises into the usual enclosing hillside, and down this flows a cascade in seven short falls.

The islands in the pond (which may be the least changed of the rock constructions) are splendid examples of the sheer artistry possible simply through the juxtaposition of choice natural rocks (Plates 116, 117). The most conspicuous characteristic here is the consistent, almost exclusive, use of flat-topped stones having strong, decisive angles and straight, precipitous sides. (The nubby nondescript rock has no place whatever in this kind of art.) Flat-topped stones, it will be recalled, we first saw used to create the feeling of quiescence in Saiho-ji's hillside garden. Later we found them used to give contrast to the pointed, soaring peak rocks of Tenryu-ji's Sung landscape. The Muromachi period seized on this stone characteristic and brought its use to the peak of rock artistry. Such flat-topped stones are usually the identification mark of a Muromachi garden or an indication of Muromachi influence.

Their inspired use in the garden art of this period seems to derive directly from the landscape paintings, notably from the brush techniques of these pictures. Such paintings often make use of straight strokes angularly combined. Sesshu was supreme in this angular technique. Of him Fenollosa says: "He is the greatest master of straight line and angle in the whole range of the world's art. There is no landscape so soft he cannot, if he wills, translate it into terms of oaken wedges split with an ax."[7]

In the painting technique these straight and angular strokes are often able to reproduce the very look and feel of rocks (which are surely one of the most difficult of all subjects to paint successfully). The Sung-Muromachi artists, nevertheless, with this type of textural impressionism, were able to bring out the very essence of rocks, whether they were pebbles, crags, or towering cliffs (Plate 113). Thus the interrelationship of the gardens to the painted landscape pictures—of stonework to brushwork—came to a full circle when the strokes of the painters were used to re-create the essentials of natural rocks, and actual rocks were used in gardens to suggest the brush strokes of the painters.

In the painting gardens (the term is mine) the stones are combined to form designs that are abstractions of landscape. Or such rock arrangements might be regarded simply as designs of pure rhythmic movement, executed in this medium. As practical components in garden making, such stone groups can be made to serve as islands, cascades, springs, hillside outcroppings, or shorelines. Or they may have no practical purpose but to serve as art, their value inherent only in their forms, textures, and colors. They may stimulate imaginative meaning in some people, but others will be satisfied to view them simply for their intrinsic beauty.

In Sesshu's Joei-ji garden there are a number of isolated stone groups placed at intervals over the stretch of mounded foreground between the building and the pond edge (Plate 115). Here they have no part in the landscape pattern (although the literal-minded, if so inclined, might see them as islets rising from a sea of ground cover). But for those with artistic perception, they seem to have been put there simply for their own inherent quality, and possibly to illustrate some Zen concept. We shall find similar groups of rocks elsewhere and get an idea, perhaps, of their Zen significance.

153

The garden which probably best exemplifies the landscape painting style belongs to Daisen-in, a small subsidiary temple within the precincts of the large Daitoku-ji monastery in Kyoto. Such small temples, clustering around a large ecclesiastical foundation, are usually residences, serving either as the retreat of a pious individual or as a memorial hall with a resident abbot. (Since Zen priests may marry, their families sometimes live with them in such temples.) Daisen-in is made up of a group of several small buildings, the principal one holding the abbot's formal reception room and also his study. Sliding panels which form the wall dividing these rooms are paper-covered and painted with a long, mural-like landscape. It is generally agreed that this painting is the work of the famous artist Soami.

The exterior walls of this main building are partly made of sliding wooden panels. When they are opened, one can step out onto a narrow veranda or outdoor corridor that goes around the building. To reach the adjacent buildings of the temple complex, extensions of these veranda corridors cross the surrounding garden, like short bridges.

A garden space surrounds the main building on all sides. It takes the form of a continuous, austere landscape, carried out in sand and stones, with a very few small trees and shrubs to relieve it (Plate 10). The portion known as the front garden, which lies across the side and end of the reception room, is merely a wide spread of white sand. Its outer perimeter is marked by two clipped hedges, one higher than the other, beyond which rise trees. The level sandy surface is kept scratched into long lines parallel to the building. This wide, level sandy area can probably be taken to represent the ocean.

Near one end of the sandy sea are two small heaps of sand, each about three feet high (Plates 6, 106). They are now permanent features, but once, evidently, they were merely piles of surplus material, temporarily left for later use. (In them, probably, we can see how the large, flattened cone of sand in the Silver Pavilion garden originated.) These two little white cones on the flat spread of sand somehow become strangely effective points of interest.

On the two opposite sides of the building the garden space is narrower and is divided at several points by the bridgelike walks to the other buildings. One rectangular space thus created is called the north garden and has recently been developed into a simple harmonizing link of sand and a few stones. The garden space is delimited by walls of buildings or garden walls covered with white plaster.

The remaining garden area is an angled space that runs around two sides of the building, opening up to the study with its paneled paintings by Soami. In this space are the rock arrangements which so vividly exemplify, in three dimensions, the style of the Muromachi landscape painters (Plate 118).

The corner itself is filled by a group of enormous rugged rocks which, to the creative imagination, form mountains with vast cliffs and peaks. Between two peaks a cascade formed by a striated rock falls from a high, hanging valley (Plate 119). It brings to mind the falling stream seen in Fan K'uan's painting of the great precipice (Plate 97).

The water from this distant fall appears to flow from a lower valley into both arms of the right-angled garden. The shorter arm holds a collection of the fine rocks typical of those in this garden, used mostly to outline a large island. It is sometimes identified as a tortoise, but the resemblance is vague, and the presence of a deep-sea creature in a mountain river is entirely inconsistent. However, the motif had become a convention and was widely used, with no reference to its original significance.

Interest in the mountain landscape and its stream returns to the longer arm of the garden, some forty-seven feet in length and about thirteen feet wide. Such proportions approximate those of the long, narrow hanging scrolls, called kakemono, which so often hold the landscape paintings.

The scene in this space is unmistakably a small river starting from the distant cascade and flowing in a sandy course down its length. In the upper area it passes around another large rockbound island, traditionally the crane, but recognizably only a group of large, powerful rocks, flat-topped and angular. The veranda edge forms the near shore of the stream, with various low, level-topped rocks against it. The farther shore is made up of pointed stones which might be distant hills. Every stone in this garden is remarkable for its uniquely individual form and its interesting surface, often marked in lines. Their placement and grouping is fully within the idiom of the Sung landscapists.

About the center of the garden picture the river falls over a sort of dividing line, a long, narrow, flat stone, level with the ground but suggesting a dam. This cuts straight across from shore to shore, dividing the scene into two distinct parts. Above is the area of rocky islands and mountains; below, the water widens into quiet smoothness. In this quiet area is anchored a small stone boat, shaped like the traditional cargo junk (Plate 10).

When the river finally reaches the bottom of the picture, it seems to veer and flow off under the building. Its flow is indicated by the sandy current and small rocks which actually disappear under the veranda floor. Thus the stream appears to be headed for the "ocean," the wide sandy sheet lying on the other side of the building.

In this pictorial composition the prevailing movement of most of the rocks is upward. But contrasted with this thrust are two cross lines. The first is the curious stone just mentioned, which lies across the center of the garden. The second is a stone bridge. This is made of a single flat rock lying over the stream emerging at the foot on the mountains (Plate 120). The bridge is large enough to carry a person across the stream at that point, but if it is to be used by people it throws out of scale the imaginative larger landscape that can be built up from the peaks and cliffs of the mountain rocks. If, however, the stone bridge is seen only as a cross line in the composition, then it can be taken to be a road or path leading up into the hills: the sort of thing that was so often a part of these mountain landscapes, denoting the presence of man in the cosmos.

Before the middle of the twentieth century the garden of Daisen-in had long remained under a temple maintenance system that removed leaves and weeds and kept the shrubs cut back a little but carefully refrained from making any basic changes. These, however, were made by nature as shaggy brownish moss came to cover the sand completely, while many of the shrubs became large and intrusive, and around the base of the rocks small plants grew into competing or even concealing forms.

With the increase of interest in these art gardens after World War II, a program of renovation was begun at Daisen-in, and in 1954 the moss and extra plants were removed and clean white sand restored. Later the main building, then about 450 years old, was put under repair so that its time-damaged timbers might be restored. This type of renewal, in which parts are exactly replaced, is widely practiced in Japan, accounting for the survival of many of the ancient wooden structures.

In the meantime there had come to light unexpected evidence that one of the corridor bridges, which then stood at the lower end of the garden, leading between the main building and another, had originally crossed it directly in the center. In doing this, it had made use of the curious and rather mysterious flat cross stone as a foundation (thus accounting for its presence). The evidence concerning this corridor, which included a roof, a single wall of half-timber, and an arched window in Zen style, as well as the flooring, was studied by various experts, including the official Commission for the Preservation of Cultural Properties. The evidence seeming to be incontrovertible, permission was given to make the restoration, and the corridor was put back into the center (Plate 121). The work was finished, along with the renovation of the building, in 1961.[8]

The new position of the corridor and its wall of course divides the river scene into two parts, the one with its mountains, the other with its boat stone. Through the window in this wall may be seen a limited view of the hills and cascade, the focus emphasizing, and making very obvious, their likeness to the painting. Controversial feeling over this move has been strong, most of those who remember the garden as a single unit seeming to prefer it that way. While each of the two parts makes an excellent landscape, and the river can still be seen to flow under the corridor, the feeling that the full sweep was better is held by many. The question in the minds of some is whether evidence may not yet come to light indicating that the corridor was not part of the original plan but was added sometime in its four hundred years of existence.

The garden of Daisen-in was probably made about 1513.[9] Yoshimasa had been dead twenty-five years, and with him had departed the glory of the Ashikaga shogunate. Civil disturbances, which had started with the Onin war, had never really ended but had spread over the whole country, until any baron or vassal who saw an opportunity to extend his domains at the expense of a neighbor did not hesitate to start a little war of his own. Kyoto itself, again and again, was the scene of fighting by lawless elements. The shoguns who succeeded Yoshimasa became pawns of the contending factions.

Since the Ashikagas had always supported the imperial court but were now themselves penniless and powerless, the court suffered actual poverty. When Daisen-in's garden was built, the reigning emperor had been on the throne a dozen years, but because there were no funds the ceremonies of his enthronement had never taken place. Nor were they to be held for nearly another decade.

Under the circumstances it is remarkable that even a small temple and garden could have been built. That they were built was due to the force and personality of the important monk Kogaku Sotan. He was one of the leading Zen ecclesiastics of his time, abbot of the great Daitoku-ji monastery, and in a happier era might have become a national figure. He was much honored by the imperial court and numbered among his followers the current shogun, Yoshitane.

26. *Casually planted small* tsubo *garden between buildings in old-palace style, Daikaku-ji, Kyoto.* ▶

27 *(overleaf). Garden view, Manju-in, Kyoto.* ▶

156

Sotan retired as head of Daitoku-ji in 1509 and went to live in Daisen-in. Then, as now, it was one of the small residence temples which cluster around large Buddhist institutions. The building must have been in a dilapidated condition, for Sotan determined to rebuild it. Fortunately he was the brother of a neighboring country baron, Rokkaku Masayori, one of those lords who controlled what wealth and power remained in the country. This brother was Sotan's patron, and it was due to his resources that the building could be completed after about four years. When it was finished, about 1513, a brief note in the account of Sotan's life states: "He planted rare trees and placed strange stones to make a landscape."[10] This is the only known contemporary mention of the making of the garden.

Nevertheless, there persists a tradition that the garden was made by the famous painter Soami, although his name is not mentioned in this connection in any record until over a hundred years later.[11] He had been one of the artists at the court of Yoshimasa, twenty-five years before, and must still have been active. The presence of his mural-like landscape painting on the temple walls indicates clearly that the artist and the monk were friends and collaborators.

It seems reasonable to assume that they planned the garden together. Sotan would have been primarily interested in it as a Zen expression. Soami would have been interested in using rocks and sand to create a Chinese landscape picture. He is known to have been an ardent admirer of the works of the Chinese painter Mu Ch'i, who is regarded by many as the greatest of all the Sung landscapists. This interest and Soami's artistic ability would account for the great success of this aspect of the garden.

But such a theme would also have fitted Sotan's desires, for he, too, had a special interest in mountains. His Zen name, Kogaku, means "Ancient Mountain." It was bestowed on him as a kind of degree when he was named as a Zen master by his teacher, at the age of twenty-three. The mountain theme appears again in a poem which was presented to him at the same time. This poem,[12] written in Chinese, is too abstruse to bear translation, but, with strong Zen implications, it refers to ten thousand peaks rising among the clouds and transcending differences. It seems certain to me that the poem must have been the basic inspiration of the garden.

Assuming that it was, and that Sotan and Soami together laid out the general plan of the garden, we still do not know the name of the stone craftsman who was in charge of the actual selection and placement of these remarkable stones.[13] He was obviously someone possessed of great experience and skill and understanding of what he was attempting to do. Other evidence of professionalism appears in such details as the presence of the "crane" and "tortoise" islands, motifs conventional at that time to the gardens of military lords. Here they may reflect a gesture of appreciation for the support given to the garden by Sotan's brother, its lordly patron.

The man who actively chose the stones to be used in creating this garden picture, and then directed their placing, must have been one of the garden craftsmen still left in Kyoto from the years when the building of Muromachi estates was in its heyday. We can guess that he was one of the school of Zen'ami, the old genius of the riverbank people. Another

◀ 28–29. *Autumn and winter views from second-floor windows, Shisen-do, Kyoto.*

guess is that he might have been Matashiro, the old man's grandson, who could still have been active. Matashiro was not only the heir to the old man's skill but was himself interested in Zen.

Where the anonymous craftsman obtained the remarkable stones that he used for this masterpiece is fairly easy to see. Certainly there would have been no chance to go searching for them in the mountain watercourses where they were originally found (which was always an expensive and time-consuming business). Nor would there have been any chance for a choice collection such as this one to have been found, had such a search been made.[14]

But there was no need. Kyoto was full of ruined estates, and we have seen how casually it had been the custom to move rocks and trees from one place to another. Among the neglected estates were those which had belonged to the shoguns, including the several unusually fine places that Yoshimasa had made when garden construction was his hobby. Furthermore, in these Ashikaga gardens must have been collected many of the finest rocks ever found, stones which had gravitated to them as gifts to the shoguns.

I think we can conclude that Yoshitane, the current shogun, gave permission to his Zen teacher Sotan to take such rocks and trees as he wished for the new temple garden from the now hopelessly deteriorated shogunal properties. Only in this way—as the choice gleanings of a whole era of collecting—can we account for the unique quality of the stones found in Daisen-in.

CHAPTER SEVENTEEN

Ryoan-ji:
Sermon in Stone

GARDENS described up to this time have all been based on aspects of nature—on hills and streams, forests, rocks, and cascades. That is, they have all been *landscape* gardens. The artists who made them might idealize their subject, so symbolizing and suggesting it, sometimes, that final relation to reality might not always be apparent. But they all have had landscape as their theme and inspiration.

We come now to something different: gardens in which landscape as the pattern was discarded. Instead, the artists and mystics who made them went to the inherent qualities of their materials for a medium in which to express their thoughts and feelings. Their feeling was, of course, some abstract concept of Zen philosophy. But rocks and sand being their materials, it was the characteristics of these materials on which the expression was formulated.

The gardens which resulted probably should not be called "gardens," for certainly they come within no definition of that word by Occidental usage. If there were a better word we should use it, but lacking a more exact term, we must continue to speak of them as gardens.

A number of such creations exist in the various Zen temples of Kyoto. But all, apparently, stem from one supreme original, that of Ryoan-ji temple.[1] This garden is so different from anything that has preceded in this discussion that it seems best to describe it briefly at once.

The temple occupies a site that was once the country estate of a Heian noble, lying on the outskirts of Kyoto. Remnants of this old lake garden, called Daiju-in, survive in a large pond with islands. We must pass this to reach the garden we seek. The wide old lake, peaceful and lovely, is mossy green under the bright sun of summer, while cicadas shrill in the leafy trees around it which shelter our path.

The garden of Ryoan-ji lies behind the walls and buildings of the temple beyond. We must remove our shoes in the vestibule and walk in our stocking feet to the broad, darkly polished veranda which overlooks it along one side. The garden was intended to be seen only from this veranda or from the open rooms, occupied by the superior, which border it. No one ever sets foot in the garden except the lay brother who keeps it raked and clean.

163

Its purpose is simply to form an outlook and an inspiration to one sitting in meditation in these rooms.

The area of ground making up this garden is about that of a tennis court—to be exact, thirty by seventy-eight feet (Plates 8, 122). The wide veranda extends down nearly the full length of one of its sides, and a small auxiliary building encloses the near end. The opposite end and side are shut in by a high earthen wall, protected along its top by a small roof of tiles. This wall was once faced with white plaster but is now stained and weatherworn to a rusty, mottled brown. Its original light color undoubtedly formed a more simple and pleasing background to the garden than does the present distracting surface of many earth colors.

The flat rectangle of ground is covered deeply with a coarse, whitish sand which is kept raked into a pattern of scratched lines. Out of this rise fifteen stones in five groups. About the base of each group is now a cushion of coarse moss, but apart from this there are no plants in the garden. High trees now rise beyond the wall, but these trees and the moss were not part of the original planning and have no significance in the design. They do, nevertheless, contribute a softening and mellowing effect which adds much to the garden's feeling.

The five groups of stones are made up, successively, of five, two, three, two, and three each. It so happens that a small stone at either end is always hidden from any ordinary angle of vision, but there is no significance in this.

These fifteen rocks, unlike those of the Daisen-in garden, are in no way especially remarkable for size, shape, or color. Some are fairly good-sized boulders, and all have character, but only one has the flat top characteristic of most Muromachi stonework, and none of the others possesses those pronounced planes and angles so typical of the stones in the painting gardens. Interest lies almost wholly in their relative shapes and sizes and in their spatial relationships to each other and to the areas of the sand about them.

This is the garden—a rectangle of sand set about with groups of stones, a bit of moss at the base of each, a brown wall, and a green backdrop of trees. The average Japanese seeing it for the first time is usually aware of something about it to which he responds, his response, of course, depending on the development of his artistic sensibilities. But foreigners looking at the garden for the first time are usually puzzled. Bewilderment, however, is not as great as it was before abstract forms in the visual arts became a familiar thing to the West.

The beauty of this garden is subtle but powerful. As a rule, full appreciation does not come immediately. It is best to sit down on the edge of the veranda with no sense of time and pressure and study the scene, first objectively, in an attempt to analyze it intellectually, then subjectively, trying to feel what the maker was expressing here.

Ryoan-ji is seen at its best when its rocks and sand are wet from recent rain and the sky is still pearly grey and misty. It may even be thought most beautiful when it is still lightly raining, for then the mystery of the stones seems to be enhanced. Wetness brings out all the subtle tones and shadowy textures of the rock surfaces; it darkens and softens the sand color and brightens and heightens the green of moss and trees. When this garden is dry, much of its beauty vanishes in a parched and dusty look. When the sun shines hard and bright, it dispels that quality of depth and mystery and the tranquility which the Japanese call yugen and hold most precious.

It is quite possible to interpret this garden, if desired, in terms of the conventional landscape. The stretch of sand with its scratched, flowing lines may be regarded as a river, and the stone groups as islets scattered in it. This accepts the scene on its man-sized scale. Or, if we choose to look at it with the eye of the creative imagination, building up a larger landscape, we see the scratched sand as sea waves and the rocks as bare, craggy islands. Just such views of the level sea with islands rising above it may be found at many places in the Inland Sea or along the old route to China by the Korean coast. But while such landscape interpretations are possible, they seem too simple. We search for additional meaning and run across the tiger story, based on the name of the garden.

This name is the Garden of Crossing Tiger Cubs, Tora no Ko Watashi. If the stones are to be taken literally as tigers and their cubs swimming the river, this name might be no more than one of those frequent explanations for the simple-minded. But Dr. Tamura suggests this name might have been given in early Tokugawa times when a wave of Confucianism from China was sweeping the country. Tigers retiring to their dens across the river would symbolize the Confucian teaching that the virtue of a good ruler protects the country, even from the danger of ferocious beasts.[2] However, I share a widespread feeling that the ultimate meaning of this garden is much older and deeper than this name suggests and is only to be grasped after a careful study of its rock arrangement.

By reference to the accompanying diagram it will be noted that the five stone groups scattered about in the sand are divided in the center into left and right halves. On the left are two groups, on the right three. Occult balance between the two sides is maintained because the two are individually larger than the groups with three.

Next, balance is maintained within each half through the size and position of the stone groups on the sand rectangle. The first group on the left, larger and nearer, is balanced by

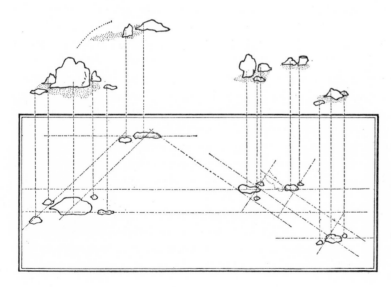

Fig. 2. Diagrammatic arrangement of the stones in Ryoan-ji garden, with their projection on the rectangle below. (After Shigemori in Kyoto Bijutsu Taikan Teien)

the smaller second group, more distant, against the wall. Within the half containing three parts, two small groups balance a single larger group.

Finally, perfect balance is maintained within each individual group. The first one on the left contains five stones; the center is a large upright rock supported by two smaller ones and by two that are almost level with the ground (Plate 123). The total effect of this group is of fine stability.

The second (Plate 124) and fourth groups achieve balance through their relative forms. Both contain one long, reclining stone and one short, upright stone which balance each other. The third and fifth groups are made up of three stones each. In both, a larger rock is balanced by two smaller ones, but the arrangement is quite different in each.

From this analysis it is plain that not a single stone could be moved or taken way from this composition without spoiling it. Harmonic balance has been created not only in the relationship of each stone to those nearest it but also in its relationship to every other stone in the composition.

Balance, however, is not the only quality present in this arrangement. In contrast to static strength, the rocks achieve movement. It hardly seems possible, indeed, that stones could convey such dynamic feeling as these do. In general, there is a strong sense of flowing movement from left to right, the conventional direction. If we think of the garden as a river, there is no doubt in our mind in which direction it is flowing. From the largest group on the left, the others seem to taper away, but direction is indicated also by a subtle obliquity of direction in the position of the stones. Those that are upright are not exactly perpendicular but slant slightly to the right, while all the long, reclining stones seem to point in the same direction. There is just one exception to this directional movement; the fourth group from the left is definitely reversed in direction and straight upright. It is as if it were standing out against the current. Through it, contrast and interest are created, and monotony is avoided.

Rhythm is obtained by the alternate upward and forward movement of every group and by contrasting movements within each group. If we start again at the left, we find the general movement of the first group is upward, of the second forward, the third again upward, the fourth again forward, while the fifth is neither but gives a sense of indefinite continuance.

The same rhythm is repeated in detail within each group. The first, although its pre-dominating movement is upward, as expressed by the large central stone, holds contrasting cross movement in its smaller stones, especially in the level cross stones lying flat in the sand. The second group moves strongly forward because of the long reclining stone, but upward contrast appears in the short perpendicular stone at the end. The same technique of movement and contrast can be traced in each group in continuous flowing repetition. Again it is obvious that it would be impossible to move a single stone without spoiling the entire effect.

Having dissected the mechanics of balance and rhythm in this composition, we realize how completely the creator knew and followed the laws underlying all design. The harmony achieved is complete: harmony of color in rocks, sand, and moss; harmony of

166

line in the shape and size of the rocks; harmony of movement in their spacing on the rectangle and relationship to each other.

After we have finished our intellectual analysis, and our minds are no longer intent on this phase, we must attempt to achieve an emotional understanding of the garden. We sit and just take in the composition as a whole, its utter stability soothing us, our feelings tranquilized by its perfections. Grey, green, and brown, the soft mistiness of rain, the rise and fall of the stones, flowing and continuous.

Somehow, without any effort, we know intuitively what the garden maker was trying to express here. It was Harmony, that Harmony which underlies the universe, the world, and man. The Harmony of force and matter and spirit. The Harmony that, to the Oriental religionist, makes the morning stars to sing together, the heart of nature to beat in rhythm, and man to know himself a brother of the rocks and wind and sun. Modern science has confirmed this feeling through intellectual research. The ancient Hebrew poet sang it in terms of his own religious concepts when he said:

"*Be still,* and KNOW that I am God."[3]

A sermon in stone, a whole philosophy bound up between the covers of an earthen wall—undoubtedly this garden is one of the world's great masterpieces of religiously inspired art.

And with it, the Muromachi garden makers reached their zenith.

Inevitably we are filled with an overwhelming curiosity to know more about this garden. Who made it and when? What was his inspiration? How did such a concept take form? Unfortunately we have no recorded answers to these questions. A few facts have come to light about the making of the garden, and from them we can probably surmise more, which may not be far wrong.

The contemporary evidence carries us back to the days of Muromachi greatness, before the Onin war (1467–77). In 1450, Katsumoto, the powerful Lord Hosokawa (who later became one of the contending leaders in that war) acquired an estate, Daiju-in, which had been the country villa of a Heian courtier. It lay not far from the Gold Pavilion and contained one of the old lake gardens. Presumably Katsumoto rehabilitated this place by rebuilding the residence beside the lake, while on the hillside behind he rebuilt an old temple which was already known as Ryoan-ji.[4]

When the Onin war broke out, the estates of Katsumoto were among the first to be attacked and burned by roving bands of the opposition, this one among them. For some years afterward the priests of Ryoan-ji found sanctuary outside the city. But in 1488, with Katsumoto dead and Kyoto trying to rehabilitate itself, his son Masamoto returned to the old estate and refounded the temple, putting up a new building.[5] All evidence indicates that the present stone garden was constructed at that time, after this building was completed.

This makes it clear that its construction took place about twenty-five years before that of Daisen-in, described in the last chapter. I have chosen to discuss the painting gardens first, however, because the designer of Ryoan-ji took an interesting step beyond those gardens in rejecting landscape as a pattern and in using only the tactile realities of rocks and sand to state its message.

At the time, then, when Ryoan-ji was being constructed, Yoshimasa was still alive and trying to complete the Silver Pavilion garden. Soami was one of the painters still living in Kyoto. Sesshu, at the far end of the country, had come back from China and may have been building the Joei-ji garden. Zen'ami, the old riverbank workman, who was called "greatest in the world in stone placement," had recently died at the age of ninety-seven. And there must have been many of the other riverbank people— the kawara-mono—who had acquired skills under him during the long years they worked on the Muromachi estates.

Moreover, there were many artists and priests still about and active who had been either at the court of Yoshimasa or connected with his family temple, Shokoku-ji, where the atmosphere of Zen and esthetics had centered. And it must not be forgotten that Zen priests were forever traveling from temple to temple, carrying news and ideas and absorbing other new things, so that ideas got around fairly rapidly. Above all, we must realize that Zen and art were, at that time, in some ways close to the same thing. Esoteric Zen concepts were never expressed in didactic words but often in parables. These parables were frequently put, again, not into words but into some form of artistic expression.

A creation such as Ryoan-ji does not come into being suddenly and independently. It is the product of a long period of developing ideas and technical practices. At this time inspiration and techniques had matured together. I believe it is the Muromachi period itself which best accounts for the greatness of Ryoan-ji. The time and place were right for it.

When we consider each of the elements of Ryoan-ji's composition we note that there was nothing new about any of them. Each part had an existing precedent or parallel. What was new was the way these older elements were combined into the supreme artistry of the whole.

For example, its small area, the enclosed rectangle, is derived from those little courts (the tsubo) left between buildings of the Heian mansion. The use of sand originated far back as a purely functional way to prevent muddiness underfoot. When, for purely esthetic reasons, sand was used as a general ground cover, its austere simplicity evidently appealed to Zen taste. We see, probably, another example of this in that spread of sand which had recently been put into Yoshimasa's Silver Pavilion garden (and which somehow has since grown into the curious monumentality of the Silver Sand Sea). In the beginning it was probably only a simple spread of sand meant to mark the monastic nature of the retreat.

As for the elimination of all plants, Dr. Mori suggests this might have been simply to control better the growth of trees, which require continual pruning in such a small area.[6] Perhaps it was a way to achieve that sense of timelessness which is a Zen ideal. Or, I think most likely, it was because the makers wanted only the characteristics of rocks and sand in their composition, with no chance for plants to interfere.

Also believed to have had an influence on this design are "tray landscapes" or miniature gardens created in low flat bowls or squared containers, often made of bronze or stone.

These containers were filled with soil or sand and little rocks, and sometimes plants were arranged in them. Called *kazan* or *kazansui* (artificial landscapes), they had been introduced from China and were very popular during the Muromachi period.[7]

Other more direct influences from China may have been operating here. There was still a good deal of trafficking between the two countries, exemplified by Sesshu's trip to China. In fact, a case might be made out for the possibility that it was Sesshu himself who brought back a basic idea for this kind of garden. One of the Ch'an monasteries where he visited may have had a spread of sand and rocks to give him the idea.

Evidence of this is, of course, the garden of Joei-ji temple. The special feature of its design, it will be recalled, is the way stone groupings have been set about on a wide level space between the building and the edge of the pond. The concept of a Ryoan-ji, set down in front of a typical pond-and-hill garden, comes to mind. Joei-ji today, with a ground cover of grass and low scrubby plants growing about the bases of the rocks, is hard to study. It is difficult, or impossible, to make out any overall design in the placement of the rock groups or to trace any theme, if there ever was one. But only a glance is needed to show that these rock groupings are in themselves fine compositions, hardly excelled anywhere.

It is tempting to imagine Sesshu coming back to Kyoto for a visit and helping to place Ryoan-ji's stones. Exact dates for both Ryoan-ji and Joei-ji are uncertain, but they seem to have been made at almost the same time.[8] I feel certain that somehow, someway, there existed a close relationship between these two. Further research may yet bring it to light.

Granted that we do not really know who preached the sermon in stone which is Ryoan-ji, we still can get a fairly clear picture of its construction. Masamoto, the young Lord Hosokawa, had selected a priest known as Tokuho Zengetsu to be in charge of the temple's reconstruction. Both patron and priest must have had their imaginations stirred by a proposal to create here something new and excitingly different.

The physical simplicity of Ryoan-ji's plan would have had its appeal in that period of postwar difficulties. The garden is small, the stones are few. There would have been no problems in gathering up those needed for this design. While none is a nubby or ordinary stone, neither are there any of those one-in-a-thousand so conspicuously assembled for the Daisen-in garden. There would have been no need to look toward other gardens, for stones like those at Ryoan-ji could be collected almost anywhere with only reasonable effort.[9] Or they might have been left over on the spot from some earlier garden.

Nor was the physical effort of placing the stones very great. They are simply set in the sand, not piled together in difficult forms. They are all small enough to be handled by a few men with ropes and bars. The difficult part of making this garden was its artistry—the spacing of its rocks and their relationships in such subtle details as slant and height and direction (Plate 125). Placement would have been slow, a matter of much trying and rejecting, of many fine shiftings and minute adjustments.

It is easy to visualize the scene: the newly constructed building with its veranda; the level ground before it with the view of the old lake garden below. (The ground was not yet sanded nor enclosed by its wall.) Awaiting orders on what to do next, at one side would be a group of kawara-mono—experienced riverbank workmen—with a good idea of how things should be done. Among them were two, Kotaro and Hikojiro, who were probably the foremen. And moving about among the heaps of waiting rocks, selecting and pointing out the stone to be handled next, was the man directing the work. It might have been Soami, as tradition avers. It might have been the head priest, Tokuho Zengetsu. It might have been some other priest or artist of Kyoto whose name has not come down to us. Or might it have been Sesshu . . . ?

During the progress of the work friends would have dropped in to watch—other priests and artists from nearby monasteries. And coming often would have been the patron, Masamoto, whose suggestions would have been politely asked for.

Progress would have been slow. I have watched a young Japanese student of esthetics sit with a tray of sand and a collection of small stones, trying to reproduce the balanced harmony of Ryoan-ji—only to give it up at last with a resigned shake of the head.

But finally, all was perfected. The ground was smoothed, the wall built, the sand spread and raked into long, straight lines. Then the rain fell, brightening and darkening the colors. And as its pearly, misty light filled the garden, there appeared that feeling of yugen, tranquility, and the mystery of beauty in harmony.

Kotaro and Hikojiro, aware that they had participated in the making of a masterpiece, cut their names roughly into the back of one of the stones, as artists put a seal on a painting. The two names can be easily read today. Ryoan-ji may be the only signed piece of garden art in the world.

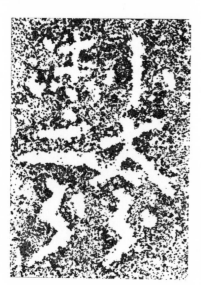

Fig.3. This rubbing of characters cut into the back of one of Ryoan-ji's taller stones reveals that they can be read as the names of two men, Kotaro and Hikojiro. It is believed that these names were cut into the stone as a sort of signature by two of the workmen who helped place the stones. Research through contemporary records has shown that two men by these names did work in Kyoto's gardens in the late 1480's. (From Kyo no Niwa, Kyoto Meien no Kai, 1959)

Painstaking research by Mr. Shigemori, through contemporary records, discloses that there were, indeed, in Kyoto at that time, two garden craftsmen called Kotaro and Hikojiro.[10] They must have been outstanding in this work to have been mentioned at all. But we cannot consider them as among the persons who might have wholly carried out the garden concept. The kawara-mono were people without the advantages of education and culture. They could learn techniques by doing, but they could not create subtle parables of philosophy.

At that time, some of these men were already beginning to think of themselves as professionals, persons who could take full charge of a job. Later some did become real professionals, assuming responsibility from designing to completion. But when scholars, artists, and mystics finally turned over garden making to such men, a new era had begun.

Ryoan-ji, fortunately, was never plundered of its rocks as were so many gardens when the dictator Hideyoshi was gathering up stones from everywhere. Instead, when he visited Ryoan-ji to see the cherry blossoms, which evidently grew elsewhere on the estate, he was so impressed that he had a sign put up ordering his men not to touch trees or rocks.[11]

The rocks have weathered to ancient greys, while moss creeps about their bases and trees spring high beyond the aging wall. For nearly five hundred years Ryoan-ji has presented its mystery to the world, unchanged and unchanging.

CHAPTER EIGHTEEN

Gardens of Power and Glory: Kokei and Sambo-in

THE weary decades of the sixteenth century dragged on, marked by fighting and disorder. It was not a single, long-drawn campaign but scattered, intermittent fighting, as one baron or another found opportunity to enrich himself at the expense of a weaker neighbor. The emperor lived, as always, in Kyoto, but eventually his palace was hardly habitable and even food was often a problem. The city was shabby and shrunken, only a ghost of the former glorious capital.

It was during this century, sometime after 1542, that Europe heard firsthand details of Japan through shipwrecked Portuguese sailors. Shortly after the discovery came Portuguese Jesuit missionaries and traders and, not far behind them, other traders, Dutch and English. The Jesuits were to play an important part in Japanese religious history, while the Dutch and English made some contributions to general Japanese knowledge, notably of firearms. But on the whole these Europeans had remarkably little influence on the cultural and artistic life of the nation, and none at all, as far as we can see, on the gardens.

Peace was brought once more to Japan by a succession of three great generals. The first was Oda Nobunaga, a small baron of central Japan; the second was his lieutenant, the one-time peasant, Hideyoshi; the third was Nobunaga's ally and neighbor, Tokugawa Ieyasu. The first of this trio, by luck and skill, was able to establish himself in Kyoto and there receive the imperial commission to pacify the country. Under him disappeared the last of the Muromachi shoguns. When Nobunaga was murdered, Hideyoshi stepped into his place, and when Hideyoshi died, Ieyasu became his successor.

Nobunaga, a typical provincial baron, is of little interest compared to his lieutenant, Hideyoshi. This man is probably the most remarkable that Japan has produced. He was born in 1536 as one of the lowest of Nobunaga's retainers, son of a peasant and foot soldier. The boy grew up small, dark, monkey-faced, and mischievous, his unprepossessing physical appearance being a handicap all his life. Yet behind his monkey face he possessed a sagacity that was to make him the true ruler of the nation. The unsettled time made it possible for genius to find its level; he rose from Nobunaga's lower to higher servant, then to advisor, and finally to trusted general. It is believed a large part of Nobunaga's success was due to Hideyoshi's advice.

172

Nobunaga built the castle of Azuchi in 1578. With a great keep, bastions, and moat, it was the first such structure ever seen in Japan. The fundamental idea, it is believed, came from Europeans, with whom Nobunaga was friendly. In spite of its moats and walls, the Japanese castle was very different in appearance from European strongholds (Plate 127). Its high central tower was faced with many small, tile-roofed gables, while golden dolphins glittered as roof finials. Separate buildings within the compound included living apartments which were lavishly decorated with sliding partitions covered with gold leaf and painted in rich colors. This exuberance in gold and color was influenced by Chinese Ming architecture. It set the mood of decoration for the whole following period.

The Muromachi esthetic, with its canons of austere simplicity, was much too severe for popular acceptance. It survived, in modified form, in the tea ceremony and in some Zen temples, while the new rulers reveled in richness and brilliance.

Other barons quickly erected castles like Nobunaga's. But when Hideyoshi came to power he built the strongest, largest, and most gorgeous of them all in Osaka. It was an expression of his megalomania, for everything Hideyoshi undertook had to be on the largest and most magnificent scale imaginable.

One of Nobunaga's first acts after taking over Kyoto had been to order the dilapidated imperial palace rebuilt. He also started other reconstruction, but it was Hideyoshi who brought the city to its next great period. New streets were laid out, a moat and ramparts built, and many new buildings erected. Most impressive of these was the great castle-palace which Hideyoshi built as his own headquarters in the city. It was called the Mansion of Assembled Pleasures, Juraku-dai, and stood on the site that had been occupied by the first great imperial palace of Heian, seven hundred years before. This area had long been virtually a wilderness. The last of the rebuilt enthronement halls had again burned, and fire had swept the other buildings also. Now, evidently, it was an available site near the center of the city.

Juraku-dai was more of a palace than a castle, although according to a contemporary record it included a typical high barbican which "towered like a mountain."[1] Several pictorial maps which still exist show the general layout of the extensive grounds—about two miles square—within their moats and walls.[2] Features included a large lake, an artificial hill, numerous trees, and many buildings scattered about, with a certain amount of landscaping around them.

To build the artificial hill, over four thousand loads of earth were requisitioned,[3] and the feudal lords, as well as various large religious institutions, were called upon to furnish trees and fine rocks. Even the gardens of private citizens were forced to give up their treasures. Hideyoshi was carrying on here that career in garden plundering which has made his name a byword in Japanese garden history.

Juraku-dai had been planned for the express purpose of entertaining the emperor, as Yoshimitsu, two hundred years before, had been host to the sovereign in the Gold Pavilion. That earlier event was now studied to learn proper court procedure on such an occasion, for no one then living had taken part in a great imperial visit such as this.

The date was set for early May in 1588.[4] This is the season in Kyoto when the azaleas reach the peak of their color and brilliance. These flowers have never been one of those traditionally celebrated in Chinese poems and other literary works (as are the pine and bamboo). Hence we do not find them mentioned. But remembering the love of color at this period, I think we shall not be far wrong in guessing that azaleas had been extensively transplanted into Juraku-dai, and the imperial visit was timed to coincide with their blooming—even as the visit to the Gold Pavilion took place in the season of the cherry blossoms.

On the great day of the visit, Hideyoshi hurried early to the palace and there, in his official capacity as regent, carried the long train of the emperor as he walked to the imperial ox coach. He then rode back in a lesser coach. The procession of princes, nobles, and ministers accompanying the emperor was longer than the mile which separated the imperial palace from the gates of Juraku-dai. Vast crowds lined the way, for such a sight had not been seen in the capital for many weary years of poverty. Great days had come again to Kyoto.

The visit had been planned for three days but was extended to five. The entertainment, as at the Gold Pavilion, included banqueting, music, dancing, and poem writing. At the poem party, the subject chosen was the traditional one of "pines," inspired by the pine symbolism of unchanging life and prosperity. Probably it was focused on some finely shaped pine trees which had been moved into the garden.

Wrote the Emperor Goyozei: "Well does it repay me, having waited until today to see the pine branches in unchanging prosperity, age after age."

To which Hideyoshi replied: "It is because my Liege Lord has deigned to visit me that the beautiful pines show themselves so green against the eaves."[5]

Hideyoshi lived in Juraku-dai only four years. Then, nominally turning over his office of regent to a nephew, he retired to Osaka Castle. But several years later he began another large new castle-palace at Fushimi, a southern suburb of Kyoto. Juraku-dai was dismantled after a few years. Many of its fine garden stones went to Sambo-in, a temple where Hideyoshi was sponsoring the reconstruction of the garden. Some of the Juraku-dai buildings went to the new castle, and others were given away to certain favored temples.

The great Buddhist foundation of Nishi Hongan-ji received the building that had served as Hideyoshi's private apartment within the immensity of Juraku-dai. Known as the Pavilion of the Flying Cloud or Hiun-kaku, it is a small structure somewhat like the Gold Pavilion (Plate 134). Its interior shows strong influences from the tea ceremony, which Hideyoshi enjoyed, for evidence exists that when there was no need to make a public impression he preferred simplicity to gorgeousness.

Today, the Pavilion of the Flying Cloud is perched rather forlornly on the rocky banks of a little pond, in a small garden belonging to Higashi Hongan-ji. The garden is known as Tekisui-en and is in no way a suitable setting for the building. Originally it had stood either on an island or on the lake shore of Juraku-dai, for one of its porticos forms a boathouse. Pleasure boats could come entirely inside the building and be reached by interior steps.

The tiny pond of Tekisui-en is today spanned by an enormous stone bridge, cut and shaped from a single piece of granite. It is over twenty feet long, three and a half feet wide, and nearly a foot thick. It must have been one of the garden adjuncts moved from Juraku-dai, and its massiveness is typical of the rocks used in the great castle gardens. The use of cut-stone bridges is one of the innovations of this period.

Hideyoshi's new castle-palace in Fushimi is thought to have held within its walls the most magnificent array of buildings ever assembled in Japan. The hillside on which it stood was later planted extensively to peach trees, and from this it has come to be called Momoyama or Peach Hill. The word Momoyama is used to designate the style of art and architecture of Hideyoshi's period and is almost synonymous with gold and rich colorings.

Like Juraku-dai, Fushimi Castle had but a short existence. Only twenty-five years after Hideyoshi's death it was dismantled, and its splendid halls, gates, and other buildings were given away to various temples. The best of these, including the great audience hall (Plate 133), went to Nishi Hongan-ji, where they still stand, the most resplendent examples of Momoyama architecture and art remaining.

Sir George Sansom describes these halls: "On the walls, mostly of bright gold, there are blue-eyed tigers prowling through groves of bamboo, or multi-coloured *shishi*—mythical beasts like lions, but amiable and curly-haired—that gambol among peonies against a golden background. There are gorgeous landscapes, thick with old pines and blossoming plum-trees, where bright birds perch on fantastic rocks or float amid ripples of deep blue. There are groves and banks and gardens, rich with brilliant leaves and flowers; bearded and sinuous dragons winding their complicated length through sepia clouds; gaggles of wild geese sweeping across the moon; scenes of the Chinese court peopled with ancient worthies. As a rule these apartments display, suite after suite, such profusion of colour and detail, such a deliberate effort to overwhelm the eye with splendour, that they come perilously near to vulgarity. But from this they are generally saved by a certain bravery, a boldness of stroke and a brilliance of design. Their full mastery can only be appreciated through comparison with less competent works of the same school."[6]

Power and wealth, subtly expressed in such paintings (Plates 130, 131), was also the dominant theme of the gardens belonging to the castles. The finest to survive today lies within the grounds of Nishi Hongan-ji. It is just outside the great reception hall that was once part of Fushimi Castle and was moved to its present spot about 1632. After this hall had been transferred, beam by beam, the garden that had stood adjacent, it is believed, was also moved, rock by rock, and reassembled in its original form beside the reconstructed hall.[7]

This garden is called the Tiger Glen or Kokei, for the tiger had become a symbol of Hideyoshi and his power and glory. The name was derived from China, for the original Tiger Glen was a valley in the Lu-shan mountains where Hui Yuan had built his monastery and gathered together the White Lotus members.[8] Japan had never known much about real tigers until Hideyoshi campaigned in Korea, where they may still live in the wild. It seems clear from the attitudes and anatomical details of the blue-eyed tigers that prowl the golden screens of Momoyama that Japanese artists worked mostly from pictures of Korean painters (Plate 130).[9]

The Tiger Glen garden suggests a wild mountain gorge where the roar of a tiger might, perhaps, have been heard at night (Plate 132). It is a dry garden, occupying a comparatively small area some ninety-five feet long and sixty feet wide. Its general plan is very like that of Daisen-in, with a stream entering through a mountain cascade and then flowing through a gorge. But Kokei is infinitely removed in spirit from the esoteric painting gardens. It was intended to express the power of the military and harmonize with the splendid hall adjacent. In this it succeeds admirably by the use of enormous stones, crowded together.

Its dry cascade is topped by four huge, pointed rocks that are lifted to extra height by being set upon an earthen terrace. It is believed this cascade is now the largest arrangement of garden rocks in Japan and probably the largest ever made. The "water" that pours through it is not as graphic as that of Daisen-in, but the feeling of powerful rushing is still strongly present. Other rocky peaks in the background continue the effect of the mountain wall behind.

Unfortunately, as of this writing, the cascade and background rocks are largely obscured by trees and by too many other extraneous plants, so that their full quality cannot be seen. Furthermore, the whole garden is overshadowed by certain immense tile slopes that roof a large building just beyond. In the original garden neither of these probably existed, and the effect of the design must have been considerably heightened.

The stream flowing from the cascade curves around two large islands, the traditional crane and tortoise. The latter, as usual, is identified by its upraised head, which is so large and graphic we can almost make out eyes and a mouth. But otherwise the islands are without traditional form. They are linked to each other and to the shore by a series of large stone bridges. It would be possible to use these bridges in taking a short stroll across the islands from one end of the garden to the other. But there would be no point in doing so; the path begins and ends nowhere.

Two of these bridges are monolithic cut stones, like the one taken from Juraku-dai to Tekisui-en. The central bridge is about fifteen feet long and proportionately wide and thick. In connecting two of the islands, it forms the central point of the garden picture and creates a strong cross line in the design.

In this garden there appears the foreshadowing of a new era in garden making, in the use of pre-existing units, combined without regard to their significance. For example, the presence in a mountain gorge of islands from the far Eastern Ocean, together with the fact that these once mystic isles are here linked by bridges, shows that there was no real knowledge of the tale. Crane and tortoise islands had become stereotypes under the name of Horai, a vague paradise, and were now part of a formula for all military gardens. Other rock stereotypes, such as the Shumisen and the three-gods arrangements, can also be identified. It is evident that men of learning were not supervising the making of such gardens.

We know little about the men who made the Fushimi Castle garden. We are aware that they were professionals, for by this time certain rock craftsmen had come to regard themselves as artists and showed this by taking professional names—as was the custom with painters. The maker of Kokei is said to have been Asagiri Shimanosuke.[10] This is certainly

30. Garden entrance: bamboo gate suspended by ropes, Koetsu-ji, Kyoto. ▶

31 (overleaf). Bamboo fence designed by the famous artist ▶
Koetsu for his own garden, Taikyo-an, Koetsu-ji, Kyoto.

a pseudonym (with a slightly overdone sound) since it means "Morning Mist, Man of the Island." Nothing is known about him, although there have been some attempts to identify him with certain tea masters of the time.

But if the castle gardeners were lacking in scholarly background, some of them, nevertheless, were possessed of great ability in understanding the problem of design in this garden. The tiger valley theme is carried out by making the mountain gorge it represents on practically a natural scale. That is, it is all on the human scale. There is no attempt here to lift, imaginatively, a few rocks into a whole mountain. Such an attempt could never have been successful with the military patrons, who had little esoteric imagination. And it would not have harmonized with the immense building beside it.

Instead, this corner of the glen was planned to be seen as an actual part of a mountain. Although the rest is out of sight, the mountain's presence is powerfully felt as we look at the massive stones of the glen. No work of man, even such a work as this large building, could overwhelm hills created by this suggestion. The building and the tiger spirit thus take their places in proper relationship to it.

To conceive and execute such an original concept indicates a high degree of creative artistry on the part of whoever designed this garden. Although he had to use traditional patterns, he was perfectly aware of the problem, and his solution shows a concept close to genius. The early Momoyama gardens held only a foreshadowing of decadence.

An unusual aspect of Kokei garden is the extensive use of the sago palm *(Cycas revoluta)*. Old drawings show that it has always held many of these, and they must have been renewed as necessary. Since these are semitropical plants which normally grow only in the southernmost part of the Japanese islands, Nobunaga is said to have favored them as impressive exotics at Azuchi Castle. A few appear among the paintings on the gold sliding partitions from Fushimi Castle. With their massive trunks and heavy fronds they harmonize well with this type of garden. Cycads doubtless grew in the Fushimi Castle grounds and were transferred to Kokei along with its stones.[11]

One more of Hideyoshi's important gardens survives, that of Sambo-in temple (Plates 77–78, 126). It lies just over the Eastern Hills from Kyoto and but a short ride from the site of Fushimi Castle. Its vicinity has long been famous for cherry blossoms—as it still is. Every April the profusion of flowering trees in the neighborhood creates petally clouds of pink against the blue of the spring sky, and crowds of people come out to enjoy the sight.

This spot was evidently a favorite with Hideyoshi, for Gien, the abbot of Sambo-in, mentions in his diary[12] that Hideyoshi visited the temple several times. On one occasion he offered to rehabilitate its old Muromachi garden. The two men even talked over details of the reconstruction on later visits, but nothing came of this until early in the spring of 1598. Then Hideyoshi suddenly decided to hold one of his grand outings in that vicinity. He ordered the temple and garden prepared immediately for use as his headquarters.

There were only six weeks in which to get ready. The building itself was hastily decorated and the garden refurbished as much as possible. The outing took place successfully. The camp for most of the guests was on a hilltop nearby. Outing parties in April, such as

◀ *32. Cryptomeria trees beyond a hedge, Koetsu-ji, Kyoto.*

this, "to view the cherry blossoms," are really prolonged and often riotous picnics of several days, the flowers serving merely as an excuse for much drinking, entertainment, and gaiety.

With the affair over, the complete reconstruction of the garden began. Three hundred workmen arrived in charge of Kawara-mono Sen, one of the Fushimi head garden men. His gang must have started moving rocks from Juraku-dai and doing other heavy work, including the excavating. When it came time to begin putting in the stones, another head garden man arrived from Fushimi. He was called Yoshiro and was also a riverbank man.

Like old Zen'ami of Muromachi days, Yoshiro appears to have been one of the river-bank people who were endowed with artistic ability and talent in this field. On him was to fall the almost impossible task of putting into this garden, finally, the incredible number of stones that Hideyoshi had designated for the project. After the first completion of the garden, rearranging these stones was to be his work from time to time for over twenty years. He finally succeeded so well that near the end of the period, in 1618, he was given the special honor of a name-title, Kentei, Excellent Gardener, by which he is generally known. He was also praised by the emperor Goyozei.[13]

Almost the first rock to be brought from Juraku-dai was one known as the Fujito Stone. Today it may still be seen in the Sambo-in garden, large, squarish, rather light-colored, not unlike a roughly cut monument (Plate 128). On the far side of the pond it looms against the green background as the single most conspicuous stone among all the stones there.

For reasons now unknown, this rock seems to have been regarded at that time as the most desirable garden stone in the whole country. It has an authenticated history of transfer through several gardens, having originally stood in one of the old Hosokawa estates. Later, Nobunaga caused it to be placed in a garden he was making for the last Ashikaga puppet shogun. To expedite this transfer, it is recorded: "Nobunaga had the stone wrapped in silk, decorated with flowers, and brought to the garden with the music of flute and drums and the chanting of the laborers."[14]

This is an astonishing procedure, unique in Japanese garden annals. Later, Hideyoshi acquired the stone by paying a thousand koku of rice for it—perhaps an almost equally astonishing way for him to acquire any rock. He first had it placed in Juraku-dai. Later it was taken to Sambo-in. Its travels serve to illustrate exactly how garden stones moved from one estate to another. In the end, Sambo-in became the final resting place, not only of the Fujito Stone but of over seven hundred others, most of them, probably, having some history of movement from garden to garden.

By summer after the cherry picnic, Gien was able to send word to Hideyoshi that the garden was basically completed. Water had been run through the cascade and the plants set out. It is probable that Hideyoshi never saw it, for shortly after the flower-viewing party of the spring he had become ill. In late summer he became worse, and in September he suddenly died. Instead of a second fine outing the following spring, his delayed public funeral took place in Kyoto in June.

After his death, the political world was full of intrigue to secure his power. Sambo-in was of no interest to anyone but Gien and the gardeners. They, however, continued to work over it lovingly, as on a masterpiece. For the next twenty years it received the attention of Kentei. During that time a number of things must have been changed. For instance, we know that the cascade was remodeled three times until it was considered exactly right. And certain details of bridge, island, and hall that Gien said he had discussed with Hideyoshi do not appear today.

As we enter this garden, the thing which instantly attracts our attention is the vast number of stones. It is easy to believe the whole seven hundred and even more are there. They are used lavishly wherever there is any excuse for them and also where there is none. Quantities border the shore, and others are heaped on the islands. The flat area between the shore and the buildings is strewn with them—for no possible reason except for display—while the background hillocks are set with stones much as a merchant might lay out his wares.

Almost every one of these stones is an extraordinarily good one, of fine shape, interesting color, and texture. Among them can be noted many with flat tops, the sort typically favored by the Muromachi garden makers, showing that they probably came from gardens of that period. Examination shows that the finer stones are in the foreground, while the rougher ones are in the rear. However, although so lavishly used, great skill went into their arrangement. Indeed, only great skill (and infinite patience) could have juggled so many into place without creating a jumbled and choked appearance, and this definitely is not the feeling the garden gives.

The stones are usually well related and grouped, except for the specimens laid out on display. Many of the arrangements have both strength and character when taken by themselves. The twenty years that Kentei spent in working over this garden must have gone into arranging and rearranging these hundreds—trying one here, another there, shifting and changing, finally to get everything as right as possible.

When the garden was pronounced finished, it was generally agreed to be unsurpassed anywhere. If the long period of retouching took away some of its vitality and strength, it left it, nevertheless, the most finished and debonair of the Momoyama rococo gardens. Few important changes seem to have been made in it since, and apparently it has always been well maintained. As we see it today it is probably very much as Kentei left it, about 1618.

Its chief weakness results from this same concern with detail. While it is possible to stroll through the garden, crossing the several bridges, Sambo-in was primarily meant to be seen from the porches of a line of buildings which look out upon it. From these there appears a certain lack of unity in the overall design. At whatever point we stop to view it, we have the feeling that it might appear better were we to move on a bit. This is curiously attested to by the fact that no two photographs ever seem to have been taken from the same spot—as would necessarily have been the case were the design better unified. Nevertheless, from whatever angle Sambo-in is viewed, it always presents a pleasing picture, in itself no small achievement.

One new feature appears in this garden for the first time—a new style of bridge. It is made of logs, earth, and sod, its foundation consisting of four strong log legs standing in the water. Arching over these is the floor, made of saplings, and piled on this are sod and small plants, with a gravel walk. The whole structure is necessarily large and bulky, tending, in this particular garden, to be out of proportion and out of key with its elegance. Such bridges, of course, do not last indefinitely and must occasionally be rebuilt, so no originals remain.

Although Sambo-in is a temple garden, it has more the feeling of a palace than of a place for retreat and meditation. There is about it more than a hint of the old, courtly shinden style of mansion, done in a miniature Momoyama way. For instance, there is the suggestion of the old end pavilion in a projecting little porch near the water. There is also a streamlet, so characteristic of the Heian estates. It arises behind the buildings, flows around and under them, and finally crosses the near side of the garden to enter the pond. This late adaptation may give us a somewhat better idea than anything else existing today of what the streamlets were like behind the Heian buildings (Plates 77–78).

It is evident, then, that the theme of this garden was pleasure, elegance, and richness. The number of stones and their extravagant use tend toward the same end as do the golden ornaments of the great halls—"a deliberate effort to overwhelm the eye with splendour." But, as in other good examples of Momoyama art, Sambo-in is curiously saved from vulgarity by a certain delicacy, a restraint that vanishes in later gardens of this kind.

Out of the intrigues that followed Hideyoshi's death the leader who won his power and became shogun was Ieyasu, head of the Tokugawa family of central Japan. He had been Hideyoshi's ally and was a powerful baron. Like Yoritomo, four hundred years before, Ieyasu decided to center his actual government away from Kyoto and so began to strengthen his new castle at Edo. This was situated at the head of the present Tokyo Bay, some three hundred miles from Kyoto. He decided, however, that his new prestige demanded that he should also have his own castle-palace in Kyoto, to use during his visits there and to serve as headquarters for his governor in that district.

Thus he began the construction of Nijo Castle in 1602.[15] It occupied an extensive area just south of the old Juraku-dai, which by then had been almost dismantled, its buildings distributed to various institutions, its garden rocks gone largely to Sambo-in. The plan for Nijo Castle called for a large garden to center a wide inner court. To build this, the same garden men from Fushimi who had recently finished the basic work at Sambo-in were probably called on. The Nijo rockwork has been attributed to Kentei, largely because it shows many of the same characteristics as that of Sambo-in.

The general effect of the two gardens, however, is quite different. Similarities include the use of an unusually large number of stones and the manner in which they are set up to make an impressive display. Some of the larger and rougher rocks that had been left behind at Juraku-dai when selections were being made for Sambo-in were probably picked up for Nijo. Probably, too, the Muromachi estates were given a last gleaning, for many of the Nijo stones, as at Sambo-in, have the flat tops of Muromachi.

Some fifteen years after it was first built, Nijo Castle was given a thorough renovation so that it would serve, in 1620, as a fitting family residence from which a bride could take her departure for her new home. She was Kazuko, the sixteen-year-old granddaughter of

184

Ieyasu, and she was to become the consort of the young Emperor Gomizunoö. Such marriages between the sovereign and a daughter of the house which held actual power had long been customary. But few of these imperial brides had come from any but the family of a high court noble.

When, a few years later, she had become a mother, she was elevated to the rank of empress. Her family then decided it was a proper time to entertain the imperial couple as Hideyoshi and Yoshimitsu had done. The time for this visit was set for the autumn of 1626.[16] Nijo Castle was expanded by the addition of several fine buildings to house the imperial party. The garden was also revamped or extended so as to face these new buildings, as well as the older ones. In consequence, it presents a full face in three directions, a most unusual layout. The renovation work done at this time was under the supervision of Kobori Enshu, the shogun's commissioner of public works, who was later to become more widely known.

Today, Nijo Castle, now an imperial property, has the status of a "detached palace." But it is maintained virtually as a museum. Its walls, gatehouses, and moats are little changed, but the great donjon tower brought from Fushimi Castle was struck by lightning in 1791 and burned. Ieyasu's four great audience halls are maintained in their former splendor. They are massive Momoyama-style structures, their rooms walled, as usual, by richly painted sliding partitions. The four buildings are set obliquely on a straight line, so that the southwest corner of each gives toward the garden, which is set in the spacious courtyard.

The garden, which covers about an acre, is larger than it appears in centering the wide level space (Plate 129). Beyond it now stretches the empty area once filled by the new structures that housed the imperial guests for a few days. (Later these halls were moved to become part of a new imperial residence.) In its central position, surrounded by wide stretches of smooth pebbles, the garden seems like a massive set piece of rock and stone. It creates almost the same effect as that given by a large central fountain decorated with statuary in a European pleasance.

Older pictures show that the pond was frequently left dry, revealing its heavily pebbled bottom. The rocks rise from these pebbles as from a water surface. That is, no extra depth of water was planned on so that the bases of the rocks would be concealed. In many garden ponds where the stones are simply laid on the bottom, the effect when the pond is dry is very bad.

There is, in fact, such a strong feeling of dry technique about this garden that it has been suggested it may have been originally planned to be a dry composition like the Tiger Glen. There is also good reason to think that in the beginning there were few or no trees (although there may have been cycads, of which a few remain). Certainly the present trees have not been there a long time, and there are no large old stumps to indicate long periods of previous growth. Today, the presence of the water reflecting the masses of leafy green trees gives this garden a much softer and more picturesque feeling than older photos indicate it was originally intended to have.

While the Nijo garden was meant to be seen primarily from the buildings, it is also possible to stroll through it. The several bridges that cross to the islands are all in the large monolithic style of the period. The lake is very irregular in outline, and the islands are big enough to add to the complexities of the vistas. Water enters from the moat through a cascade in the background area.

When viewed close at hand, the stones of Nijo are so large as to be out of proportion to the size of the garden. However, if they were smaller, they probably would lack character when seen from the buildings. The arrangements show a high degree of artistic skill, but there are some overwrought effects obtained by strong contrasts—tall stones rising very high, or low, broad, massive stones which may have a short, slender upright rock beside them. These effects may also have been planned to give emphasis to the design when seen from a distance. Another device used to obtain clarity is the deliberate use of empty space between the arrangements. The effect, however, when noted from a distance, often tends to seem merely scattered.

While this garden forms a naturalistic landscape in a stylistic way, it is primarily concerned with the arrangement of its stones. Its makers were more interested in the art than in landscape. It has lost inner meaning and has become just an ornament to grace an expression of Tokugawa military power.

CHAPTER NINETEEN

Tea Gardens: The
Dewy Path

WITH the Momoyama period blazing away in color and gold, it is still important to follow the course of the old Muromachi spirit of simplicity and understatement, that spirit which had produced the great black-and-white landscape paintings and their three-dimensional parallels, the Muromachi painting gardens.

The Muromachi esthetic was much too subtle and refined to hold appeal for country military barons and their rough followers. But it did represent something that lies, I think, deep in the Japanese character and will not be lost. In the beginning this had been a simple love of nature. Under Zen it developed into a highly conscious esthetic of naturalism and esoteric art. When the flamboyant taste of Momoyama rose like a gorgeous sunrise, this feeling took a new direction and before very long came to a fresh flowering that was able to appeal to the many and eventually touched almost every phase of the national life.

This new form was *cha-no-yu*, the Japanese tea ceremony. Arising from a Chinese religious background, it bacame, in Japan, a secular exercise in esthetics, with influences that are still strongly evident. Among its immediate adjuncts were developed the tea utensils, the tearoom, and the tea garden.

"Tea garden" brings to the Occidental mind the picture of an outdoor party of sociable tea drinkers—vaguely, something like English tea in the garden. Nothing could be further from the ceremony of cha-no-yu. It is a decorous, almost solemn ritual, always, in its pure form, performed indoors. The tea garden, or *cha-niwa*, is only the special outdoor approach to the tearoom. Basically, it is a garden path.

The tea plant *(Thea sinensis)* is a species of camellia, a native of China (Plate 140). It has tiny, fragrant white flowers which are single miniature camellias with large golden hearts. The plant is a low, compact shrub with glossy evergreen foliage. That a drink made from its leaves had the power to induce wakefulness was known in China from very early times. Tea was a common beverage in the T'ang period and was concurrently known in Japan as a rare imported foreign delicacy. There is a record that the emperor Shomu served tea to a hundred monks in his palace at Nara.[1] At this period the tea leaves were combined with other fragrant things and, after being dried into a cake, were roasted and boiled. This method still survives among the Tibetans and Mongols.

187

Later the tea leaves were powdered, hot water was added, and the mixture was whipped into a froth. This method was developed in the Sung period and is the way the ceremonial tea of Japan is still made, since the ritual had its origin in Sung China. Tea made from the steeped leaves was a later development of the Ming period and is now commonly used throughout the Orient. The Western world knows only this form because few Europeans came to China before the Ming period.

In Sung China the Ch'an monks drank whipped tea before meditating in order to defeat sleepiness. The drinking was made into a ceremony honoring Bodhidharma, reputed to be both the founder of Ch'an and the discoverer of tea. It took place before an image of this saint placed in a recessed altar. The monks gathered before this altar and drank the tea in succession from a single bowl. This detail and the atmosphere of a quiet religious ritual are still features of the Japanese ceremony.

We find art associated with tea drinking in the Gold Pavilion when Yoshimitsu served tea to his friends. The occasions seem often to have been to display and discuss the fine pieces of Sung art then being brought to Japan. These gatherings were formal and elaborate affairs. They developed out of earlier tea gatherings in which the chief entertainment had been a tea-tasting contest. In this the guests took turns sipping various kinds of tea and then identifying them. A prize went to the winner.

The tea plant, by then, was well established in Japan, and the beverage was used by farmers as well as nobles. Groups of farmers are known to have gathered in country cottages to plan protests against the hard conditions of the times, and on these occasions tea was drunk, but without ceremony.[2] The simplicity of these cottage gatherings also had its influence on the final form of the tea ceremony.

For among the Zen monks who were artistic advisors to Yoshimasa in the Silver Pavilion was one named Shuko (or Juko, 1423–1502) who had come from a country background. It was who finally formulated the drinking of tea into a ritual more in accord with Zen ideas of simplicity and esthetics. We do not know just what Shuko's ceremony involved, but it took place, it is believed, in a small room at the back of one of the buildings in the Silver Pavilion garden—the Togu-do, which is still standing. This little room of only four and a half mats (nine by nine feet) is often said to have become the prototype for all Japanese tea-ceremony rooms. It is marked by a plaque on which Yoshimasa himself brushed in the name Shuko-an—that is, Shuko's Retreat.

Shuko held that the basic purpose of a tea gathering should be to inculcate four cardinal virtues: urbanity, courtesy, purity, and imperturbability. (These, to be appreciated, I think, must be viewed against the widespread crudities of the time.) In other words, Shuko's idea was to create an atmosphere in which a little group of people might together attain to serenity and harmony of spirit and, in such a mood, discuss beauty and art and come to some new light about them and perhaps about existence.

The exact form of the tea ceremony has probably undergone much variation since the time of Shuko. But a description of a typical tea ceremony of the present day will aid in understanding its influence on many things, including the garden.

The host invites several friends, five at most, for a cha-no-yu gathering. At the proper

188

time the group assembles at a covered waiting bench provided near the garden gate. When a signal is given, they pass along the path of the small garden surrounding the teahouse and enter the low door of the tearoom.

This room may be one of the regular rooms of the house which has been especially fitted up for the purpose. More often it is a small, separate rustic building in a secluded corner of the garden. One wall of the tearoom is occupied by a shallow recess called the tokonoma. Its floor is a low shelf a few inches above the mats. For the occasion, a painting or an example of beautiful calligraphy has been hung on the back wall of the recess, and an arrangement of flowers, or perhaps a fine bronze incense burner, placed on the low shelf below. This recess, so altarlike in its form, is indeed an altar to beauty and is derived from originals dedicated to Bodhidharma in Chinese monasteries.

The guests enter the tearoom silently, with the utmost decorum. One by one they go to the tokonoma to look at the painting, the flower arrangement, or any other art objects displayed there. The picture and the flowers have always been selected and presented to strike some significant keynote of the occasion, hinting at the reason for the gathering (perhaps an anniversary) or commenting on the beauty of the season. After noting this message the guests quietly take their places on the floor cushions down the length of the room, facing the kettle, which is singing over a container of glowing charcoal at one side. The guest of greatest honor is seated nearest the tokonoma.

Now the host enters, carrying the tea equipment. He takes his place before the hearth and begins to make the tea. All his movements are slow and graceful but simple and direct. They are minutely prescribed, but long practice makes them seem spontaneous. He lifts a bit of powdered green tea leaf from the caddy, using a bamboo spoon, and puts it into the tea bowl. This bowl is larger than a teacup and is generally of some rough pottery material in keeping with the prevailingly rustic atmosphere of the room. Hot water—perhaps half a cup—is lifted by a small wooden dipper from the boiling pot and poured over the tea in the bowl. Then, with a small bamboo whisk which looks not unlike a stiff shaving brush, he beats the mixture until it is frothy.

A few cakes on small plates stand before each guest. The most important guest has begun to nibble at his cake as the tea making goes forward. Now the frothy bowl, strong and bitter, is placed before him. The cakes serve to counteract the bitterness of the drink. He picks up the bowl and drinks, his movements, like those of the host, slow, simple, and direct but minutely prescribed. When the bowl is empty he takes occasion to look at it more closely, turning it over and admiring its form and glaze. Finally, he returns it to the host with a slight bow. It is then wiped clean and a second portion of tea is made for the next guest. This is repeated until all have been served.

In the classical ceremony all the guests drank in succession from the same bowl, in which enough tea for all had been made. In recent decades, in the interest of hygiene, the use of the individual serving has been substituted, but the same bowl is still used in succession by each person.

Such is the tea ritual itself. When those taking part are thoroughly familiar with it, no feeling of strain or malaise is present, in spite of its decorum. Cha-no-yu is extremely

189

popular today as an exercise in good form and self-control. Thousands have memorized its movements and can use them when social usage demands it. But most have little idea that anything very important lies beyond the ritual. Since the means is mistaken for the end, the occasion is ordinarily finished when the last bowl was been drunk.

But those who have a real comprehension of what the tea ceremony stands for know that the ritual is merely an introduction, its purpose to create an atmosphere of mellow tranquility in which the world and its confusions have been put aside and the mind freed for a time to turn to finer things. The conversation which follows the ceremony is the thing that really matters.

When a group with such understanding has finished the last bowl, a certain informality descends on the tearoom. Someone casually breaks the silence by making a remark appropriate to the occasion. Perhaps it is a compliment to the purpose of the gathering or a request to look more closely at some article of the tea equipment—spoon, bowl, or caddy. This is followed by other talk in the same key. The relaxed feeling which has been created by the ritual is not lost during the next hour. Inappropriate subjects, such as business or politics, are never mentioned, nor does the conversation ever become heated.

Shuko's tea ceremony was the vehicle that saved Muromachi esthetics during the disintegrating early years of the sixteenth century. Men who sought peace and beauty, instead of becoming monks as in the earlier period, now turned to the tea ceremony and became "tea masters." They gathered into it all of those distinctive canons of taste that had marked the Muromachi ideal. And they became, like the scholarly monks and artists of the earlier period, arbiters of taste and authorities on cultural matters in general. When the brilliant new Momoyama art appeared, their position was not threatened, for they represented something that seems to be fundamentally congenial to the Japanese temperament. And as the latter part of the sixteenth century swept forward in new vigor and strength, the tea ceremony also reached a high point of development.

There were many tea masters in this period, but the great name among them is that of Sen no Rikyu (1521–91). Like many geniuses in an art, he came from a family which excelled in that art, a family of connoisseurs and tea men. His grandfather had served the Ashikaga shoguns as a tea master, taking the name of Sen'ami. Sen became the family name of his descendants, who today are still the leading teachers of the tea ritual in Kyoto. When the Onin troubles descended upon the capital, Sen'ami's son Yobei settled in the seaport city of Sakai, near Osaka. Sakai was scarcely troubled by the civil wars, for it was much like a European free city. The Sakai merchants were well-to-do and not without their own culture. Yobei seems to have prospered. His social status was that of a high-class merchant, for he was a dealer in art and in adjuncts of the tea ceremony, as well as a teacher of the ritual.

Yobei's son Soeki, later known as Sen no Rikyu, was born in Sakai, probably in 1521. He began to take lessons in the tea ceremony at the age of seven, and, his talent being soon recognized, he was taught by Shoö, who had been the pupil of Shuko and was then regarded as the greatest master since.

At sixteen, Rikyu presided alone over his first ceremony, an event equivalent to his debut in the art. Young Sen seems early to have set up his own establishment. It was probably first in Sakai, but when Nobunaga had restored peace to Kyoto, he moved to that city. His name became widely known, and in middle life it reached Nobunaga, who called him to preside over his own gatherings.

While Nobunaga was known as a patron of the tea ceremony, it seems clear that he could have had but little appreciation of its real meaning. In his hands it became another means for ostentation. When he invited the Sakai art dealers to bring their choicest tea treasures for his inspection, he purchased all they showed him, paying more than they asked. Then he sent them back for more.[3]

Hideyoshi was also a patron of the tea ceremony, and under these two leaders it became nothing less than a popular fad. Part of its appeal was probably genuine enough, for, like the Zen meditation of an earlier day, it provided warriors with short periods of escape from the turmoil of military life. Probably, too, its practice gave provincial captains a pleasing sense of being cultured and refined.

In this period the tea ceremony often had to struggle to maintain its tenets of simplicity and quiet. The historic example of its going to the opposite extreme is known as the Great Kitano Tea Party. It was held by Hideyoshi about the time he moved into Juraku-dai. Notices were set up in Nara and Sakai, as well as Kyoto, announcing a monster gathering of tea devotees to be held in the pine grove of Kitano Shrine. Everyone interested was invited to come on the appointed days—a period in mellow autumn. Those who wished were allowed to erect temporary shelters to hold tea gatherings and display tea treasures.

Nearly four hundred people accepted this invitation. Enclosures, marked off by striped curtains in the traditional way, were set up by individuals, and tea ceremonies began as devotees met their friends, entertained, and were entertained.[4] Hideyoshi's collection of tea utensils was displayed in four sections, and he himself served tea to some of his highest vassals. Later he went from place to place, looking at the various articles on display.

The Great Kitano Tea Party is one of the wonderful paradoxes in Japanese art history. It was a perfect manifestation of the Momoyama spirit and completely at variance with the true spirit of cha-no-yu. Rikyu and many of those present must have been aware of this, but such opinions were kept discreetly unspoken. Nevertheless, Rikyu evidently felt that Hideyoshi was capable of some comprehension of its inner meaning, for occasionally he administered a lesson. Such a one is illustrated in the story of the morning-glories.

According to this tale, Rikyu one summer grew fine morning-glories in pots. They were so beautiful that word of them reached Hideyoshi, who expressed a desire to see them. Rikyu therefore invited him to an early-morning tea ceremony. When Hideyoshi arrived at the garden there was not a blossom in sight. Angry at what seemed a deliberate affront, he stalked into the tearoom, to find there a single perfect blossom, perfectly displayed. Rikyu was a master of flower arrangement, which he held to be one of the essentials for a tea man. He had removed all the bright display of other flowers, leaving this one perfect blossom to hint at the whole world of their beauty.

Rikyu's ideas on the form of the tea ceremony, the tearoom, and the garden have come to be regarded as classical standards. He is credited also with being the one who made it possible for cha-no-yu to become generally popular. His ideas on its simplicity brought it within the reach of all. These ideas are expressed in some of the poems attributed to him, including the following:

> Just one kettle
> Is enough for cha-no-yu—
> How lacking in surety to yearn
> For many utensils![5]

> Ceremonial tea:
> It is only to boil water,
> Make the tea
> And drink it—
> Nothing more.[6]

Since the object of the tea ceremony was to build up a serene detachment from the world, every feature of the setting was designed to contribute to this end. Rikyu imagined the tearoom to be a sylvan retreat, a hut far off in the hills or by the shore. One of the poems he quoted expressing this idea is translated:

> In the distance,
> Neither flowers nor maple leaves
> Are to be seen;
> Only a thatched hut beside the bay
> In autumn's twilight.[7]

This, of course, was but an echo down the centuries from those retreats in the mountains to which the Chinese poets, monks, and artists had escaped in earlier years and which had been perpetuated by such persons as Po Chu-i with his Grass Cottage on Lu-shan. Since Po's writings have always been great favorites in Japan, I think it not improbable that the description of the Grass Cottage itself, as Po wrote it down, may have been one of the influences in developing the form of the tea hut.

It will be recalled that the Grass Cottage was a small thatched structure in which the woodwork was hewn but not painted, the walls mud-plastered but not given a white finish, the windows filled with bamboo lattices and oiled paper, while the doorstep was a natural stone. Such, even today, is the Japanese tea hut (Plate 137).

But humble as was such a shelter, Rikyu taught that it should show the innate beauty of its simple materials—the exquisite grain of the wood, the warm color of the sand in the plaster. It must also possess the subtle refinement which would inevitably be impressed on such a place were it the retreat of a cultured and artistic person. Moreover, it must be free from any of the grubbiness usually associated with rustic surroundings. Perfect cleanliness is one of the basic principles of the tea art.

The garden which surrounds the tea hut is now usually spoken of as the "dewy ground"

33. Autumn foliage above a wall, Saiho-ji, Kyoto. ▶

or "dewy path"—that is, *roji* (Plate 138). The word comes from a passage in one of the Buddhist sutras which Dr. Harada has interpreted as being the spot where men are reborn after fleeing from the fiery abode of avarice.[8] The tea garden is thus a way of escape, a transition between the solitude of the tearoom and the distractions of workaday life. Continuing Rikyu's ideas, the tea garden represents just such a path into the wilds as one would take to reach the tea-hut retreat.

The technique of the tea garden calls for suggestions which will build up a feeling of having gone far and left worldly cares behind. Sometimes the path is divided into inner and outer portions by a light gate in the middle (Plate 139). The outer portion represents the part nearest civilization; the inner, that part farthest away, where nature is wilder. But the tea garden is the least artificially artful of all Japanese garden forms.

Especially sought in it is a quality known as *wabi,* which may be translated as rustic solitude. Yugen or tranquility is also desired. A third quality, *sabi,* implies the patina of age found in the color of weathered stones, the mosses and lichens acquired through many years. All these give that sense of timeless serenity which is the essence of the tea setting.

Having no set form nor lasting stone arrangements, no ponds nor hillocks to resist the wear of time, tea gardens have not survived the years as well as have some other Japanese garden forms. Rikyu seems to have built or aided in the construction of many, but not a single one of these, nor any of his period, remains in a form which can certainly be regarded as original. The one which comes closest to it, probably, is at the little country temple of Myoki-an in the village of Yamasaki, a few miles south of Kyoto (Plate 142).

Rikyu apparently had a country house near here, and there is evidence that he probably planned a tearoom and garden for the priest of this temple. A map of the vicinity made at the end of the sixteenth century shows a tearoom there at that time.[9] Its outstanding characteristic then, as now, was a large tree, called the Sleeve Brushing Pine. According to legend, this name came from the fact that the garden was so small Hideyoshi could not get past the tree to enter the tearoom without brushing his sleeve against it. There is reason to think that Hideyoshi may actually have come to this garden for a tea ritual during one of his campaigns nearby.

The present Sleeve Brushing Pine is not old enough to have been the original in the garden but is estimated to have been planted about a hundred years after Hideyoshi's death, probably replacing the original both in kind and in position. This is a form of continuity widely practiced in Japan.

The teahouse of Myoki-an temple is a tiny structure, a sort of lean-to projecting from the south side of the temple building. The entrance, which tea guests must use, is an outside door, small and typically low, hardly more than a hole. Through this, all members of the party must crawl in equal humbleness, as an object lesson in the democracy that prevails within the tearoom. (This would have had special significance in a stratified society like Japan's at that time.)

The Myoki-an tea garden extends around three sides of this room, being a small space of mossy ground with shrubs and trees. It is crossed by two paths of stepping stones leading

◀ *34. Pattern of stepping stones among pebbles, Katsura, Kyoto.*

to the tearoom door, one from the east and one from the west. The Sleeve Brushing Pine grows in the eastern half of the garden near the building. As things are at present, the path skirts the pine with ample room for anyone to pass it. But in the Momoyama period the arrangement may have been different. The original pine may have leaned across the path. Or possibly the legend was founded only on the limited size of this garden as compared to the great areas around Hideyoshi's palaces. By later standards, however, the Myoki-an garden is rather spacious, a fact regarded as one of its surviving Momoyama characteristics.

Fig. 4. These pages from an Edo-period book show a stylized representation of a tea garden of the early nineteenth century. Guests entered through the gate in the left foreground and went to the covered bench to wait until called into the tearoom. (Beyond the bench was a privy, with a kettle of warm water available to wash the hands.) When the host sounded a gong, the guests filed into the inner garden, right. At night the gate to the inner garden was lighted by a stone lantern. The well by the gate was used for the tea water. Continuing toward the tearoom, the guests stopped at the stone laver, lower right, where a wooden dipper was used to pour water over the hands in ritual cleansing. This area, too, had a stone lantern. The guests entered the tearoom through the low, square door (here shown closed). This means of entry necessitated a humble posture. (Drawing by Akizato Rito, illustrating Tsukiyama Teizoden, *Part II, 1828)*

A second garden associated with Sen no Rikyu survives only in its stone water basin and a story. This basin originally stood in the garden of a temple near Osaka which had a fine view of the Inland Sea. The story about the original garden is not authenticated, but it is one of those anecdotes which might and really should be true.

According to this story, when Rikyu designed a tea garden for this temple he caused two hedges to be planted one outside the other in such a way that they entirely obscured the

196

beautiful view of the distant Inland Sea. It was only when a guest bent over this stone water basin, to dip up water for his hands, that he could see the view between an oblique break in the two hedges. Rikyu's followers, puzzled at this, asked for an explanation. Rikyu quoted the poem:

A bit of water here,
There, between the trees—
The sea![10]

That is, bending over the bit of water in the basin, the owner of a questing mind might see this mind reflected within its small compass and so epitomized. Then, looking up and suddenly catching a glimpse of the splendid infinitude of the ocean, the viewer could realize, in its relationship to the bit of water in the basin, that man is likewise a bit of the Infinite, the same in substance and spirit.

Three other things were contributed to Japanese gardens by the tea masters of Momoyama—the stone lantern, stepping stones, and the stone water basin. These are not found in gardens before the early sixteenth century but appear extensively afterward.

The problem of how to make a naturalistic path both artistic and practical must have received a good deal of attention from the tea men. A path worn through moss is neither attractive nor the best thing to walk on, since invariably its edges become ragged and worn, while the ground grows muddy and slippery in wet weather.

Whoever thought of laying down a line of flat stones to walk on, leaving the moss to grow up, untrampled, around them, hit upon an idea that was both practical and artistic (Plate 138). We do not know who this was, and no garden is known to have been the first to have stepping stones in it. The inventor might have been Rikyu, for he had sufficient originality to have thought of it. But at any rate, stepping stones were used in tea gardens of his time, for one of his notes mentions them.[11] The idea seems to have had immediate appeal. Not long afterward, stepping stones began to be used extensively in larger gardens also (Plates 38, 40, 45, 46).

In time a whole art and science of stepping stones was developed, until today garden makers in Japan know precisely how to place stones both for the practical purpose of walking and to give the most attractive effects. Rikyu is said to have advocated laying them with greater emphasis on their practical use than on their artistic appearance. A later tea man, Oribe, reversed this. Western garden makers could study to advantage the technique of the Japanese in placing stepping stones.

In the Momoyama period the tea ceremony was frequently held at night, so that some way to light the path became desirable. Fires burning in suspended iron baskets had been the usual mode of garden illumination, but the flaring brightness of these torches was not in keeping with the mellow atmosphere of the tea garden. Again we do not know who first had the idea of moving an old stone lantern from a temple compound into the tea garden, but it was a logical thought. The flickering yellow light of a candle (originally a tiny saucer-lamp of oil) behind the paper-lined openings is subdued and surprisingly effective in the dark.

From early Buddhist days lanterns carved from granite had been popular votive offerings

197

to temples and later to Shinto shrines (Plates 43, 135). The idea was probably brought to Japan from Korea when Buddhism and its adjuncts were first being introduced. Such lanterns are not found in China, so they are probably of Korean origin. A fresh interest in these lanterns was aroused during Hideyoshi's campaigns in Korea, for his generals sent home a number of fine ones as loot.[12] From the surviving early lanterns it is seen that many of the best designs were made in the Kamakura period, when stone carving in general reached its peak. Good designs were also made in Muromachi, but later designs are often not so artistic.

While the stone lantern was put into the tea garden for utilitarian purposes, it must at once have become a matter of esthetic consideration. In the beginning the tea masters took old lanterns from neglected temples, their mossy, weatherbeaten appearance harmonizing with the rest of the garden. In a short time, however, lanterns had become such popular garden adjuncts that new ones had to be made to fill the demand (Plate 40). Excellent old designs were copied, the reproductions being called by the name of the temple in which the original stood. At the same time certain tea masters took to designing their own lanterns. So much originality was displayed that finally many lanterns showed little relationship to the shape of the original temple lanterns.

Since most domestic water came from private wells, a well was included in the conventional tea garden as the source of the tea water. The wellhead and pulley were incorporated into the design.

Insistence by the tea masters on cleanliness, especially on washing the hands before entering the tearoom, resulted in the invention of the stone water basin or laver. It is believed that originally a wooden bucket with dipper or a teakettle with warm water may have been placed in a convenient spot for this purpose. Soon, however, a more artistic and permanent arrangement must have been sought, and the appropriate idea of a stone with a depression cut in its top to hold water was thought of (Plates 44, 136).

The stone, at first, was left in its natural form. Later, it was sometimes carved into formal shapes. The early basins were seldom more than a foot or two high; so to reach the water it was necessary to bend or squat before it. A large flat stone in front to stand on was arranged. Gravel covered the surrounding ground where the water fell, preventing a muddy spot. Soon it became customary to place a stone lantern near the basin to light it at night. The arrangement of laver and lantern with their supporting stones then became the chief feature of the tea garden (Plate 141). Such groupings are all that have come down to us in many older gardens.

The tea garden held a few other ornamental stones. These were placed casually, here and there, to appear as if cropping out naturally. Considerable artistry went into this casual placement, but on the whole there is none of that conscious display of stone art which marks the landscape garden.

The ground in the tea garden is covered with moss (if it can be made to grow). Ferns and other small plants cluster around the base of the rocks. Nothing showy or exotic like the cycad is used but only such trees and shrubs as grow wild in the hills or at least look as if they did. Nor is anything with bright and showy flowers allowed, for this would distract from the atmosphere of quiet serenity. Shrubs in tea gardens have graceful forms and usually glossy foliage, but they seem modest and unassuming. Broadleaved evergreens are preferred because they give a feeling of timelessness. The only exception to all this is the inclusion of the traditional "plum" *(Prunus mume),* which blooms modestly in the spring. The small-leaved native maple may also be allowed to bring a bright spot of color in autumn because it is part of the natural Japanese hillside.

These influences, emphasizing quiet green growth, without flowers, have affected all gardens since the time of the early tea masters. The bright masses of flowers mentioned by Lady Murasaki as part of the Heian estates disappeared with that period. The lack of flowers usually surprises Occidental visitors who are aware of Japan's interest in cut-flower arrangements. Flowers for this purpose are grown in nursery gardens, or in a hidden corner, not in the pictorial landscape area.

The tea garden receives the most meticulous care. Every dead leaf and twig and every cobweb must be removed and the moss kept green and clean. Just before guests arrive, the whole garden is usually sprinkled, so that it may be fresh and clean. This custom has been copied in other gardens, the glistening dampness indicating a proper preparation for honored guests. To clean such gardens a small twig broom is used, and even a long pair of chopsticks is found useful to pick out dead leaves from inside a shrub or hedge.

However, cleaning must not be overdone. This is illustrated in the story of how Rikyu taught his son to clean the garden. The boy had gone over every shrub and tree and had swept the moss not once but several times. Still Rikyu was not satisfied. The lad protested there was not a single leaf or twig left to be removed, that he had done everything possible. Rikyu then stepped to a small maple tree, bright with the colors of autumn, and shook it gently, sending down a flutter of tiny scarlet leaves. They lay on the mossy carpet like red flowers, adding the final touch of naturalness to the garden's beauty.

Rikyu's story ends in tragedy. No one is sure what caused the estrangement between him and Hideyoshi. It is thought most likely that the old tea master, then seventy, administered some lessons too severe for the despot's pride. Enemies took advantage of the coolness and whispered that there was a plot to put poison in the tea bowl. Word reached the old master that his life was expected to end.

The final scene reminds us of the death of Socrates. A last ceremonial tea gathering was arranged for a few close friends. All the details in the tokonoma spoke of the fleetingness of life and favor. When the ceremony ended, the equipment was distributed among those present. They left, but one remained to assist in the final rite of the "honorable departure." It was performed in the tearoom which will always be associated with the man who was forced to take his own life within it.

The cloud under which Rikyu died darkened the tea cult for a considerable period and marked its end as a popular fad under Hideyoshi. But its true appeal was too great to be ended by the barbarity of a despot. It was several decades, however, before it again regained some of its general popularity.

The three grandsons of Rikyu each set up his own center of tea instruction in Kyoto, and these three schools have continued in existence to the present day. Each is still operated by members of the Sen family. They are known as Ura Senke, Omote Senke and Mushano-koji Senke, the names being derived from their respective locations. The grounds of each

199

include examples of classical tea gardens. A water basin said to have been used by Rikyu is in one.

Today there are thousands of small tea gardens belonging to private persons. One of the advantages of such a garden is that it can be developed where land is limited. The tea garden has had a strong and continuous influence on all other garden making since Rikyu's day, so that the atmosphere of the dewy path now permeates most of the gardens in Japan which are less than three hundred years old.

CHAPTER TWENTY

Imperial Estates:
Katsura and Shugaku-in

THE tea cult appealed not only to artists and tea men and those who wished to escape from the pressures of a military society. It found a response also among members of the court and even among the emperors. To this is due much of the beauty and interest found in the two largest and finest of the imperial gardens surviving in Kyoto, the great estates of Katsura and Shugaku-in.

Katsura, a typical great landscape in the old courtly style, covers some eleven acres, including a large lake, walks winding over bridges and around mossy hills, and some of the most classical architecture in Japan. It is beautiful because all this is so perfectly cared for, and it is interesting because it shows how the tea cult could affect even large places like this with tea-garden details—stepping stones, teahouses, lanterns, lavers, and most of all the quiet green understatement of the tea path—superimposed on a great estate.

Katsura is especially admired today because its beauties are all to be seen at their best. As an imperial estate, it is always perfectly maintained. And during the three hundred years of its existence, it has never suffered serious damage from fires, storms, or vandals, nor have basic changes been made in it since it was originally completed in the seventeenth century.[1]

Katsura is the creation of two men, father and son, who were members of a little coterie of talented men in the early 1600's, tea masters, artists, and cultivated noblemen. Prince Toshihito (1579–1629) was born a younger brother of the emperor Goyozei, that sovereign whom Hideyoshi had entertained in Juraku-dai. At the time of that visit, the emperor's young brother was ten years old. He must have been an engaging youth, for Hideyoshi, having then no heir, decided to adopt him as his "nephew." Later, when Hideyoshi became the father of a son, the young prince was settled in a mansion near the Imperial Palace in the capital. Proper tutors were provided, and the prince grew into a man of cultivated tastes, expert in music and literature and, later, with strong interests in tea, architecture, and garden making.

He was given a country estate on the Katsura River, not far from the old resort of Arashiyama. Since the days of Lady Murasaki, over five hundred years before, this district had been favored by the courtiers as a site for country houses. It will be recalled that in her novel, Prince Genji owned a retreat at Katsura—even as the real Fujiwara regents possessed such a place. Today, scholars are inclined to accept as a fact the probability that the present Katsura garden was developed on the site of this old Fujiwara estate. This probability is strengthened by the fact that the present basic outline of the main lake, with its very large hilly island, is accurately described by the novelist as one of Genji's estates.

It was not until Prince Toshihito was forty years old that he started to take a great interest in his country property. Then, in 1620, he began extensive improvements which brought the basic outline of the garden to what it is today. The prince evidently accepted the old courtly tradition that garden planning was a proper activity for a gentleman, for the evidence is all that he planned the place himself. Details of the garden's development have not yet been fully established, but it is certain that the prince had as advisors and helpers a number of talented men who are known to have been working in Kyoto at that time.[2] Among his friends was the famous Kobori Enshu.

This man was a gifted tea master and an important official under the Tokugawa government. He was in charge of much of the new construction which the Tokugawa shogunate was sponsoring in Kyoto in the early seventeenth century. Enshu is known to have built a number of important gardens, and to him later times have attributed most of the others of the period, including Katsura.[3] But modern scholars are now certain that Enshu was personally too busy with official work to have done more than offer friendly suggestions to the prince.

However, he had two younger brothers and a number of students who had become accomplished in his field. It appears that some of these men, especially the second brother, Kobori Masaharu, did work at Katsura. The general supervisor carrying out the technical side of the prince's ideas was Nakanuma Sakyo.[4] Although the prince remained the primary designer, the effect these people had on the garden's final form turned it into a sort of joint product, a reflection of the Kyoto of that time, apart from the Momoyama military fashions.

Through the eyes of Suden, abbot of Konchi-in temple, we catch a glimpse of what was going on at Katsura between 1620 and 1625: "Hundreds of workmen made the stream, the mountain, the pond, and the 'southern palace.' Jewel-like pavilions were constructed."[5]

Katsura's lake covers about two acres, and because the ground surface was originally only a few feet above the Katsura River nearby, the lake bed had to be dug some five or six feet below its level to create a flow. The only cascade in the garden, therefore, is but a few inches high. The steep banks of the lake resulting from the extra depth provide the garden with interesting variations in contour.

The lake is one of the most beautiful in Japan. It is not a single wide expanse of water but is made up of several long vistas winding off to unseen destinations. These reflect cloudy masses of foliage sweeping down to the surface and long wavering lines of tree trunks. In places the shore is softened by ranks of iris or by little ferns hanging among the rocks. In summer, mounds of a native water lily build up what seem to be new islands of green.

35. Contrast of textures—cobbles, moss, and sand; Sento Palace, Kyoto. ▶

36. Modern checkered pattern of square stones in moss, designed by Mirei Shigemori; Tofuku-ji, Kyoto. ▶

And just as Lady Murasaki describes it of one of Genji's gardens, it is found that a boat starting up one of the watery vistas goes "straight toward a toy mountain which seemed to bar all further progress. But in reality there was a way round. . . ."

The toy mountain is a very large island, and the way around it is the channel which separates it from the farther shore. This island was originally left when the lake was excavated, and surplus soil was piled on it to a height of thirty feet, making it a real hill. The island is two hundred feet long and ninety feet wide and holds a heavy growth of old trees and bushes as well as several small buildings. To one following the mossy path that winds over this hill, there is no feeling at all of being on a "toy" mountain.

Other details that tie this garden in with Genji's estate are "the little wood on the hill beyond the lake," "the bridge that joined the two islands," and "the mossy banks that seemed to grow greener . . . every hour." These could be details added by the prince to continue the Genji tradition, for he is known to have been a great admirer of this piece of literature. One of the woods is made up entirely of small-leaved maples. Another is covered with stiff cycads (a touch of Momoyama preference). Other slopes have winter bamboo, cryptomeria, pines, and pasannia trees growing on them.

The prince evidently liked so well the idea of a "bridge that joined two islands" he used it twice. In two different places long islands extend into the lake, almost end to end. They are joined together and to the shore by bridges of various kinds to form what are really long peninsulas. These, along with the large hilly island, create the picturesque winding water channels into which the lake is divided.

Katsura today has sixteen bridges, although the principal one in the original design is missing. Made of wood, it has disappeared, but its location is clear. It spanned a large arm of the lake leading directly from the villa to the Shokin-tei pavilion on the opposite shore. To reach it at the present time, a rather long, meandering walk is necessary. Known to have had vermilion-red rails, this wooden bridge must have been in modified Chinese style.

Of the other bridges all that span the main channels are high enough for a boat to pass under. One is in the log-and-sod type of construction, as seen at Sambo-in (Plate 144). Another is a single long piece of granite in the Momoyama manner. Still others are wide flat stones, either natural or trimmed to rectangular form.

The green banks which, in spring, seem to grow greener every hour, as Murasaki says, are sodded. Other banks show an entirely new feature—straight walls of cut and trimmed stones. These walls line three sides of a rectangular arm of the lake where stands the tea cottage called Shoi-ken. Still another innovation is a formalized beach (Plate 147). The lake's banks are cut to slope gradually into the water and then are covered with rounded flat stones. This idea was probably the invention of Kobori Enshu, for similar beaches are found in other gardens in which he is known to have had a hand. The general effect of these flat paving stones is rather stiff. At one point they form a little peninsula jutting out into the water. Its tip is marked by a small stone lantern which must have served as a miniature lighthouse for those boating at night.

The shoreline is protected at other projecting points by the usual large rocks. But as we

◀ *37. Paving detail, Avenue of the Imperial Visit; Katsura, Kyoto.*

come to a big bay, almost a small lake in itself, we seem to be suddenly back among the elaborate creations of Sambo-in and Nijo Castle. For here the shoreline and center islets are all outlined by elaborate groupings of very large stones in the manner of the Momo-yama gardens (Plate 146).

However, styles had inevitably changed a little, especially under Enshu's influence, and rocks around this portion of the lake are not nearly so numerous as in the gardens of the military rulers. Nor are extra rocks laid out as a form of display. Prince Toshihito was no *nouveau riche* with a need to show off his wealth. It appears, rather, that he must have kept a restraining hand on the man who was directing the placement of these rocks, emphasizing suavity and elegance, not showiness (Plate 145).

But in spite of this the rock designing occasionally got out of hand. In several places there rises around the shore a stone that is too tall to be in good proportion to the landscape nearby. These high stones have almost the effect of periodic exclamation points, and that, I think, is what they really were—an effort to underline artistry by emphatic contrast. Some of these tall stones are exceptionally fine in themselves. One magnificent example (Plate 146) stands at the end of a long monolithic bridge which arches to an islet. The tremendous face of this great rock, rising in a sheer, high precipice above the water, would once have been intended to recall the vast cliffs of Chinese Sung landscapes or allude to mystic P'eng-lai. But now this stone has no other purpose than to serve in balancing the horizontality of the massive bridge. Momoyama rock artists certainly never accepted the canons of Zen taste, which, it will be recalled, were to avoid the trite, the obvious, and the emphatic. But they understood very well the principles of unity, scale, and general harmony in a design. With these tall rocks, scale and harmony were slighted, and decadence had gone a small step further.

A famous detail was added to the Old Residence in the form of an outside platform put up expressly as a place from which to view the moon rising over the garden. The moon was inevitably a part of this estate because its name Katsura is the word for a native tree (*Circidiphyllum japonicum*) which is supposed to be seen growing in the moon. The moon-viewing platform is floored merely with round bamboo poles on which cushions were placed. On a clear autumn evening the host and his guests could sit and enjoy its soft light as it rose above the trees. They might compose appropriate verses about the scene or listen to the music of a bamboo flute.

The "jewel-like pavilions" noted by Abbot Suden are small buildings of several rooms used, as were the earlier Gold and Silver Pavilions, for study, for the tea ceremony, and for other esthetic pastimes. Unlike those earlier buildings, these are cottages, simple one-storied structures of natural wood with thatched roofs. Prince Toshihito had three such structures erected in different parts of the garden. Other buildings were later added by his son.

The first prince died when the boy was only ten years old. The young Prince Toshitada (1619–62) was taken under the care of his imperial relative, the retired emperor Gomizu-noö. He received the same sort of education as his father, so that the two men came to have similar tastes.

During the years when the boy was growing up, Katsura garden must have mellowed,

206

deepening its mood of sylvan quiet, of yugen—tranquility—and of wabi—rustic solitude. The young man was twenty-three before he began to take up the development of the garden where his father left off. He appears to have been urged on to this through a letter written by a second wife of the first prince, in which she told of unfinished plans.[6]

The part of the second prince in developing Katsura was to complete and perfect it. He added lookouts from which views might be had of fields lying beyond its enclosing bamboo forest and of distant mountains. He also added another teahouse and, eventually, a small Buddhist shrine to hold the family's mortuary tablets.

This young prince was probably the one who created two areas for sports: an archery range in the form of an alley of trees and a broad, level lawn for running horses and playing the old courtly game of kemari, a sort of football (Plate 80). Today, the lawn's wide, smooth simplicity produces an agreeable contrast to the rippling lake, the patterned masses of the trees, and the rolling banks of moss.

Twenty-three stone lanterns light the path that leads around the garden (Plate 46). Most are original designs, some being quite different from traditional forms. One or two are so low they consist only of a light-holder on the ground. Whenever the garden was used at night, they must all have been lighted by a small dish of sesame oil holding a burning wick. On moonlight nights they would have been dark, offering no competition to the sky.

Eight stone water basins serve for ritually rinsing the hands before going into a room for the tea ceremony. These, like the lanterns, are also highly original in design. One is not really a basin at all but the lake itself where, near the teahouse Shokin-tei, several stepping stones lead out into the lake. On the last stone is laid a dipper with which the water can be lifted and poured over the hands.

It must have been young Prince Toshitada who completed these details and the long path that leads past them. This path, half a mile long, goes over the garden's small hills and valleys like a gold chain draped over heaps of green velvet. A stroll along the path takes one past the various buildings and offers continuous and always varying interest (Plates 45, 46).

The resemblance of the path to a chain is heightened where it consists of a straight line of round stepping stones laid like chain links in deep moss. For variation, flat, angular stepping stones are sometimes used. They are placed in close sequence, to make walking easy. Katsura is said to have 1,716 stepping stones, and the figure seems probable (Plates 34, 46, 147). By the time this garden was made two schools of thought about stepping stones had developed. One held that ease of walking should be given first consideration. The second believed that artistry—how the path looked—was more important than how it served the walker. Both schools may be found demonstrated in the course of a stroll over Katsura's long path.

In the vicinity of certain buildings this path often becomes a kind of pavement (Plate 37). Such sections are really only variants on the stepping-stone idea, for they are a combination of large flat stones and smaller ones, fitted together between straight edges. Rocks like flagstones may make a solid walk. Or large stones may be set a short distance from each other and the spaces between filled in with smaller stones. Another favorite design makes use of lengths of granite cut into long straight pieces. Narrow lengths of granite may

207

edge a patterned walk, or broad pieces of random length may serve as the walk itself. The variety and ingenuity displayed in these pavements seems endless.

Katsura's long path in some ways is the most important thing in the whole garden. It brought to a princely estate the "dewy path" of the tea garden. Never before had paths become the major feature of a great garden. The large stroll garden thus created, with changing interests all along the way, was soon widely copied.

The infinite variety and originality displayed in the designs throughout Katsura reveal that the creative spirit was still strong among the artists and tea masters of this period. During Hideyoshi's day there had been many foreign contacts which had given great impetus to new ideas. Not only had Europeans been welcomed for a considerable period, but Japanese ships had gone to various ports of Asia and the East Indies, and a few Japanese travelers had even reached Europe. Influences from Europe were reflected back, especially in the basic idea of a castle. Comparable structures had never before been seen in Japan. Possibly it was the castle's squared and angular moats and stone walls that gave Kobori Enshu—or someone—the idea of introducing a touch of geometric formality into landscape development. We have noticed an example of this in a rectangular arm of Katsura's lake, and additional examples of straight lines and squared angles were to be added during the last phase of the garden's construction.

Prince Toshitada had probably long planned to show this fine garden to his imperial relative, the retired Emperor Gomizunoö. The latter is known to have been greatly interested in estates and gardens and had visited such places whenever he could. His visit to Katsura finally took place in 1658, when he was over sixty years old and the prince was almost forty.

To accommodate the imperial couple and their attendants the residence in Katsura was enlarged by adding a third section, now called the New Palace, Shin Goten. The rooms throughout are small and simple but very elegant in their refinement. Great attention was paid to such details as the design of shelves and the metal fingerholds in sliding doors. The paper panels which line the interior walls are decorated with black-and-white paintings in the understated Muromachi style.

Nowhere is there a hint of the flamboyant overdecoration in gold and colors which was being used so lavishly elsewhere, especially at Nikko. Katsura's architecture is the delight of Japanese classicists and Occidental moderns.[7] It has undoubtedly been one of the factors, among those other Japanese influences, which have so much affected the development of "contemporary" Western architecture.

Prince Toshitada, in preparing for the imperial visit, also expanded Katsura's main entrance by constructing a new "Imperial Gate" and an "Avenue of the Imperial Visit." The avenue is all in the new geometric mood. Its straight, wide walk, almost a road, is smoothly paved with flat stones, and on either side it is lined by a clipped hedge—a great innovation (Plate 143).

Just beyond an opening in the hedge where the palanquins of the imperial visitors turned off to enter the house, the straight avenue terminates in much the way it would if it were part of a European garden axis. Its vista to the lake behind is closed by a low mound on which grows a single small pine tree, so clipped and trained into artful grace that it has all the qualities of a statue standing on a pedestal (Plate 143). It is called the Suminoe Pine and replaces an older one by that name.

The visit of a retired emperor to a relative, such as this, would have had but little of the pomp which would accompany a state progress to the Gold Pavilion or to Juraku-dai. We can thus picture the imperial guest—a cultured and literate man—enjoying a traditional boat ride up one of the winding water vistas and soon noting with delight the resemblance of the "toy mountain" to the one in the description of Prince Genji's garden. Or we can follow him to a tea ceremony as he strolled along the winding path to one of the tea pavilions.

This emperor, Gomizunoö (1596–1680), came to the throne when he was fifteen. Very soon afterward the Tokugawa shogunate saw to it that Ieyasu's granddaughter entered the palace to become the imperial consort. She is known as the empress Tofukumon'in and was probably one of the reasons the shogunate was so often generous to this sovereign. It was this young couple who had made the state visit to Nijo Castle. On that occasion their host had been the empress's brother, the shogun Iemitsu.

As time went on, however, friction developed between the emperor and the shogunal brother-in-law. It is believed the emperor showed more independence of spirit than was acceptable to the military rulers. (The emperors had never wholly given up the hope of returning to power and intrigued to this end whenever they could.) Iemitsu did not hesitate to be annoying in ways available to him. Suddenly, in 1630, Gomizunoö abdicated, turning over the imperial office to an eight-year-old daughter by the Tokugawa empress.[8] From then on, he exercised from retirement whatever powers yet remained to the throne.

With a niece as sovereign, Iemitsu could afford to be generous. Orders were issued to have a suitable retirement palace built for the ex-emperor. When its construction was complete (1634), further orders were given to build a garden around it, and Kobori Enshu was placed in charge.[9] It is believed that he and Gomizunoö consulted together on the plans.

This palace, known as the Sento Gosho, therefore dates from about ten years after Prince Toshihito had completed his part of Katsura, and the two show many similar features. The Sento Gosho stands close to the Imperial Palace in the center of Kyoto, covering some nineteen acres, all enclosed by a high wall. Earlier *sento* (retirement) palaces had stood on this site, and there were remnants of previous gardens, which were incorporated into this one. The Tokugawa empress had her own establishment somewhat apart from the emperor's but connected to it by a long covered corridor. All the buildings were later burned and replaced, not once but several times. And at each reconstruction the garden was renovated a little, so that now its original planning is often blurred.

Today, however, the garden is very peaceful and lovely, with its pond and a small stream meandering among its ferned and wooded embankments (Plates 16, 21, 35, 40, 47). A long bridge draped in wisteria is of special beauty. The stream is brought by a canal from the Kamo River and falls into the lake over a high, broad cascade, easily visible across the old green water. The larger portion of the lake is so shaped and divided by the bridge that the garden seems to have three areas, each somewhat differently developed.

209

The northern pond, by the empress's palace, holds heavy stonework, probably put in for an earlier palace. The central pond is decorated by the cascade, while the southern lake is marked by just such a paved beach as at Katsura.[10] The latter device may be a sort of signature of Kobori Enshu.

Some twenty years later, when Gomizunoö was middle-aged, the shogunate provided means for him to develop a country estate of his own. It stands near the village of Shugaku-in, northeast of Kyoto.[11] The estate still covers some seventy-three acres, most of it a steep wooded mountainside rising to a ridge. The slope looks out to a far-sweeping view of distant mountains. Within this wild acreage three small areas were turned into developed gardens, but the rest of the forested mountain has been left untouched.

It is believed the ex-emperor planned the development of this site himself. Its preliminary completion in 1655 was marked by a state visit,[12] but it is thought he had been going there, disguised as a woman, for some time previously. The spirit that could carry off such an escapade is probably what had once put him in the bad graces of the Tokugawas. But when originality and daring were directed to the planning of a garden site, they produced something new and different—and unique in all Japanese landscape design.

The Shugaku-in villa was never intended to be an estate for long visits, although once or twice it served as a residence after fires had destroyed the palace. It was planned, rather, to be what would now be called a weekend place. Visits to it were made in spring and autumn, when the weather is always at its best in Kyoto. The trip there and back may sometimes have been made in a single day, but the long ride from Kyoto, in a two-wheeled springless ox coach, over mountain roads, probably caused the visits to extend at least overnight and usually for several days. Since the court never "roughed it," elegant little cottages were built. One group served the emperor and his gentlemen; another, the empress and her ladies. For the latter, a hermitage already on the spot was rehabilitated. The building still bears the empress's Tokugawa crest.

These two groups are each enclosed by a high fence and known as the "lower garden" and the "middle garden." They are usually referred to as teahouses, but this term is derived more from their rustic atmosphere and sylvan location than from their use. Each group inside its high fence is surrounded by a little landscape garden, very charming but more or less conventional (Plates 150, 152). Outside these enclosures stretches the immensity of the pine-covered slope.

The third development in Shugaku-in, called the "upper garden," is a large landscape focused on the far-sweeping view to distant mountains (Plate 151). A path leads from the two lower gardens to an outlook point, where a viewing pavilion is placed. En route to this, the path traverses rice fields which are still part of the property and are worked by estate farmers. It is said that the ex-emperor liked to watch these men, for at this period, for the first time in history, interest in proletarian activities had begun to penetrate the upper classes.

The wide graveled path that goes through these fields is now bordered on either side by a row of unusual dwarfed pine trees. Their height is not over five feet, while their trunks are a foot or more in diameter, and their spread is perhaps eight feet. Shortly before the path reaches the crest, it is enclosed by a high clipped hedge which shuts out all preliminary glimpses of the view and greatly increases its dramatic effect when finally the crest is reached.

A pavilion at this point is appropriately called the Cloud Touching Arbor or Rin'un-tei. The outlook includes a view back toward Kyoto set in its green valley with a winding river and rice fields and the old grey city, spread out like a map. In front, above wooded foothills, the distant mountain ranges fade away to horizons of blue and purple. Gomizunoö, who had spent sixty years within the rigid confines of the court, may have felt here that his spirit had freedom to roam unrestricted.

Although the distant view is on a magnificent scale of miles, landscape skill has brought it within the man-made design of the garden. The use of "borrowed scenery"—glimpses outside the garden—was not new in Japanese garden technique. But it had never been used on any such scale as this and seldom turned into the principal feature of a garden. For sheer boldness of conception and largeness of execution, the way this view is here framed and focused must be one of the greater achievements of landscape artistry anywhere.

It was accomplished entirely within the conventional pattern of the Japanese landscape garden, which requires that a view have three parts—background, middle ground, and foreground. Here the background mountains are given a middle ground in the form of a large lake that sweeps across the center of the picture. The water lies well below the pavilion, which serves as the conventional viewing point. The foreground is a steep slope that descends from the front of the pavilion to the edge of the lake. It is covered by closely planted azaleas, camellias, and other shrubs, which are kept clipped into a flat-topped surface some feet above the ground.[13] From season to season this flat surface presents a smooth spread of variable colors.

The lake, which has an area of about six and a half acres, is fed by several mountain streams. It is supported on the valley side by strong walls and embankments. From the high position of the Cloud Touching Arbor the lake's outlines are a masterpiece of harmonic integration into the total landscape, as its long, simple shores follow and repeat the line of the distant ranges. These shorelines are doubled for emphasis by an island which juts in from one side, creating two apparent channels that curve gracefully. But along these shores there is nowhere a quirk or jiggling line to distract from their simplicity.

According to tradition, Gomizunoö developed the plan of Shugaku-in on a clay model. It seems possible, even probable, that he did, for one can think of no better way to have the shore harmonize so completely with the distant mountaintops. The lines are so right, in fact, one must be alert to note the artistic skill which created them. The artist Joko—for this was Gomizunoö's art pseudonym—is revealed as a better designer, perhaps, than has been generally recognized.

The shoreline simplicity is preserved by being merely sodded. There is not a rock in sight from this point, for even the largest would not have been distinguishable from the pavilion, and rocky shores would only have looked fuzzy.

The far side of the lake is paralleled by a path that emphasizes the lake's lines, and beyond this is a hedge that closes off the middle ground from the distant background. It also conceals the immense walls which hold the lake against the hillside. This combination of hedge and sodded shore, extensive lake and distant view, makes Shugaku-in appear to foreigners more like an Occidental park than a Japanese garden. Yet it all conforms to the traditional pattern and was completed two hundred years before European parks were really known in Japan. Shugaku-in serves also to impress on foreign visitors the fact that Japanese gardens are not all small or miniature.

The outlook over the lake is softened and decorated by occasional groups of trees around the shore and on the island. They were supposed to be kept in proportional size, but in recent years certain deciduous trees, planted in the nineteenth century, have become too large and too numerous. As of this writing, they conceal and interfere very seriously with the layout. The best time to see the total design is when these trees are bare and leafless.

Shugaku-in held other resources for pleasure. The lake was used for boating, and a long stroll path, like those in Katsura and the Sento Gosho garden, winds down from the Cloud Touching Arbor. It passes two waterfalls, crosses by bridges[14] (Plate 18) to the islands, and then follows the farther side of the lake to return to the main gate and again to the first of the enclosed residence gardens. It passes a teahouse built by Gomizunoö and the sites where others once stood.

Gomizunoö continued to visit Shugaku-in regularly for over twenty years. But at last, in his eighties, he became too feeble for the long trip. It was then he had one of its small tea pavilions, the Shishi-dai, moved to the Sento Gosho garden to remind him of the distant beauties of his mountain estate. He died at the age of eighty-five in 1680.

The list of imperial gardens in Kyoto is completed with the present Imperial Palace, usually referred to as the Gosho. It stands within an imperial park, a modern area of grass, trees, and graveled walks near the center of the city. This park is a mile long and half a mile wide. It was once filled by the mansions of the nobility, crowding around the palace. After the emperor left to live in Tokyo in the middle of the nineteenth century, these houses were taken down and the open park developed.

This present imperial area lies some distance east of the site of the original Heian palace, the great Daidairi of the eighth century. It will be recalled that after the Daidairi had burned, been rebuilt, and burned again, several times, the emperors finally came to make their homes permanently in various outside mansions. Often these were the houses of their powerful and wealthy fathers-in-law. One such mansion, belonging to the Fujiwara family, became in time the permanent home of the sovereigns. It stood approximately where the Imperial Palace is now.

The palace is an extensive group of large buildings which include ceremonial and audience halls, a shrine to hold the sacred regalia, living quarters, and other structures, all enclosed by a high wall. The existing buildings date back only to 1855, when they were last rebuilt after a large fire.

The number of serious fires that have swept Kyoto and the imperial residences over the centuries seems almost unbelievably large. Some of these fires originated with earthquakes. Others were caused by lightning, which is very frequent in Kyoto. Others, again, were

38. Variety of color and texture in stepping stones, ▶
Tsusen-in garden, Shinju-an of Daitoku-ji, Kyoto.

212

certainly incendiary in origin, and still others, one suspects, were due to sheer carelessness. The extremely flammable materials from which the palace halls are made—wood, with bark-thatched roofs—joined with the lack of any protection against lightning until modern times, and without any adequate fire-fighting system, account for the extreme destructiveness of these fires. As a result, over the centuries, the imperial residence has been burned, moved, and rebuilt again and again.[15] Gardens were usually reconstructed or renovated at the time the palace buildings were rebuilt.

Within the present imperial enclosure there are several gardens. The main one lies before the great ceremonial hall, separated from it by a wide stretch of white gravel (Plates 148, 149). The garden is spacious, dignified, and charming, with its lake, islands, bridges, and tall enclosing trees. But it belongs to no period, although a formalized paved beach and a path like those at Katsura probably date part of its construction from about Katsura's period.

The emperors made their home in Kyoto for over a thousand years (794–1868). With the coming of the modern age and their restoration as true heads of state, they removed to Tokyo, the new Eastern Capital. Visits to Kyoto, however, continued to be frequent, and the palace there is always kept in readiness. But always, for the most important ceremonies of their lives, the enthronement, the sovereigns return to their ancestral home. The ceremonies are carried out with ancient rites in this ancient setting.

◀ 39. The "dewy path" to a teahouse, with pine needles as winter protection for moss and a rope-tied stone to indicate guests should follow the alternate path; Ura Senke school of tea, Kyoto.

215

CHAPTER TWENTY-ONE

Impressionism in
Buddhist Landscapes

THE creative years that marked the end of the military period produced one more original style of garden which may be added to the innovations of Katsura and Shugaku-in. This was a style developed in the small open courtyards that lie before the reception room—called the *hojo*—of a Zen abbot. The hojo gardens of this period came to consist of a flat spread of sand, on which were spaced a few trees, shrubs, and rocks. These materials were not arranged to present a full landscape picture but only to suggest one. Because there was only a hint, an evocative impression, the hojo gardens, I think, can be rightly regarded as a form of "impressionistic" art.

The use of sand and rocks immediately brings to mind those earlier gardens in Zen temple courtyards, Ryoan-ji, and the painting gardens. While the influence of these earlier forms was certainly somewhere in the background, the new style was different. The older gardens had been created in a rarefied atmosphere of inspiration and art too high to be long maintained. The hojo gardens represent something more down to earth and familiar. Their hints are of Japanese landscape, not the steepness of Sung. Nor are they esoteric like Ryoan-ji. They are just suggestions, filled with those understatements so dear to the Zennist.

By the end of the fifteenth century Japan had begun to do in art what she has always eventually done—turn away from a foreign form (here Sung painting) to a Japanese expression growing out of it. Thus the painter, Kano Masanobu (1454–90), who was a fine Muromachi-Sung artist, nevertheless at the very peak of the Muromachi years took the first steps in forming a new school of Japanese painting. His ideas were further developed by his gifted son Kano Motonobu (1475–1559), who fully established the Japanese Kano school of painting.

The greater part of Motonobu's life fell during the years of historic poverty and turmoil. He lived in Reiun-in, a small subtemple of Myoshin-ji, one of the large Zen foundations in Kyoto. It stands in the very center of art and garden interest; up the road a short walk is Ryoan-ji, while both Daisen-in and the Gold Pavilion are not far away. Reiun-in still possesses paintings by Motonobu which decorated the panels of its sliding screens and which show, in part, the abbreviated quality of his style. In this temple he must have done a good deal of the work that gave definite direction to the new Kano school, and here, no doubt, the new directions in art had a center.

In a neighboring small subtemple called Taizo-in is a garden which tradition attributes to Motonobu himself.[1] It is, however, a painting garden of the Muromachi type, very small, as the exigencies of that unhappy period made necessary, but an excellent little piece of art (Plate 154). A pond of sand holds typical Muromachi rocks formed into a tortoise island reached by a bridge. Other rocks at the back suggest hills. Landscape is still plain here.

But in Reiun-in temple itself, where Motonobu studied Zen, is another garden, quite different in its feeling from Taizo-in. Reiun-in had been founded about 1526 by a famous cleric, Daikyo. He was greatly admired by the emperor Gonara, who wished to visit the temple to discuss Zen philosophy. Although this period was the most poverty-stricken in the whole history of the court, the coming of the emperor was still a great occasion. In preparing for it, the temple managed to get a new reception room by moving a building in from Toganoö. It is a very small hall, as is the garden that was built beside it. Both building and garden were completed by 1543, in time for the imperial visit.

The Reiun-in garden is a mere strip of land, about ten feet wide and thirty-two feet long (Plate 155). It lies between the narrow porch of the reception room and a high, grey plaster wall marked by five horizontal white lines. These show that the institution has received imperial honors. Gathered and arranged in this narrow space are a few choice rocks, as fine and unusual as those in Daisen-in. Most are of typical Muromachi style, with flat tops, and were probably gifts from some ruined estate nearby. Among them now grow a small tree and trimmed azalea shrubs. The sand that covers the foreground is largely overgrown by moss, with a few ferns about the base of the stones.

This garden is said to have been made by a priest, known as Shiken Seido, of the nearby temple of Daitoku-ji.[2] He specialized in garden making and was also a painter and leader of the chants. His painting is said to have been in the style of Soami, but his garden style, while it vaguely recalls Daisen-in, is more simplified and suggestive. He probably was under the influence of Motonobu.

The fine rocks of Reiun-in are placed to create mostly a pleasing harmonic design. The largest stone is upstanding, with perpendicular markings which might be falling water in the manner of Daisen-in. The other stones taper away to the right, arranged so that each is an individual unit of form. They are not grouped, except as a whole. A few flat stones disappear under the edge of the veranda, to indicate the direction of water flow. The effect is pleasing but vague.

If the new simplified and suggestive garden style developed slowly, it is probably because so few gardens of any kind could be made in the mid-1500's. But as peace and prosperity returned, building began again. One of the gardens of this period which show development of the new style is that of Juko-in (or Shuko-in), a subtemple of Daitoku-ji. Its garden is sometimes attributed to the tea master Rikyu, who is buried there, but it is believed it was built later, when the quarters of the abbot were completed, about 1566.[3]

This rectangular flat garden is larger than those of the impoverished earlier period, being some eighty-five feet long and forty-two feet wide. Much of this area is covered with sand,

217

the greater proportion showing the tendency in all these gardens for the sanded area to grow larger and larger with time. Against a hedge of green oak stands a line of smallish rocks, so numerous they have inspired the popular name Garden of a Hundred Stones. Neither large nor very distinguished in shape, they are arranged in what seems to be a chain of islands. Two groups are connected by a bridge. It is large and monolithic, the only thing in the garden which hints that its construction took place during the Momoyama period of power and glory.

The new style of Zen gardens came to its full development when peace was once more established over the nation and reconstruction was going forward everywhere. After 1600, although the Tokugawa shogunate made its permanent headquarters in the castle at Edo (later called Tokyo), some three hundred miles east of Kyoto, it continued to contribute generously to the rebuilding of the old capital.

Tokugawa aid to temples was placed in charge of a priest named Suden.[4] In his younger years, this man had been a knight-follower of Hideyoshi, then of Ieyasu. On turning monk, he had become one of Ieyasu's trusted advisors and secretaries in the field. When he was put in charge of all relations between the shogunal government and the temples of the country, he was politically the most important ecclesiastic in Japan.

Suden chose to administer his duties from Nanzen-ji, in Kyoto, where he had formerly lived. To serve as his headquarters there, he revived a subsidiary temple, Konchi-in. Ieyasu gave one of the buildings from Hideyoshi's Fushimi Castle to serve as its main hall. After this fine structure had been moved to its new site, about 1611, the garden which now lies beside it was built (Plate 153).

It is a large, flat, sanded rectangle, enclosed on one side by the hall and at the end by a small chapel dedicated to Suden's spirit. Instead of the usual enclosing wall opposite, there is a long, gently sloping bank, heavily wooded. Its trees and shrubs shut in the garden completely. At the foot of this bank stand two massive rock arrangements, one tall and upright, the other lower and more horizontal in feeling. Lying in the sand between them, almost like a paving block, is a large flat stone, nearly square. It is quite clearly intended to suggest a bridge, although it does not touch either island.

The two stone groups are identified as the inevitable crane and tortoise. It will be recalled that these two concepts, called Horai, were almost universally used in gardens of military men, and both Suden and his friend Kobori Enshu were of the military class. The two creatures, the tortoise and the crane, which had served the Immortals in the ancient tale, had long since become symbols of longevity and themselves equivalent to the isles of eternal youth. It was natural that military men, whose lives tended to be short and rough, should yearn for a remote paradise of beauty and everlasting youth. Other details of the myth had faded, and only a few scholars might have been able to identify the tortoises with Horai and P'eng-lai.

Today, looking with an informed imagination at the crane and tortoise groups in the Konchi-in garden, we can see the two creatures more clearly than usual. The tortoise, as always, is fairly graphic, with upraised head and flippers. But, for the first and only time I know of, there is in the other group something that might suggest, graphically, the crane. Two tall erect stones and one long, flat rock—could these be the lifted wings and body of

218

a giant bird? Probably not—it is only a fleeting impression. What we really see is a group of large, natural stones, placed together with strongly contrasting perpendicular and horizontal lines.

There is good reason to think that Kobori Enshu, the tea master and government building commissioner, had a good deal to do with Suden's Konchi-in garden. Both men were important Tokugawa officials at the time, and friends. They had common cultural interests and were part of the little group of which Prince Toshihito, builder of Katsura, was another. (It will be recalled that a description written by Suden is one of the few contemporary comments we have on the construction of Katsura.)

In building a garden, Suden would undoubtedly have asked Kobori Enshu for suggestions. Evidence that Enshu was obliging is found in another garden which has a layout very like that of Konchi-in. This other belongs to the temple of Raikyu-ji, which lies near Matsuyama Castle on the island of Shikoku. Enshu had become the Lord of Matsuyama when his father died and he inherited this castle. Thus holding in his own right both wealth and power, Enshu is known to have been a patron of Raikyu-ji temple. The similarity of its design to that of Konchi-in points to him as the obvious creator of both, although no record states this in so many words.[5]

The most noted of the new-style Zen gardens is probably that of the main Daitoku-ji monastery, one of the larger and more important of the Zen foundations in Kyoto (Plate 156). The many subsidiary temples clustering around it are famous for their gardens—among them, it will be recalled, Daisen-in and Shuko-in.

The Daitoku-ji abbot had as his main hall a large and imposing building that dates to about 1636 for its completion.[6] The garden lying beside it was finished a little later. Since it is a masterpiece, it is unfortunate that we are not certain who made it. Enshu is often favored, although he is known to have been very busy with his official duties about that time. A former abbot, his friend Ten'yu, has likewise been credited, since he was also a garden designer. The abbot at that time, Tokuan, is considered a third possibility. He is known to have made a garden somewhat like this for Shoun-ji temple in the town of Sakai. The fact that three men are known to have had the capacity to do such a piece of work speaks well for the talent of the time.

To be in proper scale with the large hojo building, the garden is also large, a rectangle about one hundred twenty feet long and forty-two feet wide. Over sixty percent of its space is covered with whitish sand. The wall that encloses the garden holds a monumental gateway which was originally a part of Hideyoshi's Juraku-dai mansion. This gate is never opened.

Over this enclosing wall was once visible a splendid view of the mountains behind Kyoto. The city has now encroached on the temple neighborhood, but the notched green peak of Mount Hiei can still be seen rising into the sky. A view of the pine-bordered Kamo River, flowing picturesquely through the intervening valley, was once part of the scene.

The outer corner of this garden points toward the hills. It is filled by a large mound of clipped greenery which could suggest that a spur of the distant hills had come down into the foreground. Embedded in the face of this green mound are three large upstanding stones, set close together but with perpendicular slits between them. The tall central stone is over seven feet high and three feet wide. The stone on its left is slightly lower but broader, while the one on its right is only three feet high. (They form a perfect example of the basic triangle, so frequently seen in Japanese art.) These three rock faces, smoothly set into their green hill, suggest a cascade in a way that is one of the most original achievements of rock art in Japan. "Water" falling here is plainly indicated by the thin slits between the rocks and by slight perpendicular markings.

This "water" forms the rippling sandy stream that flows through the rest of the garden. The sand is scratched into formalized ripple lines by the teeth of a bamboo rake, this work being redone every morning by the brother who takes care of the garden. (It has probably been done almost daily for over three hundred years.) The man is highly skilled at his work, his rake swinging from side to side as evenly as if the scratches were being made by a machine. The opposite side of the garden becomes the shoreline, indicated by occasional rocks, a few shrubs, small trees, and patches of moss.

The touch that pulls all this picture together is a large "sand bar" that lies in the stream at the end opposite the cascade (Plate 158). It is made of two flat rocks which rise slightly above the surface and are surrounded by a spreading patch of coarse brownish moss. Against the white sand this dark patch offers enough contrast to balance the upstanding weight of the cascade and bring together the whole layout.

The newcomer, seeing this garden for the first time, finds its curious details puzzling. The three stones in the mound of green, the scratched sand, the spreading patch of dark moss have little meaning to one unfamiliar with the idiom. Their interpretation into a suggested landscape, as I have given it here, is something that must be put together by contemplation and imagination.

In connection with the garden of the Daitoku-ji hojo, mention should be made of another, a tiny garden which lies across the eastern end of the hojo building like the base of a letter L. Here is a sandy strip, only a few feet wide, enclosed by a green hedge. Although this strip is separated from the main garden only by a stone gutter, it is always regarded as separate and sometimes called the East Garden. Probably it was made at a different time and under different circumstances.

This strip now holds a line of three small rock arrangements made up respectively of seven, five, and three stones each. One more stone has unaccountably got into these groupings, but the place is usually referred to as the Seven-Five-Three Garden—that is, Shichi-Go-San. Its purpose was to serve as foreground and frame to the fine view of the distant Eastern Hills, today blocked out by the encroaching buildings.

As time went on, the age-old impulse to recreate in merely natural and picturesque forms reasserted itself, while the original and imaginative ideas of the tea men and Zen artists began to fade. Toward the end of the seventeenth century, Zen gardens were not really suggestive art any longer but only pleasing decorations in a simplified style, using the flat, sandy pattern. This is clearly seen in the garden of Nanzen-ji's abbot (Plate 157).

Suden had exerted himself on behalf of the central Nanzen-ji foundation and about 1611 had obtained the gift of a fine large hall to serve as the abbot's hojo.[7] It had been part of the imperial palace which the Tokugawas were then rebuilding and was no longer needed. Its fine decorations reveal its palace origin.

The garden that now lies in front of this hall was not created until considerably later. The monastery was probably trying to assemble the other buildings needed to complete such a major institution and had no time for gardens. It may not have been until almost the end of the seventeenth century that this one was finally made. Its area again is large, and the fact that a full seventy percent of its space is sanded corroborates its late development. The sand covers all of the garden except one corner.

The passage of time is also shown even more clearly in the style of the rocks and the way they are laid out. The large stone on the left is impressively huge, but it is neither distinguished in form nor especially interesting. No hint of Muromachi style remains. This is true of the other half dozen rocks which are laid out toward the right. All are in a reclining position, and each is placed individually on the sand. There is no lack of harmony between them, although the presence today of a number of large, clipped shrubs introduces competing forms which interfere with the original spatial relations.

We do not know who made this garden, but it seems certain it was not the work of an artist or tea man. Instead, it seems to have been done by professional garden makers who were commissioned to make a Zen garden. By then, these men were working without supervision, having taken over the entire field of garden making from planning to the last detail. They were able to reproduce the outward form but had lost the sense of meaning.

CHAPTER TWENTY-TWO

The Gardens of Edo:
Literal Landscapes

THE scene shifts now from the old city of Kyoto to the new town growing up in the eastern part of the country around the shogun's headquarters, Edo Castle. The site of Edo possessed no such scenic beauties as that of Kyoto, since the castle had been put there strictly for strategic reasons. However, it possessed one beauty—a view of Mount Fuji, some fifty miles away, visible on clear days, small, pointed, snow-capped, as a million pictures were to show it during the next centuries.

In the early days of their power the Tokugawa shoguns put all their efforts into strengthening Edo Castle itself. Its ramparts were complex and angular, designed to baffle an attacking enemy—as they still baffle the traffic of a modern city.

Every military lord was required to spend several months each year in Edo in attendance on the shogun. The remainder of his time was usually put in at his castle seat, but when he left Edo he had to leave his family behind as hostages. This was one of the means which the Tokugawas employed to discourage thoughts of rebellion against their domination over the other feudatories.

The city residences of these barons and their many retainers were clustered near the main gate of the castle. But it was not long before some of the wealthier lords began laying out parklike estates on the edge of town. Several of these places still survive as unusual and historic public parks. The earliest and greatest, called Koraku-en, was built by the vice-shogun Tokugawa Yorifusa (1603–61).[1] He was the youngest son of Ieyasu and about the same age as his nephew Iemitsu, the ruling shogun. Both of these top officials were interested in having a suitable place in which to hold ceremonial tea gatherings for important people, outside the palace and away from the stiff ceremonies of the shogunal court.

To aid Yorifusa, Iemitsu secured a site for a tea garden. In a typically high-handed manner, he simply had two temples and a private estate removed from a choice area of land which possessed many large trees and some rising ground—features not often found near Edo. It was possible also to create a cascade in the traditional manner by bringing fresh water from the upper river. Construction of a suitable building and its garden was begun

40. Tea garden with light bamboo fence, Sento Palace, Kyoto. ▶

in 1629 and sufficiently finished the next year so that a ceremonial tea gathering could be held, with the shogun participating.

Koraku-en garden soon became Yorifusa's hobby. By obtaining additional land, it eventually covered sixty-three acres. As a member of the ruling house and a lord of enormous wealth, Yorifusa was able to develop here a garden in the grand manner of the military rulers. The Kyoto pattern was followed, with a large lake, islands, and hills. Since Koraku-en was under construction at about the same time as Katsura in Kyoto, it was inevitable that the two should show similarities. Chief of these is the long circuit path that leads around the garden.

The man selected to lay out the basic design of the garden was Tokudaiji Sahyoe, a member of the lesser court nobility of Kyoto. He was connected with a family that had been traditionally associated with garden planning. For the lake, he chose an irregular swampy area, which made it possible for the lake to be very large. The natural rising ground was augmented by the excavated material, making it possible for the hills to be unusually high. And since handsome rocks were not to be found near swampy Edo, they had to be brought by barge all the way from Izu, miles distant. Their high cost thus made doubly impressive the large number assembled.

They were used lavishly in the Kyoto manner to build the cascades and to reinforce the hillsides, as ornaments and islets, and as steps and stepping stones. One enormous rock, squarish in form, was set up in the water at the end of the large central island. It suggests the head of the traditional tortoise and is called, after the garden designer, the Tokudaiji Stone (Plate 161).

The long stroll path that led over the hills and around the lake took one past many features which gave added interest to the walk. Some of these were famous scenic areas reproduced in miniature. The appreciation of scenery, which had always been a characteristic of the literati, had now become a popular fad. Since the barons with their long processions of retainers were constantly coming and going across the country, there was plenty of opportunity for everyone to look at scenery. Mount Fuji came to be represented in many of the provincial gardens of the time (Plate 164).

The reproduction of famous scenes in Koraku-en took one in imagination to many of the most famous places in Japan. Later, noted beauty spots in China were added. Many of the reproduced scenes were near Kyoto. A small bridge across a maple-filled gully was named "Bridge of Heaven" after the one at Tofuku-ji temple. A green knoll became Mount Atago on the western side of Kyoto, and a boulder-filled stream was called the "Oi River" after the one that flows through Arashiyama. More than thirty such scenes, along with such buildings as a Noh stage and various pavilions, are mentioned as having been developed in this garden.

This continual harking back to the old capital makes it clear that a sentimental nostalgia for its beauties and amenities was a fashionable attitude of the day in the new (and somewhat raw) city of Edo. Most of its leading citizens were men of action who would, in reality, have fitted but poorly into the leisurely life of the old capital. Such men probably

◀ *41. Lantern-lit walk leading to evening tea ceremony, Ura Senke school of tea, Kyoto.*

were Iemitsu and Yorifusa, who thought in terms of concrete accomplishment. This is reflected in the fact that when they wanted to create a famous scene in a garden, it had to take a literal form.

When a "mountain" was to be built in Koraku-en, an actual mountain in miniature was created. Material from the lake bed was piled into a high, double peak, about thirty feet above the lake level, and its steep, grassy sides left almost bare of trees or bushes. It still stands, unmistakably a "miniature" artificial mountain. In the Zen gardens of Kyoto only a hint had been needed, perhaps a single rock. Even in Katsura the "toy mountain" which seemed to bar the way of pleasure boats was a heavily wooded, mounded island, its artificial construction wholly concealed.

After the death of Yorifusa, his son Mitsukuni (1628–1700) maintained the garden for a time as his father had left it. This second lord of Mito, living in a period of peace, was deeply interested in scholarly research.[2] He has come down in popular tradition as a champion of the common people, for it was said he wandered over the country in disguise, studying the condition of the common folk.

By this time, Japan was experiencing its third wave of Chinese influence. The first, it will be recalled, had come in the earliest period, bringing T'ang civilization and Buddhism. The second, in the Muromachi period, had brought Zen philosophy and Sung art. This third wave, in the Tokugawa period, carried a great interest in Confucianism.

The teachings of Confucius (or his reinterpreter Chu Hsi) fitted in well with the ideas of the shogunate, for Confucian emphasis on proper conduct could mean conformation to the existing state of society (with the Tokugawas in authority), and its stress on the duties of relationship, especially the duty of a follower to his lord, conformed to Tokugawa concepts of an ideal society. (In time, these studies into social philosophy and history led to questions being raised over the legality of the Tokugawa dictatorship. And in the end this regime was overthrown largely by the knowledge brought to light as a result. But such a conclusion was not foreseen in the seventeenth century.)

Differing from that of the past, interest in Chinese studies did not result in more travel to China. By the latter half of the seventeenth century the Japanese seclusion policy had been put into full effect, and the country was almost completely isolated. Japanese subjects were forbidden to leave their own shores on pain of death if ever they tried to return, and all Europeans were barred, except for a few Dutch who were allowed to live and trade in Nagasaki. The Chinese were not excluded, however, and certain scholars, mostly refugees from the downfall of the Ming government, found their way to Japan. They were usually received as honored teachers of the Confucian doctrine. One of these, Chu Shun-shui, was taken under the patronage of Mitsukuni. It is believed that a good many of the Chinese details in the Koraku-en garden were added through his influence.

The miniature mountain was renamed "Lu-shan" after those peaks in South China where the White Lotus Society had been founded. A Confucian chapel was built and a reproduction of the causeway across the lake at Hangchow. The original causeway, it will be recalled, is broken at intervals by picturesque half-moon bridges, which complete their circle in the mirror of the lake.

226

The miniature reproduction in Koraku-en was only a narrow dyke of cut stones, built in a wide part of the stream. A stone arch was part of this dyke, some two feet long and a few inches high. Even the most kindly disposed observer of this dyke cannot see in it any of the romantic beauty of the original, with its willows and reflections. But since no seventeenth-century Edoite had ever been to Hangchow (Plate 4), this attempt at a literal replica evidently satisfied.

The name Koraku-en was probably also given at Chu's suggestion. It is based on a Confucian axiom[3] which states that the wise ruler takes his ease only when his country is prosperous and contented. The Japanese words *ko raku* mean literally "afterward, ease" (*en* means garden), so the name has been generally translated as the "Garden of the Philosopher's Pleasure." At first Mitsukuni accepted this name, but later, when he had discovered the common people were *not* prosperous and contented, he could no longer be at ease on this extravagant estate. A Japanese visitor to the garden in 1678 was profoundly impressed by the way Mitsukuni had literally accepted the implications of the name and was allowing the place to go to ruin.[4] A small part of it survives as a Tokyo park.

In its day, Koraku-en set the fashion and became the model for other large estates. But since most sites near Edo lacked any flow of fresh water, and their owners, unlike Yorifusa, could not afford to bring rocks from long distances, certain ingenious adaptations were worked out. To take the place of rocks, shrubs were clipped into irregular forms to suggest piles of rocks. Such angular groups created a certain mass and weight in the garden landscape, but on the whole the device was not very successful and deceived no one. Extreme forms of clipping such as this are now seen only in a few out-of-the-way places where old ways survive.

The lack of fresh, flowing water near Edo caused garden makers who desired a lake to turn to the only source of water available, the bay and the tidal river. Along their shores were laid out a number of extensive estates. The land was flat and marshy, very easy to dig and fill, so that when lakes were excavated they could be unusually large. At high tide the brackish water seeped into the excavations, and at low tide the high level was maintained by gates which prevented the water from draining out. Cascades, which had been such a traditional feature of Kyoto gardens, disappeared.

Surviving garden lakes of this type usually hold a few mounded islands, with sparsely clipped trees, shrubs, and few or no rocks. They possess no really high ground, so the great width of the water makes the predominant feeling one of open horizontality.

To harmonize with such lines, new types of stone lanterns were soon devised. In contrast to the pillarlike form of the traditional stone lantern, the new designs were usually low and broad. One of the most popular forms, the *yukimi* or snow-viewing design, stands on low legs, usually three, has a short light-holder, and is topped by a cover that is very wide and almost flat.[5] Its horizontal lines usually harmonize well with the wide lake scenery.

The best surviving example of a tidal lake garden is the Beach Palace, Hama Rikyu, in Tokyo. It is a square island of ninety-six acres, one side facing the river, the other three enclosed by a walled canal. The main lake covers six and a half acres, but there are two

227

others, entirely secluded, one of ten and one of four acres. The latter were used for duck hunting. The path which leads around Hama Rikyu's main lake crosses the inlet which admits the river water, with the tidal water gate holding back the flood.

Hama Rikyu was built in the middle of the seventeenth century by the lord of Kofu, Matsudaira Tsunashige, a relative of the Tokugawas. Later it became a shogunal estate; later still, an imperial property. After 1868 it was often used for the entertainment of important foreign visitors. Among them was President U. S. Grant, who lived there during his stay in Japan while on his trip around the world. It is now another of Tokyo's unique city parks.

During the next decades, gardens made by the feudal lords at their provincial seats usually took on the same flat, spreading look that characterized the Edo gardens. This appeared even when the district in which they were built had natural hills, flowing water, and fine rocks. One of the best of these provincial estates lies some four hundred miles from Tokyo in the town of Okayama on the Inland Sea.

It was originally begun in 1687 by the lord of Okayama, Ikeda Tsunamasa. Although his castle stood on a high bluff overlooking the river,[6] he chose to build his garden on the opposite shore, to be reached by a bridge. There, along the river, a wide, flat area was not unlike the sites of the Edo gardens. The garden was thus a sort of detached park, planned as a retreat, not as the setting for a residence. However, the area held a number of buildings, some quite large, for various gatherings, others smaller, for the tea ceremony. Because, like Katsura and Koraku-en in Tokyo, it was visualized as a sort of enormous tea garden, it was first known as the Teahouse Garden, Chaya Yashiki.

Like its two predecessors, the garden at Okayama was planned as a stroll garden, its paths leading to various beauty spots and the pavilions (Plates 159, 160). The largest of these buildings (now reconstructed) overlooks an enormous lawn of some five acres, with a broad open lake beyond it and, in the distance, picturesque natural hills. It is said that where the lawns are now there were originally scenes of rural farms and rice fields. One such small rice field still remains at the side.

The central lake, of several acres, is broad and open like those of Tokyo. It holds three small islands, low and rounded and covered with grass. Scattered clumps of bushes and a few carefully trimmed trees grow on the islands. One is reached by an arched bridge and holds a tea hut. Larger trees are confined to the periphery of the garden, so the total effect is very like that of the open Tokyo estates.

Four lesser lakes, scattered at the sides, are all connected by watercourses. These streams are confined between embankments of cut stone and have cobbled bottoms. With their clear, flowing water, winding ornately through the garden, these watercourses become one of its most distinctive attractions.

Later lords of Okayama enlarged and added to the garden until it now covers nearly twenty-two acres. The only rising ground in the whole layout is a low artificial hillock at one side of the lake, added as late as 1863. It is another grass-covered miniature mountain, nestling against tall trees and set with a few stones and low bushes.

Stones are used sparsely in this garden, not from necessity but because it was the style.

The shores of the islands are ringed by low, rounded rocks, almost like a string of beads. Others, here and there, suggest the casual "thrown away" stones of the tea masters. However, because the natural stones in this vicinity are granite, the rocks are often of excellent shape and have been placed with considerable artistry.

Two rocks in this garden are of special note because of their history. When originally found, they were much too large to move, so they were split, one into thirty pieces, the larger into ninety-six. These parts were carefully marked, taken to the garden and there reassembled into their original form. They were held together by a mixture of lime and clay. Whether or not the cracks resulting from this treatment were originally conspicuous is uncertain. But today the cracks have weathered and the edges crumbled until, as a result, the smaller rock is not much more than a curious stone heap. The larger one, which was set up to form a bluff some twenty feet high above a small lake, is still intact but is overgrown by vines which attempt to cover its broken surface.

The garden was renamed Koraku-en in 1871, probably by the same reasoning that caused the estate in Tokyo to be given the name. A few years later, in early Meiji, it was presented to the prefectural government for a public park. The community evidently is very proud of this cultural monument and maintains it in excellent shape.

One other landscape development which took place in the provinces should be mentioned here, although it did not directly involve garden construction. This is the group of shrine buildings at Nikko which honor the deified spirit of Ieyasu. In its setting on the mountainside and its approaches, this became a landscape project on a major scale.

The mountain town of Nikko, some ninety miles north of Tokyo, is surrounded by magnificent scenery. The mountainsides are covered with forests of evergreen and with other trees which turn the slopes to brilliant hues in autumn. In spring the lower hills are lighted by masses of pink and lavender bloom from acres of native azalea bushes. Near Nikko a small river dashes through a deep canyon. Above the town a large mountain lake reflects surrounding peaks (Plate 163). The lake outlet is a high waterfall that tumbles down a great cliff, like those in Sung landscape paintings (Plate 162). Here, on a vast natural scale, are all the traditional elements of the Far Eastern landscape garden. The district has now been turned into a national park.

Before his death in 1616 Ieyasu had selected as the site for his grave a spot just above this town. After his burial there, for twenty years an elaborate assemblage of buildings was under construction, making up the memorial monument. The buildings are set in informal axial positions on a series of ascending terraces. This follows the traditional layout first devised for Chinese mountain palaces, then followed by Buddhist institutions. The buildings include sanctuaries, worship halls, a five-storied pagoda, a drum and a bell tower, gates and walls around the terraced courts, and minor auxiliary buildings. At the top of the hill the grave itself is marked by a bronze stupa.

These wooden buildings have been kept continuously in perfect repair for over three hundred years. Their exterior surfaces are always protectively lacquered in brilliant colors against the almost constant rain and mist. But the dampness has greyed the stones and marked with lichens the steps and walls that support the terraces. Large lanterns of bronze

229

or stone line the central walk, and several torii gates mark the sacred character of the place. In some of the terraced courtyards rises an occasional great cryptomeria tree, while a forest of these conifers covers the hillside surrounding the buildings.

The temple structures themselves are in the rich style of Momoyama castle-palaces. But by the time they were built, the style had been over-elaborated to the point of debasement. Each building at Nikko is almost incredibly decorated, every inch of the surface, inside and out, being covered by paintings or by deeply carved designs of flowers, birds, and animals. All are brightly colored with vermilion, blue, green, white, or black. Gold leaf is lavishly used on many portions. The technical workmanship of these decorations is marvelously executed, but the whole has been described as "fiddling and aesthetically ill conceived."[7] Only the setting among the great cryptomeria trees prevents them from appearing tawdry and cheap.

Yet their cost was staggering. It was borne by the various feudal vassals as "contributions" to honor the memory of Ieyasu. The excessive expense, it is believed, was encouraged largely to keep the barons poor and unable to finance any lingering thought of rebellion against the Tokugawa overlordship.

One baron, however, who wished to avoid a monetary assessment, was Matsudaira Masatsuna. He conceived the idea of making his contribution the planting of young cryptomeria trees along all the roads approaching the shrine. Over the next two decades his men worked at planting some twenty-five miles of roadside. They also enriched the forest around the shrine. Thousands of trees were set out, and today, over three centuries later, hundreds still survive. Most of them are magnificent specimens, their massive straight trunks like cathedral pillars, the soft grey-green of their needles forming cloudy masses overhead. The gift of the ingenious lord has given to all the rest the setting, which saves it from vulgarity.

CHAPTER TWENTY-THREE

Small Gardens
of the People

NIKKO was the last of the great expressions of military power and glory. While the barons continued to build town and country estates for a considerable period, a fundamental change was taking place in Japan. It was a change that nobody understood, but it became increasingly clear that the barons, for all their lands and rice incomes, were becoming poor, while the merchants and artisans were getting rich. The economic forces involved were complex, but we can say now that the country was changing from agriculture to industry, from barter to money. This shift eventually marked the end of the great garden estates and turned the emphasis onto smaller gardens for ordinary people.

The change was slow in making itself felt. With the country closed to the world, it was a time of unbroken peace—although a peace sternly maintained under military feudalism. Society had been settled, as nearly as it is possible to do such a thing, into a static condition, with every individual fixed into the place where he was born. The broadening influences that had begun to appear under Hideyoshi's widespread contacts were checked and choked by repressive policies.

The unbroken peace brought into existence a new leisured class, the warrior, who now was no longer called upon to fight. Every baron had a large number of such men among his followers. They were the knights, the gentlemen of society, for as always in a military system they occupied a privileged position. In Japan these men were known as samurai.

Below them, in greatly lessening importance, were the farmers, artisans, and merchants. Men of the samurai class continued to receive incomes from their lords, but any military service they rendered was purely nominal. Many occupied important executive positions in the fiefs and government. Others filled up their time with study. A few gave up their samurai status to go into the business world. But still there was a great deal of leisure time. It was largely among this group that there appeared those infinitely time-consuming hobbies which have seemed to the Western world to be characteristic of Japan.

Prominent among such hobbies was the art of growing miniature trees called bonsai (not to be pronounced "banzai"). Real bonsai trees are always grown as pot plants in containers, never in the ground (Plates 171, 172). They are usually less than a foot high, and often only a few inches.

Bonsai plants should not be confused with dwarfed trees in gardens, which are kept pruned to be in scale with the garden's size. Such dwarfed trees are seldom less than five or six feet high and usually serve more as shrubs than as trees. They may attain as much as twelve or more feet, but this can still be considered dwarfed if the tree will naturally grow twice that height. These small garden trees are usually trained into highly artistic forms which sometimes bear but little resemblance to the natural shape of the species. Or the natural form may be stylized and exaggerated to suggest ancient specimens. As gardens became smaller and smaller, trees of reduced size were used more frequently.

With no fresh ideas in art to be explored and developed, there was only one way for the old arts to move—round and round. They finally wore for themselves highly polished grooves of formalism and acquired preciosity. It must be emphasized that only the traditional arts suffered this stultification, those that had always been patronized by the upper classes. While this was happening, however, new and vivid arts were rising from the proletariat, notably those of the wood-block print and the theater. But only as the older arts touched the people, as painting did, for instance, in the decorative work of Korin, could they maintain vitality. Gardens were one of the things that suffered stagnation.

With money coming into the hands of rising merchants, who had a strong inclination to spend and enjoy it, the shogunal government attempted to correct such a deplorable situation by a series of edicts and sumptuary laws meant to push the rising commoners back into their places. But the trouble was too fundamental to be cured by such means. The chief effect of these laws was to keep middle-class wealth from being too apparent. Merchants, for instance, forbidden to wear silk and bright colors, went about apparently clad in sober cottons. But underneath, they often had on the gayest of silken fabrics.

It is plain, therefore, why almost no great estates were constructed in the latter part of the Tokugawa period.[1] The barons had no means to build them, the court in Kyoto was poor, and the commoners were not allowed to do such things. There was no way to get around this situation. A large garden is always a very obvious expression of wealth and is not to be concealed by high walls.

Traditionally, the wealthy mercantile townsman had to live under conditions almost as sober as his cotton robes. His residence was usually the rear portion of his place of business, in the most crowded part of the town. His garden could occupy only a small piece of land between buildings. Such commercial establishments, like all others of size in Japan, were made up of groups of individual structures. Inevitably, small spaces were left between them. These served as light-wells and offered the only land available for gardens.

The predecessors of these tiny interior areas had been the little tsubo gardens of a Heian mansion, built in just such open spaces between buildings for the pleasure of the ladies of the household. And wherever else this compound style of building was used, notably in the construction of large temple foundations, such spaces had also been developed as tiny gardens. For the merchants, then, such gardens were entirely within tradition.

42. Small stone pagoda on grassy knoll, with an umbrella ▶
as a sunshade; Shoren-in or the Awata Palace, Kyoto.

Many such small interior gardens may still be found in business houses in the older parts of cities, especially in Kyoto, which clings to its old ways (Plate 165). They are usually not quite so small as the Western world has pictured them, for while a few may be only six or eight feet square, most have at least the dimensions of an average room, and some may occasionally be considerably larger, perhaps up to forty feet long.

Most of them manage to suggest that they are a corner of a greater outdoor area (Plate 169). That is, they follow the principle worked out so magnificently in Hideyoshi's Tiger Glen courtyard by suggesting more than can be seen. The component parts—rocks and plants—are never reduced in size. Miniatures would simply emphasize the smallness of the area. Instead, all are on a natural and normal human scale, compatible with the size of the area. When we look at them, we feel that beyond this small corner there must be more land out of sight, more rocks, more trees, more moss.

Being so closely associated with buildings, these interior courtyards take on a certain architectural formality. No foot ever steps into them except for maintenance and cleaning. They are surrounded either by open sliding window-walls, by solid walls, or by a tiny, narrow veranda which serves as a hall. The ground is never crowded, for empty spaces create a greater sense of size than would a clutter. Each rock and plant stands in well-integrated relationship to the others, like the furnishings of a room. In a small area this may mean but one or two plants and rocks. The plants are usually glossy-leaved evergreens, rather formal in growth, such as the hollies or small native palms or certain dwarf bamboos. They must be able to grow under the trying conditions of the deeply shaded court.

Deciduous and blossoming plants are mostly ruled out of these gardens by the difficult growing conditions and by the fact that such plants usually have an unattractive rest period. Flowers may be introduced in season, as into a room, by a pot of chrysanthemums or by a small flowering tree in a container. But for the most part flowers have no more place in these gardens than in larger ones. The ground is usually covered with coarse sand or by moss, if it will grow. Or it may be just kept smoothly dampened. The garden is carefully cleaned every day, the dead leaves removed, the spider webs whisked out.

Special forms of these small gardens are the vestibule-like entrances to an inn or an old-style restaurant (Plate 170). If the entrance should be at the rear, or down one side of a building, the passage to it may be no more than a narrow alley. Yet in such an unpromising place an attractive flagstone path may be laid and planted on either side with high shrubs, flatly pruned so as not to obstruct the way. The whole thus becomes an inviting little garden path.

The vestibule gardens may be almost on the street or even actually inside the building. But some kind of wall or gate gives a sense of privacy, and the entrance path is curved to enhance it. Within the curve are placed one or two rocks and a few plants. The whole is usually lighted by a lantern. When visitors are expected, everything is watered down so as to look clean and glistening and give a feeling of preparatory welcome. The tradition of the tea garden is very evident here.

When foreigners came back to Japan in the latter part of the nineteenth century, the

◀ 43. *Stone lantern under red maple, Koto-in of Daitoku-ji, Kyoto.*

little gardens of commercial establishments were often the only ones they ever saw (Plate 174). The report grew up abroad that Japanese gardens were only the size of a pocket handkerchief. Enough has been said to make clear that this was anything but the case.

For centuries, however, Japan and China have had real pocket-handkerchief gardens in the miniature landscapes made of small plants and stones placed in low, wide containers. The containers are usually ceramic, or very fine ones may be of bronze or sculptured stone. The Occident, which has taken up this idea, calls them "dish gardens," and the rocks are often omitted. That such miniatures are very ancient, going back at least to T'ang China, can be realized when we recall the artificial landscape made of wood which has been in the Shoso-in treasure house in Nara since the seventh century. And there is evidence that such little landscapes have always been popular.[2]

Even today, people going on outings in the mountains watch for stones of interesting shape to carry home and use for such tray gardens (Plate 173). Any rock that might suggest a mountain peak or towering cliffs may be set up in a wide, shallow container filled with water and called Horai. Or the stone may be placed in a square pot of soil, among plants, and become the center of a miniature landscape.

When an extraordinarily good stone was found, it was considered valuable enough to be passed on as an heirloom. A fine example may be seen in Kyoto in Reiun-in,[3] a small subsidiary temple of the Tofuku-ji monastery. This special rock, not over twelve to eighteen inches high, is like a sculptured representation of great peaks and precipices (Plate 166). It has long been set up in this tiny temple garden, in a square stone container on a pedestal, where it is the garden's only feature apart from its setting of rocks and shrubs. This stone had long been a cherished possession of the lordly Hosokawa family of Kyushu and was presented to this temple as a memorial to Lord Hosokawa Yusai by his son, in the early Edo period. It is generally called the Much Cherished Rock or Iai Seki.

Although no great estates could be built in the later Edo period, merchants and artisans who were making money were able to acquire residences away from their downtown places of business and have gardens of limited size. Samurai, who had long had small gardens as part of their establishments, now had time to give more attention to such things. The result was a great increase in gardens of the people.

But Buddhism, which had been one of the great and vital forces of an earlier day, had come upon hard times. Confucianism now occupied the attention of scholars and received the patronage of the wealthy. A few small Buddhist subtemples were built in the eighteenth and nineteenth centuries, and within their precincts were created what may have been the best gardens of the period. But among them all not one is outstanding. The exciting inspiration provided by Zen philosophy and Chinese Sung art had run its natural course, and nothing had taken its place.

But traditions lingered, and among the literati gardens were still regarded as a form of fine art. From the standpoint of technique, however, the best that could be done toward understanding how the masterpieces had been made was to try and discover the rules. To most people of that time, it seemed inevitable that they must have been made according to rules. The notion of free and inspired creation was beyond general comprehension. We have a revealing insight into the widespread thinking of this period in comments (made before 1735) by a well-known courtier and tea man, Konoe Iehira. These remarks were noted down by Yamashina Doan, a priest who served as a sort of Boswell.

Says Iehira: "The garden of Ryoan-ji is beyond my understanding. I do not know whether it is good or not, but there does seem to be something superior about it." And, referring to Daisen-in, he goes on: "There are some things about it I cannot understand, but certain rules seem to have been followed. I wonder what they were."[4]

There was one group that did not wonder what they were. They believed they knew. These were the professional garden makers whose predecessors, in Kyoto, had been at the business of making gardens since the days of Muromachi. Families or guilds engaged in this work sometimes possessed notations on techniques handed down from father to son. Supplemented by oral instructions, these were regarded as trade secrets. Since these men knew how to build ponds, hills, streams, and cascades and how to assess the artistic value of a rock and use it to create harmonic abstractions of form, they assumed they had inherited the secrets of Muromachi greatness. But techniques alone were not what had produced the Muromachi masterpieces.

The scholars, philosophers, and artists who had used gardens to express their esoteric ideas and feelings had lost interest in this medium. Perhaps they felt it had been exhausted. By the middle of the Tokugawa period, garden making had finally been taken over completely by the men who made it a business. They contracted to do a full job, including the preliminary designing. They supplied the skill and the materials. Nurseries to grow plants were established. Men were sent into the mountains to find good stones and bring them back to base yards, where they could be held until sold. Rock merchants also kept a stock of ready-made stone lanterns, water basins, and other cut-stone articles (Plate 167). The business of these garden makers was mostly with the well-to-do commoners who were able to put small gardens around their new homes in town or country.

We find pictures of these early gardens of the people in books of the period. The production of inexpensive printed books was one of the important accomplishments of the Edo period. Each page of text or pictures in these books was printed from a single hand-drawn and hand-cut wood block. It will be recalled that early in this period historical research had been sponsored by scholars like Mitsukuni. But soon delvings into old manuscripts had become a widely popular form of study. It led to the appearance of books on such subjects as the Noh drama, tea ceremony, fencing, and, in due course, gardens.[5] Books on all of these subjects had a good sale, as ordinary people found in them details of activities that had previously been known only to the upper classes.

Among publications on gardens was the old *Sakuteiki,* that collection of notes made in the Heian period, written as from one noble gentleman to another. Other early manuscripts were also found and published.[6] Eventually, certain notes on techniques which had come down in the gardening guilds were brought to light and published, along with the oral instructions that had accompanied them.[7] These and later garden publications have become known collectively as the Secret Books and Oral Transmissions on Garden Making.

The outstanding book in this group, the one that has been reprinted many times, is *Tsukiyama Teizoden* (Creating Landscape Gardens), published in 1735. Its writer, Kitamura

237

Enkin, seems to have been a practical garden man who was also able to write for those wanting to know more about his subject. The book embodies the general contents of several earlier publications. He claimed no originality for his main text but says in his introduction, "I set down here what was taught by the masters of former times."[8] But he also included a section on such matters as how to raise goldfish, grow moss, and train pine trees—all skills that appear to have been part of his own experience. He included also a discussion on tea gardens, a subject that had not previously been written about in print. The tea garden, or adaptations from it, was becoming increasingly popular because its small size and simplicity made it practical.

A third section of Enkin's book is devoted to pictures of existing gardens. They were drawn for him by an artist, Fujii Shigeyoshi, who sketched with a brush and black ink in the current style. This style shows its derivation from the Sung landscape paintings, and the pictures often have considerable charm. Among them are views of such famous places as the Gold Pavilion, Saiho-ji, and Daisen-in. Many of the other gardens depicted are not

Fig. 5. Two pages from an Edo-period book showing the garden of the Kawaguchiya, a merchant's establishment in Kyoto, about 1735. The drawing reveals that by the eighteenth century certain commoners had attained enough affluence and influence to own opulent little landscape gardens such as this. The garden, though in Kyoto, shows a marked Edo style, with its grass-covered artificial mountain and the rather curiously rendered stones around the base of the hill. (Brush sketch by Fujii Shigeyoshi, illustrating Tsuki-yama Teizoden, *Part I, 1735)*

238

identified, but one in Kyoto is named as the Kawaguchiya. This identifies it as the establishment of a merchant. The inclusion of such a picture indicates that by the time the book was published some commoners had attained enough freedom and affluence to possess such opulent little landscape gardens as this (Fig. 5).

Some ninety years after Enkin's book was first brought out—that is, in 1828—another book was written which stated that it was intended to be a supplement to Enkin's work. The two books are thus always published as Part I and Part II of *Tsukiyama Teizoden*.[9] The new author, Akizato Rito, explains that his purpose is to give more detailed and specific information on garden making than did Enkin. It is evident he was writing for readers who were more or less in a do-it-yourself frame of mind. That is, interest had changed from a general curiosity about old secrets and the fine estates of others to a desire to have a garden, if necessary, by making it.

Akizato, the author, was himself a member of the leading guild or school of garden makers and was well qualified to do such a book, at least by the light of his day. As might be expected, he makes much of classification, dividing gardens—the small home type with which he is exclusively concerned—into two forms, the flat garden and the artificial hill garden. These he again subdivided into three degrees of elaboration, the *shin, gyo,* and *so*

Fig. 6. This design for a flat garden in the semi-elaborate gyo *category was drawn by Akizato Rito for use in his 1828 book on garden making. It is one of a series of such plan-pictures which he created to illustrate the different possibilities open to the owner of a small plot in making a garden. Such drawings from the Secret Books, when they first became known in Europe and America, aroused an interest in Japanese gardens which has never abated and at the same time built up a considerable misconception of what they are really like. (From* Tsukiyama Teizoden, *Part II, 1828)*

239

forms. He drew up special pictorial plans to illustrate each of these six types and also three styles of tea garden. All of his pictures are oversimplified, almost diagrammatic, in order to make them easy to understand and to follow (Fig. 6).

To illustrate some of his points he also included sketches of certain existing gardens. Among them was a little tea-style entrance garden which he himself had made for a wealthy brewer's house. His brush drawings, because of their simplification, have even more appeal than those earlier ones by Shigeyoshi in Part I of *Tsukiyama Teizoden*. They have a quaint, almost fantastic quality of unreality about them, like a child's playhouse garden (Fig. 7).

The classification mentioned above, into *shin, gyo,* and *so* types, is one that still haunts writers on Japanese garden subjects, although the garden makers themselves never seem to have paid much attention to it. The three words were originally invented to designate three styles of writing Chinese characters and may be taken to mean "elaborately complete," "partly simplified," and "greatly simplified." The gardens so described are similarly elaborate or progressively simplified as to the number of their hills, rocks, trees, and other

Fig. 7. On these pages from Tsukiyama Teizoden, *Part II, Akizato Rito pictures the residence and gardens of the Omura Soemon family in Suruga (the present Shizuoka Prefecture) about 1825. The house had originally been a samurai establishment, the small landscape garden at the right probably having been constructed, at the time the house was built, to be an outlook for its main room (here shown with all its exterior sliding doors closed). The central rock in this garden, shaped like Mount Fuji, was found in this natural form and considered a great treasure. By the time Akizato Rito made this sketch for his book, the family had become well-to-do sakè brewers. The small garden at the left, with stepping stones leading to the family entrance, was made by Akizato himself. (He belonged to a leading guild of garden makers.) It shows a marked resemblance to the tea-garden path.*

240

details. The words are now usually used in a certain backward-looking way to classify gardens. Katsura, for instance, with its elaborate stonework, is called *shin;* Daisen-in is *gyo;* and Ryoan-ji, with its simple fifteen stones, is *so.* But of course the creators of these gardens never thought of such a thing. Dr. Tatsui sums up and dismisses the whole matter in these words, "[Their use] was only a fashion of the time, without any particular meaning. There exists in every Japanese garden a special expression or superiority of its own, but never a style such as *shin, gyo,* and *so.*"[10]

While the Secret Books are interesting because they reveal how social changes were reflected in gardens, they are of particular interest to foreigners because almost all that Europe and America knew of Japanese gardens for many years after the country was reopened was indirectly derived from them. This came about through the works of Dr. Josiah Conder, who published the first authentic information on this subject outside Japan.

Conder, a young Englishman, came to Japan in the 1870's to teach architecture in the Imperial University of Tokyo. He developed a keen interest in Japanese flower arrangement and in the gardens, which led him to make detailed studies and write about them.

His principal book, *Landscape Architecture in Japan,* was published in 1893. Many of its pictures were reproductions from various Secret Books, which Conder studied extensively. The pictures and his report on the curiously poetic names for rocks and trees and the astounding conventions said to rule the garden craft of Japan aroused an interest in them which has never abated. It also led to considerable misunderstanding and sometimes to the construction of the curious things called Japanese gardens seen in other countries.[11]

In spite of his really great efforts to learn about the gardens, Conder's knowledge of his subject was extremely limited, for it was derived almost entirely from the Secret Books and from the decadent Tokugawa gardens in Tokyo at that time. He had heard about some gardens in Kyoto (Enkin mentions several), but there was no reason for him to think them important, since no one else did at the time. It was not until nearly forty years later, when the researches of Harada, Tatsui, Tamura, and Shigemori began to appear, that the true history of Japanese gardens came to be known and the West to get some accurate idea of what they are like.

Conder made one of his greatest mistakes in giving a mandatory quality to the rules and conventions which he set down. Since many of these rules were derived from geomancy, they held the flavor of the imperative. But, again, Japanese gardeners never took this very seriously. Akizato himself makes this clear, a point Conder seems to have overlooked: "Though these are called rules," he wrote, "they are simply intended to show the general principles to which people should adhere. These laws are not fixed and immutable. A stone by such and such a name need not be placed here and another there unless desired. They are only suggestions to be developed appropriately. People fettered by formal ideas should realize this and strive to improve their art."

In spite of all the repressions of the Tokugawa period, formalism did not smother the life of the country without being protested. From the beginning there had been individuals who, in their life and work, stood out against the currents of conformity. But as any attempt at political protest was quickly suppressed, these endeavors took place mostly in literary and artistic fields. In certain sections of the country, especially those belonging to the great lords who had been Ieyasu's superiors and had only submitted to him through force, it had never been forgotten that the Tokugawas were really usurpers of the imperial power. As time went on, a slow public opinion grew up that the emperor should be restored to his rightful position.

Leaders of this movement expressed their protests in guarded ways. One minor method was for them to build their gardens in styles differing from the prevailing modes. Since these leaders were usually scholars and literary men, the style of these little nonconforming gardens came to be known as the literary men's style or *bunjin-zukuri,* which was no style at all.

One of the first men thus to protest was Ishikawa Jozan, poet, scholar, and tea man, who lived in the early part of the Tokugawa period. He expressed his defiance of the formalism then beginning to restrict the tea ceremony by advocating the use of steeped tea instead of the powdered and frothy beverage of the classical ceremony.

Jozan built himself a small hermitage in the hills back of Kyoto which he called Shisendo. There he spent the last forty years of his life, during which the place became an object of pilgrimage to other literary men. It has remained a shrine to his memory ever since. Today the little house and garden have been converted into a temple. The garden may be considerably changed from the way it was in Jozan's lifetime, but it still holds a feeling of informality and nonconformity to any style (Plates 28-29, 168).

Another of the small literary men's gardens surviving in Kyoto is that of Rai Sanyo, a historian who lived near the end of the Tokugawa period. His house stood on the banks of the river looking across the stream to the wooded folds of the Eastern Hills, fading to misty blues in the north. His study was called the House of Purple Mountains and Crystal Streams after an old line of poetry describing Kyoto. Back of the study is a tiny garden which he built. Its chief feature is a wide depression, its walls lined by stones, with small ferns and moss growing between them. In the bottom of this depression, reached by stone steps, is an old wooden wellhead, brimming with water, which induces a growth of emerald moss on the ancient wood. Here, it is said, Rai Sanyo poured many dippers of cold water over himself before beginning his daily tasks, to purify his body and spirit for the work to which he was dedicated.

He wrote guardedly against the regime in power, pointing out the true place of the emperor in the nation's history and leaving the inference clear that his powers had been taken away. His message was an important force in bringing about the next era in Japan's history.

44. Stone water basin with traditionally laid bamboo dipper, Ura Senke school of tea, Kyoto. ▶

CHAPTER TWENTY-FOUR

Western Influences in
the Meiji Period

THE restoration of the emperor to his rightful position in 1868 was the culmination of forces which had long been building up. During more than two hundred years Japan had been tightly shut against foreign intercourse, and every effort had been made to keep its internal conditions static and unchanging. This attempt at the impossible, like holding down a steam vent, had very nearly reached its limit by 1853, and the Tokugawa overlordship had almost run its course. The forces which were moving rapidly and inevitably toward a change were simply hastened by the coming of Commodore Perry.

During the closed period, it will be recalled, Chinese had not been barred from Japan, and a few Dutchmen had been allowed to live at Nagasaki, strictly for trading purposes. Yet through these two small doors there had dribbled a surprising amount of knowledge about the outside world. A few Japanese scholars had taught themselves to read Dutch books, while other foreign books, which had been translated into Chinese, circulated widely.

From time to time, during the closed period, various European powers had attempted to open trade with what was often called the "Hermit Nation." But they were always refused, for Japan's old fear of foreign domination had become a deep obsession. It can be imagined, then, with what consternation news swept over the country, in 1853, that a flotilla of well-armed "black ships" lay at anchor in a bay near Kamakura. Its commander was politely but firmly demanding that Japan open its doors, that a treaty of trade be made between Japan and the United States—a nation that had come into existence since the days of Ieyasu.

The foreign ships went away for a year, and Japan had a chance to consider its helpless position as a country which had remained medieval while the world moved into a new age. When the American ships returned, the treaty was signed and several ports were soon opened to foreigners.

At first foreigners naturally assumed that the shogun was king. Only as they slowly became familiar with the language and history did they learn of the emperor secluded in

◄ *45. Winding path among azaleas, Katsura, Kyoto.*

his palace in Kyoto. Their insistence, finally, on dealing with him directly was one of the main, although indirect, causes of the Tokugawa downfall.

The end of the shogunate was simple yet dramatic. Keiki, last of the shoguns, evidently realized better than most of his countrymen that a new day was at hand. When an opportunity arose, he suddenly, without persuasion, handed back to the emperor the commission of generalissimo which had been given to his ancestor. A few of his followers would not accept this sudden end to their prestige, and there were several brief battles, but no important struggle took place.

In 1868 the young emperor Meiji was restored to his rightful position and moved his residence to the city of Edo. That town was then renamed the Eastern Capital, Tokyo. The old city he had left, which had been known for over a thousand years simply as the Capital —Miyako—was now renamed Kyoto. It is still one of the two head cities of the Japanese empire, and the emperors return to it for the most important occasion of their lives—the enthronement ceremonies.

There began, then, that remarkable period of change which finds its best parallel in Japan's own history some thirteen hundred years before when the country was first coming into contact with Chinese civilization and was busily assimilating its new ideas and material productions. In the nineteenth century it required several decades for the country to adjust, even moderately, to the profound differences in government, economics, and society which were inherent in the changeover from a military feudalism to a modern state.

But when it became possible once more to think about such things as garden making, it was, as always, the rich and powerful who first took it up. This time, such persons were not courtiers nor feudal barons but the businessmen and financiers of Tokyo and Osaka— those men who had long controlled the wealth of the country but had previously been prohibited from using their wealth in this traditional manner. In the early Meiji period, among the names of those interested in gardens were Iwasaki and Mitsui, names still outstanding in the world of Japanese finance.

The garden-minded first turned their attention to the old lake gardens in Tokyo, many of which had had to be abandoned or neglected by their impoverished feudal owners. Thus Baron Iwasaki (who had been given his title in the new era in recognition of his manifest position) acquired an old estate known as Rikugi-en. It had been constructed originally in 1702 as a typical large Tokyo lake garden with islands and encircling path.[1] Baron Iwasaki completely rehabilitated this place but did not change its basic character. As a result of this restoration and of continued good maintenance, Rikugi-en remains today one of the best surviving examples of its kind (Plate 184). It has been given to Tokyo as a public park.

Changes were made later in some of these gardens, as when Baron Iwasaki acquired another place called Kiyozumi Teien. He added a lake and filled it with water from the Sumida River. Then, in a way that recalls how Tokugawa Yorifusa had had stones brought to his Koraku-en garden two hundred years before, he collected rocks. As the controller of large commercial interests, he made use of his ships to bring back as ballast many large stones from all over the country (Plate 177). These were very successfully set up around the shores and islands of Kiyozumi in the Kyoto style and today form one of the best

246

exhibits of stonework in stoneless Tokyo. A line of huge stepping stones through the water is one of the well-known features of this garden.

One corner of Kiyozumi was selected by a later Baron Iwasaki as the site for a large Tudor castle. (It was designed by the English architect, Josiah Conder, whose book on Japanese gardens had recently been published.) This castle impressed the whole city.[2] But in time it became only one of many such foreign-style mansions which, like it, were often wedged into spacious Japanese landscape gardens.

These houses are an example of the way Japan, at that time, was enthusiastically copying all manner of things from the West. Many were taken over with little knowledge of their use or background. The large foreign mansions, for instance, were seldom lived in but were largely prestige symbols, used to entertain foreign visitors. When European flower beds and rose gardens were also copied around some of these houses, there seemed, at first, to be but little comprehension that they were really a branch of the same outdoor art as Japanese landscaping.

But by the 1890's there was enough knowledge of European garden styles for certain Japanese garden designers to think of trying to combine the two. The earliest example of this is the Shinjuku Imperial Garden (Shinjuku Gyo-en) in Tokyo, built partly as a setting for large entertainments, such as the emperor's annual chrysanthemum party. This site held another old Japanese landscape garden, its lake comparatively small, and there were two other ponds. The main landscape garden was left little changed. But in developing large adjacent areas new ideas from the West were used. The broad rolling lawns of English landscaping were an important part of this project, which was carried out by Yoshichika Kodaira, a landscape architect in the service of the Imperial Household. In his hands the two styles came together harmoniously, for the work was done with artistic understanding. Later, in other parts of the grounds, a formal French garden was built, designed to be the setting for a proposed French palace which was never constructed. Here there was little real fusion of the two styles; they were simply blended as they stood side by side.

Another imperial garden may show Western influence in its glorification of a single flower. This is the garden of water irises, a part of the inner precincts of the Meiji Shrine. Begun in 1894, it was also under the direction of Mr. Kodaira. But the emperor Meiji himself, it is said, took a great interest in it, planning it for the pleasure of his empress.

In June, when these flowers bloom, the effect of this garden is that of a river of flowers flowing through a small winding valley. Originally there may have been a natural stream here. To prepare it for growing the iris plants, the stream bed was widened by making it into a series of shallow water terraces. The depth of the water is barely enough to cover the mud. Each terrace is perhaps fifty feet wide and as long as the particular contour of the grade permits. Each is a few inches below the next and is supported by a dyke of small poles driven one beside another into the ground.

In random planting, clumps of *Iris kaempferi* grow close together on these terraces. From a short distance the flowers appear almost like a solid mass of bloom. Every color is seen, from palest lavender and blue-violet to deepest purple, often with lines of bright gold. Deep maroon and pinkish flowers are also present, while an occasional all-white seems like a fleck of foam on the floral tide. The slopes of the little valley are planted to the Japanese maple, its small, delicate foliage forming a lacy background of brightest green.

A path follows this stream and, about halfway up, crosses to the opposite shore on a bridge of zigzag planks only a few inches above the water. Such primitive bridges are traditional to swampy areas, where irises may grow wild. They are made by laying the end of the second plank alongside the first on a low H-shaped support, producing a zigzag effect.

The iris stream empties into a lake where nymphea water lilies grow—flowers not known in Japan until introduced from the West. These lilies flourish in spacious perfection in this lake, each plant forming its own enormous circle of leaves and flowers.

With sumptuary laws a thing of the past, wealthy men in the old commercial city of Osaka also desired to possess the amenities of a fine villa set in a large garden. When certain good residential sites became available in Kyoto, interest turned in the direction of that city of traditional beauty. Thus, in the 1890's, after a break of several centuries, garden building on a large scale again began there.

After the emperor Meiji left the city where his forebears had lived for so many centuries, it seemed as if it might be destined to become a city of the past, old, proud, and—in time—shabby. But the subtle canons known as "Kyoto taste" had become a measure of final excellence all over the nation, a synonym for everything that was best in art, design, and craftsmanship. Objects made in the city's studios and handicraft shops, the products of its kilns, looms, and dye vats, were eagerly bought by the whole country. In addition, every traveler, native or foreign, came to visit its ancient and historic beauties, leaving behind substantial sums. The town thus survived on a solid basis of prosperity.

In the new era Kyoto had not succumbed to foreign fads and fancies but had gone its immemorial way, the way of the court and of tea. It clung to old forms, old ceremonies, and old festivals. It loved restraint, subdued colors, and nature. The beauties of its encircling green hills, its palaces, temples, and gardens hidden behind ancient walls remained little touched (as they still are), even though the downtown portion of the city slowly developed a modern metropolitan exterior.

As 1894 approached, when the old capital would be eleven hundred years old, it was felt that something appropriate should be done to mark the anniversary. The emperor Kammu, that active and able ruler who had caused the capital to be removed from priest-ridden Nara, had never been properly honored by the city he founded. It was decided, therefore, to build a great shrine to honor his spirit as the tutelary deity of the city. Its form was to be, as nearly as possible, a replica of the great Hall of State which had been the finest building in his new capital.

Today this memorial is known as the Heian Shrine. It is a lofty structure showing Chinese influence, with two large and elaborate end pavilions set forward as wings on either side with connecting arcades. The main hall faces on a broad, graveled forecourt enclosed by a monumental front gate and more arcades.

It will be recalled that just outside the original imperial enclosure, the Daidairi, lay the large landscape garden fed by the Divine Spring, Shinsen-en. Many maples, cherries, and

248

willow trees grew in it, and the Pavilion of the Imperial Seat was a large Chinese structure in which the court sat to watch entertainments.

Along one side of the new Heian Shrine was built a large lake garden (Plates 178, 188) as nearly comparable to the original Shinsen-en as practical.[3] It is reached by passing through three smaller gardens beside and behind the central building. These feature flowering plants. To give some flavor of the original garden, a Chinese pavilion stands in the water at the far end of the lake (Plates 17, 186). Seen through the cherry blossoms of spring, its high, pointed roof, like that of a pagoda, may seem like a glimpse into the past. But on approaching closer it is found that the pavilion can be reached by a covered bridge from either shore, so it becomes a way to carry the path across the lake.

Heian Shrine's gardens hold an unusually large number of seasonal flowering trees and shrubs. These serve as special attractions from time to time for the large number of visitors always coming to this shrine. They also remind one of the great interest in flowers on the part of the Heian court.

In Japan's floral calendar the earliest blossoms are the "snow flowers" (Plate 183). The wet snow of Kyoto's mild winters clings to bare stems like white petals or heaps up on broad-leaved evergreens in masses of flowerlike beauty.

At the time of the lunar New Year, about February first, the pine, bamboo, and plum are honored as the "Three Friends of Winter" by being used in decorative combinations. They symbolize hardiness and survival in the cold. The "plum" (*Prunus mume*) is included as one of the three because it is the first tree to bloom in spring. Its rose or white flowers may sometimes be seen through a late snow. This hardihood, joined to its delicacy and fragrance, early caused the Chinese to regard it as the symbol of the superior man. Its fragrance they likened to his subtle but unseen influence on those around him.

Another very early flower is the camellia, also sometimes seen peeping through a late snow (Plate 180). This plant, however, is never grown in private gardens nor those of a Shinto shrine, but it is used extensively around Buddhist temples. The red native species has a tendency for the flowers to break off and fall while they are still fresh and perfect. This fact was early seized on by Buddhist priests to illustrate their preachment that in the midst of life we are in death. The Japanese, who love life and gaiety, do not like to be reminded of this, hence the plant is left alone (except by certain skeptics who grow modern tight-stemmed varieties as an up-to-date hobby).

By the middle of April the cherry trees are in full bloom. The garden of the Heian Shrine has long made a specialty of this tree, growing many different varieties. The weeping tree has small pink flowers, strung tightly together on pendant branches which seem to flow downward like a fountain of delicate color (Plate 187). Near the end of the blooming period, when a light breeze moves the trees, it seems to create a whirl of snowflakes, which settle down to form a pool under the tree. Rows of the large, single, white Yoshino cherry grow around the lake shore, where hidden floodlights at night turn their masses of flowers into cameos against the dark sky and cause them to be reflected in the polished black onyx of the lake.

Japan regards the fresh foliage of spring as another part of the floral cycle. The buds of

249

pendant willows seem to form a green haze. Later, leaf buds appear like freshly carved jade. The foliage of the Japanese maple in spring is often as warmly colored as it will be again eight months later. But the spring colors tend toward pinky apricot and terra-cotta tones, softer than the autumn colors of sharp gold and scarlet.

The dominant flowers of late spring are the azaleas. These plants are used in great abundance for two purposes, the more important being for their green forms. The species with small leaves can withstand much clipping, hence it is used to create controlled masses of green among rock designs. The azalea is also used for its color (although I have seen the gardeners go through their clipping routine just as the flower buds are about to open). However, while most of the year the plants play their green roles inconspicuously, in late April they are apt to break their green bonds and become floral rowdies, rioting in scarlet, magenta, crimson, and gold.

The Japanese, who themselves like to go on little binges under the cherry trees, smile tolerantly and enjoy the brief period of brightness, forgetting for the moment their traditional disapproval of anything but sedate greens, grays, and browns in the garden.

In May comes the wisteria, a native plant that may be found creating wild purple masses on the green walls of canyons. The vine is usually trained over trellises and bridges that cross the water (Plate 175). The flowers hang in high pendant strings that sway in unison when the breeze blows. Big black bumblebees roar softly among the flowers, and, as the breeze increases, the hanging ranks sway back and forth, back and forth as if in a mounting ecstasy of rhythmic intoxication.

Early summer is the season of the iris (Plates 22, 179), a plant that has strong traditional associations with the military and sports activities of the old Fifth Month (June). Summer is also the season of the nelumbium lotus, but, like the camellia, it has associations with Buddhism and is thus usually confined to Buddhist precincts. However, the lotus is also a commercial plant, producing food in roots and seeds, so that it may be found growing extensively in wet fields of huge leaves and flowers.

July and August find the garden luxuriantly green and pulsing with tropical heat. The cicadas, true voice of summer in the Far East, shrill in ear-splitting complaint as the sun mounts. On such torrid mornings, the lover of morning-glories rises early to see what the night has brought to his plants. While these flowers may sometimes be found making a tangle of color around a cottage door, they are more often grown by hobbyists and fanciers in pots for forcing. Skill will induce pot-grown plants to produce, on the first day of bloom, one or two giant flowers, each ten or more inches across. Or the plant may be induced to shoot its entire force in a floral broadside on a single morning, opening over twenty flowers at once. Morning-glory shows are held in cool summer dawns, the proud growers displaying their pots on steplike shelves covered with a red cloth. Flower colors vary from light to dark, from white to palest pink, to blue and purple, to crimson or even the brownish color of tea. The colors may be plain or rimmed, throated, or shot through with white.

September is a month of spent quiet after the heat. Viewing the moon, not flowers, is the traditional pastime. In countries like China and Japan, where the rains come largely in summer, the wild flowers bloom in early fall, not spring. Traditional, therefore, to this season is a group of little wild flowers known as the "Seven Grasses of Autumn." Five are small annuals, one is a shrub, and one a true grass.[4] The last, a *Miscanthus,* lifts its tall, sparse plume in every swampy spot. In poems and pictures it has long been a symbol of autumn. The bush clover, a *Lespedeza,* is sometimes seen in gardens, where its long, graceful branches are covered with tiny pink pea blossoms.

Late October finds the hillsides reddened by the changing colors of natural growth. Prominent among these is the Japanese sumac (its juice the source of lacquer). But Japan knows restraint even in its native autumn colorings. There is never the mass of brilliant foliage which marks the season in eastern and southern American forests. The native maple trees bring a flame into the garden, but their size prevents them from ever being more than a flare among the greenery.

The Japanese floral year closes in November when the chrysanthemums open. Then every little town and big city park holds its flower show, the plants being displayed in small temporary booths of bamboo. These shows tend to feature newly developed varieties of this plant, with many identical pots of a single kind displayed. These are generally the product of a single grower, for the shows are usually not competitive. The pots are set up on a series of low shelves so that one looks down upon them. The flat spread of similar flowers may suggest a length of floral-printed fabric covered by a repeated motif. Foliage is quite as important as blossom in these displays. Other chrysanthemum plants are grown as "cascades" of tiny flowers, and sometimes plants are trained to look like miniature bonsai trees. But there is never an attempt to produce mere hugeness in the size of the flowers.

In the 1890's, when the old monastery of Nanzen-ji in Kyoto decided to sell off some o its empty land, and other parcels nearby also came onto the market, there grew up in this neighborhood a community of fine villas set in spacious gardens. Most were developed as the retreats of wealthy and cultured Osaka owners who desired the finest of traditional architecture and garden art.

About the same time, a water tunnel was completed through the hills to Lake Biwa beyond, bringing an unlimited supply of water to these estates. Its plentiful rush through their cascades and streams is one of their special characteristics. Another feature is the beauty of the green Eastern Hills, the Higashiyama, in the background. Occasionally the tip of an old pagoda or a glimpse of some other old building can be seen, reminders of how temples and gardens have clustered along the foot of these hills for centuries.

The Heian Shrine garden and most of these new estates are the work of one man, Jihei Ogawa, whose professional art name was Ueji. He was born about the time of the great change of Meiji, as a seventh-generation member of a family which had had its garden-making establishment near the Heian Shrine for three hundred years. Although the construction of gardens during that period had not been extensive, it had never really ceased, as court nobles, temples, shrines, and other owners managed building or reconstruction. But, like the other traditional arts of the period, it became restricted by rules and conventions.

Ogawa grew up in the new age, feeling its sense of freedom from old repressions and conventions. In the 1890's, when his great opportunities began with the building of the Heian Shrine, he threw off many of the rules that had hampered his craft but retained its long-developed artistic techniques. He never became interested in Western gardens, but he did find interest in some of the new plants introduced.

I had the interesting experience of interviewing him in 1931, about a year before his death. We sat in the rustic Japanese cottage in the grounds of his establishment where he received his clients, surrounded by mossy rocks and lanterns which were waiting for buyers. An old man in a dark kimono, he talked through my interpreter, Chuichi Mori, a student of architecture, esthetics, and his own garden art, from the Imperial University.

"In the old days only certain plants were allowed in the garden, and these only in certain places," he told me. "But I decided there was no reason why any plant should not be used, even a foreign one, provided it was harmonious with its surroundings."

I was able that summer to visit a number of the gardens that were still wholly his work, and his point could be seen very clearly. An Ogawa garden could be identified almost immediately by its plants. Their freshness, their variety, and the way in which they became an important factor in the garden's appeal were unmistakable. Heian Shrine's garden is an outstanding example.

In laying out the various Nanzen-ji villas Ogawa usually functioned not only as the contractor but also as personal director, supervising the placement of each rock and tree. Often he was also the designer of the entire project, from bare hillside to finished estate. Occasionally the tradition of the gentleman-designer lingered, and the garden was said to be the work of the owner. But it was Ogawa who carried out the owner's ideas, and his individual touch showed through plainly. After a garden was finished, it was customary to leave it under his supervision almost indefinitely, so that some of these places came to show accumulations of his touch for thirty years.

Today, several of these Nanzen-ji estates have been turned over to the city of Kyoto and can be visited by special arrangement. One which shows the feeling of its owner-designer is Murin-an, developed in 1896 by Prince Aritomo Yamagata, working with Ogawa. Prince Yamagata had been a soldier and statesman of the Meiji Restoration, and his title was given in recognition of his great services. He was also a many-sided artist, skilled in the arts of the Noh drama and in poetry but especially interested in garden designing. In this he was really one of the "literary men" who created gardens free from conventional styling. He preferred to have them show their natural setting, was not interested in rock art, and considered water the most important element in the garden. He had previously built in Tokyo the garden of Chinzan-so, still a beauty spot.

Murin-an is devoted almost exclusively to an exposition of the beauties of water (Plate 176). It is a comparatively small garden of 3,140 square meters (about 3,755 square yards), not much more than a good-sized back yard, yet it gives a feeling of almost unlimited spaciousness and naturalism. This is because its main outlook is focused on a fine view of the Eastern Hills, seen through an opening in the trees which otherwise entirely enclose the garden.

46. Long path around the lake, Katsura, Kyoto. ▶

The water seems to flow down from these distant hillsides, entering the garden over a low, three-level cascade. It then broadens right and left into a pondlike spread, with two levels separated by a low fall. It flows out from this in two streams, the main one swinging downward to join the second in a broad sweep across the front of the house. The swing of the stream to the foreground was something new in designing and is attributed to Ogawa during a later period of completion.

Another Nanzen-ji estate, now belonging to the city, is that of the late Mr. Tokushichi Nomura. He was a devotee of the tea ceremony and a banker of Osaka. This garden is devoted to the tea theme, following the general outlines of the large, conventional pond and stroll garden leading to tea houses about the grounds (Plate 182). The estate covers about four acres centering around the wide, peaceful spread of water. It is developed with fine trees, beautiful shrubs, and ground cover in the Ogawa manner. The rocks include one very large stone that was brought to the site in pieces and reassembled. The cracks resulting from this are, as yet, inconspicuous.

The residence faces the lake. On the opposite shore a large pavilion overhangs the water, and adjoining this is a boat shed in which was kept a barge with a tearoom built on it. The boat could be poled out into the middle of the lake on moonlit nights. Three other teahouses are separated by sylvan settings, and some of their lanterns and water basins have special or historic interests (Plate 185). When Mr. Nomura occupied the house, a pair of black-tailed Japanese cranes lived in one corner of the lake, a modern expression of a very old concept.

Most of the estates developed around these mansions had a place set aside for large garden parties. (It is understandable that the proud owners liked to show them off occasionally.) These party spots were in the Western style, with broad lawns and sometimes a sheltering pavilion. But in spite of such occasional innovations, the gardens made by Ogawa were wholly Japanese. They represent, I think, the final flowering of a very old tradition which, in other hands, had mostly withered to dullness and mediocrity.

Perhaps in one sense, these Ogawa gardens are also decadent because their sole aim is to be as much like nature as possible—nature in its most enchanting and ideal moments. There are no sermons in stone nor landscapes that tell the story of man's life-progress. It could be asked: Is it really the function of art to carry such messages? Do inner meanings make art greater? Something like an affirmative answer seems to be inherent in the art of Muromachi, both in its painted landscapes and in those developed in stone. But perhaps this is not universal but coincidental.

Again it can be pointed out that the Ogawa gardens, as imitations of nature, are really a sort of three-dimensional photography, achieved through techniques carried to their highest attainments. Is this enough to account for their universal appeal, their ability to delight, not only through such things as perfect harmonic relations but also through some inner quality that strikes a universal response?

Questions like these must be answered individually and subjectively. Art, whatever it may be, has never been wholly defined nor confined.

◄ *47. Sanded path skirting a grassy bank, Sento Palace, Kyoto.*

The line of professional garden men has not ended with Ogawa, although he was probably the greatest of them all, a practical man first but also, I believe, an artist, probably endowed with genius. He lived at a time when originality had been all but smothered, and the new air of freedom had hardly begun to blow. Nevertheless, there is one piece of his work that displays a curious parallel to, or foreshadowing of, the future.

This is a rock composition in the lake of Heian Shrine's garden—a garden, it will be remembered, which was created to recall things long past, not to foreshadow things to come. The composition is a line of round stepping stones, their geometric forms strongly contrasting with the naturalistic environment of the rest of the garden, yet somehow not at all inharmonious with it (Plate 178). The stones are flat, low cylinders which seem sometimes to float on their own reflections. They are actually the tops of very wide, round old granite pillars which once served as the supports for a city bridge.[5] Each pillar top rises about eighteen inches above the water.

The progression of these stone circles makes a pattern in the quiet water of the lake that is not at all functional but purely esthetic. The stones do not even extend fully across to the opposite shore but end somewhere out in the water. And the distance between certain of the circles is so great it must be crossed by a leap. This pattern of circles moves with oblique angles and asymmetry, bringing to mind some of the geometric designs that were coming out of Europe's new art.

It is hardly conceivable that Ogawa had heard of this new art nor practiced it if he had. Here is a masterly example of a parallel reaction against too much naturalism. The source of Ogawa's inspiration can be found, I think, in the type of designs used in Japan's popular decorative arts. It is possible to see designs with similar feeling almost anywhere—on fans and fabrics and printed signs. Such designs appeared frequently in the older wood-block prints, where they were incorporated into everyday scenes. Both Ogawa and the Western artists may have received ideas from a common source, Japanese popular decorative motifs.

CHAPTER TWENTY-FIVE

Modern Developments from
a Long Heritage

WHEN, after some three hundred years of stagnation, new life finally entered the Japanese garden, it came, not through the old garden makers, nor from gardens elsewhere in the world, but in the immemorial way of the past, through artists and their art.

During the decade before the Pacific War, Japanese military elements, already looking forward to that war, had tried to prepare the country for it, both psychologically and financially, by building up feeling against Western ways and Western things. It was an attempt to move backward (in all but the mechanics of modern warfare, of course), and the only important result, I believe, was to slow down new Western influences and make them somewhat less visible. With the war lost and the nation launched into a period of postwar recovery and prosperity, Westernization never moved ahead so rapidly, making up for lost time.

Artistic influences, along with everything else relating to Japan and the rest of the world, have always moved over a two-way street. In the middle of the nineteenth century, after the country had been reopened to the West, exhibitions in Europe of Japanese wood-block prints revealed to the West an approach to art that was almost wholly new. These prints made a profound impression on the group of rebellious young artists who were then beginning to create a new style in art, one that turned away from realism. Much of their work was deeply affected by these prints.

In the late nineteenth century, while Japan was adopting and adapting much of the West's material culture—and with it, inescapably, much of the spirit that lay behind it—Western architects had come, just by coincidence, to realize the possibilities of new building materials. In searching for the best ways to handle steel, cement, and glass, they turned from the forms which Western major construction had used for centuries—that is, the piling up of brick and stone with the aid of arches and vaulting—and arrived at the use of steel framing, with curtain walls of glass and lighter materials.

Somewhat later, Western architects discovered that Japan had long used this basic type of construction in its wooden post-and-beam architecture and had perfected it in logicality and proportion.[1] The Japanese had also fully developed the use of modules (unit sizes) to aid in ease of construction. The buildings of Katsura, exemplifying these things, in particular, have come to be greatly admired.[2]

When the use of steel and glass and gadgets reached the point in the West where environments became too mechanical and inhuman to be tolerated, natural untouched materials were added to re-establish contact with nature. Uncut rocks and wood with its woody qualities revealed by natural finishes and fine graining were incorporated. Ideas for the use of these materials often came from Japan, where they had long been emphasized in construction and decoration, especially by the tea masters.

When the new methods of building with steel and glass finally made it possible for Western structures to expand their windows and other openings from what had been virtually slits to whole walls of glass, Western interiors for the first time were made aware of nature outside. The way in which Japanese buildings have always integrated outdoors and indoors, with their exterior walls made of movable panels, and their gardens designed to be seen wholly, or in part, from the building, brought new lessons in such indoor-outdoor integration.

All the new things that the West was developing were, of course, quickly reflected back to Japan. There they found open minds and often, on the part of artists and architects, full understanding of what was being attempted. The postwar period in Japan, with its tremendous programs of construction and its release from older restrictions, gave Japanese architects opportunities for work and experiments such as they had never known before. They found that they could often pick up the fumblings of the West and carry them forward with comprehension and competence. And the interest which the world was showing in their Japanese heritage stimulated a more intensive study of its possibilities.

Results are evident in some of the gardens built to go with the new buildings in Tokyo and other cities. Since land in the urban areas is usually very limited and expensive, these gardens often have to be small. They have even been built on rooftops, as is done in the United States under similar limitations. Most roof gardens, perhaps, are simply recreational areas, but others are put in for esthetic reasons (Plates 196, 205). It is not uncommon to find that an unsightly rooftop, visible from upper windows, has been converted with sand, a few rocks, and bamboo fencing—and even sometimes a few plants—into an attractive and entirely practical little landscape garden.

Since small city gardens are often no more than an open court, closely related to buildings, their designers have turned to earlier solutions of similar problems for ideas. Answers have been found in the small dry landscapes of Zen temples, in the courtyards of castles and palaces, even in the tiny light-well gardens of old-style mercantile establishments. All these stem from a central tradition and show similar techniques.

But when these techniques are used to develop modern ideas in design, the results often appear quite different from the original forms. Natural landscape is seldom the theme in these new gardens, and even hints of it are mostly missing. The new gardens vary greatly, of course, but some are almost pure abstractions of form, color, and texture, achieved through their materials. Most of them use only the traditional rocks, sand, and plants. They have not gone in for "mixed media," including pieces of metal, as in some of the adapted

258

gardens in the West.[3] Water is often omitted, perhaps for practical reasons. When used, it is usually in pools of geometric form, harmonized into the architectural design.

An example of such abstract designing is seen in the grounds around the building of the Japan Academy of Arts (Nippon Geijutsuin Kaikan) in Ueno Park, Tokyo.[4] It was created in 1958 by Isoya Yoshida, who also designed the building. This structure follows the lines of Heian-period architecture, as seen in the hand scrolls of that period, with round pillars and plain inset walls. The garden harmonizes with this older feeling while being a distinctly new development (Plates 194, 195).

Professor Yoshida, an eminent architect and member of the Japan Academy, studied in America and Europe as well as at the Tokyo Fine Arts College. He is devoted to Japanese art and has endeavored to incorporate its traditional details into his modern architectural designs and also into the gardens which he sometimes creates to go with his buildings. In the grounds of the Japan Academy he consciously brought together a number of details from classical Kyoto gardens, integrating them into a harmonious whole. Only a student of such matters, probably, could identify them, so well have they been blended, and only a few experts might suspect that the design was composed of divergent details.

One boundary of this garden is enclosed by high mounds of azaleas clipped into fairly smooth surfaces. This is derived from Emperor Gomizunoö's Shugaku-in estate, where, it will be recalled, smoothly top-trimmed shrubs cover the hillside between the Cloud Touching Arbor and the lake shore below. Another side of the academy grounds is enclosed by a brushwood fence made of stalks of dried bamboo twigs bound by coir string. This fence is a reproduction of one at Katsura which is widely admired.

Most of the level ground around the building is covered by a green lawn. But within a rectangular area, enclosed by the buildings and the brushwood fence, there has been put a sand-and-stone garden. Here the ground is deeply covered by the same whitish sand that is used at Ryoan-ji itself. It was brought from Kyoto's Shirakawa river, so that its coarse, sharp texture would hold the parallel scratches made by a wide-toothed rake.

Several fine rocks from Wakayama Prefecture, traditional source of "blue stones" for gardens, are carefully spaced out in one corner of the sanded area. Of interesting shape and texture, they still are not exceptional for size or form. Rather, they are small enough to blend easily into the overall design without becoming too emphatic. The use of such small stones is a definite understatement.

Separating the sand-covered end of the rectangular area from the grassy lawn is a flat band of dark stones like a strip of black paving. Part way down its length the straight line is broken by a stepped angle. A similar surfacing of black stones along the base of the building holds back the sand and forms a walkway outside its low windows. The stones used for these dark strips were brought from the Kamogawa river in Kyoto. Their form suggests flat black cobbles, and they have been fitted close together into a matrix to create a smooth surface. This will be recognized as a reproduction of the paving on Katsura's "Avenue of the Imperial Visit," which Prince Toshitada built to honor the coming of Emperor Gomizunoö.

Green lawn, white sand, and black paving strips form together a strong and simple

259

design that is clear-cut and very modern. It might suggest a Mondrian painting, except that its geometric sharpness of outline is softened by a few plants. Behind the brushwood fence rise stalks of bamboo. Several small flowering trees are also set at one end of the sanded space among other low planting, while here and there, about the other lawns, a few more small trees and shrubs have been carefully selected and placed for their design qualities.

Katsura and Ryoan-ji, the two gardens most called upon for details in this design, also furnish ideas to many other garden makers. Katsura, with its endless originality of detail—rich harvest of the group of artists who worked with the two princes—is one of the most popular sources (Plate 189), while Ryoan-ji has become almost a cult.[5]

It has not been forgotten that in Ryoan-ji abstract designing was brought to a peak of expression some four hundred years before Europe invented "modern" art. But more important than pride is the fact that there is something about the austere spread of sand and the perfection of natural rocks as abstract forms that fits perfectly today's artistic mood.

In 1960 Professor Yoshida created another garden which illustrates the beauty and interest that can be obtained by using nothing but plant forms as units in a design.[6] This garden is part of the museum called Yamato Bunkakan, near Nara. The building sits in a natural pine forest above an old pond. To display its art objects in the best way possible, the square exhibition hall has no windows in its outer walls, but its inner walls, which enclose a large four-sided light-well in the center of the building, are all of glass. The garden, in this inner enclosed space, is exactly comparable to the little interior gardens developed in old mercantile establishments (Plate 193).

Within this interior space the only things grown are huge stalks of giant bamboo emerging sparsely from the square of earth. The ground surface is covered smoothly with sand, and this surface is so well maintained that almost no fallen leaves ever deface its plain whiteness. The giant stalks shoot upward above the roof of the building to full tree height, varying in diameter from three to perhaps ten inches.

The heavy green lines of these stalks make a powerful design as, almost parallel, they bend slightly. But as in the garden of the Japan Academy any geometric severity is softened by leaves, for a haze of light-green foliage fills the space. Most of the bamboo's leaves grow above the roof, but a few branches shoot out from lower nodes. These are never allowed to become so thick as to obscure the main design, and most of the leaves fall off in winter, letting in the thin sun. In summer, when shade is pleasant, they thicken with new growth.

Not all Japanese postwar gardens show such perceptive artistry as do the two above, although there are many of great excellence. But as in other large world cities, almost anything can be encountered in Tokyo's private gardens. The traditional landscape pattern of rocks, water, and trees is popular and is usually carried out with skill and charm (Plate 198). Combinations of this naturalistic style combined with practical Western details are the usual rule. Results are often successful, sometimes ordinary, occasionally unfortunate.

Among the most prolific of modern garden builders are the new hotels, inns, and spas. The foreign-style hotels tend to use modernistic developments (Plate 191). But at popular hot springs it appears as if the native Japanese, in search of relaxation, forgets his pursuit of new ways and falls back comfortably on the old ones. Inns and spas build gardens usually in the traditional style. But sometimes they adapt these to modern ideas, as when, in creating the usual large tub of natural, flowing hot water at a hot-spring resort, the water is led into an outdoor pool built with smooth, rounded rocks and surrounded by a garden (Plate 192).

Professional landscape architects, who now are trained in the techniques of the West, as well as in their own traditions, are much interested, among other things, in developing public recreational areas—a fairly new concept in Japan. National and state parks have come into being and receive attention, along with city playgrounds and college campuses.

One of the most interesting examples of city park development is the treatment of the land around old Edo Castle, now the Imperial Palace, in the very center of metropolitan Tokyo. The five hundred and more acres of this walled and moated area constitute a huge, permanent hub around which the traffic of the modern city must move in a great whorl, for no roads cross it.

When, in the early seventeenth century, Tokugawa Ieyasu made Edo Castle his headquarters, he soon brought it to a great peak of power. Triple moats encircled it, the outermost being some nine miles around, with the swampy edge of Tokyo Bay as part of the defenses. Water for the moats came twenty miles by aqueduct from a river. On the inner moats, vast stone escarpments rose above the water. The gigantic pieces of granite of which these walls were made had been brought almost four hundred miles by barge from near Kobe. The whole vast structure of the castle has been called one of man's greater undertakings, worthy of being compared even to the Pyramids.

The town houses of the feudal lords and their many retainers lay just outside the castle's main gate, but they were still inside one of the larger moats. The area was known as Marunouchi ("within the walls"), which is still the name of Tokyo's financial district. To supply the wants of these residents, merchants and artisans from Osaka and Kyoto quickly opened branches nearby, and Edo became a boom town. The center of the commercial city was a bridge, known even yet as Nihon-bashi. Their business houses extended into a district called Ginza, Street of the Mint, which today is Tokyo's main shopping thoroughfare.

But after the Tokugawa rulers were gone and the emperor had moved to Tokyo, all the houses of these barons were cleared away, leaving for a time, a wide, weedy space. But soon the growing business district crowded to the edge of the largest moat. Today its many-storied office buildings look out across the wide expanse of water. Squared at the outer corner where it turns, it forms what is really a large lake in the center of the city. On the inside, the medieval bastions of the old castle stare back. Their high walls curve downward and out, in the graceful manner of this type of Japanese masonry, the line suggesting the underwater prow of an ancient ship of war. The tops of these walls are now crowned by pine trees, carefully trained to hang over them (Plate 197).

The moats enclosing the sides and back of the palace are equally picturesque. They present an ever-changing picture as one follows them around, for instead of all being great walls, the inner defenses are sometimes high, steep banks topped by lesser walls. These banks are overgrown with natural grass and shaded by scattered old pine trees. The moats vary their directions, with many angular turns and different widths, creating sometimes

261

deep green vistas. Wildfowl still come to rest on the quiet water, and in places the lotus pushes up its great leaves and flowers in season.

All this makes a restful outlook for the streets and houses of a city deficient in green areas. Long ago buildings crept all around the castle, and its outer defenses were opened to streets—but without benefit of much planning. A railway beltline now uses part of an outer moat as a right of way.

The castle's inner area, of several hundred acres, is mostly a park with fine trees. There is also the sacred rice field where, in spring, the emperor performs a ritual of immemorial antiquity when he ploughs a furrow to bring a blessing on all the fields of the nation. The castle's original towering donjon was burned in the seventeenth century and never rebuilt. Near the present palace buildings lies the Fukiage landscape garden, reported to be one of the finest gardens in Japan, with small lakes, hillocks, and beautiful plants.

But the public never sees it. Only ambassadors and authorized officials, along with a few others on imperial business or with an invitation, set foot across the two successive bridges that mark the entrance to the enclosed area. The outer bridge, a structure with double stone arches, leads from a broad open space formerly called the outer precincts of the palace. It is really a flat island surrounded by moats and once held many of the feudal mansions, but afterward it was taken over as an exterior part of the palace park. Its level area was partly visible across the moats, but it could only be entered by people coming on foot to bow in homage outside the bridge.

During World War II the palace buildings were severely damaged, but new ones have since been constructed. There was considerable pressure for a time to fill in the large moat, at least partly, and make more room for traffic. But public sentiment backed the landscape architects who held that central Tokyo needed beauty and parks in spite of its traffic problems.[7]

In the end, the moats were left intact and the wide area known as the outer palace precincts was turned into what is now called the Palace Plaza (Kokyo-mae Hiroba). Its acreage was grassed and planted with many young pine trees and the public allowed to come in. No doubt more people will come as shade develops. One boulevard was allowed to traverse it, permitting a stream of cars to by-pass the central area for a distance. Already the half mile or so of this empty green roadside has become, for motorists, a few moments of relief from the jungle of downtown Tokyo. As time goes on, the wisdom of keeping this space clear is certain to become more and more appreciated.

In Kyoto, meantime, garden developments were taking a quite different direction. True to its ancient attitude of rather lofty indifference to the somewhat frenetic atmosphere of Tokyo, the old city went serenely on its way, even after World War II (from which it was spared as an art city). While its people are far from ignorant of developments in the modern world, they select rather slowly what seems to them worthwhile. In the past, at times, it has appeared as if Japan were trying to swallow the entire modern world all at once, an attempt with sometimes peculiar consequences.

48. Flight of stone stairs, Joshoko-ji, Kyoto. ▶

The foreign visitor who has just arrived in Kyoto and is passing through its modern downtown streets with their neon and automobiles may wonder why, after all, he came. But he will find, after reaching his modern hotel, that he can wander through a side door into quaint little rear streets lined with the fronts of old-style business houses or the tiny windows of craft shops. He will see in the river long streamers of freshly dyed silk being washed, fluttering in the current like the enormous tails of goldfish. He can stroll in the evening to brightly lighted places of entertainment or go to tiny restaurants overhanging the river. As a sightseer he will be taken behind high old walls to come unexpectedly on the temples, palaces, and gardens that accumulated in the city during its thousand years as a capital.

Art is still produced and appreciated in Kyoto, and patrons are willing to pay for it. Arbiters of taste include the teachers of the tea ceremony—even though the head master of a tea school may represent his business in the Rotary Club. Sen no Rikyu's descendants flourish, with their three schools of tea. They meticulously keep up their traditional buildings and gardens, but these are not held as mere museums of the past. In the Ura Senke school, for example, is a new room in which the tea ceremony can be carried out in a modern setting—one in which it is unnecessary to sit on the floor. Every detail of this new room has been developed with careful thought, that it may accord with the basic canons of the old taste, even while making use of new ideas in design and materials.

The designing done in this school is largely the work of Mitsuhiko Sen, one of Rikyu's descendants in the fifteenth generation. An architect and designer, he also created a garden which lies just outside another new building which he planned for his father's school (Plate 190). This garden is merely a narrow strip of land, its surface covered with sand. A single fine rock is placed at one end, and behind it grow a few stalks of small bamboo. In spite of its resemblance to a temple garden, it is simply a piece of modern art, used as a decoration for the open wall of the room.

The most outstanding example of how art re-entered the Japanese garden through artists is to be found, probably, in the work of Mirei Shigemori, who has made more than a hundred gardens in the last three decades. Mr. Shigemori is not a professional garden man but an artist and a scholar for whom gardens have been a chief but not an only interest. He studied in the National Art Academy in Tokyo, where he must early have been made acquainted with the trends in Western art toward abstraction and nonrepresentation, for these things are overwhelmingly present in his work, while it remains, nevertheless, completely Japanese.

For him and other Japanese artists there could have been little about abstraction and nonrepresentation that was really new, for they have always been present in the art of the Far East. To mention one of the best known examples in painting, there is Sesshu's famous "splashed ink" landscape, painted about 1495, when he was seventy-six years old (Plate 201). While this picture can be recognized as another Chinese landscape, it was the work of a man who had been painting for a long lifetime, was the complete master of his art, and was reaching through to his subject in search of inner meanings.

◀ *49. Gate leading out of a moss garden, Sanzen-in, Kyoto.*

265

As for abstraction in garden art, we have already seen Ryoan-ji. But even geometric nonrepresentation was not unknown. In the Silver Pavilion garden we recall the design of parallel straight lines which is kept molded into the top of the Silver Sand Sea (Plate 204). While this design is generally taken to suggest formalized ocean waves, it can mean anything the observer cares to make it—or nothing.

Mr. Shigemori started making a few gardens about 1924. In 1936 he undertook an extensive study of Japan's gardens, covering all of the more important ones. Altogether he measured and mapped about five hundred, most of them, of course, private. For the history and background of the older and more noted places (such as I have included in this book) he went directly to contemporary sources, discarding local traditions.[8] In many cases these traditions have been found to be quite inaccurate.

The results of his researches and measurements were published in 1939 in twenty-six volumes.[9] Many fine pictures of each garden were included. By printing in each volume a section called "Sources" made up of quotations and extracts from the actual records, his work possesses an authenticity rare in Japanese writing on this subject. I have drawn upon it heavily for my historical material.

These historical studies made clear how vitality had drained from Japanese garden art after the middle of the Edo period when the professional garden men took over. In the late 1930's, the time when he came to this realization, he felt there was little prospect that these conditions would improve. It was then he decided to follow the earlier artist-masters and go into the creating of gardens as a serious art expression. Commenting on his efforts, he says: "When I began this work I desired that each garden should be a different and creative work of art. I was afraid this was going to be impossible, but because of what I had learned during my researches I found I could do it. Classic traditions are precious, but we should not imitate what has been done already. The older garden makers understood this very well."[10] And he quotes from the *Sakuteiki:* " 'While we are influenced by the gardens of the past and must consider the desires of the garden owner, we should still strive to create something different whenever we undertake a new piece of work.' "

In 1964, twenty-five years after this decision, he gathered together some of his efforts into a volume of pictures and description, calling it *Japanese Gardens Designed by Mirei Shigemori.*[11] It was a sort of one-man art show presenting forty-seven of the hundred and twenty or more gardens he has made. In the preface he states that he is presenting these examples of his work in the hope that critics and historians will judge it. He asks his critics to go, if at all possible, to the gardens themselves, and not to judge from the pictures alone. After I had seen some of the actual gardens I found this a justified request, for even the finest photographs cannot give the feeling of actual rocks, water, and plants. And photography is especially apt to falsify perspective and spatial relations.

The value of such a book, however, is great. The pictures were made shortly after the gardens were finished, or at least they show them as the designer wanted them to look. Gardens with plants change rapidly, of course, and even the rock-bound gardens of Japan are bound to change a little. Shigemori often uses plants as an important part of his design, so these pictures will preserve the original appearance. No such record exists for any of the older gardens.

Shigemori states that, like most artists, he has seldom been satisfied with his work when it is completed. He hints of the difficulties of working before and after the war period and of satisfying owners who held ideas different from his own. He refused certain commissions, he says, because of such differences. Around the world, other artists and landscape architects may find it significant that, even under these conditions, well over a hundred patrons were willing to pay the not inconsiderable amounts necessary to carry out his highly original ideas.

Traditionalists who love the serene old landscape gardens that reflect idealized nature are due for a shock when they look at the gardens shown in this book. The experience could be like hearing atonality in music for the first time. For while all the traditional materials of the older gardens have been used—and nothing more—they are put together in a way that reflects accurately the concurrent feeling in art of the period (Plate 200). Water, rocks, sand, moss, trees, shrubs, pavements, water basins, lanterns, even stone boats, and the old straight line of "night mooring stones" are there. The designer has called upon the whole historic repertoire of devices made known to him through his studies. But he has assembled them differently. While landscape is indicated in some of his designs, it is usually a stylized abstraction. In others, there is no hint of landscape at all. And in the selection and arrangement of the rocks, he uses a whole new personalized idiom for expression.

Down the centuries, the way the stones have been arranged has revealed most clearly the individuality of the garden maker. Shigemori does not violate basic principles of design, but he may seem to be doing it when he throws out every traditional rule of the rock art as it is related to depicting nature. He makes clear, in discussing the individual gardens shown in this book, that he had a basic and appropriate theme in mind for each one, and the rocks carry this out. It will be realized that this way of approaching a design, with a theme to develop, parallels the way the Zen artists approached their work. But Zen itself is not one of the things in which Shigemori is interested, although much of his work has been done for Zen temples. Such temples, in fact, seem to favor him particularly, which may not be surprising in view of their traditions for fostering creative art.

One of his earlier temple projects was the redevelopment of the hojo garden of the Tofuku-ji monastery in Kyoto. This institution belongs to the Rinzai sect of Zen, which was introduced into Kyoto in 1237 from Kamakura, where the sect was founded. Later, the Tofuku-ji attained outstanding importance, which was recognized when it was included among the Go-zan or "Five Mountains" of Kyoto. The Go-zan were the five leading Zen institutions of the city.[12] Tofuku-ji possesses many fine works of art, among them paintings by Sesshu, who is believed to have lived there for a time.

In 1938, not overwhelmed by its six centuries of existence, Tofuku-ji set up a "hundred-year plan" for its future. As part of its redevelopment under this plan, Mr. Shigemori was asked to construct a new garden for the abbot's reception hall. This typical building has a long porch that overlooks a sanded rectangle enclosed by a wall.

In developing this rectangle, Shigemori decided to recall the old importance of Tofuku-ji by creating the "Five Mountains." In one corner he built a series of low mounds covered with thick green moss. When one looks down on them from normal eye level, their general effect is that of an undulating chain of forested hills. Nothing about these contours

267

suggests in any way the tall, peaked "miniature mountains" of the literal-landscaping period. In fact, without some explanation, the average visitor would probably see only a series of green mounds contrasting with the sand and rocks of the rest of the garden.

In the remaining three-fourths of Tofuku-ji's rectangle Shigemori assembled four groups of large stones. They are notably huge and rugged and arranged with strong up-and-down contrasts. High upthrusting peaks rise above prone giants, half buried, while smaller stone groups reflect similar contrasts. The four groups are given the old name of Horai and the specific names of the four magic isles that were once believed to lie off the coast of China—in Japanese, Horai, Eishu, Hojo, and Koryu. In the mid-twentieth century this motif seems to have been used only as a pattern for placing the larger rocks, and not with any reference to its traditional significance as Isles of the Immortals. Instead, Mr. Shigemori explains that these rocks are intended to suggest power. He was strongly aware of the atmosphere of Kamakura in the background of Tofuku-ji and wanted someway to convey this feeling in the garden. He decided that great stones and strong contrasts would bring to mind the strength and power of the Kamakura period. The design is not in any way a depiction of landscape.

The motif of the Mystic Isles was followed with some reference to its meaning in the garden of the small Kyoto temple known as Zuiho-in. This name means "Felicitous Mountain" and is a descriptive reference to the old isles of eternal youth. In 1961, in developing a garden for this little temple, Shigemori chose to depict the mountain by raising a single great peak above an assemblage of other stones, all supported by a mossy base (Plate 199). Although the resultant design is a sort of magic landscape, the design is carried out not with any hint of realism but as a stylized abstraction. The rocky peak does not really look like a mountain but is more, perhaps, like a monument. And the surrounding rocks are not mountainlike but are supporting masses.

Perhaps Shigemori's most original garden design belongs to a small castle in the town of Kishiwada on the outskirts of Osaka. The present castle is an exact reproduction in ferroconcrete of the original, which was put up about the time of Hideyoshi.[13] Few of Japan's original castles have survived the years because their towering wooden heights were peculiarly vulnerable to lightning or, later, to bombing. Before World War II, the city of Osaka had rebuilt Hideyoshi's great castle and used it as a museum. Other cities owning castle relics recognized how uniquely successful as visitor destinations were these picturesque white structures, and a number have been restored. Kishiwada completed its rebuilding in 1953, and the mayor engaged Mr. Shigemori to develop its grounds as a park.

The little castle on its hilltop, only two stories high, with its tower a third story, stands on its original tall stone platform. The citadel area around this stone foundation is a level space of some 15,000 square feet, partly enclosed by walls. It was desired to have in this space some type of park development that would withstand the wear and tear both of time and of public usage—that is, which might serve on occasion for such municipal events as exhibitions and outdoor entertainments. These considerations eliminated the possibility of creating a typical green park.

Looking down on this open space from the tower balcony, Mr. Shigemori conceived the idea of making the high spot where he stood one of the main viewing points for the garden. The thought had its modern roots in the outlook from an airplane. While most Japanese gardens are traditionally laid out to be seen from some main viewing point, or sometimes, as in a stroll garden, from a series of them, never before had one of these points been up in the air.

As he cast about for a motif on which to hang further developments, the military background of the site brought to his mind an old story of the Chinese general K'ung Chu-ko of Ming, who was famed as a strategist. On one occasion he arranged his forces into eight different camps, seven of them set around the central headquarters. The seven peripheral groups were known by the characteristically Chinese names of Heaven, Earth, Wind, Cloud, Dragon, Tiger, Bird, and Snake camps. With this idea as a starting point, Mr. Shigemori devised the plan of setting up eight different stone groups to represent the eight camps. From this is derived the name Garden of Eight Camps or Hachi-jin no Niwa. There were thus to be two main ways of looking at the garden: one, an overall view from the tower, looking down, and the other, a ground display of eight different stone compositions, like eight different pictures.

The design, intended to be seen from the tower, took the form of a linear outline figure projected onto the level space below (Plates 202-3). The lines from which it is created are low rock walls, about two feet wide and one foot high, made of natural stones carefully fitted together. They are set onto a ground cover of sand and from above stand out with great clarity. The design created by these walls is a large, angular free-form figure made up of three concentric walls, each an angular figure in itself, but together making a complex, highly sophisticated example of modern designing. It has, apparently, no other meaning than itself.

Set about within this figure are the eight stone groups which, from above, attract little notice. But on the ground, as one follows the path which delineates the total design, one realizes that each group was intended to be seen and appreciated as an abstract design from just the point where the path leads. The rocks in each group are of a similar material, a sort of chlorite shale from the island of Shikoku which has a natural greenish color. This is enhanced when it is damp.

In representing the eight camps, each group may suggest to the imagination the name of that camp. Thus the headquarters in the middle centers around one stone towering high above the others—the commander? In the Dragon Camp a suggestion of hard saurian folds may be felt. The rocks of the Cloud Camp seem to be amorphous shapes floating on sandy ether. The Heaven Camp is a group of tall slender stones, all pointing upward. And so on with the others.

A few large pines and other trees and shrubs grow outside the design area with apparent casualness. They serve as an unobtrusive background of green to the central design.

While visitors are not supposed to walk through the design area, which is marked off by tiny bamboo fences and narrow strips of grass, the whole space could, if desired, be used for almost any purpose and trampled in the process. But it could then be quickly restored, undamaged.

Thus, after a history of some thirteen hundred years, the designing of gardens in Japan is still a vital artistic activity. During this long period, the art of the garden has been used to create landscape settings and parks and to make intimate gardens. But the garden has never been a means for merely displaying the products of horticulture. Growing plants outdoors has been recognized only as one of the tools of garden making, not as an end in itself.

Rather, the making of a garden in Japan has always been regarded as an effort of artistry. Sometimes it has served as an individual expression and has achieved high art. It has also been used to express various concepts, especially religious ideas. Always it has served to provide simple delight in the beauty of natural things.

The Japanese garden, in time, became a unique achievement far outstripping its prototypes in China, both in variety and in depth. Its influence is now beginning to be felt seriously in the West, its day as a quaint toy entirely over. It seems probable that these gardens will have an important effect on others around the world as they become better known and understood beyond their own country. This will be especially true of the rock art, which has already fascinated a few artists outside Japan. In time, I believe, the use of natural rocks to create designs will be recognized as one of the world's important art forms.

PART FOUR

Plates Illustrating the Text

50. *A large hilly island in the Pei Hai lake of the former Imperial Palace in Peking is crowned by a white stupa in Lamaistic style. The island shore is partly bordered by a carved white-marble balustrade and shaded by willows and other trees. An impressive three-arched gateway marks the entrance to the island from a wide bridge.*

51. In the lake of the Summer Palace, some miles outside Peking, stands a marble bridge in high-arched "camel back" style. Such arches were first developed in the Chinese countryside to allow boats moving through the canals to pass under with their sails raised.

52. Surviving great gardens of China have come down the centuries like a long reflection out of the past, for there were few important changes either in architecture or in garden design. In the park of the former Imperial Palace in Peking, along the north shore of the Pei Hai lake, the lotus still lifts its great leaves and flowers in midsummer. On the shore of the lake are various structures in imperial style, among them five small pavilions that were thought to suggest the claws of an imperial five-toed dragon.

53. Lotus petals form a traditionally stylized seat for the deity Amida in the Phoenix Hall of the Byodo-in temple at Uji, near Kyoto. The statue was carved in wood by the artist Jocho in the eleventh century.

54. *The true lotus lily, Nelumbium nelumbo (L) Druce, has large flowers with papery petals, usually pink but sometimes white. Golden stamens cluster around a curious flat-topped receptacle, dotted with holes, in which are the seeds. The plant grows as a native from the mouth of the Volga River across Central Asia and India to China and Japan and even as far south as Australia.*

55. *The young leaves of the lotus plant suggest a jade bowl with fluted edges. They have a bluish translucent waxen surface which, through surface tension, causes any drops of water that fall into the bowl to form rolling crystal globules. Both leaves and flowers rise on long stems above the level of the water.*

56. The garden of the Taj Mahal exhibits typical Persian formality, with its central approach axis in the form of a wide canal, intersected halfway up by a cross canal. At the point of intersection the water is formed into a large square pool. Within this is a square marble platform with a shoulder-high terrace rising above it. The center of the upper terrace is filled with a deep square tank. In this seem to float four white water lilies. They are carved from marble, and out of the center of each flower can be projected a small jet of water.

57. *In certain old Japanese gardens one can still sometimes see the outlines of a giant tortoise holding an island firmly above the flood—a remnant of the ancient tale of the giant tortoises ordered to stabilize the Isles of the Immortals. Drawing by Samuel Newsom of an islet in the lake of the Gold Pavilion, Kyoto.*

58. *High-stepping horses, all exuberantly going somewhere, seem to exemplify the spirit of China's Han empire, which reached from Korea to Afghanistan and rivaled in power and extent its great contemporary, the Roman empire. The Han spirit of expansion and innovation affected the art of gardens, among the other arts of the period. Stone bas-relief from a Han tomb. (Musée Guimet, Paris)*

59. *The fantastic Lu-shan mountains in South China were among those furnishing inspiration for the introduction of hills and rocks into Chinese landscape gardens. This came about partly through the White Lotus Society, whose members had their headquarters in the Western Forest monastery of Hui Yuan in these mountains. The painting shown here is a subjective representation of the cliffs and falls of Lu-shan as painted much later (in the twelfth century) by Chiang Shen, after Fan K'uan. (National Palace Museum, Taipei)*

60. *Double white lotus blossom. The early Aryans of India called the flower the dawn lily and associated it with the birth of the day. It thus became a religious symbol long before the Buddhists took it over to represent the power of the soul to rise from the muddy waters of evil to the sunlight of a better existence.*

61. *Not far from where ancient Chinese civilization began rises the mountain called Huashan. Like all the highlands of Asia, it is not volcanic but formed by vast uplifted folds of the earth's crust, cracked and tilted into almost incredible peaks and precipices. Wherever a foothold exists on these slopes, pines and other conifers take hold. Clouds may close in whitely around the peaks, shutting out all view. When they lift, the landscape below is revealed through tenuous veils of drifting mist. Such scenery has inspired China's landscape painters for centuries and, through them, the landscape garden makers of both China and Japan.*

62. *Rocky islets holding pine trees, such as these, are prototypes of those constructed in Japanese gardens. The view here is of islands at Matsushima (Pine Islands), near Sendai.*

63. *The beauties of nature have furnished a pattern to garden makers in Japan since the formal building of gardens around palaces was introduced from China in the seventh century. River scene near Kyoto.*

64. The shrines of Ise, sacred to the ancestress of the imperial house (whom scholars recognize as also the Sun Goddess), are simple wooden buildings with bark roofs. Prehistoric chieftains lived in such structures, and at their death the buildings were turned into shrines for their spirits, thus preserving the form of the structure down the ages.

65. Early Japanese veneration for spirits felt dimly to exist in rocks as well as in living things still finds a direct expression in this ancient pair of rocks on the shore not far from Ise. Now regarded as a married pair, they are linked by a sacred rope of rice straw. All deities of the native Shinto religion are such nature spirits. The torii *gate erected to frame this view is the most frequent symbol of Shinto.*

66. Splendid forests still surround the shrine of the Sun Goddess at Ise. Such groves may be taken as Japan's earliest gardens. At the edge of this forest the modern world is still checked, and time seems to flow backward. After they have paid their respects before the shrine, devotees linger to enjoy the beauty of great trees, the glossy green of undergrowth, and glimmering vistas of the river. Such pleasure seems to be a real, if unrecognized, part of the religious feeling present. The photo shows a procession of ritualists near the shrine.

67. *In constructing huge grave mounds for their principal personages, Japanese of the protohistoric period practiced unconsciously, on a large scale, the techniques of landscape development. The mounds that enclosed the tombs were partly built up with soil taken from the surrounding moat. It is believed that the mounds were originally covered with grass and the entire area enclosed by a belt of trees. This picture shows one of three mounds in the Uwanabe group of such tombs near Nara, made in the fifth century* A.D. *There is evidence that they held the consorts of Emperor Nintoku. Out of veneration for the imperial line, these mounds and most others of their type remain unexcavated.*

68. *This stone monument, known in Japanese as a Shumisen, represents Mount Sumeru, the vast peak which, according to Buddhist belief, separates earth from heaven. The monument was originally made of four stones, but one, placed between the bottom and the middle stone, is now missing. Chiseled on the stones are the wavy outlines of mountains, rising range on range to the peak. The structure is hollow, so that water introduced through a hole near the top can be made to gush from four small holes near the bottom. The monument is believed to have been made in the seventh century, possibly in the reign of the empress Suiko. It may be the only surviving example of a Shumisen in the Chinese and Korean style, dating to T'ang times. It is now in the grounds of the Tokyo National Museum.*

69. *A rear view of the Shumisen shows the opening into its hollow interior. Water could be introduced through this opening (say by a bamboo conduit) to fall into the bowl-like bottom stone and spurt out through small openings, turning the monument into a fountain.*

70. *Excavated from about the same spot as the Shumisen of the Tokyo National Museum (Plate 68) is a stone figure of two men, one seated on the lap of the other. One man holds a cup from which water can be made to flow. The faces of these two men are not Japanese, for they have large, prominent noses and round eyes. They may represent "barbarians," often entertained as guests by the Japanese for political or diplomatic reasons. The carving stands in the grounds of the Tokyo National Museum.*

71. *With flowers suggesting lilies-of-the-valley, the Andromeda shrub (Pieris japonica) still grows extensively in Nara Park, for the tame deer there will not nibble at its leaves. A number of old poems reveal that this shrub was also grown in the early gardens of Nara.*

72. *This detail from an eighth-century painting shows a lady seated on a rock, presumably in a Nara garden, beside a picturesque tree. The rock, much convoluted and totally unnatural, is painted in a provincial imitation of the contemporary Chinese T'ang style. The picture reveals an awareness of Chinese garden fashions and styles of painting on the part of Nara artists. It is part of a screen painting belonging to the imperial treasure house at Nara known as the Shoso-in. (Shoso-in Museum, Nara)*

73. On a snowy morning in the ninth century a scene something like this may have been visible within the precincts of Kyoto's first imperial palace enclosure, the Daidairi. The building shown here is part of the present-day Heian Shrine, erected to commemorate the 1,100th anniversary of the founding of the city. Insofar as knowledge permits, this building is a replica of an end pavilion of the great Hall of State.

74. *In spring, clouds of pinkish cherry blossoms hang over the shore of the ancient Hirosawa Pond, near Kyoto, and drift down to the quiet green water. Lakes like this were the principal feature of fine country estates in the Heian period and served their noble owners as places for gay boating parties.*

75. *This bit of pond in Kyoto is all that remains of the Divine Spring Garden, Shinsen-en, the first great imperial pleasure park of the capital. Still supplied by natural water sources —the divine spring—it was forgotten for centuries. Recognized, it became a small public park. Recently a shrine to the emperor Kammu was erected on an island in the pond.*

76. *Heian courtiers, in pleasure boats designed after the Chinese style, were often part of the early Japanese garden scene. Some of those enjoying the outing played the flute; others composed poems on the beauty of the landscape. Such a scene is annually re-enacted in Kyoto when groups devoted to the study of old music and poetry don the costumes of the Heian period and go out on the river in decorated boats. The event usually takes place in late May at Kyoto's riverside resort of Arashiyama.*

77–78. *A cascade and streamlet, flowing from behind and among the buildings of the Sambo-in temple (sixteenth century) may give an idea of the appearance of the earlier streamlets of the eleventh century. It is likely, however,*

thta too many rocks have been used in this later reproduction. These two views, taken from slightly different angles, form a panorama of this section of the garden.

79. *The forecourt garden of a mansion of the Heian period is shown here, as depicted in a conte*
porary painting. The entertainment being presented is a cockfight. The master of the house sits in
main hall with friends and attendants, while the ladies of the household peep from behind the curta
at his right. The central space of this front garden was kept clear for events such as this, but naturali.

東對

東中門

...andscaping was developed around either side. At upper right is seen the typical little stream issuing
from between two buildings and flowing into the foreground. On the other side are trees, a hillock, and
flowering plants. The picture is part of a scroll called Nenju Gyoji (Calendar of Festivals) belonging
to the Tokyo National Museum. It is believed to be a copy of a twelfth-century original by Mitsunaga.

80. *As in a scene from* The Tale of Genji, *members of the Kyoto Peers Club, modern descendants of Heian courtiers, gather in a quiet garden to play the ancient game of courtly football called* kemari. *For this occasion they wear the costumes of their ancestors. Open courts for this game were often included in the grounds of noblemen's estates.*

81. *An actual remnant of the glories of the Heian period is the 900-year-old Phoenix Hall (Hoö-do) belonging to Byodo-in temple near Kyoto. Built in 1052, it still houses its original gilded image of Amida. The structure is in the style of a* shinden *mansion, showing Chinese influences. However, the side wings and end pavilions are not enclosed buildings but only extended ornaments.*

*82. The twelfth-century Eifuku-ji temple garden in Kamakura, once
described as being as beautiful as Amida's paradise, is now overgrown
with large reeds, and its lake is once more filled in by rice fields. Only
this modern stone marker announces the site.*

83. The long, winding "dragon pond" of Sekisui-en garden in Kyoto was built by Taira Shigemori in the twelfth century. The shape of the pond marked a trend away from the old open boating lakes of the Heian courtiers. In the center are some of the straight-line "night mooring stone" arrangements.

84. Today the old pond of Moötsu-ji lies dreaming, long shadows of ancient cryptomerias still stretching across its mirror surface. The gay red bridge that crossed it in the twelfth century and the buildings on its shore have vanished, but their foundation stones can still be found. The bridge started across the water at about the point where this picture was taken. The central island which it crossed is now submerged. The bridge then continued straight on to the opposite shore, and the path led to the main entrance among the distant trees, left. The stones that outlined a rocky peninsula are still visible at right, while lying off its point are the remains of the tortoise island, with its high headstone.

85. *The sense of serenity in the woodland dry cascade and pool of Saiho-ji's garden is induced largely by the horizontality of flat-topped stones which create a feeling of repose. Although it appears as if water might flow through this cascade after the next rain, no water has ever been there. The entire cascade and pool are the work of man, and every stone in sight was brought from another location. Proof of this can be seen under the two large stones, center right, where the soil has washed away, revealing the bed of small pebbles on which such stones are always placed for stability.*

86. Saiho-ji possesses its own example of the straight-line "night mooring stones," crossing a small pond which lies apart from the main lake. The suggestion that these might be foundation stones of a former building is discounted by the fact that they are irregular in position and unsuitable in shape. The traditional name suggests that they represent a convoy of junks moored in some safe haven for the night. But it seems more likely that this name is a later explanation made up when the original meaning (if any) had been forgotten.

87. Mosses have taken possession of Saiho-ji's garden, attracting more interest than do such showy plants as the azalea and the lotus. These mosses carpet the ground in hummocky waves of emerald, jade, and bronzy green, while grey-green lichens on the tree trunks create a mysterious haze through the shadows. Over forty varieties of moss are said to grow in this garden, and they account for the temple's popular name: Koke-dera or Moss Temple.

88. *Floating in a sea of moss in Saiho-ji's hillside garden is a tortoise island. To the eye of the imagination the creature is quite clear: head back, flippers barely moving. But in the cold light of realism he disappears, and we see only a pile of lichen-covered stones which might have been discarded after some building operation. The head is the large stone at the right.*

89. *"Heaven above, Hangchow below," runs an old Chinese saying. Villas and gardens still line the shore of the lake at Hangchow, doubling in its waters the azure, turquoise, and rose colors of their glazed tile walls and the tip-tilted corners of their little pavilion roofs.*

90. *The amenities of Chinese garden art in the Sung period are revealed by this twelfth-century painting by Su Han-ch'en showing a terrace with potted plants, a picturesque tree, and an ornamental rock. The time is early spring, and the flowering apricot has put out its first blossoms. The lady has set up her dressing table outside, although her maid seems to find it still chilly. Early spring flowers have been placed among the cosmetic boxes. The painting is generally known as "Lady Before a Mirror in a Garden." (Museum of Fine Arts, Boston)*

91. Suggesting P'eng-lai, the mystic island where the Immortals lived, this seven-stone arrangement in Tenryu-ji's garden may have been the work of a Chinese rock craftsman who had come to Japan. Its soaring abstraction is in strong contrast to the serene stability of the native Japanese rockwork of the period, illustrated by the stones of the Saiho-ji garden. Here the rocks duplicate in three dimensions the style of the Chinese Sung landscape painters. This may be the only remaining example of contemporary Sung rock art.

92. The stone bridge in Tenryu-ji's garden is made up of three flat natural stones laid end to end. Where the ends meet, they are supported by other rocks rising from the water. The bridge crosses an inlet which leads to the cascade, left. In the water, right, is the rocky islet that completes the trio of arrangements.

93. The cascade of the North Hill Villa, made about 1224, is probably this one that survives today in the garden of the Gold Pavilion (later name of the estate). At its foot is the famous carp stone, attempting to swim up the rapids and so become a dragon. The rocks at the right of this cascade are in their original form; those at the left have become disarranged and have not been restored.

94. *Tenryu-ji's small garden, originally constructed in 1256, appears here in a composite view.*
The famous Chinese Sung-style rock bridge, cascade, and island lie opposite the peninsula and rock
the foreground but are not clearly visible. At right can be seen some of the sand that forms a foregroun

95. *This popular-style silk-fan painting, done by an anonymous*
Chinese artist in the 1930's, catches the traditional and nostaligic
beauties of the scene around Hangchow's lake. It shows the causeway
with its willows and half-moon bridge, the pagoda-crowned hills,
and a garden in the foreground.

ween the building and the shore. The middle ground of the picture is the lake with its islands and ficial hillocks. The background, now formed by trees, was originally a fine view of the river and a ull hill called Kame-yama. In summer a native water lily sends up its small pads and yellow flowers.

96. A personal knowledge of China's picturesque mountains gained by the artist Sesshu on a trip to China, together with his famous re-creations of Chinese masterpieces of landscape art, gave rise to paintings such as this and found reflection in the gardens he made on his return, doubtless inspiring those made by other landscape painters. Fan-shaped painting after the Sung-period master Hsia Kuei. (Collection of Nagatake Asano, Tokyo)

97. *Landscape painting of the Sung period showing the vast precipices of China's mountains as depicted by one of its greatest artists, Fan K'uan (990–1030). The same tremendous heights were suggested in the gardens of the period by the use of soaring, precipitous rocks. (National Palace Museum, Taipei)*

98. *Chinese children at play in a twelfth-century garden at K'ai-feng. Flowers of the double rose mallow surround a tall rock which was probably typical of the rock artistry of that period and eventually entered Japanese gardens also. Painting by Su Han-ch'en (c. 1115–70). (National Palace Museum, Taipei)*

99. When the lake of the Gold Pavilion was drained in 1956 for removal of accumulated silt, the large rocks which form individual islets could be seen as they rest on the bottom. Usually they are more than half submerged.

100. Autumn view of the Gold Pavilion lake as seen from a small porch projecting from one end of the the building. This porch has been likened architecturally to the classical "fishing hall" which terminated the forward arcade of a shinden-style mansion.

101. Exaggerated perspective makes the lake of the Gold Pavilion garden appear larger than it really is, an effect achieved by filling the foreground with interesting details, while the distant reaches seem too far away for details to be noted. The tip of the central island that divides the lake into near and far sections is seen at the right, marked by a small pine tree which is kept carefully dwarfed to maintain proper proportions and perspective.

102. Today's replica of the original Gold Pavilion, like its predecessor, stands out with sudden delicate clarity when seen under the conditions considered classic for its viewing: with snow heaped on tree and rock and roof above the frozen lake.

103. *Something of the ineffable, calm beauty of the Gold Pavilion lake is caught here, with the porch of the building at left. The island at the right is the "Coming Tortoise," with its long headstone pointed left and one flipper plainly visible beyond. The "Going Tortoise" (out of sight, right) is headed in the opposite direction.*

104. *This is the original Gold Pavilion, Kinkaku-ji, as it stood for five and a half centuries, dingy with its years, before it was burned in 1950. It had been constructed in 1398 by the Ashikaga shogun Yoshimitsu. On his death the estate was converted into a memorial temple called Rokuon-ji, as it is still called.*

105. One of the bridges in the Silver Pavilion garden reveals its stylistic relationship to a similar bridge in the Tenryu-ji garden. Its plank stones are laid end to end and supported where they meet on a natural stone pillar rising from the water. This view also shows some of the original Muromachi rockwork surviving around the central island.

106. Small heaps of white sand, left over at some time after the ground had been covered, have become permanent features in several of Kyoto's Zen temple gardens. Those seen here are in a side garden of Daisen-in. It is believed that such a ground cover and surplus sand were probably the origin of the present sand structures in the Silver Pavilion garden. As time passed, they grew in size almost imperceptibly as additional sand was brought to renew the covering.

107. *The building known as the Silver Pavilion, which has given its popular name to the whole garden, is a rustic two-storied structure built about 1490. It is a copy of the Ruri-den, which was constructed in the Saiho-ji garden nearly two hundred years before by Muso Kokushi. Legend has it that there was originally a plan to use silver foil on the ceiling of the upper story, a chapel, as gilt was used on its predecessor, the Gold Pavilion.*

108. The use of flat-topped rocks, with an occasional peaked stone for contrast, is typical of the best Muromachi rock art. It is seen here around the main island of the Silver Pavilion pond, constructed by Yoshimasa in 1483. The two kinds of rocks used display the combined influence, respectively, of the Saiho-ji and the Sung styles. The present monolithic bridge replaced one at this point originally built of wood in the "arched dragon back" style.

109. The hillside spring of the Silver Pavilion's upper garden was copied after a similar spring at Saiho-ji, made several centuries before. Here a single large rock to the rear and two wing stones hold back the dirt of the hillside. The water, seeping through below, lies in a small circle of stones, with its excess trickling out between those in front. It then flows away in a small rill. This spring was long buried under silt washed down from above but was excavated when research indicated its probable presence here.

110. A romantic view from the second story of the Silver Pavilion showing the ground plan of the garden.

111. *The garden of the Silver Pavilion holds two curious ornaments made of white river sand. The truncated cone, called the Moon Facing Height, is about five feet high and sixteen feet in diameter on the ground. The terracelike level of sand just beyond is the Silver Sand Sea, about two feet high. Originally the latter was probably an ordinary spread of sand before the building, while the cone is believed to have grown from a heap of surplus sand.*

112. *This typical landscape painting of the Muromachi period is of the kind that Zen landscape gardeners also tried to suggest in rocks, sand, and plants. The artist was Sesshu, a Zen monk, now regarded as having been Japan's greatest painter. Like most of these Zen landscapes, the picture may be interpreted as representing man's spiritual life. The viewpoint, symbolized by the resting pilgrim at right, is that of one who has climbed to high places and now looks back on what lies below, and ahead to what is still to be achieved. The vast peaks and spires of the mountains represent spiritual enlightenment or the understanding of man and the universe. The dark valleys with their villages and boats stand for the mundane life from which man seeks to lift himself. Weatherbeaten pines along the way tell of individuals who have stood firm, although torn and bent by life's storms. The waterfall stands for life itself, ever falling, ever renewed. A monastery on higher ground shows that some men are trying to achieve permanently a certain height in their daily thinking. The tiny figure of the pilgrim in this vast cosmos shows that man, although he may be small, is still an intergral and harmonious part of the whole. This painting is one of four in a series entitled "Landscapes of the Four Seasons" and represents summer. (Collection of Shojiro Ishibashi, Tokyo)*

113. *Sesshu is known for the way he achieved the massive effects of mountains and rocks in his paintings by using strong, often angular brush strokes. In the Zen gardens the same effect was obtained by using strong, distinctive rocks with flat tops, straight sides, and pronounced angles. The interrelations between real landscape, the paintings, and the painting gardens thus came to a full circle when the strokes of the painters re-created the essentials of rocky landscape while actual rocks were used in gardens to suggest the brush strokes of the painters. (Collection of Soichiro Ohara, Okayama)*

114. *Sesshu (1420–1506), like other artists of the time, tried his hand at different art forms, including garden making. Portrait by Unkoku Toeki. (Joei-ji, Yamaguchi Prefecture)*

115. *The garden at Joei-ji temple, in Yamaguchi Prefecture, is possibly one of those made by Sesshu. The rock groupings, in typical Muromachi style, are set about a wide space between the temple building and the pond. The space is not level but mounded and now covered with coarse grass. Small clipped shrubs growing near the rocks tend to conceal their more subtle artistic relationships. At the present time it is difficult to note any such relationships, for changes that are not now discernible could have been made in the course of the five centuries since the rocks were arranged.*

116. *The crane islet in Joei-ji's pond probably survives with little change from its original form. It shows the flat-topped rock artistry of Muromachi at its best, with the similarity between the decisive brush strokes of Sesshu and the flat surfaces of the stones clearly evident.*

117. *View across Joei-ji's pond with a distinctive island made of two stones in the foreground. The cascade coming down the hillside in the background is crossed by a stone bridge. At left is the tip of the crane island.*

118. *The garden of Daisen-in temple as it appeared before 1961. Every stone used here is remarkable for its unusual and precise form. The stones are probably the choice gleanings of a whole era of earlier collecting. The straight flat stone that crosses the river formerly presented something of a mystery in the design. Then it was discovered that it marked the point where the garden was originally divided into two parts by the construction of a wooden bridge above it. Many critics still prefer this unified full-length view of the scene.*

119. *In this detail the dry waterfall in the Daisen-in garden seems to emerge from a typical high, hanging valley, as seen in many Sung landscape paintings. The fall is suggested by a curiously striated rock set upright between two higher peak rocks.*

120. A closer view of Daisen-in's peaks and precipices shows the waterfall between two peaks, slightly right of center. The bridge is large enough to serve as a human crossing for this sandy stream, but if it is regarded as on the human scale the landscape loses its large imaginative elements and becomes merely an arrangement of unusual rocks placed in strong harmonic relations. Regarded as an artistic concept, however, the bridge becomes a line of contrast to the upthrust of the great peaks.

121. Here the restored wooden bridge of the Daisen-in garden, with its arched Zen window, is seen from the lower side. On its opposite side the bridge has a seat under a thatched roof from which the mountain view beyond may be contemplated. The foreground here depicts the quiet portion of the river with its stone boat floating below the window. The main hall of the temple, left, has been opened to show the painted panels on its inner walls, done by the artist Soami.

122. *In this general view of Ryoan-ji's rectangle of white sand and its five stone groups, photographic elongation makes the length of the garden appear out of proportion to the width.*

123. Detailed view of the first or left-hand grouping of five stones in Ryoan-ji's garden. Of the stones in this group, two are nearly invisible, since they lie almost level with the ground.

124. *Here the stone group of two which normally lies second from the left in Ryoan-ji's garden is viewed from the back. It has been allowed to accumulate a large surrounding growth of dark moss which gives it extra emphasis. Beyond it lie the three groupings which are normally seen as on the right of the viewer.*

125. *An attempt to follow the Ryoan-ji garden pattern can be found at the nearby subtemple of Takai-an of the large Myoshin-ji Zen foundation. It reveals the inherent difficulty of the concept, the finding and placing of the stones, and, by contrast, the success of the Ryoan-ji garden.*

126. Sambo-in, the most elegant and debonair of the Momoyama rococo gardens, is said to hold over seven hundred stones. Most of them were taken earlier from other gardens to decorate Hideyoshi's great castle-palace of Juraku-dai and from there moved to their present site. Among them can be noted many of the typical flat-topped forms preferred by Muromachi garden makers and taken from Muromachi gardens. In the Sambo-in garden, stones are used in great numbers on the pond edge, the islands, and the hill slopes, and still others are laid out simply for display. Yet in spite of this lavishness, because of the great skill in arrangement the garden does not present a jumbled appearance. The whole garden has a delicacy that is missing from later examples of the same type.

127. *The central donjon of a Japanese castle "towered like a mountain" over its surroundings. Himeji Castle (built in 1608), one of the few remaining original structures of this style, shows typical gables, balconies, and dolphin finials on the tower. Cherry blossoms, now growing around this castle, were regarded as a symbol of the warrior.*

128. Although of undistinguished form, for some reason that is now unknown this "Fujito Stone" seems to have been a famous rock in Hideyoshi's day, one that was greatly coveted for garden use. It has an authenticated history of transfer through at least three previous gardens. Hideyoshi bought it for its present position in Sambo-in, instead of demanding it, as was his usual custom.

129. Trees growing in the garden of Kyoto's Nijo Castle today appear to be fairly recent additions. When the garden was built, it was probably a massive set piece of huge rocks, like Kokei, the Tiger Glen garden. Perhaps it was even without water, for the pebble-covered pond area serves adequately in the design as a pond bottom. Like a great fountain before a European palace, this garden stood in the center of the castle courtyard, surrounded on three sides by buildings. The addition of trees and water, while it brings prettiness to the garden, takes away its original massive feeling of power and austerity.

130. *Tigers were almost unknown in Japan until Hideyoshi sent his forces to Korea. Then they became a favorite symbol of military power and glory. The theme is exemplified in the garden of the Tiger Glen, Kokei. These beasts are sometimes depicted on the golden screens and sliding doors of Momoyama, occasionally with blue eyes. This example of such a painting, attributed to Kano Tan'yu, appears on a sliding door. (Nanzen-ji, Kyoto)*

131. Peonies are traditionally regarded in China as the most gorgeous of all flowers and in Japan became another symbol of earthly pomp. Here tree peonies decorate sliding door panels of fine wood, the surface otherwise untouched. Painting by Kano Sanraku. (Daikaku-ji, Kyoto)

132. *Kokei, the Tiger Glen garden, makes use of massive stones closely arranged to form a mountain gorge on almost a natural scale. Here, one can imagine, the tiger roars at night. This concept expressed the power and glory of military might, for the tiger was a symbol of power. The garden is without actual water, but a stream of sand seems to enter through a rock cascade (background, center) now largely concealed by trees. The river is crossed by monolithic bridges, the central one about fifteen feet long. This garden was originally part of Fushimi Castle and is believed to have been moved, stone by stone, and set up in the grounds of Nishi Hongan-ji temple, Kyoto. Cycads, which are exotic to Kyoto's latitude, are a special feature of this garden now and, it is assumed, also grew in it at Fushimi Castle.*

133. Hideyoshi's great audience hall, originally a part of Fushimi Castle, was later moved to Nishi Hongan-ji temple. Just outside it lies the Tiger Glen garden, Kokei. The garden was designed to harmonize with the overwhelming size and richness of this hall, where Hideyoshi received his vassals and foreign diplomats. Wall paintings on gold backgrounds show gardens filled with ancient trees, flowers, and birds.

134. Hideyoshi's private apartments in the Pavilion of the Flying Cloud, Hiun-kaku, originally stood on, or in, the lake of Juraku-dai, his great Palace of Pleasures. The pavilion, now moved to a site at Nishi Hongan-ji temple, contains steps leading down to a boat landing inside the building. The interior of this private residence exemplifies the simplicity of taste fostered by the tea ceremony. It reveals an aspect of the dictator different from that shown by the gorgeousness of his public halls. Around this building on its present site is the little garden of Tekisui-in.

135. *Stone lanterns were among the things sent home from Korea as loot by Hideyoshi's generals. This is one such, now standing in the small garden of Ryuko-in temple of the Daitoku-ji monastery.*

136. *A depression to hold water has been cut into the top of a large natural rock which is placed so that it can be used from the porch of the adjacent building. This is an example of how influences from the tea garden have spread into gardens of other types. The laver shown is in the precincts of the Kompira Shrine, Shikoku Island.*

137. *A classical thatched tea hut made of beautiful unpainted boards and sanded plaster, with a natural stone doorstep, is found in the garden of the Ura Senke school of tea in Kyoto. The fence of bamboo twigs is typical of the rustic feeling dominant in such surroundings.*

138. The Japanese tea garden is primarily a path leading to the tearoom door. It represents the footpath taken to reach the remote retreat in the wilds represented by the tea hut. Stepping stones were first devised by the tea masters of the sixteenth century to make the path more practical and attractive. Shown here is part of the tea garden of the Mushanokoji school of tea, Kyoto.

139. *A light gate sometimes divides the path in the tea garden into an inner and an outer portion. The gate represents a kind of abridgment, the outer portion of the path symbolizing that section nearer to civilization, while the inner part is developed to suggest the wilder and more remote areas nearer the tea hut in the mountains.* **This gate is in the Ura Senke garden, Kyoto.**

140. *The tea plant,* Thea sinensis, *a native of China, is a species of camellia with glossy foliage and tiny, fragrant white flowers which have large centers of golden stamens. That a drink made from its leaves will induce wakefulness was known from very early times. The tea that is served at a Japanese* cha-no-yu *ceremony is made from the young leaves, finely powdered, mixed with hot water, and whipped to a froth.*

141. *A unit made up of a stone lantern and a sculptured laver stands in a famous tea garden at Ninna-ji temple, Kyoto. When the lantern is to be lighted, its openings are filled in with oiled paper attached to small wood frames. The light was originally a wick in a saucer of oil, but now a candle is used. Its flickering light is surprisingly effective in a dark garden.*

142. *A tea garden that may have been laid out originally by Sen no Rikyu is that belonging to the little country temple of Myoki-an, near Kyoto. Three hundred years ago its chief feature was a large tree known as the Sleeve Brushing Pine. The present tree is estimated to be some 250 years old, and so must have been planted to replace the sixteenth-century original. This kind of continuity is widely practiced in Japan.*

143. The Avenue of the Imperial Visit at Katsura shows the smoothly paved surface and clipped hedges that introduced some of the earliest touches of geometric formality into Japanese gardens. Like the axis of a formal European pleasance, this vista is terminated by a mound and a small pine tree trained to such artful grace that it has all the qualities of a statue standing on a pedestal. This tree is known as the Suminoe Pine, after a large tree that formerly stood at this point.

144. One of the bridges at Katsura follows the high-arched form originated in China to allow boats to pass under. The tea masters took this arch and developed it with rustic materials, its hewn supports carrying a path of sod and gravel and little ferns encouraged to grow along its edges.

145. *The Shokin-tei (Pine-Tree Lute Pavilion) served as a retreat at Katsura for such esthetic pastimes as the tea ceremony, painting, and poetry composition. With its roof of thatch and its walls and pillars of natural wood, it was an expression of the tea masters' taste rather than the current exuberance of military and castle architecture. Rock arrangements in the Katsura garden are more restrained than at the Sambo-in, but the occasional use of a very high rock, as at the right, seems to introduce an overemphatic artfulness.*

146. One of the magnificent rocks in the Katsura garden rises above the lake in a typical balanced three-stone arrangement.

147. A section of the lake shore in the Katsura garden is developed as a formalized beach with rounded stones. At one point it extends into the water as a small peninsula. To guide boats around this point at night, a small stone lantern at its tip serves as a miniature lighthouse. The stepping stones that cross this area are placed close together, their intervals and diameters geared to the human step.

148. *The Imperial Palace in Kyoto is seen across its garden lake, with the great ceremonial Hall of State at left. The buildings themselves date back only to 1855, when they were last reconstructed, but their style is that of the Heian period. Although this palace is seldom used, it is always kept ready for occupancy.*

149. Here the garden of the Imperial Palace in Kyoto is viewed from the Hall of State. The idea of paving a section of the lake shore with round stones probably originated with Kobori Enshu. Note the boat-landing stones in this photograph and the preceding one.

150. The Imperial Gate within Shugaku-in's park leads into the first of the enclosed gardens, which was used by the emperor and his gentlemen attendants.

151. Winter view of the Shugaku-in estate from the Cloud Touching Arbor showing the distant mountains and the harmonizing shorelines of the lake. These rhythmic shorelines were doubled by placing an island of just the proper outline in the lake. The breadth of outlook here is more suggestive of an Occidental park than of an Oriental garden. But even on its extensive scale the landscape design follows the same basic pattern that governs most such gardens in Japan, with foreground (of clipped shrubs), middle ground (the lake), and background (the mountains). It is believed that the emperor Gomizunoö planned this garden himself, working with the help of a clay model.

152. *The emperor Gomizunoö's estate of Shugaku-in extended over a whole mountainside, reaching to the top of the ridge above. Within this immensity were two small developed gardens, each holding one or two cottages which served as a sort of weekend retreat when the imperial owner and his empress made visits to the estate in spring and autumn. Here the second of the enclosed gardens was used by the empress and her ladies.*

153. The Zen garden of Konchi-in temple holds a crane islet, the only rock composition using this theme that gives it a graphic touch to suggest a large bird. The long flat stone on the ground could be its body; the two upstanding stones, its wings. Such an interpretation might be a fleeting impression characteristic of these Zen gardens of the mid-seventeenth century.

154. The temple of Taizo-in, a subtemple of Myoshin-ji, a Zen foundation in Kyoto, holds a garden reputed to have been made by the artist Kano Motonobu. Typical flat-topped Muromachi-style stones form a tortoise island in a sea of sand. Two bridges link this island to the shore, showing that the meaning of the old tale of the inaccessible Isles of the Immortals had been forgotten. Landscape is still plainly visible here, with almost no suggestion of impressionism. When this picture was taken, the garden had recently been rehabilitated.

155. *The garden of the small Zen temple of Reiun-in at the Myoshin-ji foundation is only ten feet wide and thirty-two feet long. It is enclosed on one side by a high plaster wall marked by five parallel white lines which signify that the temple has received imperial honors. This is one of the earliest of the impressionistic gardens. Its extremely fine stones, in Muromachi style, form a design of harmonic elements but do not create any definite landscape. Only insofar as the rocks and plants are natural can a scene of nature be sensed here.*

156. *Daitoku-ji's flat Zen garden of sand and rocks is one of the great masterpieces of impressionistic garden art in Japan. Set into a "hillside" of clipped greenery (far left) are three large, upstanding, flat-faced stones which form a "cascade." "Water" entering through this cascade flows in the sandy "river" which covers most of the ground. The surface is kept scratched into formalized ripples with a bamboo rake swung in the hands of a skillful acolyte.*

157. *The abbot's garden at Nanzen-ji monastery, although made of the usual flat sand, rocks, and shrubs, as are other impressionistic hojo gardens, fails of true impressionism and becomes only a simplified decoration. It appears probable that with the passage of time the artists and monks who had created the earlier gardens of this type had lost interest and, with it, ability. The job was probably turned over to professional garden makers, who were emerging at that time as designers also. They could follow a pattern but lacked the capacity to give it meaning.*

158. Balancing the distant three-stone impressionistic cataract in Daitoku-ji's hojo garden is a flat island or sand bar. It is formed by two stones nearly level with the surface of the sandy river. These stones are now surrounded by a mat of coarse brownish moss which gives emphasis to them. Their presence unifies the total composition of the picture.

159. *The ideal in Japanese garden maintenance of pine trees is the tree which has been carefully hand-plucked to achieve an artistic sparseness among the needles. Here such carefully tended pines line the lake shore of Okayama's public garden, Koraku-en, now some 350 years old.*

160. Some four hundred miles from Tokyo, in the city of Okayama, the Koraku-en garden, named for its Edo counterpart, presents the same broad, open feeling—with few stones used—as did its contemporaries of seventeenth-century Edo. The tidal marshes and lack of stones around Edo had necessitated these effects, and, although conditions were different in the provinces, it was the style and was copied anyway. The view shown here looks across an island within the broad lake to the central buildings of the garden, beyond. Swans now replace the rare black-tailed cranes originally favored for such gardens.

161. *The first great estate to be built in the new city of Edo (now Tokyo) after the Tokugawa shoguns had established it as their headquarters was Koraku-en, begun in 1629. Since there are no fine rocks to be found in the vicinity of Tokyo, all those used had to be brought from a considerable distance by barge. Among such transplanted stones was a huge squarish one that was placed at one end of the central island and called, after the garden's designer, the Tokudaiji Stone. It was meant to suggest the head of a huge tortoise, of which the island was the body. Today this garden is a public park, and the lake and its environs, although reduced in size, still hold a calm, quiet beauty.*

162. *Like a Chinese landscape painting is the white leap of the great Kegon Waterfall, outlet of the lake in Nikko National Park*

163. Nikko National Park, with its Lake Chuzenji and the surrounding mountains, exemplifies on a vast natural scale the elements of an Oriental landscape garden. Near this lake the first of the Tokugawa shoguns, Ieyasu, selected a site for his grave, which is now marked by the famous Nikko shrines.

164. *A conspicuous example of the literal "artificial mountain" as developed in the Tokugawa period survives far from the capital city in Suizenji Park, city of Kumamoto, on the island of Kyushu.*

165. The small interior garden of a shop in Kyoto uses a lantern, a dry pool, and a few rocks.

167. The present-day shop of a stone merchant in Kyoto displays natural rocks, carved water basins, granite blocks, and traditional lions in Chinese style to be used on either side of a formal entrance.

166. A most unusual small stone suggesting the great peaks and cliffs of the Muromachi painters was a cherished possession of the great Hosokawa family. It was considered sufficiently important to be presented to the small temple of Reiun-in of the Tofukuji in Kyoto as a memorial to the head of the family. It was set up on a special pedestal to form the chief feature of the temple garden.

168. The garden and hermitage, called Shisen-do, of the scholar Ishikawa Jozan lie in the hills back of Kyoto. Jozan developed the garden in the nonconforming "literary men's" style—that is, it followed no style at all—in protest against the attempt of the Tokugawa shogunate to impose conformity upon the country. Today the garden may be considerably changed from the way Jozan left it three centuries ago, but it still holds a feeling of individuality, with its huge random mounds of clipped azaleas.

169. *A tiny interior garden of a modern mansion in Tokyo with a large tree among its other plants. The tree was probably already growing on the spot when the house was laid out in such a way as to incorporate it.*

170. *The entrance to a modern restaurant in Tokyo has been developed as a small garden path from what was virtually an alley.*

171. *The influence of bonsai techniques is evident in the development of this* satsuki *variety of azalea, which has been trained to assume the lines of a miniature tree. It also follows the triangular pattern of classical flower arrangement. The practice of piling up the earth above the level of the pot into a sort of miniature hilltop and then covering it by growing moss also shows the influence of the tray-garden landscapes.*

172. *Bonsai trees are often grown among rocks and moss which are placed in their flat containers to suggest a miniature landscape. Such miniatures are not to be confused with dwarfed garden trees, which are kept pruned to a size proportional to the garden area. Outdoor dwarfed trees may range from five to twelve feet, but bonsai are always grown in containers and are but a few inches high.*

173. When a stone with the contours of a mountain is found during an outing or on some other occasion, it is often taken home and set up as an ornament. This much-prized example suggests the outline of Mount Fuji.

174. Here we are given a contemporary look, through the eyes of the famous wood-block printmaker Hiroshige (1797–1858), into one of the small courtyard gardens of the late Tokugawa period. This garden was part of the Kikoya inn at Akasaka, one of the fifty-three posting stations that lined the Eastern Sea Road, the Tokaido, between Edo and Kyoto. The little garden contains a rock, a stone lantern, and an ancient cycad plant. The art of the wood-block print was representative of the rising artistic vitality of the common people.

175. One of the most famous prints by Hiroshige shows the wisteria blooming at Kameido Tenjin Shrine in Tokyo. The gay red bridge still arches over the pond, and in season the wisteria still blooms around it. (From One Hundred Famous Views of Edo)

176. Murin-an, the Kyoto garden designed for his home by the late Prince Yamagata, looks toward the green hills. Water, which seems to flow down from them, enters the garden through a low cascade at the back. It first forms a pool, then flows out in a pair of streams which wind down to meet in the foreground, in front of the house. Making this display of water its chief feature, this small garden is unconventional and original in plan.

177. Large stones brought from all over the country were used in redeveloping the old garden of Kiyozumi in Tokyo in the late nineteenth century. These rocks were brought to Tokyo as ballast in ships controlled by the garden's new owner, Baron Iwasaki, and used in the Kyoto manner.

178. *Circular stepping stones, formed by the tops of old granite columns, extend into the lake of the Heian Shrine garden, creating a pattern completely different from the historic and naturalistic atmosphere of the rest of the garden. The design inevitably suggests Western art nouveau with its asymmetry and oblique angles. Made in the late nineteenth century, this development was a curious foreshadowing of things to come.*

179. Irises growing around the lake of the Heian Shrine in Kyoto take their place in Japan's floral calendar. The plant is especially connected with martial sports traditional to the Fifth Month (early June).

181. Winter in Japan finds the semitropical sago palm (Cycas revoluta) protected by little skirts of straw, becoming a different kind of seasonal ornament. Country women, appropriately dressed, make a business of light garden maintenance. (Kanagawa Prefectural Office, Yokohama)

180. Camellias are greatly favored as plants to grow in the precincts of Buddhist temples. An unusual and magnificent specimen, a single tree with five different varieties grafted onto its trunk, belongs to the little Jizo-in temple in Kyoto. Inevitably Jizo-in is popularly known as Tsubaki-dera, Camellia Temple.

182. *The garden of the late Mr. Tokushichi Nomura, in Kyoto, holds a floating teahouse on a barge that can be poled into the middle of the lake on a moonlit night. The large rock shown here in the foreground was brought in pieces to its new site in the garden and then reassembled. The cracks that resulted from this process are inconspicuous.*

183. "Snow flowers" are regarded as the earliest blossoms in Japan's annual floral cycle. The wet snow in Kyoto clings to branches and broadleaved evergreens like masses of flowers. This picture was taken in the Silver Pavilion Garden.

184. Rikugi-en, in Tokyo, now a public park, is still a peaceful and lovely example of a large Edo-period lake garden, with wooded islands and encircling path. After the country was reopened in 1864, and garden making could once more be thought of, rich businessmen first turned their attention to these old places. Often their feudal owners had had to neglect them. Rikugi-en was rehabilitated by Baron Iwasaki but not basically changed in form.

185. A stone trough, excavated near Nara, is believed to have been part of a prehistoric sakè brewery. Now on the estate of the late Mr. Tokushichi Nomura, in Kyoto, it is used to conduct water to a hand-washing basin serving a tea pavilion.

186. A pavilion in Chinese style stands in the lake of Heian Shrine's garden. It is a reminder that in the garden of the emperor Kammu, founder of Kyoto, there was a Pavilion of the Imperial Seat where the ruler and courtiers sat to watch entertainments. Seen through the cherry blossoms, this present pavilion may be taken as a glimpse into the past.

187. Weeping cherry trees are a special feature of the garden of the Heian Shrine, Kyoto, their drooping branches held off the ground by a light framework of bamboo. The small double flowers of light pink are strung tightly together on the pendant branches.

188. Mystic reflections in this garden lake, a part of today's Heian Shrine in Kyoto, may help us to imagine some of the beauties of the old Divine Spring Garden, Shinsen-en, which was the original imperial lake in Kyoto. The present garden was built eleven hundred years later to commemorate its beauties.

190. *A new garden outside a recently constructed addition to the Ura Senke school of tea ceremony in Kyoto makes use of sand as a ground cover, with a single fine rock and stalks of small bamboo. It is meant to be viewed from the adjacent assembly room. Although its style and materials suggest a temple garden, this one has no esoteric overtones but is, rather, definitely "modern" in feeling—a decoration for the room that looks out on it. Designed by Mitsuhiko Sen about 1955.*

189. *Especially prolific in providing ideas for modern gardens has been the 300-year-old estate of Katsura, particularly in details of its paths and paving. This photograph shows part of a path in front of the Shokin-tei pavilion. The combination of rounded pebbles, slabs of granite, and a natural stone of striking form could hardly be more "modern" in feeling.*

191. Modern hotels are prolific builders of gardens, sometimes following the
traditional styles, again working in the
modern manner with abstract forms. A
garden designed by the sculptor Masayuki Nagare for the Palace Hotel in
Tokyo occupies a space between one
of the dining rooms and part of the
adjoining moat of the Imperial Palace.
It reveals the strong influence that
Ryoan-ji has had on modern art.

192. A modern hot-spring resort has
built its traditional tub of natural
flowing hot water in the form of an
outdoor pool fashioned of smooth
rocks.

193. *A garden design created by nothing but the parallel stalks of giant bamboos is a modern idea developed in the museum building called Yamato Bunkakan, in Nara. The garden is a square open space in the center of the building, its walls entirely of glass. In form it is exactly comparable to the little interior gardens originally developed in old Japanese mercantile establishments. There is nothing in the garden but the sparsely set bamboos. Designed by Isoya Yoshida in 1960.*

194. *An abstract design using angular strips of black stone paving in strong contrast to white sand suggests a Mondrian painting. This garden is part of the grounds of the Japan Academy Hall (Nippon Geijutsuin Kaikan), Ueno Park, Tokyo. The pavement which separates the lawn area and the building from a stretch of sand is made of flat black stones (which here appear grey because of surface sheen). A few special rocks are placed at one side in Ryoan-ji fashion. Designed by Isoya Yoshida in 1958.*

195. *The similarity in feeling between modern architecture and that of ninth-century Japan is revealed here in the Japan Academy Hall, which is developed in the Heian style. This portion of the grounds is enclosed by a long mound of azaleas, created to suggest the hillside cover of the emperor Gomizunoö's Shugaku-in estate in Kyoto.*

196. *The rooftop garden of a Tokyo department store shows touches of Japanese garden techniques in the way the shrubs are clipped and massed.*

197. *The many-storied office buildings of Tokyo's financial district crowd to the edge of the old inner moat that surrounds the Imperial Palace grounds, once Edo Castle. Across the water the medieval bastions rise in high escarpments, curving outward and down in the graceful manner of this type of Japanese masonry. The tops of these walls are now crowned by pine trees trained to lean over them. Around the hub formed by the palace grounds the city's traffic must flow in a great whorl. But public sentiment has resisted pressure to fill in the moats.*

198. *This new garden of a private residence in Tokyo carries out the traditional dry-landscape style, with sand simulating water, fine rocks, and beautiful trees. The making of such traditional landscapes is still done with skill and charm. Designed by Shuji Hisatsune about 1960.*

199. *Here a mid-twentieth-century garden still makes use of the ancient Chinese motif of the Mystic Isles of the Immortals. But it is used here only to interpret the name of the small Kyoto temple Zuiho-in (Felicitous Mountain), for which the garden forms a setting. No hint of realism remains in the design apart from the single tall peak. The design shows the effect of concurrent art ideas on the traditional rock art of Japan, with the rocks creating not landscape but abstractions of mass and form. Designed by Mirei Shigemori in 1961.*

200. This modern garden pavement symbolizes a shoreline which separates the grassy area (here newly planted) from the spread of raked sand. Created for his own garden by Mirei Shigemori.

201. With a national background of art that includes work such as this, Japanese artists have had little difficulty in comprehending similar trends in Western art. The picture is Sesshu's famous "splashed ink" landscape, painted in 1495, when the artist was seventy-six years old. (Tokyo National Museum)

202–3. *Pure abstraction is seen in a modern garden near Osaka. The outline of low rock walls against sand was laid out to be seen from a high spot, the tower of Kishiwada Castle. The design also includes eight groups of stones set about on the ground and intended to be seen from normal eye level. The lower photograph shows one of the stone groupings at eye level, and also a length of the low stone walls that define the abstract pattern of the garden. The garden and castle are now a city park, the materials of indestructible rock and sand having been chosen to withstand the usage of time and the public. Designed by Mirei Shigemori about 1953.*

204. *Nonrepresentation in Japanese garden art is seen in this detail of the design that is kept molded into the surface of the Silver Sand Sea, the terrace of sand in the Silver Pavilion garden. This design is usually said to represent formalized ocean waves, but each person may have his own interpretation—or none.*

205. *This modern garden of rocks and gravel, on the roof of the Tenri Building in Tokyo's Kanda district, is widely open to the sky. Its designer, the sculptor Masayuki Nagare, calls it the Sleeping Garden (Nemuri Niwa). Beyond its enclosing walls rise the tips of various Tokyo towers, giving visitors a chance to ponder such anomalies.*

Acknowledgments:
With Nostalgia and Appreciation

Now that this book is being published and I can look back over the years that have gone into its preparation, I realize that there must have been several hundred people who were helpful in connection with it. Many were strangers to me: the friendly people one encounters casually in Japan when following up an interest. Such people often go to unbelievable lengths in assisting the visiting foreigner: the pedestrian who turns around and walks back several blocks to show the way, the abbot who invites a sightseer to stay and have a cup of tea. During my six years' residence in Japan such incidents were numerous and heart-warming.

My expression of gratitude to people more directly concerned with the book's development must be addressed first to those who helped with my earlier book on this subject: the modern scholars whose research has produced authentic information on Japanese garden history—Dr. Jiro Harada, Dr. Tsuyoshi Tamura, Dr. Matsunosuke Tatsui, and Dr. Eisaku Toyama—and then to a new generation of researchers who are carrying on this work, with Dr. Osamu Mori in the forefront. To this new group I am grateful for many new details.

But most of all I owe thanks to Mr. Mirei Shigemori, whose 26-volume work on Japanese gardens is not likely soon to be overshadowed. To him I must also express special appreciation for personal answers to questions on obscure points; many of these were put to him when I returned to Kyoto for further research in the postwar period.

In my development of the historical settings of the gardens I describe, many friendly authorities have helped me, smiling as they allowed me to pick their brains of pertinent bits of information not found in books. Others have been most gracious in allowing me to quote from their writings or to use their translations. Thus I must mention with appreciation the late Mr. Arthur Waley, who allowed me to quote extensively from his works; Dr. Alexander Soper, who as a neighbor in Kyoto made available to me many of his own unpublished translations and who looked over early portions of the manuscript; the late Dr. D. T. Suzuki, another neighbor, who discussed Zen; the late Dr. Ryusaku Tsunoda, who had the rare ability to find English words for many subtle aspects of Japanese culture; Dr. Homer Dubs, who helped with early China; Dr. Wing-tsit Chan, who aided with Chinese philosophy; and Dr. Jon Carter Covell, who guided me to a better understanding of Oriental painting.

In Hawaii, where most of this book was written, the learned men and women of the University of Hawaii, although I have never been connected with it, have been universally kind and obliging. But to name them all would be almost like preparing a faculty catalogue, and I shall mention only one or two. Dr. Jean Charlot and Professor Prithwish

Neogy of the Art Department have read the manuscript and offered suggestions in their special fields. The staff of the Oriental Library has always been patient and willing. And Miss Joyce Wright, head reference librarian, has never disappeared when she saw me coming.

But the greatest help in every way has come from my friend Dr. Hiroko Ikeda, scholar in the cultural treasures of her native land, deeply versed in Japanese literature, able to discern the finer points of translation in two languages, skillful in finding her way through the intricacies of Japanese references. Without her help I could hardly have accomplished my objective.

The Honolulu Academy of Arts has also been helpful, especially through its librarian, Miss Marion Morse, who often went to endless trouble to turn up something I needed.

For illustrative material I owe thanks to many persons and organizations, most of whom are named in the List of Illustrations. The illustrations were, however, collected over many years from many different sources (including, in a few cases, my own camera) and it has not been possible to include a credit in every case. I apologize in advance for any oversights, which certainly indicate no lack of gratitude on my part.

And, after all these, there have been so many others: Chuichi Mori, the graduate student in fine arts and architecture who, long ago for a fabulous month during my first visit to Japan, introduced me to the gardens of Kyoto and revealed to me something of the esthetics and techniques that went into their making; Dr. Masaru Victor Otake, who did interminable translating for my original book and has lately refurbished some of his earlier poem renderings; Miss Hiroko Ueno of the Miyako Hotel information staff, who, during my return visits, followed up for me many obscure contacts and acted as my liaison; Kay Lewis, my vigilant typist; and Ralph Friedrich, a keen-eyed editor, who caught many a slip. Finally, in a different context, I must make one more important acknowledgment: of the help given by Richard C. Tongg, my collaborator on earlier Hawaiian garden books and longtime practicing landscape architect of Hawaii. Over the years he has introduced and established the art of Oriental rock arrangement in gardens of these islands. On some of his jobs I have worked as director, developing the design, selecting the stones, and overseeing their placement. Such actual participation has given me insight into the rock art that has been invaluable.

To think back to all these wonderful people, to retrace my visits to the gardens and relive their times in imagination is to know that it has been a joyous journey. I hope those who follow me will find it so too.

Honolulu, 1968   LORAINE KUCK

Notes

CHAPTER I

p. 19   1. This record is found in *Sui Yang Ti Hai Shan Chi* (Sea and Mountain Records of Sui Yang Ti) in the *T'ang Sung Ch'uan Ch'i Chi* (Collection of Fictional Works of the T'ang and Sung Dynasties). It is reprinted in *Chung Kuo Ying Tsao Hsueh* (Bulletin of the Society for Research in Chinese Architecture), Vol. IV, June 1934. Dr. Alexander Soper has kindly allowed me to use his translations.

p. 20   2. *Sui Yang Ti Hai Shan Chi,* as above.

3. *Sui Yang Ti Hai Shan Chi,* as above.

4. Alexander C. Soper, *The Evolution of Buddhist Architecture in Japan,* 1942, page 186.

5. For a good account of the garden palace called Yuan Ming Yuan, see Carroll Browne Malone, *History of the Peking Summer Palaces Under the Ch'ing Dynasty,* 1934.

p. 21   6. Princess Der Ling, *Two Years in the For-bidden City,* 1931.

7. *The Book of Ser Marco Polo,* translated and edited with notes by Col. Sir Henry Yule, 3rd edition, 1926, page 365. A translation in part is also found in Osvald Sirén, *Gardens of China,* 1949, page 108.

8. The flower referred to in Chinese as "Second Month Orchid" is not an orchid but *Arychophragmus violaceus,* sometimes also called moricandia. See Dorothy Graham, *Chinese Gardens,* 1938, page 127.

9. Eleanor von Erdberg, *Chinese Influences on European Garden Structures,* 1936, Chapter 2. The *chinoiserie* movement was stimulated by the famous letter of Père Attiret, written in 1734, describing the imperial gardens in Peking. It is partly translated by Hope Danby in *The Garden of Perfect Brightness,* 1950, page 69.

10. For a full description of the gardens of the Pei Hai see Osvald Sirén, *Gardens of China,* 1949, Chapter 8, with many illustrations.

22   11. Sui Yang Ti was raised in southern China, near Hangchow, an especially beautiful part of the country. This makes more under-standable his desire to own an extensive forested park. It may also explain partly why he under-took to build the Grand Canal, one of his largest projects, for it would then be easy for the court to travel in comfort on houseboats directly from his capital in the north to Hang-chow.

CHAPTER 2

1. Metropolitan Museum of Art Publica-   p. 23 tions, *Egyptian Expeditions,* Vol. 2. See Plates LXXIX and CX in "The Tomb of Rech-Mi-Re." Plate CX is shown in color as Plate XX in the accompanying color folio. See also Nina M. Davis, *Ancient Egyptian Painting, Selected, Copied, and Described,* Vol. 2, Plate LXIX: "The Pool in the Garden," and Plate LXXVII: "Usheret Enjoys the Cool of His Garden."

2. Georges Perret and Charles Chiepez, *A History of Art in Egypt,* 1883. A suggested re-construction of such an estate is shown in Vol. 2, Figure 12.

3. Rom Landau, *Islam and the Arabs,* 1959,   p. 24 page 31.

4. Daniel David Luckenbill, *Records of Assyria and Babylonia,* 1927, page 170.

5. William Cullican, *The Medes and the Persians,* 1956. See Plates 41 and 42.

6. Ralph E. Turner, *The Great Cultural Traditions,* 1927, Vol. 1, page 367.

7. O. M. Dalton, *The Treasure of the Oxus,*   p. 25 2nd edition, 1926, page xxxiii.

8. Arthur Upham Pope, *Persian Architecture,* 1965, page 272, note 7.

9. Landau, as above.

10. A quotation from Megasthenes is given   p. 26 in the *Cambridge History of India,* 1922, Vol. 1, page 411.

11. Pope, as above, page 45.

12. Kalidasa, *Meghaduta* (The Cloud Mes-

senger), verses 71 through 74. I am indebted to Professor Prithwish Neogy for calling this record to my attention and making a special translation from the Sanskrit of the poem.

p. 27   13. Donald M. Wilber, *Persian Gardens and Garden Pavilions,* 1962, page 75. Taken from Babur's memoirs.

14. C. M. Villiers Stuart, *Gardens of the Great Mughals,* 1930, Chapter 3.

p. 28   15. Edward J. Thomas, *The Life of Buddha as Legend and History,* 1927. Original sources are the *Majjhima Nikaya* and the *Nikaya Mahavagga.*

16. The Sukhavati scriptures are translated in *Sacred Books of the East,* Max Müller, editor, 1894, Vol. 49, Part 2. On pages 93 and 95 of the Small *Sukhavati vyuha* the lotus lake is mentioned, while on page 692 of the Larger *Sukhavati* is the statement about the reborn souls on the lotus flowers.

17. Robert Treat Paine and Alexander C. Soper, *The Art and Architecture of Japan,* 1955, page 212.

p. 29   18. Langdon Warner, *Buddhist Wall Paintings: A Study of a Ninth-Century Grotto at Wan Fo Hsia,* 1938. Plate XXIII shows the Sukhavati Paradise of Amida.

19. According to I. H. Burkhill in his article "On the Dispersal of Plants More Intimate to Buddhism" in the *Journal of the Arnold Arboretum,* October 1946, the nelumbium lily has an immensely wide provenance extending from the mouth of the Volga across Central Asia and even as far south as Australia. Long before the Buddhists took over a water lily as a religious symbol, the Aryans, in their Himalayan foothills (probably as far back as 2000 B.C.) had given some lily a place in their sun worship. They called it the dawn lily because it opened at dawn, and they associated it with the birth of the day. From this it came to be connected with birth in general, and its flower cup was regarded as the birthplace of great and holy beings. It was also thought of as a seat of honor. Whether or not this was the nelumbium lily, or indeed any· single water plant, seems to be uncertain.

CHAPTER 3

p. 33   1. Account based primarily on Ernest H. Wilson, *China, Mother of Gardens,* 1929, and on George B. Cressey, *China's Geographic Foundations,* 1934.

2. *Book of Songs.* Translated by Arthur p. 3⸱ Waley as Number 24 from the *Shih Ching.*

3. I am indebted to Dr. Wing-tsit Chan for p. 3 calling this to my attention. The characters illustrated are found in Frank Chalfont, *Early Chinese Writing,* Vol. IV, No. 1, Plates VII and XI, Memoirs of the Carnegie Museum. The "tree" is found as a bronze character. See Jung Keng, *Chin Wen-pien,* Sec. 6, page 1a, Special Publications No. 1, Institute of History and Philology, Academia Sinica, 1939. The "garden" character occurs on the Stone Drums. See Ting Fu-pao, compiler, *Shuo-wen Chieh-tzu ku-lin,* pages 27–28b.

4. *Shih Chi,* 26th year of Shih Huang Ti. p. 3⸱

5. *Shih Chi,* 35th year of Shih Huang Ti.

6. *The Works of Mencius,* Book 6, Part 1, p. 3⸱ James Legge's translation.

CHAPTER 4

1. *Shih Chi,* 8th year of Han Kao Tsu. Also p. 3⸱ found in Pan Ku, *History of the Former Han Dynasty,* Vol. 1, translated by Homer H. Dubs, 1938, page 118.

2. Far from the capital, certain of these murals survived in the Ling-kuang Palace in Shantung Province, long after city palaces with such pictures had been destroyed. They were described in a poem, "Lu Ling-kuang-tien," written by a visitor, Wang Yen-shou, which may be found in partial translation by Arthur Waley in *The Temple and Other Poems,* 1923, and is quoted in part by Laurence Sickman and Alexander Soper in *The Art and Architecture of China,* 1956, page 38.

3. Sickman and Soper, as above, page 219. p. 3⸱

4. Account based on Soper, *The Evolution of Buddhist Architecture in Japan,* page 12. He quotes from *Hsi Ching Tsa Chi* (Miscellaneous Accounts of Ch'ang-an) and *San Fu Huang T'u* (Records of Three Imperial Districts).

5. *Han Chiu I* (Later Han Records), Part 8, page 5a. Dr. Homer Dubs has kindly allowed me to use his unpublished translation.

6. Sickman and Soper, as above, page 218.

7. Among them the *Hsi Ching Tsa Chi* and p. 4⸱ *San Fu Huang T'u,* as above.

p. 40   8. The emphasis in these early records is largely on the birds and beasts found in the natural parks. Among animals mentioned are the elephant and others which must live in a mild climate, while exotic birds and beasts from the tropics seem to have survived without much trouble. As long as the forests remained, the climate of North China seems to have been much warmer, with less extremes, than today.

9. Account taken from W. Percival Yetts, "Chinese Isles of the Blest," in *Folklore*, Vol. 30, March 1919. The sources are found largely in the third-century book *Lieh-tzu*.

p. 43   10. Yetts, as above.

11. Yetts, as above, based largely on the *Shih Chi*.

12. *San Fu Huang T'u*. My description also includes details from the *Han Shu*. See also the chapter "Architecture" by Chu Chi-chien in *Symposium on Chinese Architecture,* edited by S. Zen, 1931, page 119.

13. *Shih Chi,* Book 12. The author of this history, Ssu-ma Ch'ien, was Emperor Wu's court historian and could have seen personally what he describes.

p. 44   14. Taken from the *Liang-tu Fu* (Rhapsody of Two Capitals) by Pan Ku. Translation by Michael Sullivan in *The Birth of Landscape Painting in China,* 1962, page 29. A statue which fits this description stands on the large island in the North Sea Lake of the Sea Palaces in Peking. See illustration 72 in Sirén, *Gardens of China.*

p. 45   15. The quotation is given in an article (in Japanese) by Kazuo Kosugi entitled "Antecedents of Artificial Garden Islands in the Asuka Period," in *Houn* (Magazine of Fine Arts), No. 13, July 1935, page 72. It is taken from the *Ch'ang-an Chih* edited in the Sung period by Sung Min-ch'iu. He describes a "Mount Sumeru" erected on a terrace during the reign of Yao Hsing (died A.D. 416) of the Later Ch'in. Translation by M. V. Otake.

Apparently similar structures called "Terraces of the Immortals" were also built, at least later. The Japanese priest Ennin described one that he saw, built in A.D. 845 by the Taoist emperor T'ang Wu-tsung. The four sides of the terrace were faced with large rocks, among which grew trees. On top was a high building with five towers. The whole soared like a mountain above the flat plain. See *Ennin's Travels in T'ang China,* translated by Edwin O. Reischauer, 1955, page 251.

16. Account based on *San Fu Huang T'u,* p. 45 Book 4, "Parks and Gardens," translated by Homer H. Dubs.

CHAPTER 5

1. *The Book of Songs,* No. 81, translated by p. 46 Arthur Waley from the *Shih Ching.*

2. Confucian *Analects,* translated by James Legge, Book VI:21.

3. Shih Ch'ung, "Preface to Chin Ku p. 47 Poems," found in *Ch'uan Chin Wen* (Complete Chin Prose Works), Vol. 33.

4. Shih Ch'ung, *Ssu Kuei Yin Hsu* (Preface to Homesick Poetry), found in the *Wen Hsuan* anthology, Vol. 23, "Prefaces."

5. "Notes on the Origin of Chinese Private p. 48 Gardens" by Wu Shih-chang. Translated and condensed by Grace M. Boynton in the *China Journal,* Vol. XXIII, July 1935. The original article (in Chinese, "Wei Chin Feng Liu, Yu Ssu Chia Yuan Liu") is found in *Hsueh Wen,* Vol. I, No. 2, Peking, June 1934.

6. Translated by Alexander Soper in "Early p. 50 Chinese Landscape Painting," *Art Bulletin,* Vol. 23, 1941.

7. Tsung Ping's biography is found in the ninth-century history of painting, *Li Tai Ming Hua Chi,* VI, by Chang Yen-yuan. Translated in part by Soper in *Art Bulletin,* as above.

8. A full translation of Tsung Ping's commentary is given in *Art Bulletin,* as above.

9. Account based on Arthur Waley, *The* p. 53 *Life and Times of Po Chü-i,* 1949, Chapter IX, and on *Po Shih Ch'ang Ch'ing Chi* (Record of the Grass Cottage), Book 26.

10. *Po Shih Ch'ang Ch'ing Chi,* as above. p. 54 Translations are by Alexander Soper.

11. E. Zurcher, *The Buddhist Conquest of* p. 55 *China,* 1951, page 241. Based on *Kao-seng Chuan,* Book VI, 532.2, found in *Taisho Daizokyo,* Vol. 50.

12. "Notes on the Origin of Chinese Private Gardens," as above, page 20.

13. "Notes on the Origin of Chinese Private p. 56 Gardens," as above.

14. Hsieh Ling-yun, "Planting Trees in a Southern Garden." Special translation by

A. E. Dien. The hibiscus mentioned would have been the red *Hibiscus rosa-sinensis,* a native of southern China. It is still used as a hedge plant in mild climates.

p. 57   15. *Poems of T'ao Ch'ien,* translated by Lily Pao-hu Chong and Marjorie Sinclair, 1935, page 20.

16. From *One Hundred Seventy Poems,* translated by Arthur Waley, 1919. Chrysanthemums were T'ao Ch'ien's favorite flowers, and probably from this poem they have become known as the symbol of the scholar.

17. In the selection and use of natural stones in Oriental gardens, taste and style have inevitably entered. The result has been various schools and periods of rock artistry. Even the work of individual masters can be identified when enough of it survives for study.

CHAPTER 6

p. 58   1. *Chin Lu Hui Yeh Chung Chih.* Found in *Chung Kuo Ying Tsao Hsueh* (Bulletin of the Society for Research in Chinese Architecture), Vol. IV, June 1934. Translation by Alexander Soper.

p. 59   2. Alexander Soper, "Early Chinese Landscape Painting," *Art Bulletin,* Vol. 23.

3. *Shih Shuo Hsun Yu* (New Ideas from Old Writings), Vol. 2, page 25. Referred to in "Notes on the Origin of Chinese Private Gardens," in *The China Journal,* Shanghai, July 1935, page 18.

p. 60   4. *Wei Shu* (History of the Wei Dynasty), Book 93, "Biographies." Available in *Chung Kuo Ying Tsao Hsueh* (Bulletin of the Society for Research in Chinese Architecture), as above.

5. *Lo-yang Chia-lan Chih* (Record of Sangharana [Buddhist Institutions] in Lo-yang), Book 2, leaf 6.

6. *Lo-yang Chia-lan Chih,* as above. Translation by Alexander Soper.

p. 62   7. Waley, *The Life and Times of Po Chü-i,* 1949.

8. *Po Shih Ch'ang Ch'ing Chi* (Record of the Grass Cottage), Book 26. Translation by Alexander Soper.

CHAPTER 7

p. 65   1. *Nihongi: Chronicles of Japan from the Earliest Times to* A.D. *697.* Translated by W. G.

Aston, 1896; revised 1956. See chapter on Empress Suiko, year A.D. 607. While there is mention in the Chinese records of an earlier envoy from Japan, it is not known which of the various Japanese chieftains he might have served.

2. Several of these Chinese-style structures, p. 6 built of wood in the seventh and eighth centuries, have withstood the vicissitudes of 1,300 years and stand to the present day. They include the main building and pagoda of the Horyu-ji monastery and a "Hall of Dreams" made for a Japanese princess. For these T'ang-style buildings in Japan, see Paine and Soper, *The Art and Architecture of Japan,* 1955, Chapter 18.

3. *Nihongi,* Suiko 608.

4. *Nihongi,* Suiko 608.   p. 6

5. *Zoku Gunsho Ruiju* (Classified Series of Collected Texts, Continued), 1923–28, Vol. 3, page 53.

6. Kokusai Bunka Shinkokai (Society for p. 6 International Cultural Relations), *Tradition of [the] Japanese Garden,* 1962. See Plates 3 and 4, with notes by Sutemi Horiguchi.

7. *Tradition of [the] Japanese Garden,* as above, Plates 6–8, with notes.

8. Yukio Kobayashi and Yoshiro Kondo, *Sekai Kokogaku Taikei* (World Archaeological Records), Vol. 3: "Japan," 1959.

9. *Nihongi,* Suiko 613.   p. 6

10. For example, Emperor Kosho's palace was called "Palace in a Pond" (Ike no Koro no Miya). See discussion by Mirei Shigemori in *Gardens of Japan* (Vol. I in the series *Arts of Japan),* 1949.

11. For the excavation and a possible interpretation of this piece, see Teiichi Shigeta, "Asuka no Shumisen" (A Shumisen of the Asuka Period), in *Shigaku Zasshi* (Magazine of History), Vol. 15, January 1904, pages 47–54.

12. Seiroku Noma, "Asuka, Hakuho, Tem- p. 6 pyo no Bijutsu" (Art of the Asuka, Hakuho, and Tempyo Periods), in *Nippon Rekishi Shinsho,* Vol. 35, 1958, page 31.

13. *Nihongi,* Suiko 620.

14. *Nihongi,* Suiko 626.

15. Shigeta, as above.

16. There is a possibility that this Shumisen was not a part of Soga's garden but something made about fifty years later during the reign

of Empress Saimei (655–61). Three times during this period mention is made in the *Nihongi* of the construction of a Shumisen. All were set up in connection with lavish entertainments for foreigners or for a group of the unconquered "northern barbarians" who were being wooed by diplomacy. The site of the Shumisen made in the fifth year of Saimei fits the one on which the stone monument was found, as well as does the site of Soga's garden. It has been suggested by Mr. Shigeta that perhaps it was not water but something stronger to drink that gushed from the bottom stone. Mr. Kosugi (see Note 15, Chapter 4) believes that by this time all religious association with such a Shumisen had been forgotten.

Also excavated near the "mountain" was a stone figure of two men (now set up near the "mountain" in the Tokyo National Museum grounds). One of the men holds a cup from which water can be made to pour. The faces of both these men are non-Japanese, with large prominent noses and round eyes. Could they represent two of the "barbarian" or foreign guests at these entertainments?

p. 69 17. It may also embody the current idea of the garden island called after one of the Mystic Isles, P'eng-lai or Horai-zan. Since, in China, Buddhism was first conceived of in terms of churchly Taoism—the Chinese language lacking equivalent words for Buddhism's esoteric concepts—it is probable that for long Sumeru was imagined as very similar, or even identical, to the Mystic Isles. Mr. Shigeta points out (see Note 11 above) that for this reason the Nara Shumisen could probably just as well be regarded as a Horai-zan island of the period. Mr. Kosugi suggests that the form of the stone mountain might have been developed from the mountain-style incense burners which were developed in the Han period and represented one of the isles.

18. Noma, as above.

CHAPTER 8

p. 70 1. This plan is completely different from the medieval plan of Tokyo, which was laid out around a castle, with curving streets designed to baffle and mislead an attacking enemy.

2. G. B. Sansom, *Japan: A Short Cultural* p. 71
History, 1943, Chapter 6.

3. Osamu Mori, "Japanese Gardens: Their History, Makers, Schools, and Styles," page 5. This is the English summary of Dr. Mori's *Nippon no Niwa*, 1960.

4. The translations of this poem and the ones p. 72
following in this chapter, except the two by Aston, are by M. V. Otake. *Man'yoshu*, Vol. 20, No. 4512: *Ike mizu ni / Kage sae miete / Saki niou / Ashibi no hana o/ Sode ni kokire na.*

5. *Man'yoshu*, Vol. 20, No. 4513: *Iso kage no / Miyuru ike mizu / Teru made ni / Sakeru ashibi no / Chiramaku oshi mo.*

6. *Man'yoshu*, Vol. 20, No. 5411: *Oshi no sumu / Kimi ga kono shima / Kyo mireba / Ashibi no hana mo / Saki ni keru kamo.*

7. W. G. Aston, *A History of Japanese Literature*, 1899.

8. Poems of the *Kaifuso* were written in the p. 77
Chinese language adapted for Japanese understanding. Their transliteration into English is virtually impossible.

9. In a poem by Fujiwara Yatsuka, in the *Man'yoshu*, Vol. 19, No. 4271.

CHAPTER 9

1. Paine and Soper, *The Art and Architecture* p. 78
of Japan, pages 197 ff.

2. R. A. B. Ponsonby Fane, *Kyoto: Its His-* p. 79
tory and Vicissitudes, 1931, Part 1: "The Capital and Palace of Heian," page 100. This book comprises reprints of four papers originally presented in *Transactions of the Japan Society of London*, Vols. XXII (1925), XXIII (1926), XXIV (1927), and XXV (1928).

3. *Keikokushu* (Anthology of Chinese Prose and Poetry). Available in *Gunsho Ruiju* (Classified Series of Collected Texts), Vol. 125, Tokyo, 1928–37.

4. *Honcho Monzui* (Models of Chinese Prose). Available in *Kochu Nihon Bungaku Taikei*, Vol. 23.

5. This is the festival of Kuramazaki Shrine. p. 80
It is held annually at the river resort of Arashiyama, near Kyoto, usually on a Sunday late in May.

6. The mythical hoö bird was supposed to come to a country only when it was peaceful, prosperous, and happy; hence it was an omen

of peace and good fortune. The name is sometimes translated as "phoenix," but there is no connection between the hoö and the Egyptian phoenix. Daikaku-ji temple still possesses a large blue-and-gold head and neck of a hoö which served as the prow of such a pleasure boat.

p. 80   7. Translated by M. V. Otake from the original by Fujiwara no Shunzei (1114–1204), in *Shin Zoku Kokin Wakashu: Osawa no | Ike no keshiki wa | Furi yuke do | Kawarazu sumeru | Aki no yo tsuki*.

8. Account taken largely from Mirei Shigemori, *Nihon Teien Shi Zukan* (Japanese Garden Histories, Illustrated), 1936–39, Vol. 1: "Joko, Asuka, Nara, Heian Jidai" (Ancient, Asuka, Nara, and Heian Periods), section on Saga-no-in.

p. 81   9. Translated by M. V. Otake from the original by Fujiwara no Kinto (966–1041) in *Hyakunin Isshu* (One Hundred Poems by One Hundred Poets): *Taki no oto wa | Taete hisashiku | Nari nuredo | Nakoso nagarete | Nao kikoe kere*.

p. 82   10. Account founded largely on Mirei Shigemori, *Kyoto Bijutsu Taikan: Teien* (Survey of Kyoto Fine Arts: Gardens), 1933, section on Shosei-in.

11. Translated by M. V. Otake from the original by Ki no Tsurayuki (884–946) in *Kokin Wakashu*, Book 16 (Songs of Pathos), No. 825: *Kimi masade | Kemuri taenishi | Shiogama no | Ura sabishiku mo | Mie wataru ka na*.

p. 85   12. Account founded largely on Shigemori, *Nihon Teien Shi Zukan*, Vol. 1, as above, section on Kanju-ji.

13. *Kanju-ji Engi* (History of Kanju-ji). Manuscript copy dated 1506. Reprinted in Shigemori, *Nihon Teien Shi Zukan*, Vol. 1, as above.

CHAPTER 10

p. 86   1. Murasaki Shikibu, *Genji Monogatari*, made available in English through the fine translation of Arthur Waley as *The Tale of Genji*, 1935. Murasaki lived from about 987 to 1031 and wrote the story while at court, around the year 1000. Modern critics rank it as one of the world's literary masterpieces.

2. A sketch of Murasaki's life, with excerpts from her diary, is given by Mr. Waley in the introduction to *The Tale of Genji*.

3. The following selections are from *The Tale of Genji*, Part III, "A Wreath of Cloud," Chapter 3, pages 430–31. Quotations by permission of Mr. Waley. As a creative translator Mr. Waley endeavors to use terms which his readers will understand. His references to "beds" and "borders" of flowers are not to be taken to mean quite what they would in a European garden.   p. 8

4. *The Tale of Genji*, Part III, Chapter 6, pages 478–79.   p. 88

5. *Sakuteiki* (Treatise on Garden Making).   p. 91 This work has been traditionally attributed to Fujiwara Yoshitsune, but modern scholarship now believes it was written by Tachibana no Toshitsuna (died 1094). See the article on the *Sakuteiki* by Dr. Osamu Mori in *Nippon Rekishi Daijiten* (Japanese Historical Dictionary), 1958. According to Japanese scholars, the present text of the *Sakuteiki* may have been somewhat edited and added to in a way that is hard to detect. But on the whole the book is believed to cover rather exactly the legacy left to Japanese garden art by the Heian court. All later generations of garden makers have read it and been influenced by it. I have used a translation by Mr. Hogitaro Inada made for Dr. A. C. Soper, who generously loaned it to me.

6. *The Tale of Genji*, Part II, "The Sacred Tree," Chapter 9, page 351.

7. For the style of the shinden mansion, see   p. 92 Paine and Soper, *The Art and Architecture of Japan*, 1955, page 206.

8. *Nenju Gyoji* (Calendar of Festivals). This scroll painting is owned by the Tokyo National Museum. The existing scroll is believed to be a copy of an original painted in the twelfth century by Mitsunaga.

9. Rocks which once supported just such a   p. 93 bridge are in the lake of the ruined twelfth-century Moötsu-ji temple near Hiraizumi.

10. *The Tale of Genji*, Part I, Chapter 2. Special translation by M. V. Otake.

CHAPTER 11

1. Account taken largely from Shigemori,   p. 94 *Nihon Teien Shi Zukan*, Vol. 1, section on Sekisui-en.

97   2. Traced by Mr. Shigemori, as above.

98   3. Minoru Shinoda, *The Founding of the Kamakura Shogunate*, 1960, carries a full modern account of the struggle.

99   4. Account taken largely from Shigemori, as above, section on Moötsu-ji.

100   5. Account founded largely on Shigemori, *Nihon Teien Shi Zukan*, Vol. 2A: "Kamakura, Yoshino Jidai" (Kamakura and Yoshino Periods), Part 1, section on Eifuku-ji.

  6. *Azuma Kagami* (Mirror of the East), which was kept between 1180 and 1266. "East" here refers to Kamakura, which is east of Kyoto.

  7. This reveals the way in which all the great feudal estates were to be constructed, a system which goes back to the emperors of China. A baron might almost measure his power by the number of men and the amount of material he could commandeer for such projects. If a vassal felt himself strong enough to refuse, he might do so, risking reprisals. On the other hand, powerful leaders sometimes took this means of keeping their vassals too poor to consider rebellion.

103   8. Certain scroll paintings made in the Kamakura period show artisans at work, revealing how little changed up to World War II were many of the craft processes.

  9. *Prunus mume,* often mistakenly called plum in English.

104   10. *Azuma Kagami,* 3rd year of Kenkyo (1194), 8th month, 20th day.

CHAPTER 12

106   1. *Entairyaku* (diary of the prime minister Nakasone Kimikata). It covers the years 1311 to 1359.

  2. A booklet given out by the temple lists the botanical identification of at least nineteen species.

109   3. Shigemori, *Nihon Teien Shi Zukan,* Vol. 2A: "Kamakura, Yoshino Jidai" (Kamakura and Yoshino Periods), Part 1, section on Saiho-ji. Reference is made to *Saiho-ji Chitei Engi* (Legendary History of Saiho-ji), a temple document which is a compilation of traditions, legends, and stories of its early history. The compilation is purported to be the work of the chief priest Kyukei in 1400, but Mr. Shigemori

doubts that it was made so early. Perhaps the collection of stories was started by Kyukei.

  4. A certain royal Prince Shinnyo is said to p. 110 have had his hermitage near here in the ninth century and to be buried on the hillside above, according to the *Saiho-ji Chitei Engi.*

  5. The account of the stone marker with its engraved record *Saiho-ji-ki* (History of Saiho-ji) appears in the *Saiho-ji Chitei Engi.* The high priest Jikusen (1292–1348), who erected the marker, was a Chinese Zen monk who came to Japan and became head of Nanzen-ji temple. Corroboration of the marker's existence is found in the *Heikizan Jitsuroku* (Record of Heikizan Temple). Under date of Choroku 4 (1460), 9th month, 30th day, the author states that he visited the temple and saw the marker.

  6. Documentary evidence against Muso as p. 111 builder of the whole of the Saiho-ji garden is found in the "history" engraved on a stone marker (Note 5, above). Jikusen (1292–1348) was a contemporary of Muso Kokushi and doubtless a friend, since both were important priests in Kyoto at the same time. He stated on the marker that Saiho-ji was built in the Kenkyu era (1190–98).

Internal evidence gives additional weight to the earlier date. Muso lived in a period filled with political intrigue and fighting, in which there could have been no time, no money, nor even much interest in such occupations as garden making. Certainly such a large, expensive, and slowly constructed piece of work as Saiho-ji could hardly have come out of this period. However, means to fix up the old garden and put up a few small buildings could have been found by Chikahide, who was still wealthy. But that is about all.

Muso's reputation as a garden maker grew up in later times. Records of his life bring out clearly that he was a great lover of nature. But his part in garden making seems to have been limited to sponsoring small new buildings in old temple gardens where he was staying. Such pavilions he added to Zuisen-ji, in Kamakura, and to Saiho-ji and Tenryu-ji, in Kyoto.

CHAPTER 13

  1. Chang Hao, *Ken Yu Chi* (Record of Ken p. 113 Yu). Found in *T'sung Shu Chi Ch'eng Ch'u*

Pien (Collection of Chinese Repositories). Reprinted by the Commercial Press, Shanghai, 1936. This is an account incorporating descriptions written by Hui Tsung and Chu Mien. See also the Sung dynastic histories.

p. 114   2. For Su Han-ch'en (about 1104–70) see Osvald Sirén, *Chinese Painting: Leading Masters and Principles,* Part 1, page 105. His notes are derived from *Nan Sung Hua Lu* and *Pao Hui Lu.*

p. 116   3. The belief is explained in the encyclopedia *Tu Shu Chi Ch'eng* (Comprehensive Survey of Chinese Literature) under "Lung Men" (Dragon Gate). According to this account only seventy-two of the golden carp were destined to succeed each year. As they reached the crest of the rapids, a clap of thunder and lightning burned off the fish tails, and the animals flew away as dragons.

    4. At some later time it was arranged that a thin flow of real water could be brought to the top of the cascade through a bamboo conduit, carried on temporary spidery bamboo stilts across the glade behind. On occasions, as when there are important guests, this construction is set up. The water falls in a thin trickle across the face of the upper cascade and hits a buried jar of water at its foot, making a tinkling sound. It is then conducted in a runnel to the lower fall. The touch of realism given by this water is inconsistent with the whole cascade, since water flowing with the power suggested by the massed rocks would roar, not tinkle.

p. 121   5. Shigemori, *Nihon Teien Shi Zukan,* Vol. 2B: "Kamakura, Yoshino Jidai" (Kamakura and Yoshino Periods), Part 2, section on Tenryu-ji.

    6. A summary of Tenryu-ji's history is given in Shigemori, as above. He quotes from various contemporary records, including *Tenryu-ji Kinen Koryaku* (a temple document), *Honcho Monzui, Godai Teio Monogatari, Meigetsuki,* and others.

p. 122   7. The Kitayama villa was later called Rokuon-ji temple and now, popularly, the Gold Pavilion. For its history see *Rokuon,* edited and published by the temple in 1955. Several authorities have contributed chapters, that on the garden's history being by Yoshinobu Yoshinaga.

    8. Fujiwara Sadaie, also known as the poet p. ? Teika, writing in his diary *Meigetsuki* on the 14th day, first month of 1225.

    9. Japanese trading (and sometimes raiding) on the coasts of China and Korea is discussed by G. B. Sansom in *A History of Japan, 1334–1615,* 1961, page 256.

    10. This note is now a temple document. p. ?

    11. The tradition appears in Akizato Rito, *Tsukiyama Teizoden,* 1828, for possibly the first time.

CHAPTER 14

    1. *Taiheiki,* Vol. 26. This excerpt and those p. ? cited in Notes 3 and 4 below are reprinted in Eisaku Toyama, *Muromachi Jidai Teien Shi* (Gardens of the Muromachi Period), 1934.

    2. This chapter was originally written in a p. ? house which stood on part of the Flowery Palace estate. No trace of the garden remained except, possibly, a large and beautiful rock in an adjoining missionary garden. This rock was later purchased by Shokoku-ji temple (originally an Ashikaga foundation) and moved to one of its subtemple gardens.

    3. *Gukanki,* the diary of Konoe Michitsugu, 2nd month, 28th day of Eiwa (1348).

    4. *Gukanki,* as above, 11th day, 3rd month of Eitoku (1381).

    5. The history of the imperial palace in p. ? Kyoto has been traced by Ponsonby Fane in *Kyoto: Its History and Vicissitudes.*

    6. Oral communication from Mr. Mirei p. ? Shigemori, November 1961, after he had studied the lake bottom while it was drained.

    7. Sansom, *Japan: A Short Cultural History,* Chapter 18.

    8. A photograph of a temple in Likiang, Yunnan Province, China, was reproduced in *Asia Magazine,* November 1942, page 643. The picture had no identification, but the location of the building was given in a communication from the editor.

    9. The legendary extravagance of Yoshi- p. 12 mitsu's time survives in a story that, on a hot summer day, he ordered this small hill covered with lengths of white silk to suggest a cooling fall of snow.

    10. For a detailed discussion of the islands p. 13 and other techniques see Shigemori, *Nihon*

Teien Shi Zukan, Vol. 3A: "Muromachi Jidai" (Muromachi Period), Part 1, section on Rokuon-ji (Gold Pavilion).

131   11. Mentioned by the poet Teika in his diary *Meigetsuki.*

132   12. Account founded principally on *Kitayama-dono Gyokoki* (Record of an Imperial Progress to Kitayama Hall). Reprinted in *Rokuon* (see Note 7, Chapter 13) and in Shigemori, as above.

135   13. This poem and others written that day are found in *Kitayama-dono Gyokoki,* as above. The translation here is by M. V. Otake from the original, which reads: *Ike mizu no | Migiwa no matsu no | Tomozuru wa | Chiyo ni yachiyo o | Soete sumuramu.*

CHAPTER 15

136   1. Quoted from an unnamed source by James Murdoch, *A History of Japan,* Vol. 1, 1910, page 593.

137   2. The incidents related are largely from Toyama, *Muromachi Jidai Teien Shi,* in which are quoted excerpts from various sources.

139   3. *Onryoken Jitsuroku* (Daily Record of Onryoken Temple). This is an official diary kept by the priest-scribes of Onryoken Temple from 1435 to 1466. Pertinent material from it is quoted by Toyama, as above, and by Shigemori in *Nihon Teien Shi Zukan,* Vol. 4: "Muromachi Jidai" (Muromachi Period), Part 3.

140   4. *Onryoken Jitsuroku,* Kansho 6 (1465), 7th month, 10th day.

141   5. *Rokuon Jitsuroku* (Daily Record of Rokuon Temple), Chokyo 2 (1488), 2nd month, 21st day. The *Rokuon Jitsuroku* is a series of diaries kept by official priest-scribes of Shokoku-ji temple covering the years from 1487 to 1651. It is virtually a sequel, on Yoshimasa's life, to the earlier *Onryoken Jitsuroku.*

6. The Japanese *ume* is usually called "plum" in English. It is *Prunus mume,* a kind of apricot, with pink or white flowers which are more scattered, waxen, and fragrant than those of the fruiting plum of the Occident.

7. *Rokuon Jitsuroku,* Chokyo 2 (1488), 1st month, 19th day.

8. The first reference to Soami as the designer of this garden seems to have been made,

about three hundred year afters it was finished, by Akizato Rito in *Miyako Rinsen Meisho Zue,* 1799.

9. For an interesting discussion of Zen'ami   p. 142 and the kawara-mono, see Osamu Mori, *Nippon no Niwa* (Japanese Gardens), 1960, page 101.

10. *Rokuon Jitsuroku,* Chokyo 3 (1489), 6th month, 5th day.

11. *Onryoken Jitsuroku,* Kansho 2 (1461), 12th month, 8th day.

12. For a full discussion of the techniques used in the Silver Pavilion garden, together with an appraisal of its reconstruction in the Momoyama period, see Shigemori, as above, Vol. 4, Part 2, Muromachi period, section on techniques.

13. Matsunosuke Tatsui, *Japanese Gardens,*   p. 145 Tourist Library, Vol. 4, series of 1934, page 194.

14. This poem is found in *Rokuon Jitsuroku,* Chokyo 1 (1487), 12th month, 28th day, the date on which it was written by Yoshimasa. Translated by M. V. Otake from the original, which reads: *Waga ie wa | Tsukimachi yama no | Fumoto nite | Katamuku sora no | Kage oshizo omo.*

15. *Rokuon Jitsuroku,* Entoku 2 (1490), 1st   p. 147 month, 2nd day.

16. Much new construction was being started at this time in Kyoto, with the Tokugawas taking the lead. Kobori Enshu was their representative. It was also the time when the great Katsura garden was being developed. See Chapter 20.

17. This poem was written by Sakugen, a   p. 148 priest of Tenryu-ji, who died in 1576. It is now in the possession of the Silver Pavilion Temple. See Shigemori, as above, section on style.

18. This is noted by Shigemori, as above, in Vol. 4. He mentions *Miyako Meisho Zue* (1632), *Miyako Rinsen Meisho Zue* (1798–1800), and *Ginkaku-ji Rinsen Zue* (1866).

CHAPTER 16

1. Japanese artists living in the fifteenth and   p. 149 sixteenth centuries include Josetsu, Shubun, and Sotan; Sesshu, Jasoku, and Keishoku; Noami, Geami, and Soami; Kano Masanobu and Kano Motonobu.

2. Account of Sesshu's life taken from Jon   p. 151

Carter Covell, *Under the Seal of Sesshu,* New York, 1941 (reprinted 1961).

p. 151   3. *Ouchi-ke Kabegaki* (Wall Writings of the Ouchi Family—that is, the Ouchi family's book of laws), under date of Entoku 4 (1492), 6th month.

4. Covell, as above.

5. Covell, as above.

p. 152   6. Ryoan Keigo, *Tenkai Zugaroki* (Record of the Heaven-Created Painting Pavilion), given in full in *Koga Biki* (Notes on Ancient Paintings), Vol. II, page 671a. Translation by Covell, as above, page 31, used with permission.

p. 153   7. Ernest F. Fenollosa, *Epochs of Chinese and Japanese Art,* 1921.

p. 156   8. A full account of this change and the evidence on which it is based is given in an article in the quarterly *Gardens of Japan* (subtitled *Garden Design and Landscape Architecture of Old and New Japan*), July 1961. The article, in Japanese, is by Kinsaku Nakane and is entitled "Daisen-in Sho-in Teien no Fukugen ni Tsuite" (Restoration of the Sho-in Garden of Daisen-in). Mr. Nakane, chief research fellow in the Japanese garden planning division of the Architectural Research Association, discovered an old plan of 1880 showing the corridor in the center of the garden. A second plan, corroborating the first, was also found, and the two constituted evidence that the corridor had been moved to the end of the garden, probably early in the twentieth century.

9. Historical account taken from Toyama, *Muromachi Jidai Teien Shi,* and from Shigemori, *Nihon Teien Shi Zukan,* Vol. 3B: "Muromachi Jidai" (Muromachi Period), Part 2, section on Daisen-in.

p. 161   10. *Ko Daitoku Shobo Daisho Kokushi Daikasho Dogyoki* (Record of the Way and Conduct of the Great High Priest Kogaku of Daitoku-ji). Reprinted in Shigemori, as above.

11. Attribution of the garden to Soami is found in various Tokugawa-period books, including *Kaiki, Yoshu Fushi, Tsukiyama Teizoden,* and *Miyako Rinsen Meisho Zue.* These seem to have copied from each other.

12. The poem is given in *Ko Daitoku Shobo Daisho Kokushi Daikasho Dogyoki,* as above.

13. In making an artistic creation of natural

rocks two steps are involved: first, the selection of the stones to be used; second, their placement in harmonic and meaningful relationships to each other. The garden maker starts with a general plan of how he wishes to carry out his idea, but he must do this with whatever units of rock are available. This use of stones in their natural forms is obviously quite different from carving or chiseling the desired form from a block. The stones available, therefore, and the selection of which stones to use are basic.

14. Any doubt about this statement can   p. 1(
easily be settled if we make a search for unusual stones in the nearest rock heap. One stone of interest among hundreds is a fortunate find.

CHAPTER 17

1. The name of this temple is sometimes   p. 1
incorrectly spelled and pronounced Ryuan-ji.

2. Tsuyoshi Tamura, *Art of the Landscape*   p. 1(
Garden in Japan, 1935, page 103.

3. The Bible, Psalms 46:10.   p. 1(

4. Historical facts presented here are taken from Tamura, as above; from Toyama, *Muromachi Jidai Teien Shi;* and from Shigemori, *Nihon Teien Shi Zukan,* Vol. 4: "Muromachi Jidai" (Muromachi Period), Part 3, section on Ryoan-ji. Contemporary records in which facts are found include *Rokuon Jitsuroku* (Daily Record of Rokuon Temple), *Heikizan Jitsuroku* (a record of the years 1459–63 and 1465–68 by the monk Unsen Daigaku), *Gaun Nikkenroku* (Daily Record of Gaun), and *Ninna-ji no Setsu* (Stories of Priests of the Ninna-ji).

Various writers of the Tokugawa period, over a hundred years after 1488, made frequent and unfounded attributions, crediting the garden to this person and that. Both the painter Soami and a seventeenth-century tea master, Kanamori Sowa, are said to have designed the garden. As a result of statements made in these late books, the garden is still popularly said to have been made by Soami. A small pond garden that was made quite some time after the stone garden, on the opposite side of the building, may have been made by Sowa, thus accounting for the association with his name. It is also thought that Sowa and Soami, whose names are similar in sound, may have become mixed.

167   5. The present building dates from 1797, when it was moved there after the building of 1488 was burned.

168   6. Osamu Mori, *Nippon no Niwa* (Japanese Gardens), 1960, page 42.

169   7. Miniature artificial landscapes were nothing new in China at that time. The kazan or miniature landscape made of pieces of old wood which is in the Shoso-in treasure house dates back to the Nara period.

8. Shigemori estimates that Joei-ji was probably made sometime between 1489 and 1492 and Ryoan-ji built in 1488 or a little later.

9. This has been done in an approximate replica of the Ryoan-ji garden which was constructed in the New York Botanical Garden in 1963.

170   10. Shigemori, as above, Vol. 4. He finds that both names occur in the *Onryoken Jitsuroku*. Hikojiro worked on the grounds of a subtemple of Shokoku-ji in 1489, and Kotaro was among those receiving wages for similar work done in 1490.

171   11. The sign is mentioned in *Ryoan-ji Manjo* (Writings on Ryoan-ji) under date of 1588, according to Toyama, as above, page 647.

CHAPTER 18

173   1. Account taken generally from Ponsonby Fane, *Kyoto: Its History and Vicissitudes*, Part 3: "Kyoto in the Momoyama Period" (first published in *Transactions of the Japan Society of London*, Vol. XXIV, 1927). The writer takes his description of the palace and grounds largely from *Taikoki* (Records of Hideyoshi) and from Naojiro Nishida, *Kyoto-fu Shiseki Chosakai Hokoku* (Reports of the Society for Investigating Ancient Monuments in Kyoto), Vol. 1, "Juraku-dai Iseki" (Remains of Juraku-dai).

2. One of these maps, belonging to the Juraku Grade School, is reproduced in Ponsonby Fane, as above, facing page 262.

3. Ponsonby Fane, as above, page 262. He quotes from *Tocho Giyo Yoroku*, which he describes as "a collection of old papers in the possession of Mr. Kiichiro Kanda."

4. Details of the imperial visit are given in

Ponsonby Fane, as above, based on *Juraku Miyukiki* (Record of the Imperial Progress to Juraku-dai).

5. Translation by Ponsonby Fane, as above,   p. 174
page 264.

6. Sansom, *Japan: A Short Cultural History*.   p. 175

7. Although no known documentary evidence supports the assumption that the garden was moved and reassembled in its original form, Mr. Shigemori states that internal evidence in its style and construction shows that it belongs to the earlier Fushimi period and not to the date of its transfer to Nishi Hongan-ji, thirty years later (1632). Shigemori, *Nihon Teien Shi Zukan*, Vol. 5: "Momoyama Jidai" (Momoyama Period), Part 1, section on Kokei.

8. The Tiger Glen on Lu-shan is known to artists as the setting for a number of Chinese paintings which show three old men standing by a small bridge, all laughing heartily. One of these three is supposed to be Hui Yuan.

9. J. Barinka, *The Art of Ancient Korea*, 1962. On page 57 typical Korean paintings of tigers in the sixteenth century are described and illustrated. Pictures by Japanese artists in the Momoyama period show a marked resemblance to these.

10. Shigemori, as above, Vol. 5. He men-   p. 176
tions having heard that the Nishi Hongan-ji possessed records stating that Asagiri was the maker of Kokei, but he was not allowed to see them.

11. During the cold months in Kyoto,   p. 181
cycads are kept alive by being wrapped in straw. The straw is bound around the leaf bundles in such a way as to create picturesque straw ruffles, so that even in winter the plants present an attractive and rather monumental appearance.

12. *Gien Jungo Nikki* (Gien's Daily Record). Sambo-in temple is always referred to as Kongorin-in in this record. Excerpts are here quoted by Shigemori, as above, in Vol. 6.

13. *Gien Jungo Nikki* (see above).   p. 182

14. Matsunosuke Tatsui, *Nippon Teien Shiyo* (Short History of Japanese Gardens), 1937. He reprints the quotation from *Chohen Shoku Onin Roku* (Supplement to the Later Volumes of Records of Onin).

15. Historical account taken from Ponsonby   p. 184

Fane, as above, Part 3, pages 271 ff., quoting, among other sources, from *Bonshun Nikki* (Bonshun's Diary).

p. 185　16. Ponsonby Fane, as above, page 273, based on *Taihei Nempyo* (Chronology of the Taihei Period). A description of this imperial visit is found in *Kan'ei Miyukiki* (Record of an Imperial Visit in the Kan'ei Era).

CHAPTER 19

p. 187　1. Mentioned, without giving his source, by Kakuzo Okakura in *The Book of Tea,* 1906 (reprinted 1956).

p. 188　2. Account founded upon an article by Kenzo Tange in *Katsura: Tradition and Creation in Japanese Architecture,* 1960, page 219. Reference is made to *Kissa* (or *Kitcha*) *Orai* (The Development of Tea Drinking) by the priest Gen'e (1269–1350), a scholarly advisor to Ashikaga Takauji.

p. 191　3. *Sokenki* (A Family Record of the Oda Clan) by Toyama Nobuharu, 1702.

　　4. Although the party was planned for ten days, external events caused it to be canceled after a single day.

p. 192　5. Translated by M. V. Otake. The original reads: *Kama hitotsu | Moteba cha-no-yu wa | Naru mono o | Yorozu no dogu | Konomu tsutsunasa.*

　　6. Translated by M. V. Otake. The original reads: *Cha-no-yu to wa | Tada yu o wakashi | Cha o tatete | Nomu bakari nari | Moto o shiru beshi.*

　　7. Translated by Yukuo Uehara. The original, by Fujiwara no Sadaie (Teika), reads: *Miwataseba | Hana mo momiji mo | Makari keri | Ura no tomaya no | Aki no yugure.*

p. 195　8. Jiro Harada, *Gardens of Japan,* 1928, page 4.

　　9. Reproduced in Shigemori, *Nihon Teien Shi Zukan,* Vol. 6: "Momoyama Jidai" (Momoyama Period), Part 2, section on Myoki-an.

p. 197　10. Translated by M. V. Otake. The original, by Sogi, reads: *Umi sukoshi | Niwa ni izumi no | Ko no ma ka na.*

　　11. *Kyaku no Shidai* (Procedure for Guests).

p. 198　12. A good example of one of these Korean lanterns stands in the garden of Ryuko-an, a subtemple of Daitoku-ji, in Kyoto.

CHAPTER 20

1. Katsura remained in the hands of the p. 2 noble family that founded it until the death of the last princess of the line in the 1880's. It was then taken over as an imperial property and has since been held as a "detached palace," Katsura no Rikyu. In effect, however, it is a museum of especially fine landscaping and architecture, to which admission may be gained by special permit.

2. Dr. Osamu Mori has done extensive p. 2 research, as reported in his *Nippon no Niwa* (Japanese Gardens), 1960. This book has an English summary in a pamphlet entitled "Japanese Gardens: Their History, Makers, Schools, and Styles," 1960. An excellent plan and a bird's-eye view of Katsura are found in *Tradition of [the] Japanese Garden* (Kokusai Bunka Shinkokai, 1962). A full discussion of Katsura is given by Shigemori in *Nihon Teien Shi Zukan,* Vol. 12: "Edo Jidai Shoki" (Early Edo Period), Part 5, section on Katsura.

3. The first recorded reference to Kobori Enshu as the maker of Katsura is dated ninety years after his death. The statement appears in the diary of Hirohata Dainagon Nagatada, 15th day, 4th month, 1736. The remark is attributed to the seventh prince of Katsura. See a discussion by Eisaku Toyama in the tea magazine *Heishi,* Vol. 8, summer 1937.

4. For a general discussion of these persons and others who might have had a part in Katsura, see Osamu Mori, *Nippon no Niwa,* as above.

5. Suden, *Katsura Teiki* (Record of Katsura Garden). Reproduced in Shigemori, *Nihon Teien Shi Zukan,* Vol. 12, as above.

6. Mentioned in Mori, as above.　　　　p. 20

7. See, for instance, Kenzo Tange in p. 20 *Katsura: Tradition and Creation in Japanese Architecture,* with English text by Walter Gropius and illustrations by Yasuhiro Ishimoto, 1960.

8. Ponsonby Fane, *Kyoto and Its Vicissitudes,* p. 20 Part 4, "The Capital in Peace," pages 351 and 357. See also Note 1, Chapter 18.

9. For a full discussion of the Sento Gosho, see Shigemori, *Nihon Teien Shi Zukan,* Vol. 10: "Edo Jidai Shoki" (Early Edo Period), Part 3, section on the Sento Gosho.

210   10. Suitable stones of the right size and shape for this paved shore were not easy to obtain. It is said that those used here were collected near Odawara by offering a measure of rice for each usable stone found.

11. This garden is open to visitors by special permit.

12. Ponsonby Fane, as above, Part 4, page 358. For the history of Shugaku-in, see Shigemori, *Nihon Teien Shi Zukan,* Vol. 8: "Edo Jidai Shoki" (Early Edo Period), Part 1, section on Shugaku-in. Its chief references are from *Reigen Hoō Shinki* (Diary of the Retired Emperor Reigen), which covers this emperor's own visits to Shugaku-in between 1721 and 1732.

211   13. These shrubs are maintained by gardeners who creep in beneath them, stand cautiously erect, shear what they can reach, and creep on to another place.

212   14. One of these bridges, in the form of a Chinese pavilion, was built during a reconstruction in 1824. Most critics feel that it is extraneous to the garden.

215   15. A full history of the wanderings and rebuildings of the palace is detailed in Ponsonby Fane, as above, pages 339 ff.

CHAPTER 21

217   1. Shigemori, *Nihon Teien Shi Zukan,* Vol. 3A: "Muromachi Jidai" (Muromachi Period), Part 1, section on Taizo-in.

2. Account founded on Shigemori, Vol. 3A, as above, section on Reiun-in.

3. Tamura, *Art of the Landscape Garden in Japan,* page 109.

218   4. Shigemori, as above, Vol. 5: "Momoyama Jidai" (Momoyama Period), Part 1, section on Konchi-in.

219   5. Shigemori, as above, Vol. 7: "Momoyama Jidai" (Momoyama Period), Part 3, section on Raikyu-ji.

6. Shigemori, as above, Vol. 11: "Edo Jidai Shoki" (Early Edo Period), Part 4, section on Daitoku-ji hojo garden.

220   7. Shigemori, as above, Vol. 8: "Edo Jidai Shoki" (Early Edo Period), Part 1, section on Nanzen-ji hojo garden.

CHAPTER 22

1. Historical account founded largely upon Shigemori, *Nihon Teien Shi Zukan,* Vol. 24: "Edo Jidai Shoki, Zoho 1" (Early Edo Period, Supplement 1), section on Koraku-en.   p. 222

2. It was through Mitsukuni's interest and support that the *Dai Nihon Shi* (Great History of Japan), a massive work of Japanese scholarship, was undertaken and carried through.   p. 226

3. Expressed in a poem by Pao Ch'en (999–1063), a famous political figure of the Sung period, who in the legal history of China has become the model for a statesman-official.   p. 227

4. Yoshikawa Keikan, in *Koraku-en ni Okeru Ki* (Record at Koraku-en), a short note quoted by Shigemori, as above, Vol. 24, section on Koraku-en.

5. The original idea of a low, broad lantern, sometimes with three or four legs, probably came from Katsura as one among the many new designs created for that estate. See illustrations, page 233, in Tamura, *Art of the Landscape Garden in Japan.*

6. The original donjon of this castle was destroyed in World War II, but one of the original corner towers of the wall survives, rising picturesquely above the river. In 1965, plans were afoot to reconstruct the castle tower in modern materials, as had been done in the case of several other castles earlier destroyed.   p. 228

7. Sansom, *Japan: A Short Cultural History.*   p. 230

CHAPTER 23

1. Only two large estates were constructed in the latter part of the Tokugawa period. Kenroku-en was built between 1818 and 1836 by the head of the Maeda family, one of the most powerful of the clans. It stood next to their castle at Kanazawa. Kairoku-en (or Tokiwa Park) was constructed between 1834 and 1840 by the current lord of Mito, Tokugawa Nariaki. In both cases it appears as if the builders were really more interested in a good water supply than in gardens, the one for his castle moats, the other for irrigation. In the Meiji period these two gardens, along with the Okayama Koraku-en, which had been rehabilitated in the middle of the nineteenth century, became known as "Japan's three greatest   p. 232

gardens." This was a popular estimate based on their newness, their size, and a general ignorance of the older gardens.

p. 236   2. Sung paintings show these miniatures in garden courtyards. Yoshimitsu provided an exhibition of them as part of the entertainment for the emperor during the imperial visit to the Gold Pavilion, according to *Kitayama-dono Gyokoki*. An example is pictured in the *Seiko-ji Engi* by Tosa Mitsunobu, dated 1487, now in the Tokyo National Museum.

3. Not to be confused with the Reiun-in of Myoshin-ji.

p. 237   4. Yamashina Doan, *Kaiki,* a manuscript in six volumes holding remarks by various well-known people overheard by Doan—especially those of Konoe Iehira, the court's prime minister.

5. Account taken largely from Matsunosuke Tatsui, *Nippon Teien Shiyo* (Short History of Japanese Gardens), 1932, section on Edo gardens. Also by the same author, an article in *Heishi* magazine for October 1938, "Edo Jidai no Zoteika ni Mochiiraretaru Hidensho ni Tsuite" (Secret Books Used by the Edo-Period Garden Makers).

6. Especially a manuscript from the library of the wealthy Maeda family entitled *Sansui Narabi ni Yakei Zu* (Illustrated Forms of Landscape and Field).

7. The district of Saga, northwest of Kyoto (where the emperor Saga had his ninth-century estate), is still a center of the nursery garden business, as it has been for centuries. Here was centered the Saga school of garden makers, and from this district came a book called *Saga-ryu Niwa Koho Hidensho* (Old Landscape Secrets of the Saga School), which claimed that its notes dated back to the fourteenth century.

p. 238   8. Enkin's main text is practically the same as that of *Tsukiyama Sansuiden* (Landscaping Records), to which was attached the name of Soami as author. Its contents cover almost exactly the material found in the book of the Saga school, as above.

p. 239   9. The new publishesr evidently possessed the original wood blocks from which Enkin's book had been printed and used them for the joint book. As late as 1918 the same sets of blocks appear to have been used for a new printing in the old way.

10. Matsunosuke Tatsui, *Gardens of Japan:* p. ? *A Pictorial Record of Famous Palaces and Gardens,* 1935.

11. Since World War II, skilled Japanese garden makers have been taken to various foreign countries for the purpose of supervising the construction of a garden, with the result that a number of very good Japanese-style gardens now exist outside Japan.

CHAPTER 24

1. Tamura, *Art of the Landscape Garden in* p. ? *Japan,* page 143. This estate was originally built in 1702 by the feudal lord Yanagisawa Yoshiyasu, who is reputed to have designed it himself. He included eighty-eight spots of literary significance arranged along its winding path.

2. The castle was destroyed by the 1923 p. ? earthquake, along with a large part of the garden. The remaining garden was later turned over to Tokyo as a park.

3. The bit of surviving pond of the original p. ? Shinsen-en had not then been identified.

4. The seven are listed in an old poem: p. ? *Hagi ga nana; obana; kuzu hana; | Nadeshiko no hana; ominaeshi; | Mata fujibakama; asagao no hana.* These, in order, are lespedeza (hagi), miscanthus (obana), pueraria (kuzu hana), dianthus (nadeshiko), patrinia (ominaeshi), eupatorium (fujibakama), and platycodon (asagao). The last is the flower known in the West as the blue Chinese bellflower, not a morning-glory.

5. This bridge had long carried Kyoto's p. ? medieval traffic, mostly on foot, across the Kamo River at Gojo-machi, one of the town's busiest thoroughfares. Becoming inadequate, it had been replaced. Whether Ogawa thought of bringing the old pillars to the Heian Shrine garden or, for sentimental reasons, the municipality decided to salvage them this way, is uncertain.

CHAPTER 25

1. Kokusai Bunka Shinkokai (Society for p. ? International Cultural Relations), *Architectural*

Beauty in Japan, 1955. See section by Y. Kojiro, "Modern Art and Japanese Architecture."

258   2. Tange, Gropius, and Ishimoto, *Katsura: Tradition and Creation in Japanese Architecture.*

259   3. Notably those made by the American, Isamu Noguchi.

4. Tomizaburo Nishida, *Tokyo no Niwa* (Tokyo Gardens), 1959. See discussion and illustrations on pages 184–87.

260   5. Reverence for Ryoan-ji is something comparatively recent. When I first started visiting it in the early 1930's, only a few artists and priests had ever heard of it or gone to see it. The last time I went there, over thirty years later, I counted twelve large buses lined up on the road outside. I found their Japanese passengers inside the temple, sitting or standing, facing the garden. Most were silent, intently studying it, some with frowning intensity, others with rapt appreciation, others plainly puzzled, and some openly frustrated and giving it up.

6. Kokusai Bunka Shinkokai (Society for International Cultural Relations), *Tradition of [the] Japanese Garden.* See notes by Y. Kojiro, page 177.

7. *Tradition of [the] Japanese Garden,* as   p. 262
above. Notes by S. Horiguchi, page 180.

8. As I visited gardens during those years I   p. 266
recall once coming on him settled in a temple reception room, all its records and documents piled around him. He was going through them in search of factual material that might throw light on the garden's history.

9. Mirei Shigemori, *Nihon Teien Shi Zukan,* in 26 volumes, 1939.

10. Mirei Shigemori, *Niwa: Shigemori Mirei Sakuhin Shu* (with English subtitle *Japanese Gardens Designed by Mirei Shigemori*), 1964.

11. *Niwa: Shigemori Mirei Sakuhin Shu,* as above.

12. The term "Five Mountains" harks back,   p. 267
of course, to the early days of Buddhism in China, when new institutions were being founded in the mountains for safety and quiet.

13. The castle was first constructed in 1585   p. 268
and completed in 1640. In 1821 the tower was struck by lightning. What remained was torn down in early Meiji. In 1920 the site was donated to the town of Kishiwada by its owner, the former viscount Nakakage Okabe.

Bibliography

NOTE: *Items in Japanese are indicated by parenthetical English translations of their titles.*

Covell, Jon Carter: *Under the Seal of Sesshu,* 1941

Danby, Hope: *The Garden of Perfect Brightness,* 1950

Engel, David H.: *Japanese Gardens for Today,* 1959

Erdberg, Eleanor von: *Chinese Influences on European Garden Structures,* 1936

Futagawa, Yukio, and Itoh, Teiji: *The Roots of Japanese Architecture,* 1963

Graham, Dorothy: *Chinese Gardens,* 1938

Harada, Jiro: *Gardens of Japan,* 1928

Kitamura, Fumio, and Ishizu, Yurio: *Garden Plants in Japan,* 1963

Kokusai Bunka Shinkokai (Society for International Cultural Relations): *Architectural Beauty in Japan,* 1955

——: *Tradition of [the] Japanese Garden,* 1962

Malone, Carroll Browne: *History of the Peking Summer Palaces Under the Ch'ing Dynasty,* 1934

Mori, Osamu: *Nippon no Niwa* (Japanese Gardens), with summary in English, "Japanese Gardens: Their History, Makers, Schools, and Styles," 1960

Mosher, Gouverneur: *Kyoto: A Contemplative Guide,* 1964

Nishida, Tomizaburo: *Tokyo no Niwa* (Gardens of Tokyo), 1959

Okakura, Kakuzo: *The Book of Tea,* 1956 (reprint of 1906 edition)

Okamoto, Toyo, and Takakuwa, Gisei: *Gardens of Japan,* translated by Hirokuni Kobatake and Roger Matthews, 1966

Paine, Robert Treat, and Soper, Alexander C.: *The Art and Architecture of Japan,* 1955

Ponsonby Fane, R. A. B.: *Kyoto: Its History and Vicissitudes,* 1931

Sadler, A. L.: *Cha-no-Yu: The Japanese Tea Ceremony,* 1962 (reprint of 1933 edition)

Saito, Katsuo, and Wada, Sadaji: *Magic of Trees and Stones,* 1964

Sansom, G. B.: *A History of Japan,* 3 vols., 1958–63

——: *Japan: A Short Cultural History,* 1943

Shigemori, Mirei: *Kyoto Bijutsu Taikan: Teien* (Survey of Kyoto Fine Arts: Gardens), 1933

——: *Nihon no Teien* (Gardens of Japan), Vol. 1 in the series *Arts of Japan* (in Japanese), 1949

——: *Nihon Teien Shi Zukan* (Japanese Garden Histories, Illustrated), 26 vols., 1936–39

——: *Niwa: Shigemori Mirei Sakuhin Shu* (with English subtitle *Japanese Gardens Designed by Mirei Shigemori*), 1964

Shigeta, Teiichi: "Asuka no Shumisen" (A Shumisen of the Asuka Period), *Shigaku Zasshi* (Magazine of History), Vol. 15, January 1904

Sickman, Laurence, and Soper, Alexander C.: *The Art and Architecture of China,* 1956

Sirén, Osvald: *Gardens of China,* 1949

Soper, Alexander C.: "Early Chinese Landscape Painting," *Art Bulletin,* Vol. 23, July 1935

——: *The Evolution of Buddhist Architecture in Japan,* 1942

Tamura, Tsuyoshi: *Art of the Landscape Garden in Japan,* 1935

——: *Koraku-en,* 1931

Tange, Kenzo, and Gropius, Walter: *Katsura: Tradition and Creation in Japanese Architecture,* 1960

Taniguchi, Yoshiro: *The Shugaku-in Imperial Villa,* with English résumé by Jiro Harada, 1956

Tatsui, Matsunosuke: "Edo Jidai no Zoteika ni Mochiiraretaru Hidensho ni Tsuite" (The Secret Books Used by the Edo-Period Garden Makers), *Heishi,* October 1938

——: *Gardens of Japan: A Pictorial Record of Famous Palaces and Gardens,* 1935

——: *Japanese Gardens* (Tourist Library, No. 4), 1934

——: *Nippon Teien Shiyo* (Short History of Japanese Gardens), 1932

Toyama, Eisaku: *Muromachi Jidai Teien Shi* (History of Gardens of the Muromachi Period), 1934

Villiers Stuart, C. M.: *Gardens of the Great Mughals,* 1930

Waley, Arthur: *The Life and Times of Po Chü-i,* 1949

——, trans.: *The Tale of Genji,* by Murasaki Shikibu, 1935

Warner, Langdon: *The Enduring Art of Japan,* 1953

Wilber, Donald M.: *Persian Gardens and Garden Pavilions,* 1962

Wilson, Ernest H.: *China, Mother of Gardens,* 1929

Wu Shih-chang: "Notes on the Origin of Chinese Private Gardens," translated and condensed by Grace M. Boynton, *China Journal,* Vol. 23, July 1935

Yetts, W. Percival: "Chinese Isles of the Blest," *Folklore,* Vol. 30, March 1919

Yoshida, Tetsuro: *The Japanese House and Garden,* 1955

Yoshimura, Yuji, and Halford, Giovanna M.: *The Japanese Art of Miniature Trees and Landscapes: Their Creation, Care, and Enjoyment,* 1957

Index

The "weathermark" identifies this book as having been planned, designed, and produced by John Weatherhill, Inc., 7-6-13 Roppongi, Minato-ku, Tokyo. Book design & typography by Meredith Weatherby. Layout of plates by Elaine Reiko Nishi. Composition by General Printing Co., Yokohama. Plates engraved and printed (in 5-color offset and 1-color gravure), together with the text, by Nissha Printing Co., Kyoto. Bound at the Makoto Binderies, Tokyo. Set in 12-point Monotype Bembo, with hand-set Cloister for display.